ACA
Publishing Ltd
英国查思出版亚洲有限公司

Published by
ACA Publishing Ltd,
Tel: +44 (0) 20 7834 7676
Fax: +44 (0) 20 7973 0076
Email: post@alaincharles.com
Web: www.alaincharles.com
New Jersey office:
Tel: +1 (732) 469 8898
Fax: +1 (732) 469 8585

ALL RIGHTS RESERVED. NO PART OF THIS
PUBLICATION MAY BE REPRODUCED IN MATERIAL
FORM, BY ANY MEANS, WHETHER GRAPHIC,
ELECTRONIC, MECHANICAL OR OTHER, INCLUDING
PHOTOCOPYING OR INFORMATION STORAGE, IN
WHOLE OR IN PART. MAY NOT BE USED TO PREPARE
OTHER PUBLICATIONS WITHOUT WRITTEN
PERMISSION FROM THE PUBLISHER.

The greatest care has been taken to ensure accuracy but the
publisher can accept no responsibility for errors or omissions, or for any
liability occasioned by relying on the content of this book.

ISBN 978-0-9555854-3-2

Cover photographs courtesy of
Dr. Robert A. Kapp (front) and Joerg Wuttke (back).

Printed in Shenzhen

Further copies of My Thirty Years in China are
available at a cost each of GBP19.95 plus GBP5
postage and packing. To order, please e-mail:

circ@alaincharles.com

Foreword

Sir David Brewer
Former Lord Mayor of
the City of London and Chairman,
China-Britain Business Council

I first visited China in 1981 when I went to open the first broker's representative office in China, for Sedgwick (now Marsh). Since then, the country has seen huge changes. Beginning with the processes of reform and opening up to the outside world initiated by Deng Xiaoping 1978, China has modernised itself and has undergone unprecedented social changes. Some 400 million people have been lifted out of poverty, more than at any time before in human history. Living standards have improved immensely for most ordinary people, and many of the most enterprising have embraced the concept that it is indeed good to be wealthy.

Over the past 30 years, the country has experienced extraordinary development in its built environment and infrastructure. Its major cities, such as Beijing, Shanghai and Guangzhou, have undergone rapid transformation, with new high-rise districts mushrooming, it seems, almost overnight. Second-and third-tier cities are not far behind. The cities are served by some of the most modern airports in the world, while China's extraordinary programme of road-building has seen a brand-new network of highways and expressways extend to virtually every corner of this vast and disparate country. New and luxurious high-speed train services connect the major centres, and China's ports, among the busiest in the world, handle increasingly huge tonnages of goods that go to fuel the world economy.

China is a powerhouse, and is becoming increasingly influential globally, both in purely economic terms and in its geopolitical importance. It is tentatively becoming a major player in a globalised economy, as it begins to reclaim the position it once held as an economic and technological leader. In 2008, in particular, China is centre stage as never before, as Beijing hosts the XXIXth Olympic Games. The eyes of the world are watching, and China is inordinately eager to acquit itself well. The importance of the Games to ordinary Chinese people, as a symbol of China's new status and of its latest stage of development, cannot be overstated.

The foreign visitors flocking to Beijing to watch the Olympic Games may find it hard to believe how different China was just thirty years ago, especially in its relationship with outsiders. For the small number of foreigners who came to the country in the late 1970s and early 1980s, 'Red China' was indeed a strange place. It was considered a hardship posting by diplomats, and contact between Chinese and foreigners was often hampered by suspicion and misunderstanding on both sides.

And yet some of these foreign visitors, drawn initially by the language, culture or a desire to do business, came to fall in love with the country, and have stayed there to live and thrive. They established businesses, typically at first operating on a shoestring out of hotel bedrooms, and built strong partnerships with Chinese counterparts. Some helped to improve relationships between China's government and their own home countries. Many found their life partner here, married, bought houses, put down roots and raised families.

For these brave souls, building a new life in a strange country was rarely easy, but it was always interesting. The collection of first-hand accounts contained in this book reflects the joys and sorrows, the triumphs and challenges involved in living as a foreigner in China at such an exciting stage of its history. The contributors are drawn from a variety of different business sectors and have a wide range of personal stories to tell. All are pioneers in one way or another.

What they have in common is that they are all dedicated and committed people who have been singularly successful in their chosen fields and that they share a deep love and understanding of China. We hope that their memories and insights will paint a vivid picture, then and now, of this sometimes puzzling, sometimes challenging, but always rewarding country that they have chosen to call home.

David Brewer

Contents

Foreword 3

A dream come true 8
■ *Sidney Rittenberg*

Sidney Rittenberg Sr. (Chinese name Li Dunbai) is a legend in China. He has personally known every Chinese leader from Mao Zedong to Jiang Zemin, and spent 16 of his 35 years in China in prison. Today he teaches at Pacific Lutheran University in the US and runs his own consulting company, Rittenberg Associates, Inc.

    Engineering a new model 11
    Social transformation 12
    Doing business in China 17

Building for the future 22
■ *Stephen Perry*

Stephen Perry is Managing Director of the London Export Corporation and Chairman of The 48 Group Club, the original 'Icebreakers' of Western trade with China.

    The new generation 26
    How the UK sees China 29
    China and the developing world 31
    A changing society 32
    Dramatic transformation 36
    Cultural exchanges 40

Growing a business 42
■ *Michael De Clercq*

Michael de Clercq studied Chinese at the Australian National University in Canberra and first travelled to China in 1975. He set up his trading company in 1978 and developed it into a consulting business specialising in sourcing, sales and growth, including mergers and acquisitions.

    First trip, 1975 44
    The Beijing Language Institute in 1978 ... 48
    Moving around 50
    Living in China, and marriage 51
    Hotels: home far away from home 54
    Leisure: weekends, friends, etc 60
    Business in China: drinking 71
    From telexes to the internet 74
    Buying from China 77
    The art of war: selling 85
    Looking back 91

A China life 94
■ *Dr. Robert A. Kapp*

Robert Kapp has four decades of involvement with China, in academia, trade relations and consulting, and is recognised for his contributions to furthering dialogue between China and the US. He currently runs his own consulting firm, Robert A. Kapp & Associates, which advises companies seeking to expand business with China.

    January 1977: a silent first visit 96

1980: the year of big changes ... 98
The 1980s: building bridge ... 101
1987–1994: an interlude away from China ... 106
The China life in Washington DC ... 107

The life of a *laowai* insurance broker ... 116
■ *Tim Mathieson*

Tim Mathieson was responsible for setting up the first insurance broker liaison office in China in 1981. Since then he has accumulated 28 years' experience in the insurance industry and today is Chief Operating Officer at Willis Insurance Brokers in Shanghai.

    A rookie businessman in China ... 119
    Rapid growth of the insurance industry ... 123
    Twelve years on ... 125

On the road ... 130
■ *Chris Ruffle*

Chris Ruffle has played a pioneering role in opening up the Chinese A-share market to foreign investors. His team at investment company Martin Currie manages specialist China funds worth US$6bn and is the largest foreign investor in the domestic stock market.

    Communications challenges ... 131
    The necessities of life ... 133
    Choice of entertainment ... 134
    Attitudes to foreigners ... 135
    Doing business ... 136
    Investing in the A-share market ... 139
    The changing face of China ... 143

Unexpected opportunities ... 146
■ *Ian J. Stones*

Since 1979, Ian J. Stones has played a pioneering role in a number of different industries in China, including the oil and gas, aviation, automotive, financial and pharmaceutical sectors. He has held a variety of senior corporate positions and today is a director and senior advisor for a number of Chinese and global companies.

    First contact with the language ... 147
    Preconceptions of 'Red China' in 1978 ... 149
    Exchange scholarship to Beijing ... 152
    Different worlds ... 155
    Bourgeois thinking ... 159
    Visits to the *hutong* ... 160
    Beijing's John Travolta ... 162
    Kung fu star ... 165
    First job, and the first of many battles ... 166
    The world's best negotiator ... 170
    Beijing's first bars and dance spots ... 173
    Getting what you needed ... 174
    Office life in the Beijing Hotel ... 177
    Rural encounters outside Beijing ... 179
    A fruit fest in quarantine ... 182
    Shanghai and Guangzhou ... 183
    Worst memory ... 186
    Biking in Guangzhou, 1984 ... 188
    A move to the auto business ... 191
    Logistical challenges ... 193
    Chrysler, and some special people ... 194
    Back channel diplomacy ... 197
    A new city, and back to my 'drugs' roots ... 198
    Autos again, and onwards ... 203
    Proliferating expats and returning Chinese ... 205
    Evolving times ... 206
    The funniest memory of all ... 208

Healthcare ambassador..........210
■ *Roberta Lipson*

Roberta Lipson co-founded healthcare company Chindex in 1981 and was the creative force behind the Beijing United Family Hospital and the United Family Hospitals concept. She has been an active member of the Beijing business community for almost 30 years.

    Transportation..........215
    Communications..........216
    A hotel room is not a home..........217
    Making healthcare healthier..........220
    'It can't be done'..........225
    Going public..........226
    Looking back, and looking forward..........228

A question of self-belief..........230
■ *Clinton Dines*

Clinton Dines came to China on a postgraduate teaching programme in 1979 and has lived there ever since. For the past 19 years he has been the senior country executive in China for BHP and, since 2001, President of BHP Billiton China. He is based in Shanghai with his wife and three children, the youngest of whom was adopted in China.

    First impressions..........232
    A new era..........239

Lifelong education..........244
■ *Caroline Chen Gaillard*

Caroline Chen Gaillard is the founder and director of the International Montessori School of Beijing (MSB), which she established in 1990. She is recognised in teaching circles in China for her expertise in early childhood education and for her work in introducing and promoting the Montessori teaching method.

    Coal heaps and cabbages..........246
    The changing face of the city..........248
    Laying the foundations of MSB..........249
    Crossing the cultural divide..........251
    A time for reflection..........253

Unwrapping the puzzle..........254
■ *Joerg Wuttke*

Joerg Wuttke is General Manager and Chief Representative of BASF China, based in Beijing. He was a founding member of the German Chamber of Commerce in China, and since April 2007 has been President of the European Union Chamber of Commerce in China.

    An auspicious beginning..........259
    Long-term commitment..........265
    A changing society..........269
    Flying the European flag..........273
    Pondering the riddle..........276

Building bridges..........278
■ *Jim Gradoville*

Jim Gradoville is President of United Technologies International Operations – China. He has lived and worked full-time in China since 1998 and lives in Beijing with his two adopted daughters. He is a past Chairman of the American Chamber of Commerce in China.

    Now versus then..........280
    Changes in the business environment..........281
    Personal life..........284
    Olympic Torchbearer..........286

Branding in China..........288
■ *Scott Kronick*

Scott Kronick has helped to build Ogilvy PR into China's leading public relations consultancy. With 21 years at the agency, 13 in Beijing, he established offices in Beijing, Shanghai and Guangzhou and has built the firm into China's leader in terms of size, client base, talent and relationships.

    The testing ground..........291
    Business highs and lows..........295
    Olympic triumph, and challenging times..........301
    Plunging into the property market..........306
    Anticipation and excitement..........311

Sidney Rittenberg
President, Rittenberg Associates, Inc

First came to China: 1945

Sidney Rittenberg Sr. (Chinese name Li Dunbai) is a legend in China. In the 1940s he was the only US citizen to join the CCP, and he has personally known every Chinese leader from Mao Zedong through Deng Xiaoping to Jiang Zemin. He spent 16 of his 35 years in China in prison, first falsely accused of spying and then the victim of inter-factional fighting within the CCP. However, he emerged undaunted and free of bitterness, with his love for China intact, and was hailed as a true friend of the Chinese people.

Today he teaches Chinese Studies at Pacific Lutheran University in the US and runs his own consulting company, Rittenberg Associates, Inc, which assists companies seeking to do business with China.

A dream come true

Sidney Rittenberg's remarkably long and eventful relationship with China makes him uniquely qualified to comment on its recent past and its likely future direction. Here he offers his personal insights on the rapid social changes taking place, on China's relations with the US and the rest of the world and on how Western companies should approach doing business in China

Sidney Rittenberg was born in Charleston, South Carolina in 1921 and attended Porter Military Academy and the University of North Carolina, where he majored in philosophy. During his time there, he was briefly a member of the US Communist Party. Following the entry of the US into World War Two, he joined the Army and was sent to learn Japanese, but switched to Chinese instead. The Army sent him to China in 1945; subsequently, he stayed on and joined the United Nations Relief and Rehabilitation Administration as a relief worker and interpreter.

With Mao Zedong at Tiananmen Gate Tower, 1 May 1967

He met and formed a friendship with Zhou Enlai, and in 1946 accepted an invitation to help train Chinese journalists working in English. He joined Zhou, Mao Zedong and other Chinese Communist Party leaders at their base in Yan'an in Shaanxi province, and for some time observed the CCP leadership at close quarters. He became a leading translator of Mao's works, and twice interpreted messages from Mao for the United States. He was the only American citizen to be accepted into the CCP, and remained a member until he withdrew from the Party during the Cultural Revolution.

In 1949 he was accused by Joseph Stalin of being an American spy with links to a supposed international network, and was imprisoned for six years in solitary confinement. Stalin's death in 1953 led to his eventual release in 1955. During the Cultural Revolution, he became a nationally known celebrity on account of his speeches and actions on behalf of the transitory democracy that prevailed for a short

Sidney Rittenberg

Sidney Rittenberg with heads of the 8th Route Army Health Department in Kalgan, 1946

while. However, he paid for this celebrity with a second period of imprisonment from 1967, this time spending ten years in solitary confinement. He was finally released in November 1977 and was formally eulogised by the post-Cultural Revolution government as a person who had made a significant contribution to the Chinese people. His ultimate vindication, and his complete lack of bitterness at his harsh treatment, made him a legend within China. In 1980, he moved back to the United States.

His reputation has subsequently given him easy access to China's leaders – a great advantage for his consulting work. As well as Mao and Zhou, he has personally known every Chinese leader, including Deng Xiaoping and the notorious Gang of Four, up until Jiang Zemin and Zhu Rongji. His wide network of friends and acquaintances extends to many current leaders at provincial level, and he has dedicated himself to fostering relations between the US and China at every level.

He met his wife Yulin in China, and she has been his lifetime partner for more than 50 years. Today, together with Yulin and their daughter Jenny, he runs the consulting company Rittenberg Associates, Inc, which assists businesses working with Chinese companies. As consultants, Sidney and Yulin have helped clients such as Intel, InFocus, Nextel, Levi Strauss, Microsoft, Hughes Aircraft and Teledesic.

Sidney is former Frey Distinguished Professor of Chinese History at the University of North Carolina, where an endowed chair has been announced in his name. He is currently Visiting Professor of China Studies at Pacific Lutheran University in Tacoma, Washington. He has appeared on numerous TV and radio programmes in the US, and delivers frequent seminars around the world on China and on doing business there. The fascinating story of his 35 years in China is chronicled in his book, *The Man Who Stayed Behind*, co-authored with Amanda Bennett of the *Wall Street Journal*.

A dream come true

Actually, I lived in China for 35 years (1945–1980), but who's counting? I was born in Charleston, South Carolina, but I grew into manhood in China. I studied Philosophy at UNC-Chapel Hill and formed an outlook on life, but the smelting and forging happened mostly in China. I like the description of me that Linda Charlton gave in the *New York Times* in March 1979, during my first return trip to the States with my Chinese wife: 'Native Son of America, Son-in-Law of China'.

Since 1980, when I moved back to the States, I have commuted back and forth to China several times each year, gaping wide-eyed at the four big, unthinkable changes that I was seeing:

1. The world's oldest country converting itself into the youngest – the fastest-growing, the most innovative, the most eagerly grasping for a new and better future.

2. The most self-isolating of the large states pushing itself into the world community, for the first time in history.

3. The wide-open market, both domestic and foreign. At the end of 2007, at Mao's old wilderness cave-capital of Yanan, on the desolate high plateau of north Shaanxi, I found the latest Sony flatscreen TVs on sale, some more than six feet long. Yanan was once held up as the national model for frugal living. A whole department of the store we were in now offers cakes and candies of every description. I asked our guide, a 21-year-old local girl: 'Do you know what was the only treat that kids in Yanan had when I lived here?' She didn't. 'It was the millet that caked at the bottom of the wok – they called it "Lenin Cookies". It was the only cookies they ever saw.' With few exceptions, all prices today are set by supply and demand in the market place. The new leaders, for the first time in this frugal country's history, urge their people to spend, to live well, to embrace globalisation.

4. Underlying it all is a change in the nation's orientation, and in how children are taught. In Mao's day, it was 'The interests of each individual must be subordinated to the needs of the Party, the Motherland, the Socialist economy'. Today, official policy says, 'The people come first!' And young Chinese, rather than striving for social recognition by conforming to the Party model, are busy inventing their own personalities and pursuing their own careers.

These changes are good news for the human race, spelling new opportunity and adding a new force for peace and progress. But they are not completed: they are a work in progress

These changes are good news for the human race, spelling new opportunity and adding a new force for peace and progress. But they are not completed: they are a work in progress, often advancing slowly, in zigzag fashion, through hard struggles between the old forces (known both as 'the conservatives' and 'the Leftists') and the new. We hear about China's 'outraged youth' who rant noisy nationalism in some of the online chat rooms. But if you walk around and talk to people in China today, you find that what is on most people's minds is: (1) earn enough to enjoy life and secure retirement; (2) live as trouble-free as possible, in peace, at home and in the world; and (3) get free from all sorts of bullying, annoying controls and harassment by bureaucrats and petty tyrants. Let's take a closer look at these changes – and at others, not so promising.

Engineering a new model

The composition of the Chinese leadership has changed drastically over the past few decades. Gone are the old guerrilla fighters and former student revolutionaries who made up nearly all of the first two generations of Chinese Communist Party and government leaders. Today, around 95 per cent are university graduates, and overwhelmingly engineers – although the first economists and lawyers have just begun edging their way in. The Party General Secretary and President, the Premier, the Vice Premiers, the big city mayors and the main provincial governors – all engineers.

These people are essentially builders, not ideologues. They jealously guard their legitimacy, national traditions and pride, but at the end of the day they are highly pragmatic. They adhere to the Chinese Communist Party today as the only existing strategiser and organiser at national and local levels. But the new leaders know that the old model of what was called Marxist-Leninist Socialism has been a miserable failure. They are seeking a new model for a society that is both equitable and democratic, drawing on the lessons of China, of all other Communist-led countries and of the more successful welfare states. They have launched a bold attempt to redistribute income more judiciously, and to transform the party, gradually, into a widely representative, democratically run organisation. Will they succeed? The jury is still out. But having seen the ingenuity and cohesiveness of the Chinese, I believe that they will – after many bumps and challenges.

Studying Chinese at Stanford University, 1943

Why the timidity about allowing free public expression and free elections at all levels? Not just the fear inspired by the 'colour revolutions', but also the hard facts of tens of millions of urban unemployed, 150 million rural migrants, a serious disconnect between the central and the local authorities and a myriad of injustices and despotic ways left over from the old regime.

In a developing country like China, with a great and widening disparity between rich and poor, rural and urban, the number one issue for leaders who want to grow the economy and reform the old political system is stability. Without a stable platform on which to stand (shades of Archimedes!), it is feared that

A dream come true

everything could return to the chaos of the Cultural Revolution, burying all attempts at enlightened reform before the country can escape from poverty and backwardness.

Are the Chinese over-cautious? Is the risk associated with more rapid democratisation really that great? We may think (as I do) that they should move faster – but it's our opinion, not our responsibility, and only indirectly our risk. Personally, I voice my opinions, but I yield to the judgment of the dedicated men and women who have the job of managing this enormously complex and seething country. From my experience, I believe them to be people of peace and good will.

In 1978, one year after my release from long years in prison, with my close friend, the famous Chinese writer Ding Ling, right after her own release

Until the Deng Xiaoping reforms, the core demand that the CPC raised for the Chinese people was: 'Subordinate personal interests to the needs of the Party, the Motherland, Socialism'. China's new leaders have turned this upside down: 'People come first' is the central Party slogan today. Literally, *Yi Ren Wei Ben*, or 'Take People as the Basis for Everything'. Fundamental political reform may result from a combination of vigorous moves by reformers in the leadership and mass action by people from below.

Social transformation

After the rigidly disciplined Mao era and the ten years' anarchy of the Cultural Revolution, I have seen the spread of greater individual liberties than the average Chinese has ever before enjoyed. Basic rights that seem like air and water to people in the West are new in China – only becoming widespread over the past decades. Things like the right to pick your school, to choose your job after school (if you can find one), to move your domicile, to travel freely both in China and abroad – and the right to go into business and earn money, either on your own or together with foreign businesses. People also have the right to criticise and complain to their hearts' content – so long as they don't write down and publish opinions that challenge basic CCP policy, or don't organise to work for their advocacy.

Changes for the man-on-the-street, or the man-at-the-wheel-of-a-cab, are mind-blowing. China is becoming a hi-tech world, exulting in how it is leapfrogging the old path of capitalist development to grow its own brand of Chinese welfare

My Thirty Years in China | 13

Sidney Rittenberg

With Yulin on our wedding day at the Summer Palace in Beijing, 11 February 1956

capitalism with socialist dreams.

My own primary concern has been that the sea of money-grubbing individualism and cynicism that followed the Cultural Revolution was drowning out the most precious heritage of the Chinese people – the philosophy of their ancients, both deep and down-to-earth, and its development and application in modern China. Modern Chinese thinking, represented by Mao Zedong during the years before he was corrupted by power, is what won them the civil wars and drove Chiang Kai-Shek's strongest of Asian armies into the sea. The reforms have produced a new economy, but they have not succeeded in generating a common vision or the urge to contribute to the public welfare – to give back to the community. At times, I have worried that the Chinese might gain riches but lose their soul.

Like a clap of thunder, the Sichuan earthquake disaster has put that worry to rest. The wisdom and the great heart of the Chinese people are alive and well – reasserted with a sudden outburst of compassion, self-sacrifice and volunteerism in response to this national tragedy. China's vigorous reformers are building on this momentum to foster the rise of civil society and to make the regime more representative, closer to the people.

This is truly becoming a hi-tech society. iPods are everywhere, along with the Cokes and burgers, while 520 million cell phones (at last count) keep up a constant cacophony of ringtones, as though some vast symphony orchestra were tuning up to play Stravinsky. More important, Chinese today are connected – leading the world in the number of Internet users, digging for information from all over the world and liaising with each other over common concerns. This is rapidly changing the fabric of society, as well as relations between leaders and led – and this is only the beginning.

Ordinary people using information technology are growing in power as a force for progress and are forging China's first civil society. Of course, there are tens of thousands of government minders and monitors and some websites are blocked – but they are a tiny drop in an ocean of websites, and they are easily outflanked by any bright young Chinese guy or gal. In Shanghai recently, a young whizzkid in a tiny little office took five minutes to load Chinese character capability into my iPhone – without jailbreaking it, he claimed.

Substantial progress has been made in elections at the village and factory level. In

A dream come true

some places, local Party leaders are being elected by the membership in consultation with non-Party people, rather than being appointed from above. Of course, these are only beginnings, and the path of progress is slow and thorny. The same official statement that declared Party membership paramount, and announced that from now on all major policy decisions and appointments would be discussed by the members before a decision was taken – the same statement demanded absolute conformity to central Party policy. This still makes it difficult for members to speak freely, even in secret party meetings.

No one who lived in China 20 years ago would recognise the rural areas today – especially the heavily populated coastal plains and metropolitan suburbs. If you go by train, you can ride all day without seeing the kind of hovel that most farmers used to live in. Most own new homes, colour TVs are common and cell phones are beginning to penetrate. The average per capita income in the countryside is still only about a third of urban incomes, but money is mailed in from relatives working in the cities and life has greatly improved. The demands of Sichuan earthquake victims for soundly built homes and schools dramatise how these are now regarded as a right of the people and a duty of the government.

No one who lived in China 20 years ago would recognise the rural areas today – especially the heavily populated coastal plains and metropolitan suburbs

In our living quarters at Radio Beijing in around 1961, with our three daughters Sunny, Toni and Jenny

Sidney Rittenberg

Acting as consultant to Mike Wallace and the CBS *60 Minutes* team in 1982

Except in remote, isolated, or especially harsh areas, a modicum of food, shelter, and clothing is no longer a problem–though health care and tertiary/college education are still big concerns. There is a guaranteed minimum average income for everyone, town and country, but it is low and frequently some of it is siphoned off by corrupt officials before it reaches the farmers' hands.

The government recognises the potential explosion in health care, and it has greatly increased investments in that area. In the villages, cooperative health care has returned, on a large scale, and in the cities the health service delivery system is being overhauled. The government has acknowledged that it was a mistake to cut hospitals and clinics off from the state budget, which both forced and enabled them to squeeze money out of patients and to profiteer from illicit fees – depriving the low-income majority of adequate health care. As for schools, rural education fees have been abolished, along with the farm tax, and the state is reimbursing local governments for the resulting loss in income.

All progress, economic or political, is a seesaw struggle between those who press for reforms and those who fear or oppose them. The momentum is forward, however, and, given the current plethora of articles published on the need for democratisation, 2009 may show further progress in political reform.

All progress, economic or political, is a seesaw struggle between those who press for reforms and those who fear or oppose them. The momentum is forward, however

A case in point in this seesaw struggle is the effort to eliminate the manufacture of counterfeit products and violations of patent and trademark guarantees. The central government is anxious to solve this problem – not primarily because of outside pressure, but because it cramps the R&D efforts of the big Chinese conglomerates. Who is willing to invest big bucks in developing new products, when they know that their compatriots in the south will steal their inventions and out-compete them? But the problem is that many local governments, as well as corrupt officials, get considerable income from the counterfeiting. They block efforts at patent enforcement and even attack inspectors

A dream come true

sent down from higher levels. Enforcement of IPR protection is a hard struggle, day by day, place by place. Hong Kong, Taiwan and Korea have all been through this stage, and have successfully dealt with counterfeiting. For a country as large and as complex as China, it takes longer. But it is happening, and will happen, because a modern economy demands it.

Doing business in China

The quality of business leaders, and the way business is done, has fundamentally changed. In the late 1980s, my wife and I approached the high-ranking foreign trade official in charge of all trade with English-speaking countries on behalf of our client, Levi Strauss & Co. Levi's, we explained, was the world's leading maker of jeans. 'Oh no,' he said. 'Apple jeans are the best known.' Apple was a small Hong Kong company that had managed to get its product into the Chinese market before anyone else. We solved the problem only by producing a copy of Webster's Collegiate Dictionary and showing him that the word 'Levi's' means 'jeans'.

Not long ago, we accompanied a client in synthetic fuels to a meeting with the Chinese Ambassador in Washington. The Ambassador walked into the meeting room (unaccompanied), shook hands, sat down and immediately began talking about the market conditions and key players, about China's specific needs and about how we might go about connecting with the appropriate persons in Beijing – with his assistance. These two meetings tell the story of the difference between the inexperienced

Yulin and I with Li Lanqing, Vice Mayor of Tianjin and later Executive Vice Premier, 1987

My Thirty Years in China | 17

Sidney Rittenberg

amateurs of 20 years ago and the well-informed professionals one encounters in China today.

Other things have changed too. Getting the support of a central government minister no longer ensures the success of your project in China – you usually have to make your deal with the particular executives or managers in charge, or with the local approval authorities. *Guanxi*, or connections, are certainly important, as they are anywhere – but they typically only get you a hearing. Whether your project works depends on your having a business plan that will succeed in Chinese circumstances, having the right team to carry it out – and making sure that you're working with the right people in China.

And that is a key question: how do you determine the right choice of partner, associate, co-investor or staff member in China? The answer is due diligence – threefold due diligence. Check out the candidate's track record for the 'Three Cs': Character, Competence and Connections.

Character, amazing as it may seem, is routinely overlooked by foreign companies going into China. Someone you meet there speaks workable English, lays on a great banquet (or even a trip to a massage parlour) and assures you that he has the keys to the kingdom: 'No problem,' he says – he can get your project done. As soon as you hear that, be on your guard. Do nothing until you check out his record. Does he keep his commitments? Does he honour his debts? Does he play straight? Is he good to work with? Is he part of some corrupt gang?

These issues are Number One. Find the right talking partner or manager, and he will help you shape your project for success. Tie up with the wrong person, and you will rue the day. Competence is also an issue – can he do what you need done, or does

With Yulin, Governor of Zhejiang province Shen Zumin and officials at a reception in Hangzhou, 1992

A dream come true

he just think he can? Finally, connections. He has to have enough standing with the approval authorities so that he can obtain the approvals, indulgences and expediting that most projects will require.

Incidentally, it should be obvious that there are great opportunities to do business in environmental protection technology, including water purification. China's leaders are at long last devoting serious attention to reining in pollution and protecting the environment – mainly because of the many billions of renminbi that pollution is costing the government every year.

Meeting Vice Premier (later Premier) Zhu Rongji in Beijing, 1991

Whatever the sector, in China today, you cannot afford to get enmeshed in bribery or other illegal doings. It may look like a good idea – some people will tell you that you can't do business in China without it – but don't do it. First, it makes you vulnerable to blackmail. (The Chinese know that the US has a Foreign Corrupt Practices Act, for instance.) Secondly, any partners you have to bribe are not worth having. Thirdly, more than 90 per cent of the time, whoever is seeking a bribe will be forced to drop his demand if you reject it and push back. They know that both the US and China have laws against corrupt dealings. There is a great deal of official and commercial graft and corruption in China, but don't think that because they can do it, you can do it. If you get involved with someone who is behaving illegally, and their opponents get the law on them – guess where that leaves you?

The raising of hundreds of millions of people out of dire poverty, the lengthening of life expectancy and China's positive role in world affairs show that, on balance, it has made enormous progress

Furthermore, avoid like the plague having your business held hostage to anyone's political agenda. There are plenty of things in China that are wrong – but the raising of hundreds of millions of people out of dire poverty, the substantial lengthening of average life expectancy and China's positive role in world affairs show that, on balance, it has made enormous progress. China is a friend to the world, not a menace.

Avoiding political agendas, however, may not be easy. With the trouble in Tibet in spring 2008, there was a great blast of media and public opinion in the West against the Chinese

Sidney Rittenberg

With Yulin and old friend Li Ruihuan, Mayor of Tianjin and later a member of the ruling nine-person Standing Committee, Tianjin, 1988

government. People forgot that every great power has serious problems in assuring equal treatment and fair play to one or another minority ethnic group, and not one of them is easy to resolve. Criticise, sure – but why pick on China, as though the failure to resolve the Tibet issue satisfactorily calls for condemnation, threats of boycott, attacks on the Olympic Torch and so on?

Every one of the mortal challenges before the human race in the twenty-first century requires prolonged, concerted efforts by all the major countries to resolve. WMD plus terrorism, global warming, energy sources – you name it. Common sense – and the instinct for self-preservation – tell us that nothing, however objectionable, must be allowed to create hatred and dissension among people of all lands that could affect their coming together to face our common tasks.

To give an example – when we threaten the Beijing Olympics or give one-sided support to Tibetan exile forces against China, it isn't the Communist Party leaders that we are upsetting – they go coolly about their business of managing this very old, very complex, very quickly changing country. Who we hurt are the 1.3 billion ordinary Chinese, who take enormous pride in their country's Olympic Games. We are stoking flames of resentment and misunderstanding that could endanger success in meeting our common challenges. In that sense, I have no doubt that if we cannot keep our cool, we are sure to get burned.

Avoiding confrontation and building close ties with the US is now at the centre of China's foreign policy – hence the low-key responses from Beijing to the ignorant fulminations in Congress against the Chinese

Here in America, we find a rising fear of competition from China and the other 'BRICs' countries (Brazil, Russia, India). Imagine – Americans afraid of competition! The fact is that we have the technology, the skills, the manpower and the capital to hold our own and continue to grow, no matter how stiff the competition. One of the expressions of this fear is to blame all our competitive disadvantages on unfair

A dream come true

trade practices by other countries. Of course, there are unfair trade practices, on their part and on ours, and they need to be negotiated and dealt with. But, apart from transitory recessions, which are more or less built into our system, the US economy is not only the largest but also one of the fastest-growing, with a high rate of increase in productivity. Whining, complaining and blaming other people won't see us through – hard work, innovation and ingenuity will, if these are supported by responsible and far-sighted government policy.

The change closest to my heart over these 30 years is the growing trend, in practical terms, towards a strategic alliance between my beloved country, America, and this fascinating emerging world presence, China. Avoiding confrontation and building close ties with us is now at the centre of China's foreign policy – hence the muted or low-key responses from Beijing to the ignorant fulminations in Congress against the Chinese. On the other hand, despite the fact that our politicians' statements on China policy tend to be based more on how they will play in Peoria than on our genuine national interests – despite all the differences, objections, trade issues, misunderstandings and fears – we now have dozens of regular strategic dialogues with Beijing, some at a very high level, and our actual relationship continues to advance with every new administration in Washington.

This is the realisation of the dream that hatched for me in the Army Chinese School at Stanford 65 years ago – and it is a wonderful thing to see the dream you chased after all your life beginning to come true.

At home with Wen Jize, Vice President of the Chinese Academy of Social Sciences, his wife and daughter Lili

Stephen Perry
Managing Director, London Export Corporation and Chairman, The 48 Group Club

First came to China: 1972

Stephen Perry is Managing Director of the London Export Corporation and Chairman of The 48 Group Club, the original 'Icebreakers' of Western trade with China. Today The 48 Group Club promotes positive relations with China in many different fields.

Personally he has been instrumental in forging relations between the two countries in a variety of areas over many years. The London Export Corporation developed trade with China through its London office to and from all of Western Europe. In 1971 the company was given an icebreaking role in US/China trade to initiate a set of major Chinese purchases from the USA. Stephen was involved in this from the start, and today continues to be involved in trade between China and the USA.

E-mail: admin@48groupclub.org
www.48groupclub.org

Building for the future

Stephen Perry, Chairman of the 48 Group Club, has spent decades working to develop a dialogue between the UK and China and to build economic and cultural ties. Along the way, he has been privileged to know many of China's national and provincial leaders. Here he looks at the legacy of the Icebreakers and sets out his personal view of China's changing role in the world

Britain and The 48 Group have a special place in international trade history, as the first Western country to open trade with the new People's Republic of China after 1949. The 1953 'Icebreaker Mission' paved the way for the trail-blazing 1954 trade mission that in turn led representatives of 48 British companies to constitute themselves as The 48 Group.

My father Jack Perry was one of the original 'Icebreakers'. Jack Perry, a businessman from east London, was the UK representative on the preparatory committee for the Moscow Economic Conference in April 1952. Others on the committee included Dr Chi Chao-ting, vice-president of the Bank of China. Dr Chi, on the instructions of Premier and Foreign Minister Zhou Enlai, was seeking new trade partners to help with the post-1949 reconstruction of China. A business partnership was established with Perry's company, the London Export Corporation.

The 48 Group led the campaign against the British government's embargo on trade with the new China, introducing new technologies and products to keep up with China's modernisation agenda and working directly with British companies to win business with Chinese customers. Its efforts made the UK China's premier Western trade partner up until the

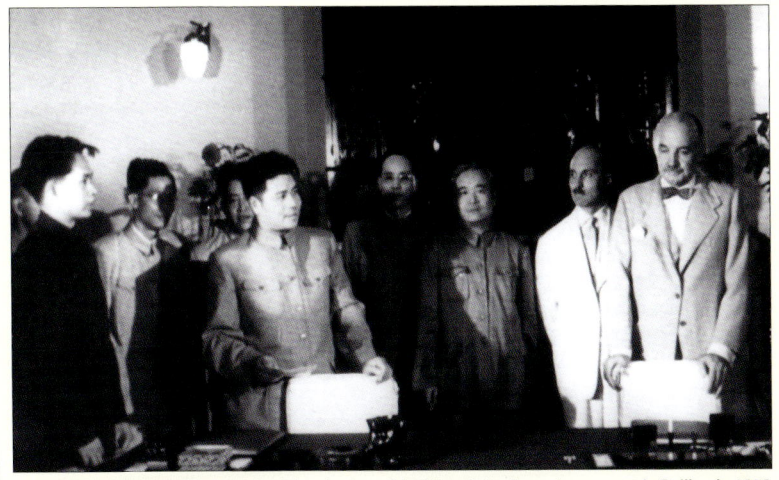

A rare surviving photograph of the signing of the historic Business Agreement in Beijing in 1953

Stephen Perry

Premier Zhou Enlai with Dr. Joseph Needham in Beijing, in October 1964

late 1970s. Crucial to its success was its close relationship with Chinese counterparts, such as the China Council for the Promotion of International Trade (CCPIT) under its chairman, Bo Yibo.

Today The 48 Group Club has more than 350 members and continues its work of promoting Sino-British relations. It organises activities throughout the UK, as well as academic and cultural exchanges, and provides an important network of contacts for those active in the China trade. The 48 Group Club's motto is 'Equality and mutual benefit' – in Chinese *pingdeng huli* – a phrase that echoes Zhou Enlai's 1953 statement of China's 'five principles' of cooperation with the outside world.

The first Icebreaker mission arose out of the Moscow Economic Conference in 1952, where people who did not agree with the concept of an Iron Curtain, but who preferred to believe in trade, interdependence and peace through trade, gathered in Moscow from countries all over the world. That's where the British delegation, of which my father was secretary-general, met the Chinese and were invited to Beijing. That led to the Icebreaker mission in the following year, in July 1953. It was a mission that was entered into against a background of no little tension, with 'Reds under the bed' scares, questions asked in Parliament and articles in newspapers condemning these people for going.

They were a broad range of people – some motivated by politics, but most of them motivated by the desire to try and open up business opportunities. These were the people who opened up trade between the two countries, these were the people whom Zhou Enlai and others thought highly of and who made the names of the Icebreakers and the 48 Group legendary in China. Today, when the President or Premier of China come to the UK, they usually take the time to meet me as Chairman of The 48 Group Club, and to thank us for what we have done, and what we are doing and what we will do.

Building for the future

In those early days, the challenges lay in getting goods to the docks for the first time, getting people to accept Chinese letters of credit, all sorts of things like that. It was getting people to accept the vision that China wasn't for fighting with, China wasn't for competing with, China wasn't for containing, but that China would, of its own strength, grow and develop into a major world nation. And that's what has happened. Some people opposed this idea; today, few still hold out hopes that China will go back to being the type of place that it was before 1949, but of course there are some who would like it to go back to the days when foreigners had a grip on China.

A lot of the tensions in the relationship between China and the West today are due to the influence of what happened in China in those previous 150–200 years. The memory of the Chinese people for what the foreigners did to them is considerable. Some people (like me) say to them that they brought some of it on themselves by rejecting overtures from the West – and they did – but there's no justification for opium or anything like that at all. If you shut yourself off from the world, you always run the risk that other people are going to open you up, although if you're a bit more subtle in your methods you don't run into such problems. This still very much influences China today as an open country. The reaction to the Western media coverage of the Olympic Torch is all about that sense of humiliation that the Chinese feel the West imposed on them – and which it still, from time to time, goes about doing again in the current day.

The 48 Group was one of the main means of doing business with China for Europe. We also helped to open up trade with the United States in 1971–72, when I started working for the organisation and went to live in America. Later we joined with the government in a single organisation, the China-Britain Business Council (CBBC), which is the main trade promotion body for China-Britain trade. This has worked well on the whole in terms of the trade agenda. The 48 Group Club was established as a place where people who were really interested in gaining a medium- to long-term understanding of China could maintain their relations, both with China and with each other. We really raised our profile in the late 1990s when the last Governor of Hong Kong, Chris Patten, started attacking China in what we considered to be a most ill-advised way, and against our long-term interests. Since then The 48 Group Club has been an organisation of some profile in the United Kingdom. Today we organise lectures, offer fellowships and various awards and generally promote a positive attitude towards China business through culture, education and sport.

It was getting people to accept that China wasn't for competing with, China wasn't for containing, but that, of its own strength, it would develop into a major world nation

We don't go around doing trade missions and that kind of thing – we're never going to start doing that. If we go anywhere in China and I say I'm the Chairman of the 48 Group, then maybe five times out of ten I will get a blank face. When that happens, I say, 'You don't know the 48 Group?' and there's a couple of moments of embarrassed silence and they say, 'No,

Stephen Perry

actually we don't', so I will say 'Here's a brochure, why don't you do some checking and find out who we are?' The next time we meet, they are very attentive and very switched on. Our name carries a lot of weight, but not everyone in Britain has really worked out how to use it. There is no comparable organisation with our history in any major Western country that is still going, and that could give the UK a huge comparative advantage in China.

The new generation

A very important part of our organisation is the younger generation of the 48 Group, the 'Young Icebreakers'. This initiative grew out of a meeting I had with Premier Wen Jiabao about four years ago, when we got onto the subject of the tensions that occasionally resurface between the British and the Chinese, and how much things have improved since 1997. It is true that when the Labour Party came into government that year it did completely turn over a new leaf in Sino-UK relations, starting with the Hong Kong handover. The British were basically misled by US President Bill Clinton's pre-election, post-Tiananmen rhetoric. Within months of coming to office, he had changed his position, but by that time Patten had already spoken. That left the British in a bit of a cul de sac, but when the Labour Party came into government in 1997, things did change. The Labour Party did invest in a better relationship, although I don't think they really thought through all the implications and possibilities of that better relationship in a rapidly changing world.

Premier Wen said, 'The future is with the young people. They can come to all this without the prejudices of the older generation, and that's where I hope you will concentrate your future work'

In my conversation with Premier Wen, we talked about the problems of the past, the memories of the Opium Wars and so on and the tensions that exist between the generations – there was a lot of mistrust on the British side towards the Chinese, and vice versa. And he said, 'You know, the future is with the young people. They can come to all this without the prejudices of the older generation, and that's where I hope you will concentrate some of your future work.'

I thought about that for a long time, and I tried to find a solution to what it meant. We've got 60 million people in the UK of whom, say, 20 million are young people; China has got 1.4 billion of whom, say, 400 million are young people. But how do you actually bring them into contact with one another? Well, there were a lot of things we could do, and in part this has stimulated a lot more lectures and talks, and in part I think it also led to the China Now Festival in the UK in early 2008. I think that what we do is stimulate people, and then things happen as a consequence of us stimulating them.

However, in the end I decided that actually the answer to the conundrum that Wen had set me was to put The 48 Group Club into the hands of young people – by 'young', I mean people aged between 20 and 40 – and that is really what the Young Icebreakers is: it's a first step in bringing together young people, British, British-Chinese

Building for the future

Jack Perry with Bo Yibo at the opening of the 48 Group Club Liaison Office in Beijing, 1985

and Chinese, who will work out what they want from this name and this history and this tradition, and they will take over the Club – they will be the Club. People ask me what I mean by that, and I say, 'Well, do you remember when Deng Xiaoping came back in 1978–79, and suddenly he took all the old leaders out, called them all "senior advisers", and made himself one?'. He said, 'You know, we changed a generation almost overnight.' And that is what we will do in The 48 Group Club, when these younger people are ready.

It's not really going to be a matter of how old the current generation is or what we need, it'll be a matter of when the young people are ready. As soon as they're ready – and, boy, do they learn fast – they'll take over. And if you ask me what The 48 Group Club will be then, I honestly don't know, because that would be to determine what young people will do. But if I had a hunch, it would be that there will be a group of young people who, over the next 20 to 30 years will become the leaders in developing a positive relationship in the UK, which means that they'll understand China very well from a number of different perspectives – sport, business, culture, education, and so on – and that they will have developed networks with Chinese of a similar background.

We've got 60 million people in the UK of whom, say, 20 million are young people; China has got 1.4 billion, of whom, say, 400 million are young. But how do you bring them together?

China is probably the most important foreign country for the British to understand and learn about, but the UK is not that for the Chinese. So, finding Chinese who are interested in the UK takes a little more work, but there are a number of different things – our stability, our education system, all sorts of things – that mark us out. The Young Icebreakers will develop with these Chinese: they'll start as friends and then they'll become business acquaintances and then, hopefully, they will grow into leaders of the future.

How the UK sees China

There is a neurosis in the way that the UK media currently perceives China, and this isn't going to go away. The British media were all bullish about China in the 1980s, seeing the beginnings of liberalisation, but then they all got their dreams broken with Tiananmen Square and suddenly all became hostile to China, and now they have an absurdly antagonistic position to the Chinese.

I don't think the BBC will interview me any more, because I just take them on every time. I was interviewed by the BBC recently for a radio programme and the presenter started, 'Do you think this brutal and ruthless regime should have the Olympics?', and I said, 'Which brutal and ruthless regime? Have you been there? Do you know what you're talking about? What would you think if the Chinese, in 2012, three months before the London Olympics, ran a radio programme in which they talked about the ruthless and brutal British regime? Why are you trying to make the Olympics such a negative thing for the Chinese?' And this is one of the problems – the media have got a paranoia about China.

Such misconceptions are not confined to the media. Very few people in Britain have grasped the real importance of the Communist Party in China and the need to engage

Politburo member Li Yuanchao delivered a 2007 Icebreaker lecture at the House of Commons in London

Building for the future

with it. Now, you can say that dealing with the Premier of China is important, and of course it is. But the Government of China doesn't make policy – policy is made by the Communist Party. I remember a Chinese Communist Party delegation coming to the UK about four or five years ago, meeting a delegation from the Labour Party and asking questions, and there was a complete lack of comprehension in both directions. The Chinese were saying, 'If someone wants to join the Labour Party, what type of political education do you give them before you accept them?', and the Labour Party people said, 'We just take their money, and hope that they'll help us and do some work at election time.' And the Chinese replied, 'Well, we don't take anybody as a member of our Party unless they've been through a very strenuous review and also education.'

The core of China is the Communist Party – it's more than 74 million people. And the Labour Party doesn't really exist any more as a living body, even when it is in government. If you suggested to the General Secretary of the Labour Party that he went to meet the General Secretary of the Communist Party of China, he would run terrified because people would think he was a Communist sympathiser; that's one of the problems for the Labour Party. And the Tory party also has no serious connections with the CPC. The CPC leads China, and its head is Hu Jintao, and the Standing Committee. We have little contact with the Party leadership, its higher bodies, or the many leading groups that develop policy within China.

The 1952 letter that began the Icebreaking initiative

For instance, the policy relating to financial services, which matter so much to the UK, is not made by the Chinese banking regulator; it's made by the Financial Services group within the Party. Business people in the UK want to get market access in China, and they have meetings with the Chinese Minister of Commerce – but he doesn't make policy on market access, he only implements the

The Young Icebreakers will start as friends with these Chinese and then they'll become business acquaintances and then, hopefully, they will grow into leaders of the future

policy, although of course he's involved in some of the deliberations about it.

Similarly, if you take foreign affairs and you look at the Foreign Affairs group of the Party – the leading group on foreign affairs – the Minister of Foreign Affairs is about number eight on the list. There's a Ministry of Foreign Affairs which deals with foreigners, and then there's a Foreign Affairs section of the Party, which is as big, or bigger, than the Ministry and actually develops policy on foreign affairs. People go talking, for example, about Darfur to the Ministry of Foreign Affairs, which you have to do, because they are the implementers, but they should also be talking to the Foreign Affairs group and the people in that, and they should have an understanding of how it all fits together. The British do not understand this: they keep knocking against doors that do not really lead to where they want and need to go.

China and the developing world

At one level the relationship between China and other developing parts of the world is very simple. All Asia's manufacturing and assembly for exports to the United States and Europe has moved to China – mainly led by foreign or overseas Chinese owners. At the same time, many of the raw materials or components for those exports come from Africa, Asia and Latin America. All of a sudden there's a big trade going on with China, fuelled by demand from the United States and Europe. This means that Africa and Latin America have become important to China, and it has consolidated those relationships. The government's policies, and its intent, are good ones – I've known them long enough to know that their deep values are positive.

There are other things at work: China needs to build resources of food, oil and other commodities, and Asia, Africa and Latin America are important in supplying these, so China will build relationships with them. Now, it's very easy, because in certain respects the Chinese are doing what the West used to do, to point a finger at them and say that they're being imperialists or colonialists. However, that depends on the price one is paying and whether it's genuine; not to mention whether or not it is accompanied by political or military interference – and if you look at China's commercial relations with Africa, not just in the past ten years but over the past 50, you'll see they have generally been fair. Most of the increase in GNP in Africa has come as a result of Chinese purchasing. Of course, there are some bad individuals and some bad policies, but if the Americans or the British were punished pro rata for the mistakes they made in places like Africa, the headlines would be full of it the whole time.

The Chinese have come in for criticism over Darfur, but generally their involvement

Celebrating the Year of the Rat, February 2008

Building for the future

there has been intended to help stabilise the situation. From the public relations point of view it has not been handled very well, but it's not been a disaster. It's mainly been the enemies of China who have tried to make it look bad in Darfur, Zimbabwe and places like that. The Chinese in general have responded pretty quickly when a real problem has been identified.

I think what is a bit more of a concern – where the Chinese can go wrong in the field, although it will be pointed out to them and I think that they'll react and deal with it – is the behaviour of individual Chinese corporations, which do not have the same values and controls

> *This big trade means that Africa and Latin America have become important to China, and it has consolidated those relationships. The government's policies, and its intent, are good ones*

as the government. Companies will need to be watched very closely by the Chinese embassies abroad, to make sure that they don't act corruptly or improperly. I've heard some stories that I don't like the sound of at all, and I hope that the Chinese have kicked the behinds of the guys who are behaving badly – or else they'll be as bad as we were. However, I don't think they will be: I think they are, at the centre, principled. Time will tell.

The important thing with China is that scrutiny may be more difficult – though, of course, all foreign companies ought to be scrutinised in Africa. A bigger arms shipper in the world, by a factor of 50 over China, is America. If people were genuinely concerned about stopping the murder of hundreds of thousands of people across the world by evil people, they would campaign to stop arms exports from America, as well as from Britain, France and other countries. The Chinese are much lower on that list; they are still doing it and it shouldn't be happening, in my opinion, but individual corporations are a bit more difficult to control.

I remember someone at a big Western corporation – I won't mention its name – once thanked me very much for something I'd done for him, and asked me whether I would like to make some money: they wanted me to arrange for the People's Liberation Army to test their bullets. So I said, 'I don't quite understand, why do you need to get them to test them? You can put them in a gun and fire them.' He said, 'No, it has to be on real targets.' I thanked him for the meal, and left.

A changing society

The way that some people in the West depict the Chinese Communist Party as being run by old men holding on to power – which is a nice picture to paint for anti-Communists – means that you end up missing the whole point: that this Party has transformed China in 30 years. Again, all the headline stuff about Mao Zedong means that people miss the real point about China. People did die under Mao, but if there had been no Mao Zedong there would have been no modern China. He unified the country and laid the basis for modern industry and agriculture, science and technology. Of course the Cultural Revolution and the Great Leap Forward had many terrible aspects to them, but when a country is coming from where China was then, things do happen that are terrible – and I'm no defender of that. But this tendency to condemn Mao and to condemn the Communist Party means that people miss what's really going on.

What's going on at this point in time is that China is being led by some really socialist-motivated people: socialist in the sense of 'We're here for the betterment of mankind, we're here for the betterment of our country, we're here for the betterment of our people – that's why we're civil servants'.

So what type of vision do they have of society? It's of a society, remarkably, that's a lot closer to the realities of the Third Way than we understood. In the United Kingdom, the Third Way was a recognition by the Labour Party that the middle class had become the largest class in the country. China's policies are aimed at transforming as many people as reasonably possible into a middle class, and giving that middle class innate responsibility and innate recognition of its duties to those who are less successful. You are looking at the creation of the first state-controlled, Party-controlled middle class in the history of the world.

People think that the private sector is something that will be a force acting on the Chinese leadership. Not at all: the Chinese leadership have invented, created and appointed the private sector themselves. Officials are not sent out as Party hacks to run the private sector, but if you are involved in the private sector in China, if you start a business and you become successful and start growing it, then you won't go too far before you find the Party, and then you have to recognise that you have to operate within the Party's parameters. And so the Party does become socially conscious, it does help in a number of ways at a local level.

As China's leaders try to build this socially conscious society, where GDP and per capita incomes are steadily rising, they are conscious of the fact that things go wrong – corruption, pollution of the environment, inequalities between town and country, north and south, east and west, between the poor and rich in the cities and so on … all these things become apparent. People say, 'Have you seen what's going on in China, how bad the pollution is?' Well, if China wasn't developing, it wouldn't have the pollution.

China's policies are aimed at transforming as many people as reasonably possible into a middle class. You are looking at the creation of the first state-controlled middle class in the history of the world

These are the results of taking 400 million people out of poverty. China has got another 400 million people to move out of the countryside, and it is going to build hundreds more towns and cities to help achieve this. They're not going to continue moving these people into existing towns, they're going to build a lot more new cities around the country. The big corporations will be owned by the pension funds and the insurance funds, but they will be controlled by the State through the pension and insurance industries. They'll be there to grow, to participate in the world, and to help raise the overall life of all the Chinese. The vision then breaks down into details of stock markets and all sorts of different things;

Building for the future

that's China's vision of where it's going, and it is proving remarkably successful at it.

The Chinese used to go around the world asking people how they did things. They still do that, but now we're getting to the point where people are starting to go to China to learn how to do things. Our education system in the UK is somewhat complacent: because we've got 100,000 Chinese students here, we think that the Chinese have some sort of dependency relationship with the UK. Well, when I brought the Chinese Minister of Education here about four or five

The Chinese used to go around the world asking people how they did things. Now we are getting to the point where people are starting to go to China to learn how to do things

years ago, he told me (and everyone else) that he intended to have as many foreign students in China as there were Chinese students abroad – that's over 300,000.

Now that is the most phenomenal opportunity, but no one in the United Kingdom was even participating in that process; they were all focused on bringing Chinese students to the UK. The big educational developments of the world will, in time, be in China. They'll have much larger numbers of people. The big developments in health and in pensions will originate in China, because they're the ones who will have been around the world,

The 48 Group Club usually receives an attentive hearing in China, where its brand name carries weight

My Thirty Years in China | 33

started with a blank piece of paper and designed systems for the modern day.

I had a meeting with the Labour Party almost ten years ago, when a group of us talked about health and pensions, and I said, 'I think you're starting at the wrong point, guys. Why don't you look at what kind of health service and pensions you would create if you were starting today, and then work out how to get there? That's what the Chinese do.' But people in the West are stuck with what they've got, and with trying to reform it – and clearly the reforms of our major institutions aren't working.

> *Three or four years ago, people said don't invest in Chinese banks because of their non-performing loans – and now Chinese banks are doing much better than Western banks*

The Chinese are not obliged to start with a National Health Service – they can create a health industry from scratch. People can say that China's health and education services are not at the Western level and that they've got a lot of problems. They may be right, but you just wait, in ten or fifteen years' time....Three or four years ago, people were saying, don't bother to invest in Chinese banks because of their non-performing loans – and now Chinese banks are doing much better than Western banks. I think that this sort of contemplation of the Chinese vision is critical for the West to understand where China is going.

Herein lies the danger: if we don't understand where China is going, and we carry on our stupid battles with them, they will still go on growing, and China could become very big and powerful. Generally speaking, the Chinese are usually one jump ahead of most people. I think all the protests in spring 2008 against the Olympic Torch were just silly stuff, and not likely to change China's direction.

Our concern is: who will be the leaders of China in 30 years' time, what will they be like, and how can we make sure that they're participating in a world that we're all comfortable with? We have a situation now where America walked into Iraq despite the opposition of the United Nations and of many nations of the world. Why shouldn't China take similar unilateral action in the future against a smaller and weaker neighbour on the pretext, true or false, that the country is pursuing a nuclear programme detrimental to China's interests? So I believe that we've got to look at the world institutions and we've got to look at how to encourage the creation of an Asian Union, and as quickly as possible. The Americans keep on trying to force an APEC-based union, which is a nonsense. An Asian Union is in the interest of all the people of the world. We ought to be talking to the Chinese and helping them to understand the importance of accountability, of being able to remove leaders if they think they're inappropriate. If we support the development of global institutions, global structures and interdependence in terms of sharing resources and the fruits of development, it makes it nearly impossible for people to start wars. Why don't the Germans and French go to war any more? Well, it wouldn't even enter their heads, because they're both part of the European Union.

For example, we could get to a situation in 30 years' time where we're fighting over oil. In 2005 the Americans rejected CNOOC's purchase of the oil company Unocal, but

Building for the future

if they'd had any sense, they would have said, 'No, you can have it – a 50/50 deal with an American company.' The Chinese would have been happy, the Americans would have been happy, and the Chinese and Americans would have learned how to work with each other. But the prejudices and the negativity towards China prevent people understanding a) its vision and b) what results from that in terms of prioritising what we need to do with China.

Dramatic transformation

It's almost impossible to describe how much China has changed since I first went there in 1972, how to work it out conceptually. Foreign trade accounted for a negligible part of China's GDP and foreigners' interaction with the country was extremely limited. Most of what trade did go on was done through the Canton Fair. There were eight foreign trade corporations that conducted all the business, nearly all of it through the Canton Fairs, and it was simply buying and selling. It's completely changed now.

I remember, in 1974, going to help a Chinese company develop ceramics suitable for the American market and taking some people to one of its key factories in Liling, about two hours' drive from Changsha in Hunan province. The cars had curtained windows and we had police outriders. When we arrived at the factory and turned in at the gates, I looked round and thought 'Those windows over there look dirty'. But they

With President Hu Jintao at Buckingham Palace during his state visit to Britain, November 2005

weren't: it was because there were hundreds, perhaps thousands, of people pressed up against the windows to see the first foreigners since 1949. They were as much concerned about our safety as anything else, because some of these people, obviously, had had bad experiences with foreigners. That China then is completely different today.

And it has been through so many stages. That's why I have the utmost respect for this Party: they've taken China through so many stages that they must have had a pretty good idea of where they were going right from the start. People often attack Chinese policies – for example, they ask the question about China's US$1.5 trillion foreign reserves, but they miss the point: when did the Chinese decide to build that level of reserves, and why? And you go back to the early 1990s: that's when they changed their exchange rate.

> *On this whole question of whether China's growth is right or wrong, I ask: was the Industrial Revolution right or wrong? Neither: it was an inevitability, a part of history*

They did it to provide a power balance with the Americans, and it has been effective. The Americans never thought that China was of any great importance until the end of 2006, the beginning of 2007. Suddenly they realised that China's reserves had grown to such an important level – by then it was approaching US$1 trillion – and when the Americans started trying to tell them what to do, the Chinese said 'No'. They couldn't have done that without having that amount of Treasury bonds.

The Chinese who I deal with today are a completely different people. In some ways I preferred the old way. The Chinese people you met were very diligent, with very high personal values. Today a lot more people are involved, with much more varied values. Some of these Chinese don't behave the way I'd like them to behave in this world – but then I guess that the same is true of the British. So, it's been a complete and total transformation: like comparing, say, Bombay 20 years ago with London today.

Of course there are downsides. Some of the Chinese leaders told me in the late 1980s that Mao had thought that China needed to triple its population in order to have enough agricultural and industrial workers and to have a big enough army to defend itself. So he emphasised population. They said it was a mistake – but he wasn't to know then that the world was going to go through a huge technological transition.

Really, they said, our population is at least double, maybe triple, what it needs to be. And that's our fundamental driver: we've got to provide jobs, health care and everything else for our population. To do that, we've got to go the way that we have. Personally, I think all the cars in China are an abomination – the pollution is horrible. But they say, 'Well, what would you do – would you not give cars to your people? They'll shout at us.' I reply, 'Well, you might have developed electric cars. ' They say, 'It's all very well for you – you're not in the business of running a car company.' And they're quite right.

On this whole question of whether China's growth is right or wrong, I ask: was the Industrial Revolution right or wrong? Neither: it was an inevitability, a part of history. I think that the Chinese have captured the problems of their development,

Building for the future

though whether they'll be able to address them or not is another question. Then there's the cynicism with which people say that China hasn't met its targets in reducing energy costs or it hasn't managed a reduction in pollution – well, five years ago, nobody had any targets or controls for these things. I think they are serious about it, and I think that this is why misreading who the Chinese really are is a big mistake, because they will solve a lot of these problems, and will solve them well before us in the West. And will they help us? Well, probably they will – so then the shoe will be on the other foot.

The major challenges for China, I think, are pollution, the environment, getting the resources it needs and maintaining good relations outside – and trying to stop the Americans or the Japanese going off on an anti-Chinese trajectory. All these things are part of the same problems: there are problems of development, problems of success. I think that corruption is less of a problem than some people do, although it is a problem. Having said that, I watched a football match in the UK recently, and I really did wonder whether the referee was bent! Corruption exists in many societies in many forms, and I think the Chinese have got to keep on top of it, to keep it under control.

China has got 1.4 billion people and it really only needs about 600–700 million, and there are big social inequalities: north–south, east–west, peasant–town, and in the towns rich–poor, and there is the contradiction with the environment and pollution. Those are the main problems that they have identified they have to deal with, and

Premier Wen Jiabao in 2004 with the late Percy Timberlake, one of the founders of the 48 Group Club

they will deal with them. There have been tensions. People say, 'Look at this, they've had 78,000 incidents of social unrest'. Well, who told you they had 78,000 incidents? They did. And why did they tell you that? Because they're saying, we have a problem and we're going to have to deal with it. And they wanted to be able to carry their people and the international community with them, because it's difficult to keep secrets any more. So they had to show that there was a real problem first, and they have done.

> There are times in development when more sophisticated forms of controls come into place, but these are the pressures that China has to deal with now

I think that, right now, if the Chinese government wanted to put a road through to get to an Olympic site, they wouldn't want a lot of planning appeals and objections, which we have in the UK. However, in 10–15 years' time, I think, you'll see a lot more of that kind of thing, because by then they'll have put in most of their roads. And when we put in our own roads, we weren't very big on appeals. There are times in development when more sophisticated forms of controls come into place, but those are the pressures that China has to deal with now.

My prediction is that there is no real pressure on the Chinese government. If the CPC stood for election today, it would win hands down, and that's the misreading of China that people make. If there was a credible opposition, instead of it being 75:25, it might be 60:40, but it would still be a landslide, and it would be because the CPC delivers, and

Guests at The 48 Group Club Icebreakers Chinese New Year Dinner held in Leeds in 2006

Building for the future

nobody else does. What alternative vision could you develop for China that would be better than what the Communist Party is delivering on? I think you would find it hard to find one person in four who would vote against them.

When I was interviewed by the BBC recently, they asked me 'What do you think of the absence of democracy in China?' and I said

Sir William Ehrman, the UK Ambassador to China, meets Mme Fu Ying, the Chinese Ambassador to the UK, at the Icebreakers 2008 New Year banquet

'What are you talking about?' So they said, 'Well, you know, opposition parties.' I said, 'I haven't met a Chinese in years who said they wanted an opposition party'. We have the type of Parliament we do, because we had to reconcile the differences between capitalists, many of whom were exploitative and uncaring, and workers, who suffered. The nineteenth century in Britain was no pretty place to be, and the parliamentary democracy we have today was originally to settle that all down, to let us deal with it through Parliament.

The Chinese don't have that background. They do have similar situations, with workers or peasants who are not happy about their conditions, but their own forms of democracy will be applied to those situations. It may or may not be a parliamentary democracy that emerges in time – although I would think that is

The concept of a harmonious society, which Hu Jintao has been promoting, reaches far back into Chinese culture and is readily understood and appreciated by the Chinese people

unlikely: I think it will be a democracy that works in a different way. I think the Chinese have got ideas about this, but people really don't ask them what form of democracy they think they will develop. Let's see what happens: I think we might be surprised. China certainly sees Western democracy as conflict-based and unable to deal with long-term issues.

The concept of a harmonious society, which Hu Jintao has been promoting, reaches far back into Chinese culture and is readily understood and appreciated by the Chinese people.

Stephen Perry

Elton John with a local staff member, in China with Watford FC in the early 1980s

As it develops, it can address the concerns and interests of all sections of the Chinese people in a genuinely democratic way, but one that stresses consensus and compromise rather than confrontation and conflict.

Chinese society is changing. You don't develop a middle class without developing pressures, and you then have to develop mechanisms to deal with those pressures. It's now about seven years since Jiang Zemin wrote 'The Three Represents'. At the time, everybody called it a lot of jargonistic rubbish – but it wasn't. He was saying, 'We have to be led by the middle classes, and we have to change to deal with the consequences of that.' You can see very clearly now what that means. It means that if people don't want a highway built on stilts through the middle of their city, like in Shenzhen, or a train that goes at superhuman speeds through Shanghai, then they'll object to it, and they may stop it happening.

The government knows that it's going to have to operate differently – and that's why we're talking about democracy, the rule of law and the role of the Party within that emerging paradigm – because they're talking to their own Party members. And they will operate differently. If they don't, the world will face a catastrophe far greater than the Indian Ocean tsunami. If China goes wrong, you're going to have half a billion people walking around the world, looking for food. We shouldn't be so critical and negative about the leadership in China: it's in all our interests to make sure that they succeed.

Cultural exchanges

In my 'day job' as Managing Director of the London Export Corporation, I've had many lighter moments in my personal involvement with China, and many fascinating experiences. For example, we took the first foreign football team to China in 1977/78, a trip that involved an incredible amount of intrigue on the British side. At that time no football team was allowed to play the Chinese because they weren't in FIFA, the international football federation, because Taiwan was

Building for the future

a member of FIFA. Our job was to break the boycott, and in the end the British agreed to do it – I don't quite know what went on behind the scenes, but there were incredible machinations. Eventually West Bromwich Albion, with manager Ron Atkinson, star player Bryan Robson and all the others, went to China, and we organised the tour for them.

Midway through the second half of the second game, there was an incredible roar, and only about four years ago did I find out what that was. The current British Ambassador, Sir William Ehrman, who was then a junior in the British Embassy, told me that it was the first reappearance of Deng Xiaoping in public. He emerged at the front of a box and waved to the crowd, and they roared their approval. This was before anybody knew that he was coming back, although there were rumours of it.

We took other football teams after that – Sheffield United, Watford twice, and Arsenal; now they all go. Sheffield United have a deal with Chengdu and Stockport County did a lot in China, although they've stopped now. We took Elton John as chairman of Watford FC, though I'm not sure that was a cultural exchange: I think it was more of a shock exchange. The Vice Minister of Sport had never seen a man wearing a diamond in his ear before. In fact, I've probably seen more cultural shocks than I've seen cultural exchanges.

We've taken a lot of ballet companies to China, we've taken orchestras, we've taken shows like *Phantom of the Opera*, *Cats* and *Les Misérables*. It was very interesting to talk about the Chinese taking *Miss Saigon*, with its characterisation of Vietnam and the Communists. It all makes for very interesting exchanges, and it's intriguing how you try to find the balance. In the end, people are pretty mature, and they find what they want to find.

Taking Andrew Lloyd Webber to China was interesting: he has a desire for the most exotic foods in the world and so when I went out for dinner with him, it was one of the most miserable experiences I've ever had! Cameron Mackintosh is fascinated by China; he absorbs everything about the country he possibly can. We took the singer Elaine Page, we've taken big, important leaders from America, and I've spent a lot of time in America with the Chinese. It's just fascinating watching all the cultures meet each other. The Chinese are incredibly polite – that's why they have problems with the Western media, because they're not used to being interrupted and they're not used to being rude about each other. They can't quite handle the insistence on forceful or even provocative questions, but I hope they learn. I'm sure they will.

> *I'm not sure that taking Elton John to China was a cultural exchange: I think it was more of a shock exchange. The Vice Minister of Sport had never seen a man with a diamond in his ear before*

I've spent over 40 years being involved in culture, sports, education, all sorts of things, and in opening doors, in making things happen. Personally, my engagement with China has been very enjoyable and it's been very interesting, very interesting indeed.

Michael De Clercq
President, TransContinental Trade & Finance Corp

First came to China: 1975

Born in Belgium, Michael de Clercq studied Chinese at the Australian National University in Canberra, Australia, and first travelled to China in 1975. He lived and worked in China for many years and then moved his family to the USA, from where he continues to travel to China about once a month. He is happily married and is the proud father of three grown-up children.

He set up his company in 1978, established his main office in Beijing and initially developed a trading business, buying manufactured goods from China and selling machinery. Early on, he made investments in industrial plants in different parts of China.

After the 1980s, he supervised a change in business direction for the company, and developed it into a thriving consulting business specialising in three areas:
Sourcing: Helping companies buy better in China.
Sales: Market analysis, Marketing strategies and Sales implementation.
Growth: Business development, including mergers and acquisitions.

Website: www.chinaperformancegroup.com

Growing a business

Language was the lure that first drew Michael de Clercq to China. Once hooked, he found himself embarking on a thirty-year relationship with the country that has involved marriage and family, numerous valuable friendships and many adventures, and the never-ending struggles and joys of doing business in a rapidly changing economy

They were aluminum crutches. Not the clumsy wooden ones that hurt your armpits, but the aluminum ones that fit on your forearms, under the elbows, and allow you to walk, really walk, with your arms. It was the winter of 1975, and I had flown into Hong Kong. I had a broken leg but that was not going to stop me: I was going to China. I was 21 and I did know then that this was the beginning of the adventure of a lifetime. Many people have asked me since what it was that prompted my interest in China, what got me started? Upon reflection, the answer is language. At the time, I spoke French and Italian, I was pretty good in Dutch and knew some German and Spanish. I was in my first year of college and I had selected Political Science and Economics courses, but I needed one more course to complete my line-up. Modern Chinese was appealing, but so was Prehistory.

I had to make a choice. I consulted my friends and, although they did not have much of an opinion on Prehistory, they were surprisingly unanimous in steering me clear of Chinese: it was way too hard and would drag my GPA score down. Moreover, they said, it was useless to someone who wanted to go into business. So Chinese it was.

I was fascinated first by Chinese characters. I discovered that the concept was not at all like the English alphabet. For example, you cannot read English unless you speak English. Not so with Chinese. You don't have to speak Mandarin to read Chinese, you just have to know what the characters mean. Each character represents an idea, a picture or a stylised combination thereof. And you can learn their meaning in any language, which means that people who only speak, say, Vietnamese, Korean, Japanese, Russian, English or one of the 47 major dialects of China can read it. This was the glue that had held the Chinese empire together, an empire that stretched for millennia over distances, dynasties and cultures.

> *It was the winter of 1975, and I had flown into Hong Kong. I had a broken leg but that was not going to stop me: I was going to China. I was 21 and I didn't know that this was the beginning of the adventure of a lifetime*

But learning Chinese was still not going to be of any use to me. The point is, what I wanted to do from day one was to develop a career in business and, in 1974, it didn't seem that knowledge of the Chinese language was going to be at all useful for that purpose. I had friends who studied Japanese and who reckoned that that was the business language to study. They had a point: China at the time was not open to trade and change was unlikely in the foreseeable future, whereas Japan was the economic miracle that everyone wanted to emulate. But I was stubborn, and probably optimistic too, and I became passionate about Chinese. I ended up changing my college courses, taking a Major in Modern Chinese and a Sub-Major in Classical Chinese, as well as Chinese Culture and Philosophy courses. After college, I sought every opportunity to put the Chinese I was learning to some use. I was lucky. And one thing led to another...

First trip, 1975
Memory fades, but some aspects of that first China trip in 1975 remain deeply etched into my brain. Trepidation is a strong marker. Everything about China was shrouded with awe-inspiring mystery. China was still undergoing its Cultural Revolution, a movement not fully understood in the West at the time but perceived to have a sinister undercurrent. The Vietnam War was just over and Maoism, an old lefty campus favorite, was alive and well, with Jiang Qing (Mao's wife) and the Gang of Four still in power. At the same time, China was known as the 'sleeping giant' and references were made to Napoleon ('When China shall wake, the world will tremble'); the country's economic potential hung like an awe-inspiring velvet curtain in the dark background.

China was not 'open' at the time. Visas were very difficult to get and were subject to some mysterious approval process, so when I finally got mine, nothing could stop me from going. Little was known of the reality of day-to-day China. I recall that my expectation was that people, men and women alike, would be dressed in blue suits, and most likely waving little red books. Prejudices were all you had to go on. And yet, I knew that the people of China were also the proud heirs of a magnificent empire – this would make an interesting combination of baggage. I was curious to see the real thing.

When I arrived in Guangzhou, I had some time to spare before connecting with my Beijing train, so I went to the Nan Yuan, one of the most famous Cantonese restaurants of the time, to experience what turned out to be a delectable meal. The staff proposed wine (*jiu*) with the meal, and I was keen to try it since I liked wines and did not know that China produced them. But by *jiu* they did not – unfortunately – mean grape wine: I had just had my first encounter with Chinese alcohol. I don't remember the brand, but it stayed with me for the duration of my 48-hour trip to Beijing. Not pleasant. I decided right there and then that I would not drink *jiu* any more. I could not have known then but the resolution did not, could not, last: over time I would end up drinking gallons of the stuff.

The train trip to Beijing was very comfortable. I was alone in my 'soft sleeper' compartment and kept myself busy looking out of the window and observing the

> *Prejudices were all you had to go on. And yet, I knew that the people of China were also the proud heirs of a magnificent empire – this would make an interesting combination of baggage. I was curious to see the real thing*

Growing a business

activities of the train. Everything was a discovery. Every detail was significant; every moment was a surprise. My guidebook was a hefty red volume of 1,568 pages published in 1967 by Nagel of Switzerland and written in French. Great for historical context, but woefully short on modern China realities. It was my constant companion during that first visit. But it contained nothing about how to turn off the blaring stream of propaganda and music that was piped into my compartment. I discovered the 'off' switch under the little table only two hours before I arrived in Beijing, and I finally managed to get some sleep.

> *On the old Manchurian border between China and Russia in Heilongjiang, the immigration team were able to address us in excellent French, as well as English – a fact made all the more remarkable by the extreme scarcity of foreigners crossing that border*

I spent about four months in Beijing, and during that time I visited Tianjin and took a round trip to Siberia, going through Ulan Baator in Mongolia, and returning via Manchuria. In Beijing, I was staying at the residence of the French Embassy as a guest of M. Arnaud, the French Ambassador to China, who was the stepfather of my friend Philippe. There were five of us young people staying together and Beijing was a never-ending source of wonderment and fun. The visits to the cultural icons of Gu Gong, the Summer Palace, the Temple of Heaven and the Great Wall alternated with trips to the *dashala* arts and crafts district, the *hutong* (the side streets), Baihuodalou (the department store), bridge games and visits to the zoo, schools, farms and museums.

Our trip to Siberia was noteworthy partially because it provided an interesting contrast between the Communists of China and those of the USSR. Both societies were new to me, and they were obviously different in two aspects. The first was consumer goods. The shops in China were full of merchandise, but the shelves in Irkustk were bare. One large shoe store there had only one style of

Christmas 1975 at the French Embassy in Beijing, complete with crutches

shoe available. The same applied to restaurants. Although many restaurants in Beijing lacked the kind of dishes that Westerners expected, food nonetheless seemed plentiful. In Siberia, the menus were a litany of 'don't have'.

The other element was, shall we say, diplomatic polish. The Russian immigration officials we encountered were generally uncouth, loud and unable to speak anything but Russian. The Chinese, by contrast, were polite and sophisticated; on the old Manchurian border between China and Russia in Heilongjiang, the immigration team were even able to address us in excellent French, as well as English – a fact made all the more remarkable by the extreme scarcity of foreigners crossing that border.

Back in Beijing, my broken leg was strong enough to allow some load bearing, so I would attach my crutches to a sturdy Chinese bicycle and spent a lot of time cycling through the mostly car-free streets and avenues. It was winter and I was wearing a northern Chinese 'great coat' (*dayi*), which was made of thick blue cotton. I combined that with a dog-fur-lined, flap-eared winter hat and a face mask, and this disguise enabled me to blend into the throngs of bicycles and to observe daily life in Beijing incognito. It was great to no longer be the subject of relentless staring. I was to use that comfortable technique again years later but for a different purpose: to avoid drawing attention to myself while visiting my fiancée.

It may seem strange now, but at the time I was expecting the people to be gloomy and sad. I had reasoned that they did not have democracy so they must feel oppressed,

Despite the broken leg, I was keen to get around Beijing to visit sites such as the Temple of Heaven

Growing a business

and therefore must be miserable. But I saw them laughing and they seemed generally happy with their lot. They would, for example, push their weight around in the extremely crowded bicycle lanes and would cuss each other when a lack of skill or bad timing caused harmless accidents and sometimes hilarious, domino-

One my visits on that first trip to Beijing in 1975 was to a local school

like cascades of bicycles falling over. To the 21-year-old I was then, the surprise was that they were people, just like me. They had feelings, tempers, good days and bad days, and were not fundamentally different from the people I knew back home. I was soon to experience another facet of that humanity.

Zhou Enlai, China's famous Prime Minister, passed away on 8 January 1976. During that first trip, I went to his funeral. This was an official affair held in one of the parks on the edge of the Forbidden City at Tiananmen Square. The enormous crowds, conveyed there by buses, were well behaved. I was part of the foreign contingent and subject to the usual intense staring and scrutiny that foreigners attracted at that time. I noticed that a lot of photographs were being taken of me, probably because I was still walking on crutches. The sorrow at the departure of one of China's greatest leaders was in evidence everywhere, and nearly overpowering. I had never seen so many people crying. Not just women, but grown men were sobbing without shame.

The sorrow at the departure of one of China's greatest leaders was in evidence everywhere, and nearly overpowering. I had never seen so many people crying. Not just women, but grown men were sobbing without shame

And although the large crowds were well organised and disciplined, the sorrow seemed genuine, the tears were not artificial, the grief was everywhere, palpable, overwhelming. I had read a lot about Zhou Enlai, his diplomacy, his skill, his influence, and I was moved by the genuine affection that the people of China had for him.

I observed it again two years later in April, during Tomb Sweeping Day (the Qing Ming Festival). In my usual outfit of big coat, hat and face mask, I had gone to

Michael De Clercq

Tiananmen square by bicycle very early in the morning to film the dawn rising over the Monument to the People's Heroes, the big granite obelisk inscribed with Zhou Enlai's calligraphy. I set myself up at the Great Hall of the People with my Super 8 camera on a tripod and started filming when first light appeared over the Museum of History. The bushes surrounding the monument were covered with so many white paper flowers and wreaths that it looked like it had snowed. These tributes had been put there overnight by Beijing residents. Numerous bicycles were already passing by. Suddenly, a movement to my right caught my eye: a guard was running down the large staircase of the Great Hall of the People and heading towards me. The early morning light had revealed my presence. Not wanting any argument, I promptly packed my camera gear, jumped on my bicycle and headed for the road. The flow of bicycles opened, embraced me and I was away.

The Beijing Language Institute in 1978

For a few months in 1978, I lived and studied at 'Yuyan Xueyuan', the Beijing Language Institute (now called the Beijing Language and Culture University). I was sponsored by the Australian government, but I did not have a scholarship. I was *zifei*, which meant on my own expenses. Optimistic as I was, I had figured on earning my way in Beijing and was confident that I could find a job that would cover room and board. No such luck. I looked everywhere but could not find anything that paid more than Rmb50 a month. Embassies would not or could not hire, and there weren't any foreign companies in the market for young foreigners. I made ends meet, with some difficulty, by writing articles for Australian newspapers which, lazy as I was, I then translated into French and sent for publication in Belgium. The pay was not bad, but actual funds were very slow to arrive. So I ended up on a rice-only diet for weeks and having to borrow money from fellow students.

Yuyan Xueyuan, however, was a revelation. Foreign students were mostly from Europe or Australia (none yet from the USA), with contingents from Africa. The Chinese students there were a combination of people selected through the old system (*gong, nong, bing*: worker, peasant, soldier) and the new system. The gong nong bing system required no academic excellence, but relied instead on recommendations from Party cadres. This meant that many students from that group were selected not because of their intellect

For one thing, our room-mates had a very different concept of privacy from ours. They thought nothing of reading your private mail, for instance, and they were accustomed to letting you know of their every move

but because of their political correctness. The new system, on the other hand, demanded academic performance, and many of these students were very bright.

Lessons were in Chinese, using the traditional, learning-by-rote system prevalent at the time in China. To the university students that we were, it was somewhat reminiscent of kindergarten methods. Separation was the way of life at that time.

Growing a business

Engaged in debate at the Beijing Language Institute

Foreigners were separate from Chinese (different norms, separate dorms); we had different dining rooms; girls, of course were separate from boys; and tall fences and sturdy gates separated us all from the outside. We were herded into national groups, two per room, Italians staying with Italians, French with French, Australians with Australians, etc., and encouraged to stay that way. Some of us felt we had not travelled all that way to bond with fellow Australians. So we asked if we could have Chinese room-mates instead. No can do. We insisted. That raised eyebrows, but the school authorities did not budge. So we did what students do: we demonstrated. The authorities were not used to that subtle form of negotiation, so they gave in.

The students who were finally allocated to us were carefully selected. Since they were going to spend unsupervised time one-on-one with foreigners in the confines of a small room, they had to be ideologically reliable, and so came mostly from the *gong nong bing* batch and were carefully coached on how to deal with foreigners. This cultural exchange was a very interesting experience for all of us. We must have seemed quite weird to them and they certainly were strange to us. For one thing, our room-mates had a very different concept of privacy from ours. They thought nothing of reading your private mail, for instance, and they were accustomed to letting you know of their every move. My room-mate and I would be studying three feet apart at our mini-desks and every time he made a move, he would be sure to let me know. He would interrupt me to say: 'I am going to the toilet!' and five minutes later he would be back with the announcement: 'I am back from the toilet!'. Mesmerising.

My room-mate had been told that foreigners always got up late, say around 10am. So it was very confusing to him that I always rose at 5am for my martial arts training. He was fond of traditions and respectful of the calendar. When autumn officially arrived, he promptly put on multiple layers of clothes and at night covered himself with thick blankets. But it was a warm autumn and every morning his bed was soaked with perspiration. Still he remonstrated with me for wearing short sleeves and for sleeping under only a bed sheet. Conversation was rather limited;

Michael De Clercq

Monkeying around with Ian Stones, one of the foreign student contingent who became a firm friend

allowed topics were English, Chinese and sports. We were apparently not supposed to talk about girls, or God forbid (well, not really God), politics. Attempts to stray off this limited agenda would lead to tense situations or, sometimes, amusing results.

Toilets were easy to find, even with a poor nose. Urinals were on the right and the squat toilet stalls (sometimes known as French toilets) on the left. For privacy there were hip-high partitions between the toilets, which made for easy conversation with your neighbour when you stood to pull your trousers up. If a girl visited the men's dormitory it was a drama for my room-mate, but if a girl dared to use our bathroom it was infamy, since the male students she was visiting would guard the door (there were no locks) and my room-mate would be denied entry. After all, girls clearly had no business in the men's dorm, much less in the men's bathroom.

I asked my room-mate what the Chinese expression for 'male chauvinist pig' was. He explained this concept did not exist in China – but was interrupted by a girl nearby who gave me at least three Chinese idioms for it

Our foreign dining room was much less crowded and had a significantly better (and more expensive) selection of food than theirs, but Chinese students were not allowed in our dining room. So some of us (very few) would chose to eat in the Chinese dining room where the lines were very long, the food was poor but the atmosphere was great – and you got to learn Chinese. Standing in line was an experience in multi-level

Growing a business

conversations. It was there that I once bumped into my room-mate and asked him what the Chinese expression for 'male chauvinist pig' was. He proceeded to explain to me that this concept did not exist in China – but then was interrupted by a girl nearby who gave me at least three Chinese idioms for it.

I was there for less than four months, but what an experience! There were lots of rules and curfews, but I made good friends. We had memorable snowball fights. We introduced the concept of parties and disco (*Staying Alive*), we taught rock'n'roll dancing with crowd-stopping success and learned the finer points of the jitterbug and the waltz. We loved to collect Chinese books, which were rare and would sell out very quickly, so you always bought multiple copies for your friends. An excellent new Chinese/English dictionary had just come out, which was a great help and which became my constant new companion.

Amenities and luxuries were few. You had access to the Friendship Store, but that was far away. There was only one Chinese restaurant within walking distance of the school, across the street and in the middle of fields where students would meet to get away from the institute. But they only had *mantou* (buns), beer and *erguotou* (a cheap though good-quality alcohol); you could not get things like Scotch whisky unless you went to Hong Kong. On the other hand, some students noticed that hemp was growing wild on the side of the road and were drying stacks of it in their cupboards. We travelled everywhere by bicycle (black Flying Pigeon models). The nearby Beijing University was a hang-out, and we patronised the Old Summer Palace (Yuanmingyuan) from time to time, notably during the Autumn Festival when we drank warm rice wine (*huang jiu*) from thermos flasks and ate moon cakes in memory of the poet Qu Yuan.

'I am in love with an American girl: her name is Democracy.' This was the text of the most memorable *dazibao* (big character poster) I saw during the winter of 1978. It was written in English and Chinese, was pasted on a wall in Wangfujing and it tackled many taboos in a single sentence. Surprisingly, it stayed up for three days. Society was changing. There was the thrill of the Democracy Wall and there was excitement in the air, a feeling that people were doing things they had never done before: they were venting their frustrations. Those were days of tremendous change, both for China and for me: 1978 was the year I set up my company in Hong Kong and, during a Christmas party that year, met the girl who would become my wife.

Living in China, and marriage

For the record I have been married twice, each time happily – and each time to the same woman. Getting married is complicated enough at home; concerns about meeting the parents, and the mother-in-law syndrome, are big challenges for any prospective groom. But in China in 1979, the hurdles for a foreigner wanting to marry a Chinese girl were quite different.

The context was a society where it was a no-no for boys and girls to hold hands in public. Kissing was a very risqué concept, and certainly was never, ever done in public. Rock'n'roll was illegal. The most visible difference between a married woman

Michael De Clercq

and an unmarried one was the hairstyle: page boy vs. pigtails. Boys and girls walked in separate groups, but were all dressed in blue. Since apartments were allocated by work unit, getting your own place was most difficult. Privacy in this crowded society was a problem. During warm spring evenings, bushes and solitary benches in public parks were a hot commodity.

A marriage prospect for a Chinese groom was either an issue of legs or one of 'three turnings and one portable', depending on the social context. The legs – no, not the ones sticking out of your trousers – referred to furniture, as in how many legs could the groom bring the bride? A bed has four legs; tables, chairs, cupboards and so on add up to more. You did your own math and made your own pitch. The 'three turnings' referred to the bicycle, the sewing machine and the tape recorder, while the 'portable' was a camera (the kind you looked down into and saw the target upside down in). I was relatively short of legs on the China side and I was not sure I wanted to compete with the turnings etc., so I instinctively used the Western approach to courtship instead. You know – impressing the girl with your personality.

> *The problem with my approach was communications: she did not speak any English and, to be honest, my Chinese was not very good. This was fertile ground for miscommunication, and I made good use of it*

The problem with that approach was communications: she did not speak any English and, to be honest, my Chinese was not very good. This was fertile ground for miscommunication, and I made good use of it. We were often in a group of four or five friends, and the conversation was fast-paced and in Mandarin. To keep up, I was constantly looking up words and idioms in my new dictionary, which I carried with me at all times. It was a large, hefty green book and my searching skills were excellent. You have never seen anyone use a dictionary as fast as I did at that time. But, despite that, I was constantly playing catch up. I kept getting the expressions wrong, and I misunderstood the trend of the conversation. My fiancée's little sister would often burst out laughing at my clumsiness. She was not at all diplomatic and quite infuriating. I told her to try and learn English and see if she could do any better – but that kind of comment only increased her mirth.

Courtship is always fraught with dangers, as we all know, but the danger at that time and place was not just ridicule, it was more ominously with the police. If the relationship was considered to be 'less than honest', the girl ran the real risk of being put in jail. To protect her, one had to be very careful. The best approach was to keep a low profile: I could camouflage myself with Chinese clothes quite easily in the winter and no-one noticed me when I rode my bike. But in the warm months the disguise was more challenging, and I had to resort to straw hats and face masks. Still, my big nose was hard to hide and I had to shave my beard. These were not easy times for romance.

Amicable relationships with foreigners were frowned upon and marriage with them was simply not done. Moreover, people found it all very suspicious. I mean: why does

Growing a business

he want to marry a Chinese girl? Can't he find a suitable girl back home? Maybe he is already married – how can we find out? Could it be that he wants to sell her into slavery after he returns home? I am not making this up: these were some of the specific concerns directed at my future in-laws. The Chinese state had a protective 'Big Brother' – or more accurately 'Mother and Father' – attitude towards its people and wanted to protect its citizens, whether they liked it or not. So the pressure was on, and the local authorities had regular meetings with the parents of the bride. My fiancée, however, was persuasive too and I got along fine with her parents, so they gave us the green light.

The next step was the other approvals. How does one register a marriage (*dengji*) when half the equation is missing? For starters, my work unit (*danwei*) did not approve my application. Could not approve it in fact, since I did not have a unit. This was a big problem because bureaucrats liked precedent, and both parties in a marriage should have a work unit that approved of them and sponsored them with the authorities. This lack of correct procedure provided ammunition for nay-sayers who were notoriously difficult to sway, so one needed to be very persistent.

The marriage bureau lacked pomp of any sort

Finally, there was the paperwork: we had to register the marriage at the district office. This lacked the pomp and circumstance you expect from such places in the West. The building was a simple, one-storey brick house with a blue door and a couple of windows. The actual procedure was simple, involving three officials and a tape recorder in a drab room watched over by portraits of Marx, Engels, Lenin and Stalin. Celebration: we got the marriage certificate! The documents were colourful, with the Red Flag and the seal of China, and we had two of them: one said she had married me, and the other said I had married her. And when I say 'I', I mean Ma Pengji – the documents were in my Chinese name. This is only noteworthy because no birth certificate, passport or other official document existed that linked the name to the person. My only evidence was my business namecard. But it was good enough for the officials, and who was I to argue? We married again a year later in Sydney, Australia. It was our chance to do it again with family and friends: a traditional church wedding at my old school chapel, signing the register and getting a certificate with real names and all.

Hotels: home far away from home

There was a time when your apartment was a hotel room, when hotel reservations were not permitted, when restaurants closed at 5pm, when there were no office buildings and when rules just had to be broken. Hotels were a big part of expatriate life in China until the 1990s: that was where you lived, worked and ate. I met Bob Hope in the elevator of the Beijing Hotel in 1979. He was in Beijing with a group that included Crystal Gayle and Big Bird, doing a US TV show. They were staying at the Beijing Hotel because it was the best accommodation in the city at the time. Since I worked and ate there most of the time, to bump into such celebrities was a bit like seeing movie stars in your apartment building or your neighbourhood restaurant back home.

Some people imagine that it would be nice to live in a hotel. After all, you have room service, you don't need to worry about changing sheets or towels and the place is cleaned every day. But the charm wears off quickly after a prolonged stay. This was especially true back in the late 1970s and in a Chinese hotel. At that time, to lodge in a hotel was not

We registered our marriage with the three officials and a tape recorder, under my Chinese name

Growing a business

a choice but a necessity. Apartments for foreigners did exist in Beijing, but they were for diplomats only. So the place you went back to every day, week after week, year after year, the place that was 'home' had to be a hotel. And, of course, it did not feel like home.

With hindsight I came to realise that the reason why Chinese hotels were such an imperfect solution was the very different nature of the parties involved at the time. On the one hand you had the guests, the expats who were paying for the accommodation, who felt they were long-term customers providing revenue to the hotel for months on end and who expected appreciation and service in return for their business. On the other, you had the hosts, the Chinese managers who had the typical gatekeeper mentality of a salaried bureaucrat in charge of a government asset. Everybody

> *The expats were adventurers: they were rule-breakers almost by definition, since their very presence in China was evidence that they were seeking new horizons away from their own traditions*

should know that the hotel was under their control, and the longer you lived there, the more you should appreciate them letting you do so. Both parties were to some extent justified in their beliefs, but this diametrical divergence of points of view was a source of seething resentment on both sides, and the more prestigious the hotel, the more exacerbated the divergence. The Beijing Hotel was the worst.

We were living in a highly controlled society, full of rules and regulations that the Chinese were used to and which they generally accepted without question. Deviation was not allowed, service was a foreign concept and you were expected to conform to their norm – not the other way around. But the expats were adventurers: they were rule-breakers almost by definition, since their very presence in China was evidence that they were seeking new horizons away from their own traditions. In a way, they were accustomed to making things happen, and did not take 'no' for an answer. They wanted their hotel rooms to be home. They wanted to customise them, hang pictures, move the furniture, invite friends, have parties. None of that was allowed and, as a result, we all had great hotel stories to tell. Horror stories, of course.

One particularly irksome rule was that you had to register your Chinese guests downstairs at reception. Once you did this, the *danwei* (work unit) of your friends would be notified of the fact that they were visiting foreigners. They would be subject to questioning and maybe worse. This system was an effective damper on impromptu gatherings of friends, and those who tried to circumvent the rules by sneaking visitors in would inevitably end up having an altercation with hotel security. The 'floor boys' were part of the system: they were meant to keep management aware of what was going on and take care of the rooms. There were usually two of them, stationed at the elevator exit of each floor. We got along with them quite well as they were our main interface with the hotel, and thus more service-driven and inclined to avoid confrontation.

A perfect example of conflict was the reservation system: simply put, it did not exist. You could not book a room in advance. If you had important visitors coming to Beijing, there was only one prestigious place for them stay, and that was the Beijing Hotel. If you could not get a reservation there, it would affect your business and maybe even your career. In retrospect, I understand that the hotel management had their own concerns as well: they wanted to keep control over their rooms in case a high-level official needed them. Not to have availability would have been a huge loss of face for them. But they would not explain this – and even had they done so, we probably would not have cared.

> *In smaller towns, hotels were few. Many were very cheap – I recall a hotel in Sichuan that charged Rmb4 per night. Often the rooms did not include bathrooms; in Anhui, you had to walk down two floors to take a shower*

Money was not an issue: the rooms were cheap (about Rmb40 per standard room) and offering more money for a reservation would get you nowhere. So we had to be creative. We put together a secret, informal pool of rooms, as many as 50 to 70 rooms and suites at any one time, which were fully paid in advance but were empty. For those in the know, if you needed rooms, you tapped into the system and found out what was available from the pool; you then paid for the rooms and took them over. Your guests bypassed the hotel registration system, and room availability was guaranteed.

Now, the rooms were paid in advance but if the hotel management found out that one was empty, they would promptly evict you and get the room back. I know because I was evicted once. To avoid discovery by the floor boys, I made sure that the rooms always looked lived in by leaving personal effects in the cupboards and moving suitcases in and out. But it was not enough: one day I found all the clothes and suitcases in the corridor. I went to see the hotel management to get the room back, but to no avail: they had concluded I was not living there and nothing would change their minds. They were furious that I had even asked for the room back.

Overall the system worked really well. So well that one day Chinatex approached me to find out if I could help them with a delegation from Bloomingdale's: they needed rooms in the Beijing Hotel, fast. I was mystified that this Chinese corporation would ask me since (a) we kept our system very confidential, so how could they know about it?; and (b) they usually had a lot of influence with the Beijing Hotel management. So I told them to get the rooms themselves – but they could not do it and they were desperate. As a favour, I got them eight standard rooms and four suites – but that was the beginning of the end. The hotel had suspected for a while that we had something going on, but they could not prove it. After the Bloomingdale's delegation, they cracked down and started taking back all the rooms they could find.

Luckily for us, the Jianguo Hotel opened soon thereafter, in 1982. It was the first foreign-invested hotel in Beijing, and you could make reservations there. As soon as it opened, most businessmen chose to patronise it and the Beijing Hotel lost, pretty much overnight, its reputation as the best hotel in Beijing. The investors in the Jianguo were not unhappy: I heard that they got their investment back in one year.

Growing a business

Then there were the other kind of hotels: those you used for short stays during trips. But in the 1970s, the hotel industry in China was in its infancy. Large, older cities like Beijing, Shanghai, Tianjin and Guangzhou had a number of quaint, antique hotels but in smaller towns, hotels were few. They were often called *zhaodaisuo* (guesthouses) and were mostly for visiting government cadres. As such, they were meant to provide shelter and maybe conference and banquet facilities, but not a lot more. Many were very cheap – I recall a hotel in Sichuan that charged Rmb4 per night. Often the rooms did not include bathrooms; in Anhui, you had to walk down two floors to take a shower. These hotels were not designed for foreigners and they certainly did not have swimming pools or health centres.

The notable exceptions to the low-quality trend of the time were the state guesthouses, such as the 'Angler's Corner' (Diaoyutai) in Beijing, which provided sumptuous, top-level accommodation with the highest level of security. This were reserved for government officials and foreign dignitaries; Nixon, for one, stayed there in 1972. But in the late 1970s the state guesthouses opened up and, for a fee, one could rent these lavish apartment-like facilities. Around 1980 I organised a high level of a board of directors meeting at the Angler's Corner, and I was impressed by every aspect of the guesthouse. To start with, one could only gain entry if the guard at the gate recognised the number plate of the long, black 'Red Flag' limousine you had to use. The guesthouse was set in a park, and privacy was achieved by providing separate houses for the guests. The rooms were huge – you could play table tennis in the bathroom, it was that big – and furnished with unique antique furniture. The facilities were not modern, but they were well maintained and luxurious. You had your own dining room and lounge, and breakfast there was the best I ever had anywhere.

China lacked modern accommodation, and the reason behind that fact was a bit of a Catch 22: there was no need for hotels because there were no visitors. Conversely, because there were few hotels, tourism and foreign trade could not flourish. In fact, in order to prevent travel problems, permits (*luxingzheng*) were required for travel within China and many areas of the country were not open (*kaifang*) to foreigners. Travelling within China could be a challenge.

The early Canton Fairs provide an excellent illustration of why this form of control made sense. The Fair was held in Guangzhou in a miscellany of buildings and across the street from the best hotel in town, the Dongfang. During the spring of 1979, the good news was that China was opening up, and it seemed like the whole world was coming. Thousands upon thousands of visitors descended on Guangzhou. The bad news was that the city was not ready – lodging was a disaster. There were simply not enough hotel rooms; the authorities scrambled to try and salvage the

> *The reason behind the lack of modern accommodation was a bit of a Catch 22: there was no need for hotels because there were no visitors. Conversely, because there were few hotels, tourism and foreign trade could not flourish*

Michael De Clercq

With our driver on an unscheduled but memorable visit to Guiyang in 1978

situation, and had to resort to desperate measures. At the time, rumour had it that trainloads of people coming from Hong Kong were asked not to disembark at the station but to spend the night on the train. Some hospitals were evacuated to make beds available for visitors.

Lodging was subject to a rationing system for the different categories of visitor, identified by the numbers on their Canton Fair invitation. If you were in the No. 1 category (i.e. USA, Europe, Africa, etc.) you got access to first-level hotels like the Dongfang. If you were in the No. 2 category (Japanese), you got access to second-level hotels like the Baiyun. Category No. 3 was for Hong Kong and overseas Chinese visitors.

This was the first time I had attended the Fair, and I was tested. When I arrived at the Dongfang Hotel in April 1979, I and, as it turned out, most likely everybody else, was blissfully ignorant of the problems and totally unprepared for what I was about to experience. When I walked in, the lobby of the hotel was packed with foreigners. The reception desk was under assault, ten people deep. Guests of all nationalities were there, including Arabs in djellabas and groups of Africans, Europeans and Americans. They were complaining loudly, red in the face, waving reservations and demanding rooms. It was loud, a Babel-like cacophony, and the hotel staff were in full defence mode: eyes glazed, polite but inflexible and, to the extent of the possible, avoiding eye contact. No keys were handed out: the hotel booking system could not cope with the demand. Some guests were despairing, others were exhausted, some were even sleeping on the marble floor.

I was faced with a huge problem: I had important clients arriving in the afternoon and securing proper accommodation for them was essential. I had verified reservations for four rooms, and I had better get them. I had an advantage over most of the crowd: I lived in China and could speak Chinese. I knew that joining the screaming throng was a waste of time and would not get me anywhere. The trick was to identify the manager and present my case privately. I determined that an older woman behind the desk was in charge and I waited until she left the area to approach her quietly. I got my four rooms 15 minutes later. Service with a smile.

Growing a business

Many other people were not so lucky, and ended up going elsewhere or sleeping in cots that were set up in the conference rooms and corridors on different floors. Some of the floors looked like dormitories. For me, it was an important early lesson in doing business in China: the unexpected is the norm. I was 24 years old, and I was learning about business at the same time as I was developing it. I started to understand the true meaning of the expression 'business is about people', because taking care of your customer's lodging and meals was just as important as negotiating a good contract.

Meals, of course, were very important. While travelling, every meal from breakfast to dinner was an opportunity to discuss business and strengthen relationships. Some meals were formal banquets with Chinese hosts, some were casual affairs with friends or family. The food varied too. Breakfast on the road was usually a choice between congee and congee or maybe *youtiao* (a fried doughstick), and the hotel restaurant would normally close no later than 8am – no sleeping in allowed. For lunch and dinner, most meals were Chinese cuisine. You could find Western food but it was rare, and in the early days it was not very authentic, in the same way that Chinese food in the USA is often 'American-Chinese'.

If you were in Guangzhou, going out to dinner was a must. Guangzhou was the best place to eat in China (*'Chi zai Guangzhou!'*) in the early days and there were many famous restaurants to sample, many more certainly than you could find in Beijing or Shanghai at the time. So after your day at the Fair, and before dealing with your telexes, you went to dinner, usually in a group of six or more Westerners from different nations – and that meant a taxi challenge. The taxi lines were very long and we had to outwit the Japanese, who always found ways to get the minibuses first. Dinners were memorable, partially because of the food, which was often excellent and sometimes challenging (I enjoyed taking new clients to the snake restaurant which let you choose your food before they killed it) and partially because of the atmosphere. For a multi-national group of people who often barely knew each other, it would make for lively conversation.

However, some guests had no concept of boundaries. In the fall of 1979, a dinner at the Datong Restaurant in downtown Guangzhou went awry when two pairs of the antique ivory chopsticks for which the restaurant was famous went missing

> *The trick was to identify the manager and present my case privately. I determined that an older woman behind the desk was in charge and I waited until she left the area to approach her quietly. I got my four rooms 15 minutes later*

from our table. The restaurant staff caught up with us as we were boarding our minibus and prevented us from leaving. At first, I was outraged at the suggestion that people in our group could have taken the chopsticks, and I told the restaurant staff to look again. But they could not find them anywhere and were adamant about not letting us go – so I asked our group again and, to my surprise, a French couple owned up and sheepishly returned the chopsticks. In China, they have a name for this type of situation: they call it 'losing face'. More about that later.

Michael De Clercq

Today, from Hainan to Heilongjiang, China has some of the best hotels in the world, and these compete hard for your business. Even better, a whole range of apartments is available for long-term guests. There is an incredible variety of restaurants in most major towns, and they do not close at 5pm any more – in fact, some of them stay open all night. Prices of course, are also world class.

Planes, trains and automobiles; bicycles, motorbikes, boats

The Chinese government obviously knows that there is a direct link between transport infrastructure and economic growth. It has invested and continues to invest a large amount of capital in roads, railways and airports. Early in 2008, I travelled on the Beijing to Tibet highway in Inner Mongolia. I found out that it now takes about two hours to drive from Beijing to Inner Mongolia, and another couple of days to reach Tibet. The highway system in China is surprisingly good now. It is vast, well built and new: most of it has been constructed in the past five years.

Previously, inter-city transportation was quite good but slow, and mostly by train. Road travel was downright dangerous. During my trips I saw horrendous accidents and, on average, I would witness one fatality per day on the road. So train was the better choice by far. On my first trip in 1975, I went from Hong Kong to Beijing on a multi-stage train trip. You first travelled from Kowloon station to a small town in the New Territories called Lowu. Then you got off and walked across a bridge to the China border.

At the immigration point, there were hundreds of people, mostly Chinese, but also up to four or five foreigners. The whole process took maybe one hour. On the other side was a village called Shenzhen, where you boarded a train for Guangzhou. The train was comfortable, especially in the 'soft seat' section where I was sitting. China did not have first or second class sections (that would have been incorrect in a classless society); instead it had 'soft seats', 'soft sleepers', 'hard seats' and 'hard sleepers'. After a stopover in Guangzhou, you caught the Beijing express. As for Shenzhen, it is the perfect illustration of what 30 years of change can do. If you visit now, you will find a large, modern metropolis with skyscrapers, spacious avenues and five-star hotels, bearing no resemblance whatever to what I saw in 1975.

> *At the immigration point, there were hundreds of people, mostly Chinese, but also up to four or five foreigners. The whole process took maybe one hour. On the other side was a village called Shenzhen, where you boarded a train for Guangzhou*

The most memorable train trip I had in China was in 1978, on a voyage from Beijing to Kunming, Guiyang and back. I was still a student at the time and was travelling with an Australian friend of mine. We wanted to see China from the 'man in the street' perspective and were roughing it. This meant going 'hard seat', but we quickly changed our minds. Partly because of the noise, partly because you could not

Growing a business

Wanxian in Sichuan province, 1978. In some parts of China, boat was the best means of transport

stretch your legs (one guy actually lay down at our feet: we could not move) and partly because of the intensity of the smoking, we found it very had to sleep. So after 18 hours in an incredibly crowded carriage full of people, chicken, ducks, bags and bundles, we decided that henceforth we would travel 'hard sleeper' instead.

The train from Kunming arrived in Guiyang in the afternoon, and there was no connection until the next day. Guiyang was not an open city and you could not get a travel permit to go there. So the authorities had a problem: they could not let us in, and they could not let us sleep in the station either. After going into a huddle, they sent a car for us and put us up in the town's guesthouse. We could not communicate very well because my Chinese was not up to par, but they were the nicest people. The next day they took us on a tour of the town and showed us the sights, including the beautiful local caves. We also did a bit of shopping: I was looking for local pottery. But foreigners were so rare there that our presence was stunning to the local folks. If we stepped out of the car into the street, there would be an instant traffic jam. And even though the crowds were never hostile, their size and intensity was strange and a bit scary to the newcomer I was then.

When they drove us back to the station, we wondered how much all this would end up costing us. Nothing, as it turned out – they were simply being gracious. There was a bit of consternation when we insisted on buying 'hard sleeper' tickets. They even said that there weren't any available, but they could not talk us out of it. So they relented – but they made us wait at the station while everyone was boarding. Just as we were becoming concerned about missing the train, they let us board and, as we got to our hard sleeper compartment, we finally understood why there had been such a delay.

They had been busy. Having given us the first compartment at the head of the hard sleeper car, they had cordoned off the neighbouring compartment so that we would not be disturbed. And in our open-ended compartment, they had put new carpets, new doilies on the tables, silk comforters on the bed and leather slippers on the floor, and had perfumed the whole area. And when we went to the adjacent toilet, we saw their final touch: they had cleaned and perfumed the toilet and, lo and behold, there was toilet paper. Talk about roughing it. We did not ask for any of these things: it was just a way of making our trip nicer, a farewell gift from our hosts.

> *The bus conductors were so polite that they would force people to give way and require them to stand up to let the foreigner have a seat. They would even get little old ladies to get up. And if you refused the seat, it would stay free until you got off the bus*

In Beijing, taxis were a major headache. You could only find them at certain designated stations and it was normal to wait as long as three hours before you could get a ride. You could not flag down a taxi from the kerbside either so, since you were not allowed to have your own car, your only alternative was the public transport system or a bicycle.

Public transport was not really an option, because it was way too overcrowded and required special skills that I did not have – such as jumping the line, shoving, elbowing and pushing people out of the way. As a result, I sometimes missed two buses in a row before having enough gumption to 'negotiate' my way onto the next one. This was especially the case if I was 'disguised' as a Chinese. If I wasn't, however, it was worse: the bus conductors were so polite that they would force people to give way and require them to stand up to let the foreigner have a seat. They would even get little old ladies to get up. And if you refused the seat, it would stay free until you got off the bus.

As a result, I cycled a lot in the late 1970s and early 1980s. Beijing is great for cycling because it is flat and easy to navigate without maps. I knew all the shortcuts through the *hutong* side streets, and would go as far as the Summer Palace on a bike. I liked to go fast: I enjoyed the exercise and I was always in a hurry. This led to daily adventures, because foreigners were still rare and therefore subject to pointing and staring at by the locals. It was even rarer to see one on a bicycle, not to mention one going really fast. Once, some guy thought this was a race and gleefully caught up and overtook me at great speed. He then turned and looked back, grinning victoriously at me. And then crashed into the oncoming cycle traffic. It pays to look where you are going.

I used my bicycle time to record mini-cassette messages to send the folks back

Growing a business

home. I would ride with one hand on the handlebars and the mini-cassette recorder held in front of my mouth. Embarrassingly enough, one message recorded the evidence of a crash, when another bicycle turned suddenly in front of me and I did not have time to turn the cassette off. The event reminds me of the current concerns about driving with a cell-phone.

Support services for bicycles were great at that time. There were many kerbside mini-repair centres all over Beijing that would not only fix a flat tyre in no time but would also fine-tune your wheels and grease your hubs – kind of like a chiropractor for bicycles. It made an astonishing difference to performance. From the bicycle, I eventually upgraded to a scooter, then a motorcycle and, finally, a car. Imported cars were subject to very high duty, so we bought them from diplomats who were leaving their China posting. We ended up with a disparate collection of vehicles – Fords, BMWs and Mercedes.

In the 1970s and early 1980s, the car to get was the Red Flag limousine, the 'Hongqi'. It was a heavy, luxurious, Russian-looking limousine with power seats and curtained windows, and was copied from the 1959 model Soviet ZiL-111. What made it outstanding and most desirable was that it was a priority vehicle. Foreigners could not get one, of course: they were reserved for high-level Chinese officials. In those days, Beijing had few cars, but lots of small and medium-size trucks, thousands of horse-drawn carts and millions of bicycles. The traffic lights were manually operated by policemen in little booths set high above the road and connected by phone to other such booths down the road. When they saw a Red Flag coming, they would switch the lights to green; the Hongqi never had to stop.

The old Red Flag limousines are no longer made, but the brand lives on at FAW in Changchun

My Thirty Years in China | 63

Michael De Clercq

This system lasted a few years, but an end was put to it as traffic increased and a few accidents occurred – including at least one, rumour has it, when two convoys of Red Flags ran into each other on the then narrow two-lane airport road. Both had priority, and neither stopped. The Hongqi brand still exists today, but that particular model of limousine has not been made in 25 years and is now a relic of the past. First Auto Works of Changchun, the factory that produced it, now also makes Audis, and is coming out with a new model, the HQE, this time inspired by Rolls-Royce.

This system lasted a few years, but traffic increased and a few accidents occurred – including at least one, rumour has it, when two convoys of Red Flags ran into each other on the then narrow two-lane airport road. Both had priority, and neither stopped

When the airport system developed, we flew a lot. It was the best way to get around this vast territory. Beijing airport was a small, drab brown building, and you had to walk across the tarmac to your plane. Nevertheless, it was an excellent hub, with the most connections to Chinese and international destinations. In those days it took about 24 hours to travel to the USA on Pan Am via Tokyo and San Francisco; now it takes 13 hours via the North Pole.

Domestic flights in the early 1980s were a bit of a concern because of safety issues: pilots were not well trained and equipment was not properly maintained and, as a result, there were some serious airplane crashes. At the time, China had a fleet of new jets for long routes, but mostly relied on ancient planes for short inter-city flights. I recall many flights aboard the Russian-built Antonov 24, which was a medium-range prop plane that carried 52 passengers. The plane itself was actually quite good, but as you boarded you passed by the tyres, which were so worn that the canvas was showing in patches. You had to hold your breath and keep your fingers crossed during landings.

Flight services were poor. It was not unusual to wait for hours for a delayed departure, and no one would bother to explain or predict the estimated departure time. And sometimes you would land in the wrong airport for some mysterious reason, and again wait there for hours.

When all else fails, you hitch-hiked, and I did this once, in Yunnan in 1978 when I was still a student. It did not work very well at first because people were puzzled at the sight of a foreigner on the side of the road with his thumb in the air. I found out that, to get cars to stop, you had to stand in the middle of the road with your hand raised, palm facing out, like a half-hearted Mussolini salute. It worked well enough, and I got a couple of friendly rides.

I like the water, and in some parts of China the best transport was by boat. Hovercraft and high-speed hydrofoil ferries in the Pearl River Delta between Hong Kong and Guangzhou sound romantic and exciting, but they were not. These craft were much faster than the normal ferry, but on the hovercraft you could not see

Growing a business

anything out of the windows and on the hydrofoil you were so shaken about that you had to endure epidemics of nausea on board. The Yangtze river ferries were a much nicer experience. I took them a few times in the 1980s. Before the construction of today's extensive network of highways and bridges in the Nanjing-Shanghai corridor, a ferry boat trip was a convenient and comfortable way to get from one river town to another.

During one particular trip I was travelling with a Foreign Trade Corporation (FTC) agent on the way to Shanghai, when in Nanjing the ferry made a slow U-turn manoeuvre. I was on the upper deck watching the river traffic, and I noticed a small tug-boat pulling a string of six to eight heavily-laden barges coming our way. I pointed out to the FTC man that, given our current course, we would collide with these barges unless we altered course. Maybe we should tell the captain.

But the FTC guy (who, typically, had a tendency to assume the role of China PR with foreigners), insisted that the river rules were complex and that the captain knew what he was doing. This was a reasonable assumption, but it was incorrect. So over the course of about ten minutes we watched the collision happen in slow motion, during which time I continued to make my dire predictions and the anxiety of my travelling companion increased. My final comment was, 'Unless we reverse full throttle now, we will hit it.' And his reply (somewhat less convinced than before) was, 'No, no, the captain knows what he is doing.'

When we collided about a minute later the ferry's siren sounded in a panic and the tug-boat veered away, sounding off with its own high-pitched siren like a dog whimpering after being kicked. Our boat came to a full stop and anchored for a few hours to assess the damage and to file reports. I fully expected that all the passengers would be transferred to another boat but no, we proceeded to Shanghai. At each port of call I could see from the deck people stopping, then pointing at the front of the boat and bursting out laughing. When I got to Shanghai, I finally saw why: the bottom part of the prow of the boat had been torn and bent, leaving the upper part sticking out like a big nose.

I had a number of other boat experiences in the 1980s, some of which may never be repeatable. One that is

Looking out for sandbanks on the Yangtze, 1979

My Thirty Years in China | 65

was when we saw two Yangtze river dolphins next to the boat. I knew that we were incredibly lucky to see these creatures, also known as *baiji*, because they were already extremely rare at that time. The captain of the boat told me he had never seen one in 40 years on the river. They are unique to the Yangtze river, basically blind and, by now, most probably extinct.

> *When the man's call became frantic, it was too late and we smacked into a sandbank. I was watching from the deck right next to the restaurant window and braced myself. The boat came to a sudden stop, but the dishes, chairs and passengers did not*

The other experience was on a trip from Chongqing to Wuhan, passing the beautiful Three Gorges of the Yangtze river and encountering sandbanks. Sandbanks are not a factor here any longer because of the Gezhouba dam. At that time, however, they were a serious obstacle in the river; they would constantly move, so they could not be marked on maps. The boat had no sonar depthfinder so, instead, a man at the front of the deck used a manual alternative, basically a long graded stick, and yelled out the depth to the captain while the boat proceeded at slow speed. Slow, but still with enough speed to be dangerous. When the man's call became frantic, it was too late and we smacked into a sandbank. I was watching from the deck right next to the restaurant window and braced myself. The boat came to a sudden stop, but the dishes, chairs and passengers did not. It was a mess in the restaurant, though no major harm was done. You could tell the captain had done this before: he managed to engage reverse thrust, got the boat unstuck and get us on our way in just a few minutes.

Leisure: weekends, friends, sports and entertainment

A tomb may not seem like an ideal setting for a fun day out with family and friends. But memories are created by doing things you can't do anywhere else, and on weekends we often went to the tombs of the Ming dynasty emperors in Beijing. Two of the thirteen tombs had been opened to the public (the Chang Ling and Ding Ling), but we went to some of the other eleven, which were abandoned, solitary and mysterious. They were close to local villages and had been left alone in their park-like settings. The tombs themselves were unopened and still hidden under mounds surrounded by large perimeter walls, inside which the crumbling buildings and pavilions were still in pretty good shape, given their age. Majestic ancient trees guarded the courtyards, having taken root centuries before in the old brick walls. We would have a picnic lunch and play frisbee and softball with our friends and kids, and would finish the afternoon by going to the Great Wall at Badaling. There was usually no one there to disturb us as we watched the sunset.

In those days, you could find remarkably quiet places in Beijing if you had a car. The Summer Palace and the Western Hills were typically peaceful weekend excursions. Tourism had not yet been developed and the concept of the weekend itself was

Growing a business

foreign. In fact, the one rest day per week that factories had would be rotated, so that there would be enough electricity to go around. One factory would take Wednesday off, another Thursday, and so on. It was only much later that the concept of weekends, especially two-day weekends, was adopted by the government. When I moved my family to the USA, a friend asked how I found living in New Jersey after living in China. To his surprise, my reaction was: 'Crowded'.

In the early days, social life in Beijing for an expat like me rotated around two poles: the Western community, which was small and primarily made up of diplomats, and a group of Chinese friends. They were like oil and water: one group rarely mixed with the other.

The small community of diplomats was lively. China was already considered a choice posting for most diplomats, and these were veterans. They knew how to entertain themselves, without nightclubs or commercial bars. They held costume parties, and were keen on singing and overall good cheer. We had great Brazilians friends. The Swiss had nice parties, and the Australians were always friendly and had a bar, 'the Downunder Club'. The British put on hilarious plays, and there was a tendency to invite everyone when dignitaries visited. In this way I had the privilege of meeting King Baudoin and Queen Fabiola of Belgium in 1981, Richard M. Nixon in 1985 and Prime Minister Bob Hawke of Australia in 1986. I also bumped into George H.W. Bush at our office in the International Club in Beijing (apparently he was looking for his old

The Ming Tombs were one of our regular venues for weekend trips out of Beijing in the mid-1980s

Michael De Clercq

Ice-skating and hockey were favoured winter sports

barber from the days when he was the head of the US Liaison Office in the mid-1970s).

We liked movies, and I got to see a number of classics like *Gone with the Wind* and *Borsalino* in Beijing movie theatres. Entry was free of charge. The tickets were given as a bonus to Chinese staff and they shared. Whenever possible, we would also go to see Peking opera shows and Chinese plays. Less frequently we saw acrobatics and the exciting *qigong* shows, which were a combination of martial arts and magic feats. When Bob Hope performed at a Beijing theatre with Crystal Gayle and Big Bird we made sure we did not miss it – but these shows were so rare they were almost unique.

In the winter, the Canadians organised an annual amateur ice hockey competition with the Russians. Ice hockey was an excellent winter sport in Beijing, because in those days, as a rule, the weather was much colder. One winter, you could skate all the way from the city centre to the Summer Palace lake: all the rivers were frozen solid, even under the bridges. Also, there weren't many alternatives: skiing, for one, was not an option. And ice hockey was fun for a beginner like me. I often played on the moat of the Forbidden City, on Hou Hai behind the Forbidden City and on the lake in front of the White Dagoba in Bei Hai Park. You had an awesome historical setting for skating, which with the Chinese was a vigorous but surprisingly gentle sport. Some of these young guys were excellent skaters and when, during a pick-up game, they knocked me down, it was refreshingly unexpected when they stopped to help me up again.

The annual game with the Russians, however, was another affair altogether. It was held at the Russian Embassy, which had its own ice hockey rink, with a knee-high wall that made for some spectacular exits from the game. There were pits for the players and chairs for the spectators, who were primarily embassy families from both the Eastern bloc and the West. Some cheeky spectators had made banners which they hung inside the rink wall, with slogans such as 'Go Free World!'. Pretty girls from the Romanian Embassy would come up to us to get autographs. We were concerned that they would get into trouble, but they said they didn't care.

Growing a business

We had some pretty good players on our team, but not many. The team was made up of anyone who cared to join. There were Canadians, Europeans and they even took me, the lone Australian, which was evidence of their desperation. They were willing to drop their standards to get another warm body on the team – and because I had my own hockey skates. The Russians were well equipped and brutal. In fact, I suspected they weren't amateurs at all. Our team, on the other hand, had a rag-tag selection of disparate equipment and jerseys. We had helmets of non-matching colours and all sorts of different gear. Some of us had no hockey gloves at all and when we got on the ice, the Russians would go for the hands, which would soon be bleeding so much you could not hold on to your stick.

We always tried to win, but we lost nearly every year. With time we improved our standard with better players, including an American-Chinese from Michigan and a really good Chinese-Chinese player by the name of Zhou, who we called 'Joe' and pretended was American too. The Russians were suspicious but could not prove anything. In 1980 there was a breach of protocol: for the first time, the Russians initiated discussions with the Canadians on the ice hockey tournament. It used to be the Canadians that called the Russians first. Why the change? The consensus was that the Russians were seeking a 'business as usual' kind of endorsement for their offensive in Afghanistan. So the ice hockey game was cancelled. That surely taught them a lesson.

In the 1990s the number of foreign companies opening offices in China increased and the business community became an entity in its own right. As the number of expats rapidly grew, the cosy relationship with the diplomats cooled. We had memorable parties of our own, such as the one held in the French restaurant Maxim's, which was booked for a costume party with the theme of 'Shanghai in the 20s'. Japanese companies were the first to develop a large presence in Beijing, and we took them on at softball. As usual, they were well organised. They had a softball league and the teams from Sumitomo, Mitsubishi and such companies had their own uniforms, with numbers and the players' names

Dressed for a 'Shanghai in the 20s' party at Maxim's

Michael De Clercq

printed on the jerseys. One year they held an eight-team tournament but were short of one team, so they invited the Americans, who were the only other group who played softball with any regularity.

I was on the team, and what a team it was! Cut jeans and torn T-shirts of all hues and colours: we looked a bit ragged. To make it worse, many of the players were late, and when we were supposed to start the first game of the tournament there were only four of us. So the Japanese umpire threatened us with disqualification unless we could field at least seven people within ten minutes. To the dismay of the Japanese, we recruited spouses (yes, females) and we were ready. You can forgive our Japanese friends for underestimating us, but we won the eight-team tournament. In fact we got a bit cocky. We thought we were so good that we challenged the China Women's National Team to a game. BIG mistake. You have never seen such a fast underarm pitch. It was not even a contest: I don't think we scored even one run, but I try not to remember.

We got into other sports in Beijing. We played tennis regularly, especially at the International Club where we had our office. But that was more of a business game – we had matches with clients and Chinese officials. We also played a lot of table tennis in which, needless to say, we faced a high level of competition. Most Chinese had the attitude that in table tennis they had some kind of genetic advantage over foreigners. We tried to prove them wrong, but put it this way: we did not always succeed. Once I happened to be in Guangzhou when the Chinese National Championships were held. I thoroughly enjoyed the show, as the three or four highest-ranked Chinese players were also the highest-ranked players in the world. Pick-up basketball (usually outdoors) and horse-riding were other activities we favoured.

Playing in our courtyard in the late 1980s. China was a great place to bring up children

Growing a business

Some things have not changed much. The big downside of outdoor exertions was and still is pollution. China burns coal to generate electricity and about two per cent of the coal ash – the finest particles – goes into the atmosphere. Tens of thousands of tonnes got dumped on cities like Beijing every year. We called it 'fly-ash': it was always present in the air. It affected most outdoor sports: for example, the basketballs were grimy and after ten minutes of play your hands would be black. On long bicycle rides you had to wear a cotton face-mask to filter the dust and, even if you did, when you blew your nose, your handkerchief would turn black. During the winter, fly-ash acted like sandpaper on the ice and would grind your ice-skate blades down at phenomenal speed. In the summer, however, it had an unexpectedly beneficial side effect: the billions of invisible particles in the air shielded you from harmful ultraviolet rays. You could play tennis without a shirt for hours in the noon-day sun without getting sunburn.

Today, China has caught up with most of the type of lifestyle we are used to in the West. There is not much you cannot do, and young adults love the discos and bars in Beijing and Shanghai

Twenty to thirty years ago, China was great place to live and to raise young children. It was safe and, despite the lack of Western amenities, it was comfortable. It was in many ways also innocent and refreshingly simple. You could do many of the activities you liked to do, and if you could not, you simply left China for an R&R trip once in a while. However, many expats considered Beijing a hardship post, and I have known a number of them to burn out, leave and never want to come back. Conversely, I also have some friends, rare exceptions, who have made China their permanent residence.

In the early days, many Chinese themselves were desperate to leave China. If they got a visa out, they tried not to come back. Today, China has caught up with most of the type of lifestyle we are used to in the West. There is not much you cannot do, and young adults love the discos and bars in Beijing and Shanghai. China has a big challenge ahead of itself in cleaning its environment, but we have come full circle and the Chinese 'expats' are coming back. Many young people of all nationalities have realised that, as a place to live and work, China is an exciting place to be. And soon, China will be putting on a great party, a kind of debutante ball for which it has prepared for years and for which it has spared no expense: the Olympic Games.

Business in China: drinking

I could write a book about drinking in China in the days when drinking was a must, when alcohol was a business requirement and when your liver had to struggle to survive. The word was 'banquet', the game was drinking, the liquor was hard and the point was business. The alcohol was mostly Maotai, or Wuliangye, but sometimes you would enjoy Erguotou or unknown, local 'white lightning' brews when travelling afar and the aforementioned brands were not available. Beer was a chaser.

Michael De Clercq

A typical banquet would involve 8–12 people seated around a large round table, in a private room with numerous dishes. And at least two glasses in front of you: a large one for beer and a shot glass for Maotai. Sometimes, there were up to seven shot glasses in front of each person. There were usually attendants on hand, whose primary job was to refill the glasses.

There was a whole protocol in toasting. The host would start, and it was *ganbei* ('bottoms up') with Maotai. The guest would toast next; after that the second host would make a toast, and so on. Protocol would then allow a free-for-all, where everyone would toast in no specific order. All this was done with great decorum, with key people maintaining their dignity and poise even after the alcohol took hold. It was definitely bad form to 'lose it' and behave improperly.

There were fines (i.e. you had to drink one shot for being late) and many unwritten rules. If you tried not to drink, you would have to drink double. If you volunteered to drink for a helpless associate, you would have to drink his shot – and then yours. It was customary to be under attack from the whole table, especially if you were the only foreigner or the highest-ranking of your group. The usual procedure was that each person at say, a table of ten, rose to drink with you, each in turn. Do the math: after ten rounds they had each had one shot, you'd had ten.

'War stories' were numerous and sometimes unusual. One I remember fondly occurred in the city of Shijiazhuang in the mid-1980s. My wife and I were invited to a banquet by the governor of the province of Hebei. It was a big affair with many tables. The governor insisted that our son David, who was about three at the time, be seated at our table. So they placed him with due honour next to the co-host of the table, and they gave him a shot glass too, filled with orange juice. Which was a big mistake – because David saw what everyone was doing and thought it was great fun, so he kept toasting the official next to him: *ganbei!* And the official felt obliged to drain his shot glass every time – except that he had Maotai in his. We finally had to remove him – David, I mean.

> *They placed our son next to the co-host of the table, and they gave him a shot glass too, filled with orange juice. Which was a big mistake – he saw what everyone was doing and thought it was great fun, so he kept toasting the official: ganbei!*

So how did you avoid getting drunk while keeping up with the toasts? How did you remain sober without offending your host? First you needed to develop some resistance to the evil brew. Second, as far as possible, you needed to avoid drinking at all: this was an imperative of self-preservation, as you could have up to seven or eight banquets a week (lunch and dinner, sometimes two dinners). Avoidance methods required practice, skill and experience.

The most effective approach was 'matching'. This involved identifying one specific individual at the table, preferably the host, and stating to all present that you would drink no more and no less than him – or her. This protected you from over-drinking,

Growing a business

but it was not foolproof. For one, you needed to make sure that your match was a moderate drinker, for another there were protocol issues i.e. you could not pick someone too low on the totem pole. You also needed to stick to your match and not waver, which in itself could be challenging in an alcoholic haze. And you had to be vigilant. I once caught an older official red-handed: he had arranged for the waitress to refill his glass with water, from an identical but separate Maotai bottle. Such shenanigans were not unusual.

You needed gumption and a sense of humour, but there were various ways to avoid drinking altogether. Some people used various tricks and sleight of hand (i.e. pretending to drink, but not really) but the most creative approach I witnessed was that of an American businessman, who each time he was being toasted, would ponderously get up and make everyone stand. He made sure that everyone was ready and then said *ganbei!* – and with a flourish, he would go through the motions of a bottoms-up toast at the same time as everyone else, but promptly empty his glass over his shoulder.

> *Whether you were buying or selling, a banquet was a friendly but important way for your counterparts to test your mettle. It was a way for your Chinese host to discover the real you that was hiding under that inscrutable Western mien*

One could also use excuses (for example, 'I'm on antibiotics') or simply refuse point blank to drink at all. This was not a good way to establish your reputation, but it usually worked with repeat players who knew you well, or with first-timers whom you would never meet again. Once in Jiangxi province, under severe assault from a very persistent bunch of banqueteers, who were literally forcing glasses of white spirit down my throat, I resorted in desperation to a Western drinking game which happily involved the whole table. After twenty minutes, they were too inebriated to notice I was hardly drinking at all.

Notable variations were introduced. In the mid-1990s, Hong Kong businessmen made Cognac (the more expensive the better) the banquet drink of choice. It was not unusual to go through four or five bottles of VSOP in one sitting. Those who sip Cognac slowly from a wide-bottomed glass would disapprove, but the French companies loved it: more Cognac was sold in Hong Kong than in the whole of the rest of the world. Later wine, meaning grape wine, became popular. And when it did, it took time for most Chinese to adapt their palates to its taste. It was considered too tart and was mixed with Sprite or diluted with ice cubes.

Whether you were buying or selling, a banquet was a friendly but important way for your counterparts to test your mettle. It was a way for your Chinese host to discover the real you that was hiding under that inscrutable Western mien. Banquets were also an extended form of negotiation. The usual line was: 'Let's have dinner and not talk business any more' – but more decisions were made during banquets than at the negotiating table. The upside of the drinking game was that, if you held your own with the firewater, you often formed valuable, long-term relationships. With time, the popularity of the drinking game started to wane. Visiting foreigners became more routine and easier to read and banquets became less popular. By the year 2000, the drinking game habit had totally disappeared from the main Eastern seaboard cities and now it only occurs sporadically in the hinterland provinces.

Communications: from telexes to the internet

It's all a matter of perspective. If Marco Polo had had the ability to send a message and have it instantly received on the other side of the world, he would have made a fortune. The notion that one could do this would have seemed unbelievable at the time, bordering on magic. But in these days of VOIP and instant e-mails on a Blackberry, the telex system we used to use in China seems positively antediluvian. Incredible new technologies have become commercially available during the past thirty years and have had a direct impact on business in China. The fact that China's growth has been in near lockstep with the phenomenal efficiency improvements of the communications industry is so remarkable that it calls for a cause-and-effect analysis. But not now: such a study exceeds the scope of this piece.

Our ability to communicate, rapidly, clearly, inexpensively and efficiently, is directly affected by the tools that are available to us. In the 1970s and early 1980s we used the telex. Later on in the 1980s, the personal computer surfaced and the fax machine became available, and communications improved and expanded. When the internet gave us e-mail in the late 1990s, the combination of a dramatic increase in both the quality and scope of communications, accompanied by a large decrease in cost, led to an explosion in the volume of communications to and from China.

The telephone, which was available from the very beginning of my China experience, was not a major factor for us in international communications because it was expensive and left no records. But it was an important tool for communicating within China with FTCs and factories. The fact that we located our main office in Beijing was partially driven by the fact that the capital was linked by phone with all major towns in China. The country benefited from the Fourth Five-Year Plan (1971–75), which had emphasised the development of communications. Progress continued rapidly over time, especially after the mid-1980s, mostly with the installation of optical lines and the advent of mobile phones, which became both an efficient tool and a status symbol.

During my formative years, the only way to communicate was by telex. It was also known as the teletype machine, and first started to be used in a global network back in the 1920s. The technology improved through the 1950s and 1960s, and the new machines in the late seventies were quite slick. But the old telex machines we used in China were owned by the State and were only available for rent. They reminded you of the ancestor of motor cars, the Model T Ford. I figured that the Chinese must have acquired the earliest models because they actually looked like they were from the 1920s. They were robust, heavy and clunky, and available in any colour as long as it was black.

The machines worked on a system of perforated paper tape and were slow and

Growing a business

cumbersome to use. If you made a mistake and realised it, you could correct it by typing back-space, back-space, back-space, crossing it out with a row of XXXXs and then laboriously typing in your correction. However, the recipient on the other side of the world would see all that – messy at best. And if you noticed a serious mistake after the whole text was finished, you had to re-type it all from scratch; word processing was not available then. Sometimes errors got through despite your vigilance. See what happens when you drop the 'r' from the main subject in the phrase '100,000 dozen shirts'.

At the Canton Fair in Guangzhou, which I attended twice a year for one month each time, there was a telex room downstairs at the Dongfang Hotel, where you could perforate your messages on a tape which you rolled onto a spool. The result was a spool less than an inch thick and as wide as your message was long. You then booked a line to your destination – and waited for a connection. Seven hours: that was my record wait in Guangzhou for one telex to New York. You could not leave the telex office because you had no idea when your line would come through, and when it did you had to take it immediately. The wait had an upside: you weren't alone. You shared the space with as many as twenty seasoned businessmen who had been at the fair many times. There was an atmosphere of camaraderie among traders. Many had bottles of whisky and were willing to share. The stories would flow, yarn upon yarn of China trade stories, of great deals and those that went sour.

Back in Beijing, for years we had to go to the electronic communications building on Changan Avenue, on the other side of Tiananmen Square, to type our messages, then line up and wait just like in Guangzhou (but for much less time since there was less traffic). We could not receive telexes, because we did not have a machine and so did not have an address. So, to receive messages, we had to ask an FTC (Foreign Trade Corporation) if we could use their address instead. We would go and pick up the telexes in the morning. This friendly system created challenges of confidentiality since the people we were negotiating with read our telexes before we did. For our counterpart to know what our client's position was

Business involved many factory visits; this one was in Shanxi, around 1980

My Thirty Years in China | 75

on pricing was an awkward approach to subtle negotiations. So we developed a code system to address the issue.

We finally got our very own private telex machine in our new offices in the International Club in the 1980s. It was a brand-new, modern, light blue Siemens machine from which we could both send and receive telexes. We were one of the first companies to have this great luxury, which required a dedicated line as well as various approvals. It meant a huge jump in productivity.

> *This friendly system created challenges of confidentiality since the people we were negotiating with read our telexes before we did. For our counterpart to know what our client's position was on pricing was an awkward approach to subtle negotiations*

But there were glitches too. Once my secretary had already left for the day and the telex line had dropped halfway through an outgoing message. I had to reconnect and resend but, at $7.00 a minute, I did not want to resend the whole thing if some of it had already been well received. So I called the central number for telexes in Beijing, explained who I was and could they please tell me how many minutes had been sent? The operator was most helpful: the line had dropped about halfway through the message, just after the words 'quota for the third shipment…' How convenient: she had a copy of my telex right in front of her. It was nice to know that there was a back-up copy of your confidential telexes with the government in case you lost your original.

The telex system was abandoned around 1990 when it was overtaken by the fax (facsimile) machine, which operated over normal phone lines and only required you to get one machine for each end. We had one of the first faxes in Beijing too, which we had brought in from Hong Kong. It was faster and more reliable than the telex, and it enabled us to send pictures and communicate with our USA office using Chinese characters. The early models used rolls of a chemically-coated paper that we had to import and which had the annoying tendency of fading when exposed to light. Valuable fax records had to be photocopied onto normal paper or else you would open your files to find illegible, washed-out curly pages. Faxes were also much more efficient partially because they tapped into the productivity of that other new tool: the personal computer. You could write your text with a word processor and send only the final printed version. Faxes were also more economical, many times cheaper than the telex.

But e-mails topped all that. They enabled us to send text, spreadsheets and other software, which could not only be read but could also be instantly modified on the other side of the world. They also allowed us to send high-density pictures and sounds – and in turn they were much cheaper than their fax predecessor.

Times were a-changing, and China was embracing new technologies with gusto. There were all sorts of benefits. We had the new ability to make much better sales

Growing a business

presentations, as well as providing customers with better sourcing services by sending them instant quality control pictures, for instance. Investments were facilitated by excellent cellular phone connections, instant number crunching with laptops and inexpensive audio and video conferences through media such as Skype. The impact on trade was considerable. We tend to take all this for granted because we adapt so quickly to tools that are designed to be used without thinking. But my experience in China was marked and coloured by the communications devices that I used in the early days.

As a final note, the depth to which technology has impacted China can be illustrated by one guy I noticed pushing a handcart full of junk in Beijing recently. The cart was the wooden kind with bicycle wheels and long handles. The man was dirty, wearing faded blue and grey clothes, ill-fitting and torn, one of the numerous unwashed poor. But then he stopped, dug in his pocket and pulled out a cell phone. I like to think he was checking on his stock investments…

Buying from China: the Canton Fair and beyond

There is no such thing as 'buying from China' today. 'China' is no longer a centrally controlled entity responsible for the supply of merchandise, and the government no longer controls each factory. You no longer have to deal with government employees to negotiate a contract, you no longer rely on the State to determine whether a given product can be made. And if you need changes, you no longer have to wine and dine officials in the hope that they will work with you. That is what China was like in the good old days of the past.

The bicycle pumps were blue. There were thousands of bright royal blue pumps everywhere in that factory, at various stages of production. It was the early 1980s, and I was doing an in-production inspection of an order for a large US customer. The quality was excellent, but the order called for red. So why were the pumps blue? The factory manager happily explained: 'I thought blue would be better for America.'

The understanding gap between buyers and factories was vast. At the time, China's export volume was small, and most of the goods it did export were commodities such as petroleum products. Even garments, which were a new export product being developed then, were handled like a commodity. Buyers placed orders from afar; they never went to the factories, but rather let the Foreign Trade Corporations (FTCs) handle the business.

The quality was excellent, but the order called for red. So why were the pumps blue? The factory manager happily explained: 'I thought blue would be better for America'

We, however, were pioneering a new concept: sourcing manufactured products from China. We were prepared to support this effort by having a 'hands-on' office in the country. We never thought it was going to be easy, but it turned out to be such uphill, unrewarding pioneering work that, in retrospect, I sometimes wondered why we did it. There were actually three good reasons. First, we knew that the fundamentals of a good export programme were there. China was ready to export large volumes of manufactured products because similar products were being produced for the China market. The factories existed. The workmanship of these products was good and labour was inexpensive. All that was needed were minor product changes and better infrastructure. For example, China had rubber boot factories, so we would work with them to buy steel-toe rubber boots.

Second, we were young, idealistic and unafraid, and we did not calculate whether this activity was a good return on our time investment. The thrill of doing something new, something that had never been done before was more than enough reward for us. We had followed the old adage of adventure 'Go West, young man'. China was exciting, it was the last frontier: we had gone so far West that we were in the East. And third, the export business provided our young company with a regular cashflow that our sales business could not guarantee.

So we forged ahead. Our initial challenge was two-fold: on the one hand we had to convince customers to buy from China; on the other, we had to convince the Chinese export authorities to work with us. Fear of the unknown was the main concern of our customers: they did not want to be guinea pigs in a new experiment. Back then, you did not find much in the stores with the 'Made in China' label on it. China was known as 'Red China' and Communism was feared, even after Nixon's visit. Taiwan and Korea were the

Machimpex Hall at the Canton Fair, the only place in the 1970s for buyers to interface with sellers

Growing a business

big suppliers then, and convincing importers to switch some of their business was difficult.

We overcame their lack of enthusiasm by providing attractive pricing, which was the easiest part of the equation: we were often able to quote 20 per cent lower than, say, Korean prices. China needed foreign exchange for its import programmes, so exports were encouraged.

'Struggling towards the Four Modernisations', Tianjin factory, 1979

There was an official exchange rate (US$1 bought about Rmb1.4 in 1978), but the government was willing to subsidise pricing in order to obtain dollars.

That was the easy part, but it only got our foot in the door. The key determinant of success in a buying programme is to get repeat orders. And to achieve that, one needed to get everything right: the quality had to be good, the packing had to be up to spec and the shipment had to be on time. So, to make this a business, we developed internal systems to ensure the reliability of three key ingredients: quality, delivery and good communications. Because the business of manufactured goods is detail-intensive, we needed direct access to the factories and we needed them to be eager to do business. We needed factory owners who cared, who took responsibility, who had a stake in going ahead.

The problem was that there was only one factory owner: the State. Under the centrally planned economy that China had in the late 1970s and early 1980s, all orders had to be placed with the State: namely the FTCs. These Foreign Trade Corporations were rigidly organised according to specific product segments, with textiles and garments, for example, assigned to 'Chinatex', leather products to 'Animal By-Products', rubber products to 'Light Industry', and so on.

Because the business of manufactured goods is detail-intensive, we needed direct access to the factories and we needed them to be eager to do business. We needed factory owners who cared, who took responsibility, who had a stake in going ahead

The system was inflexible. When we tried to source a hunting vest with a leather shoulder patch and elastic (rubber) cartridge-holders, no FTC wanted to take the order, each claiming that one or the other of the components was not under its control. We finally convinced Light

Industry to do it by using our good relations with them and assuring them that we would secure the missing components.

Buying used to be a hard sell. At first, the FTCs were national and all China business had to be transacted through one central office in Beijing. The staff of these FTCs were high-calibre individuals, and this centralised approach had one big advantage: it made ordering easy. The downside, of course, was that you were very limited in your scope of business.

> *Since we handled a broad range of products, we spent time in many different kinds of factory. For me it was a mind-opener, a discovery of human ingenuity, of things I had never known or even thought about*

The FTC procedure was straightforward: you placed orders with them and they, in turn, allocated the orders to provinces and factories of their choosing. This worked fine for commodities, which is a volume-driven business with few variables. But for manufactured goods the system was slow, inefficient and impractical, and the export volume of manufactured goods was consequentially tiny. In those days I spent time with the bright young people of the US-China Business Council, and a frequent topic of conversation was the potential size of trade. Someone claimed that trade would one day exceed US$580m, while others laughed at such a large figure. I thought it was pathetically small, but in 1979 an order we placed at the Canton Fair for rubber boots, worth about $200,000, was the single largest export contract for light industrial products to the USA on record.

In order to increase business, we had to increase the reliability factor, and the logical, natural approach to developing sustainable programmes involved gaining direct access to the factories. But the FTCs did not want us to contact factories directly, since this would undermine their own control over them. The FTCs felt practically insulted that we would even ask to know who the factories were, let alone mention visiting them. It was simply none of our business.

After a while, however, they relented. The government decentralised export authority to the provinces, and the provincial FTCs broadened opportunities by giving us access to the factories. Contracts were still concluded with the FTCs, because the factories did not have the right to export, but we could establish direct control programmes at factory level, and this was a critical step.

Direct access to factories allowed us to develop more business in a broader range of products that we would not have dared to try before. Reaction time was also much quicker, and we gained a better understanding of what motivated the factories and what was a problem for them. This created a process of continual improvements and a rise in confidence levels on both sides. It also opened up techniques of CMT (cut, make and trim) where some or all of the raw materials were imported and the factories were just doing the manufacturing. In addition, it created opportunities for machinery sales for our sales division.

Growing a business

Quality control involved a strong understanding of the manufacturing process and plunged us into the fascinating world of industrial manufacturing. Since we handled a broad range of products, we spent time in many different kinds of factory. For me it was a mind-opener, a discovery of human ingenuity, of things I had never known or even thought about. We learned about such things as the pungent, chewing gum-like process of rubber manufacturing; the highly flammable production of ping pong balls; the intricate world of jacquard knit machines; the noisy spinning and weaving process of vast piece goods factories; the wet and smelly tanning of leather; the complexity of mass garment production; the clever process of freeze-drying vegetables; the demanding details of furniture manufacturing; and many others. We were doing hands on something that people can now learn from the comfort of their homes by watching *How It's Made* on Discovery Channel.

Back in the old days, the process of getting access to the factories also touched on some delicate and controversial issues. I recall once in the mid-1980s I was travelling in Liaoning province with two American clients, both in their fifties and both top-level executives of mid-size US companies. We were on our way to a new factory not far from Shenyang, and I noticed that the representative of the FTC was a bit nervous during the car ride. He kept telling me that discipline at this factory was particularly good, and I suspected that it was a prison factory. Sure enough, the factory had tall walls topped with barbed wire, with watchtowers at the corners.

During the obligatory initial meeting in the conference room, the management and the engineers of the factory, about twelve people, were seated on one side of the table, all of them wearing blue police uniforms and caps, while the three of us sat with the FTC rep on the other. For some reason, the two Americans thought the whole thing was hilarious and they were horsing around, comfortable in the belief that no one except me understood them. I, however, was translating and trying to keep things serious, knowing that at least some of our counterparts would understand English. The Americans kept asking me to translate things like, 'Does quality control involve whipping?'. Since I had to address the raised eyebrows of our hosts with a creative translation it was hard to keep a straight face. The incident was an example of the importance of the need for good communications. The FTC should have made clear to us what type of factory we were visiting: it would have saved us time and them embarrassment.

> *There was a special smell to the Fair. It combined the smell of the warm, moist southern vegetation with that of mosquito coils, and permeated the atmosphere of the Fair buildings as well as that of the Dongfang Hotel across the street*

Another part of the buying equation was finding suppliers. In the days before the internet and Alibaba, the Chinese Export Commodities Fair, known also as the Canton Fair, or for short 'the Fair', was the main, in fact the only venue for buyers to interface

Michael De Clercq

with sellers. In the late 1970s it took place twice a year in April and October and lasted four weeks each time. Although in theory the Canton Fair also serviced imports, it was overwhelmingly an export outlet.

There was a special smell to the Fair, peculiar to the place but not unpleasant. It combined the smell of the warm, moist southern vegetation with that of mosquito coils, and permeated the atmosphere of the Fair buildings as well as that of the Dongfang Hotel across the street. The Fair was divided into well-defined, separate sections for machinery, equipment, chemicals, garments, textiles, light industry, animal by-products and so on, but which were housed in a confusing array of buildings of different heights linked by stairways, elevators and covered walkways. Exploring these halls took time but, for the right people, it was a mind-boggling treasure trove. Anything that China made for export anywhere was exhibited at that fair; you could find AK-47 machine guns, fibre-cement yachts, silk carpets and asbestos gloves all under the same roof.

At that time, China's exports were primarily commodities. Even garments were considered and handled as commodities, because of the quotas. Visitors were not buyers, they were traders – commodity traders. For them, the Fair was a twice-a-year opportunity to secure shipments of minerals, chemicals or garments at the right price, and an opportunity to make a killing. But if traders missed out, they had to wait six months for another chance.

For these commodities, China had many buyers but limited supplies, so it was a sellers' market. It was critical for traders to set up meetings with the key FTC negotiators who controlled the contracts. The atmosphere was tense and shrouded in mystery. Traders wanted to be first, and to lock in their deal. They were tight-lipped about their relationships and resorted to various ploys to secure their position, such as entering early through side doors to beat the crowds. The vast majority of traders did not speak Chinese; in fact, it was odd and unusual if someone could. The onus of language was on the FTC negotiators who either spoke English (rare) or who had interpreters. Since it was a competitive relationship issue, foreign traders wanted to be recognised immediately so some always wore the same clothes, such as bright green trousers or red shoes that differentiated them from the rest.

Since it was a competitive relationship issue, foreign traders wanted to be recognised immediately so some always wore the same clothes, such as bright green trousers or red shoes that differentiated them from the rest

For the FTCs, the Fair was a barometer of foreign trade. The amount of business transacted there was published, and the business volume was a matter of prestige. It was important to walk away with a large portfolio or orders. This meant that FTCs would routinely delay business so that they could count it as orders booked during the Fair.

With time, the Canton Fair became less important; other regional fairs surfaced and policies changed. The most important of these had to do with the progressive

Growing a business

Out on the road again: a business trip to Qingdao in Shandong province, northeast China, 1980

privatisation of factories and enterprises. This process started over 20 years ago with the empowering of managers through contracts (*chengbao*) and still continues today. This system placed the onus of performance on the manager and would reward him accordingly, but without giving him ownership. The step of ownership took much longer, but it came too.

Economic and legal reforms were critical factors in transforming China into an export giant. Through the years, it was interesting to observe how the Chinese government worked in tandem in an uneasy relationship with Chinese entrepreneurs to enact reforms. On the one side you had a conservative government reluctant to change, while on the other you had a vibrant multitude of businessmen chafing at the bit, striving to be rich and yearning for an opportunity to own their own business. Someone once made the observation that China was the only country in the world with a lot of poor Chinese. Well, that was about to change.

For businesses to thrive, the government needed to provide enterprises with legal legitimacy and protection of their property. The government also needed to reform the financial system so that banks would be able to lend to companies based on financial common sense instead of political expediency. But the government was Communist, and most of its members were unfamiliar with the concept of free enterprise. The entrepreneurs, on the other hand, seem to have had an innate understanding of it. The chicken and egg conundrum (you needed reforms to develop business, but you needed to show the benefits of business growth to convince the government on reforms) was progressively resolved, as a kind of tug-of-war occurred between the government and the entrepreneurs.

Owner-managers of factories demonstrated to the government that they were much better at generating profits, getting repeat orders and developing a business than state-owned enterprises (SOEs) were. Places such as Zhejiang province took the lead and became hotbeds of capitalism. Money was being made, taxes were being paid – things were happening. So the government, at the local level first, then progressively nationwide, started to loosen up and put in place new regulations that made life easier for entrepreneurs. Every time the government gave an inch, the entrepreneurs seemed to take a yard. They were stubborn, optimistic and had nothing to lose.

While they waited for reforms, Chinese businessmen operated in the shadows of the 'no-rules land' of the Chinese legal system. The way they ran their businesses did not give them legal cover, but neither was it illegal. There were no laws or rules to address it. To protect themselves, they used 'red-hat' companies (companies that pretended to be state-owned in order to benefit from the system and to be protected from meddling local officials) and other stratagems.

Eventually, the State recognised the value that this multitude of companies could generate, and recently it has implemented new laws and policies to facilitate their growth and protect their assets. Generalised privatisation of the SOE system has been mandated, and the process still goes on. This fundamental shift has enabled Chinese factories to compete with foreign-invested factories, improve efficiencies and provide an unbeatable cost/quality ratio that has helped to make China exports the US$800bn-a-year business behemoth that they are today.

As a result of all this, the vast majority of factories supplying the world from China today are private and many are foreign-owned. Very few are State-owned any more. China is now merely a country of origin. This means that if you had good experiences in sourcing from China you were dealing with a good factory and you must have had a good local team in place. Conversely, if you had a bad experience, blaming China for it would not help.

Many companies still think the 'Made in China' label means 'poor quality'. But that was never true. During the bad old days, 'Made in China' meant a lot of hard work to get things done. It meant indifference, slow samples, poor infrastructure, hard-to-get packaging and unreliable shipping – but never bad quality. As an example, the hunting vest I mentioned above ended up being of better quality than the made-in-Taiwan original because we made the shoulder patch from real leather instead of the original imitation leather material – which we could not find in China. And I remember a customer complaining that Chinese bicycle tyres were too good: they were made from virgin rubber, whereas he wanted them in recycled rubber: this way they would wear out faster and he would sell more.

On the one side you had a conservative government reluctant to change, while on the other you had a vibrant multitude of businessmen chafing at the bit to be rich

Quality is up to the buyer, and even though China has followed in the lead of

Growing a business

Japan and first developed its export base largely in low-end, high-volume, inexpensive merchandise, to associate China with 'cheap merchandise' is an outdated concept. I believe that China has graduated to being a high-quality source of merchandise. It is no longer a good source for low-end products with low technical inputs: white T-shirts are better bought in Bangladesh or Vietnam. While China is still a source of inexpensive goods, the quality and sophistication of these goods has improved dramatically. China is now a proven source of electronics, computers and accessories and of quality automotive products, as well as a whole range of engineered wooden products and specially processed metallic parts.

US companies, which are forced to mark their goods with a country-of-origin label (not a requirement in Europe), have realised for a long time that brand, not country of origin, determines quality. The brand is a fundamental reflection of a company's value system, its attention to detail and to quality. Consumers buying an Apple computer, a Sony camera, a Stanley tool or a pair of Levi's jeans don't really care where it is made; their buying decision is based on the brand.

During the bad old days, 'Made in China' meant a lot of hard work to get things done. It meant indifference, slow samples, poor infrastructure, hard-to-get packaging and unreliable shipping – but never bad quality

We have come a long way since 1978. As a result of its diversity of supply, China has evolved today as a complex resource for a large range of merchandise. Sophisticated procurement managers tap into China because it gives them an edge as a result of its inexpensive but qualified labour pool and the willingness of factories to operate on razor-thin margins. The larger their programme, the more they need qualified support in China. In recognition of that growing need, our company decided to offer the experience and systems we had developed for our own sourcing as a service to our clients. In doing so, we stopped acting like a trading company and became a service provider.

The art of war: selling to the China market

In the late 1980s, I heard of a young Frenchman who killed himself in Beijing because he had been negotiating a big sale for months and he just could not seem to make any progress. What often led people to despair in China during the early days was the perception that they were imminently about to break into a huge potential market, only to be confronted with the sobering reality.

If your whole business plan, or your career, was based on making some big China sale in the short term, the odds for failure were short indeed. Large companies such as Siemens and GE had strategic plans for China. They could afford to wait and engage in a form of long-term lobbying. We, on the other hand, depended on sales to make money. We did not have deep pockets and we had to cover expenses. It did not matter so much what we sold, as long as we sold something: we had to generate short-term income. What mattered to us was finding real projects, and by that we meant projects

Michael De Clercq

that had government approvals and hard currency funding.

Finding these projects at the time was an art, not a science. Since everything was planned and budgeted by the central government, research involved reading the government's five-year plan and meeting with FTCs like Machimpex and Equipmex to find out what they had the budget to buy. It would normally take months, sometimes even years to close a sale. But the fastest industrial sale we ever got took only two weeks, from the time we first found the project to the time we signed the contract.

Another search approach was to scour the lists of cooperation deals that many provinces were touting at the time. These were designed to find foreign investors for specific projects. By definition, these projects lacked both government funds and transparency. The legal structure for investment was sketchy at best, and such investments had to be rated as extremely risky. But to us, the lists were an indication of a province's pent-up need for a specific technology or equipment, and we knew that if a partner could not be found, or if terms could not be reached, and if the project was important enough, then a cash sale was possible. The process took longer, but resulted in a greater understanding of the market at large and created more opportunities.

After we found a project, we needed a strategy to close. In that process we were confronted by four challenges: understanding the precise needs of the buyer, finding a supplier, beating the competition and closing a contract without lawyers. Our main advantages were that we had an office and a good reputation in Beijing, we were quick and we were not product-specific. In other words, we could handle any product, from anywhere. In order to increase our sales business, we recognised that, despite our small

With Jim Park and Jiang Xiaoyu, now executive vice-president of Olympic Organising Committee BOCOG, 1998

Growing a business

size, we were in a position to cast a wide net and make ourselves useful to the FTCs.

Understanding the FTCs was not just a matter of knowing the detailed specifications of the equipment they wanted to buy, it also involved an understanding of their timetable, their enthusiasm for any other bids and their sensitivity to a specific country of origin. We knew, for example, that the end of December was often when the money ran out. It was 'spend it or lose it' for the FTCs: contracts had to be signed before 31 December. We also knew that product expertise was not a requirement for bidding on a sale at the time. In one case, the FTC wanted to buy a large cold storage plant for apples and was about to sign with a Japanese supplier. But the Chinese government had had serious disagreements with the Japanese government, and so the FTC had been told to suspend any negotiations with Japanese companies for the time being. By 15 December it had no other supplier, so it approached our office in Beijing.

The FTC wanted a quote for a turnkey cold storage plant, which meant that the foreign seller was responsible for the supply of the whole plant. We were familiar with this buying approach, which FTCs often used at the time to establish a clear and well-defined responsibility for performance by the contractor. Payments were structured to include a retention for performance, and the risk of technical failure of the project was much reduced. The contractor (i.e. us or our clients), on the other hand, had to be careful not to take responsibility for factors beyond our control. In this case, the FTC wanted a controlled-atmosphere cold storage plant that would keep apples fresh and crispy for months. This meant that the plant had to control carbon dioxide and oxygen levels to keep the apples 'breathing' slowly, instead of freezing them. And we knew nothing about this technology.

The FTC presented us with a clear challenge: this was a sure sale, but we need to close before the end of December. I told them I was not sure I could find a supplier by then. That was not a problem: they gave me the name, address and phone number of a US company that specialised in this field. (In the days before the internet, that was most useful information – it saved us long and tedious research using tools such as the Thomas directory.) Since this company did not have an office in China, the FTC wanted us to represent it. So we contacted the manufacturer, and they confirmed they could supply this type of plant in a turnkey format. There was one big problem: it was close to Christmas and they could not provide us with a quotation until later in January. Without a detailed quote, we had no price. Without a price, we could not negotiate a contract and the sale would be lost. What were we to do?

We gave the FTC a quote based on a budget reference and managed to structure a credible contract. Negotiations were tough and somewhat unreal; we had quoted high and gave away very little throughout the process. The FTC dismissed our bid three times before Christmas. They told us our price was much higher than that of the Japanese and that they categorically could not accept this contract. But since we did not know our own bottom line, we refused to budge. The FTC ignored us, our calls were not returned and we were subjected to total silence. So that was that, we thought, good effort but no cigar. We signed the contract on 30 December.

Michael De Clercq

To make it more interesting, it was considered bad form to bring lawyers to the table, so your reputation rested on a contract drafted without them. The FTC negotiators objected to lawyers for a different set of reasons from those why Western companies object to them today: they were not lawyers themselves, and had no training in what they felt was a useless, esoteric field. They figured that sellers who brought lawyers to the table at best did not trust them and at worst would be trying to tie them in complex legal knots. So lawyers were often presented with done deals: contracts they did not like and which they really wanted to be renegotiated but which often was impossible to do, as a matter of face.

> *The FTC negotiators objected to lawyers for a different set of reasons from those why Western companies object to them today: they were not lawyers themselves, and had no training in what they felt was a useless, esoteric field*

Lawyers had a frustrating job in those days, as a legal counsel's ability to help the sales contract process was limited. With the lack of legal infrastructure or precedent of the time, the best advice a lawyer would give was probably, 'Change this, change that and add 25 pages of legal clauses to the contract' – which was the same thing as saying, 'Walk away, don't sign.' This was not what we wanted to hear: we wanted the contract. This devil-may-care approach to the legal structure of business gave us an edge on large corporations, which were obliged to follow certain legal protocols. We instead followed a commonsense, hard-nosed approach to structuring contracts. Responsibilities were carefully analysed and negotiated, and little was left to chance.

I admit there was a strong underpinning of faith in the system. Trust, if you will: trust that the FTC would not breach the contract, that the State would not prevent the contract being honoured, that loopholes would not be found or created to avoid payment or to prevent completion. That trust was justified by the circumstances of the time. In a way, our contract risk was mitigated by the fact that we were not really selling anything: we were instead helping the FTC to buy what it wanted. There was a well-defined beginning and end to a transaction, and the performance of the equipment was the FTC's main concern. It had a vested interest in making sure that all went well.

If anything, the trust had to be mutual: the FTC needed to deal with a company that had a China office because it wanted some recourse. FTC negotiators felt they were taking a big risk in buying. They had been taught that many foreign companies were dishonest, and they had to study casebooks of transactions that had gone disastrously wrong for China in the past. It was far more important for them to understand people than to try and understand laws. This is partially why drinking games (see above) were so elaborate. Contracts for them were no more than an extension of the trust they had formed with their counterpart along with the record of each party's obligations. If their trust in a company or person was breached, they would cease contact and in extreme cases go so far as to blacklist the offending party.

Conversely, successful transactions brought more contracts. We would sometimes

Growing a business

be invited to bid on existing and ongoing negotiations. Pitching one seller against another was one of the favorite negotiation ploys of the FTCs and one that made life much easier for them. An all-out bidding war was good for them – but, of course, not for the seller. For us, it was like war. The competitor was the enemy and the sale was the battle. Pricing was not, should not be the only argument; in fact, offering a low price was not an intelligent long-term strategic plan, because for the next sale the FTC would demand a discount. So you had to be creative to win a sale.

We once secured a sale in three months from under the feet of a Danish competitor, which had been negotiating it for nearly two years. This was an egg processing plant, and it too was turnkey. The equipment we offered was good, but the quality was on a par with that of the Danes. To win the sale we offered something more: we would not only sell them the plant, but we would also buy back the output.

This was the winning argument for the buyer for two reasons: first it promised to provide them with a stream of hard currency to balance their expense in buying the plant and, second, it showed that we had so much confidence in the product made by our equipment that we would, in effect, buy it back. To secure the transaction, we signed two contracts: a sales contract and a purchase contract. To reduce our risk on the second contract, we had made a back-to-back agreement with a reputable US company in the egg business, which agreed to buy the egg powder based on an attractive price/quality ratio, which in turn was reflected in our buying contract.

A Beijing building materials delegation meets Italian Foreign Minister Gianni de Michelis in Rome

My Thirty Years in China | 89

Michael De Clercq

With Minister of Construction Wang Guangtao, Besser chairman Jim Parks and associates, 1998

This approach was known as 'compensation trade', a form of countertrade that China favoured at the time to balance its foreign exchange. Very few companies knew how to do it, but we were well positioned to make this linkage between sales and purchasing, because from the very beginning we saw China as both a source and as a market.

If China has wanted to buy something over the past 30 years, it has usually found willing sellers. But as it has opened up to the West and increased its foreign trade, its buying system has significantly changed and the China market has become quite different. We can simplify by categorising these changes into three broad phases. The first phase was when China had a highly centralised, planned economy. What the country needed was identified by the various ministries and was processed by the FTCs in Beijing. Sales to China during this phase were mostly reactive, not proactive. By this, I mean that you sold to China what China wanted to buy. There was not much point in investing in marketing, even if marketing vehicles had existed; and foreign exchange was a big concern.

During the second phase, buying power was decentralised to the provinces, which were given more flexibility in what they could buy. There was still a strong element of planning, but there was more flexibility within the plan. Although the bulk of sales opportunities remained within the plan, some projects could be secured even if they were outside of it. This increased the potential and the complexity of the market in China, as well as its size. During this phase, foreign companies needed to beef up their operations in China, and marketing became more relevant. Foreign exchange was still lacking, and various forms of countertrade were employed.

Growing a business

The third phase is the current stage. Central planning still plays a role, but for most industries it is more a guideline than a rule. FTCs are reduced to the role of agents, trade finance is in place and buyers must rely on their own means to buy. The retail market has become a real opportunity for Western companies, and market research and marketing are essential components of a sales strategy. China, at this stage, acts mostly like a market economy.

For each of these phases, the China market has been different, and a successful sales programme has required a different approach. Knowledge of the market was critical. We, at first, were generalists doing any sales we could, then the market required us to be specialists and we focused on the building materials sector. Then, as the market continued to explode, we morphed into a sales consulting company.

Looking back

Looking back thirty years and revisiting the adventures, the stories, the ups and the downs of my time in China has been a fascinating exercise for me. When you start such a project, you can't imagine what you are going to write but once you get going, you can't seem to stop. But stop one must, and much has been left unsaid. I realise, for example, that I have done nothing to convey the excitement and tension of living in Communist China, especially at the beginning, when I lived for two years on a two-week visa, and when you got an entry visa but had to apply later for an exit visa. There are stories to tell about bureaucracy, ranging from visas and travel permits to driver's licences, and about the time the police lost my passport.

A lasting legacy of my experience in China has been the understanding I have gained of the one common denominator between Western and Chinese culture: the people. Chinese or Western, the fundamentals are essentially the same. When I got down to it, I realised that the differing perspectives and points of view between China and the West are mere details, colouring in the background. The important issues are the same. Just like people in the West, Chinese people value friends, health, a clean environment and the means to achieve their material objectives. And just like us, those who achieve their objectives tend to do so with integrity.

I have been fortunate and honoured to meet outstanding individuals in this arena. People with vision and courage, both Westerners and Chinese, from different walks of life. I do not name them here, but it was interacting with these people that made the China experience so worthwhile.

> *Just like people in the West, Chinese people value friends, health, a clean environment and the means to achieve their material objectives. And just like us, those who achieve their objectives tend to do so with integrity*

One of the recurring concerns of the 1980s and even into the 1990s was whether China would undo everything it had achieved and go back to the 'bad old days'. There were strong factions within the Communist Party that were both influential and

Michael De Clercq

conservative (i.e. 'leftist'); they were anti-reform and more comfortable with a old type of environment. Nobody knew exactly how one faction prevailed over another, and dramatic change always seemed possible. But over time, I have watched with pleasure as talented low-level officials become managers of large corporations or high officials of state. I have realised that a system that allows such individuals to prosper and which takes advantage of their skills has a lot going for it. A system like that sets for itself a point of no return.

I have not written about our family adventures, which were many, fun and sometimes dangerous. One excursion in Tibet, for example, occurred during the worst flood of recent memory, and our tribulations there could be the subject of a novel.

There were anxious moments, when China or the world was in crisis and you either feared for your family and friends or you became concerned that business could not go on. These were nightmare scenarios that never materialised – but could have. During the short-lived Vietnamese border war in 1979, we really were concerned that it would escalate and that the Russians might nuke Beijing to help their ally. In 1989, I was living in Beijing with my family during the six weeks of the Tiananmen incident, and we were trying to keep our business running while the very fabric of China's society seemed to fall apart.

China's love-hate relationship with the USA was also a factor. Anti-Americanism flared up in 1999 when the USA accidentally 'smart-bombed' China's embassy in Belgrade, and again two years later when a US navy plane collided with a Chinese jet off Hainan island. But later in 2001, on September 11, outrage, compassion and sympathy prevailed instead. On that day, I was in Italy with a couple of Chinese delegations, and when I met with the Governor of Heilongjiang outside of Pisa, all we could talk about, until way past midnight, was the Twin Towers.

I wanted to write about Chinese culture and my experiences with acupuncture, *qigong*, martial arts, the game of *weiqi* (Go) and Chinese calligraphy; about how Chinese characters nearly became extinct and were saved by the wonders of computers. I wanted to review the strange similarities between Chinese people and foreigners in respect to language, alcohol, tobacco and face recognition. I wanted to expound on the reality behind the mysterious powers of *guanxi* (relationships) and describe the Chinese fascination for staring at foreigners, which was especially annoying in public toilets; the lines for buying coveted goods; and the science and importance of picking good Chinese names for Western companies.

I wanted to explore Chinese humour, the especially funny *xiangsheng* or 'cross talk' and the way that the Chinese use sarcastic finesse to express their political views, like the time in 1978 when you could buy crabs in packs of four: three males and one female, a daring and not so subtle jab at the Gang of Four. I should have written about crime and the general lack thereof, but of my close encounters with embezzlement, fraud, theft and even murder.

There is also the topic of religion, often taboo and always controversial. I had many discussions with the Bishop of Beijing, the official head of the Catholic Church in China, on the issues of faith and the underground church. There is also the difficult

Growing a business

topic of corruption. How prevalent it was, and still is; why I think it happened, and how we dealt with it ourselves.

I wanted to share with you the struggles and joys we experienced with financing. How we could not get any when we started our business. How trade finance was most creative in the absence of traditional methods. How China coped in the days when it had little to no foreign exchange reserves. The opportunities of countertrade. Foreign Exchange Certificates (FEC) and renminbi. How the government encouraged the Chinese tradition of savings, and how it used these funds. Another important subject that I wanted to share relates to our experiences in investment in China: joint ventures, cooperation, issues of management, M&As and how Chinese companies related to the process.

Then there is the rise of capitalism in China. How 'money' had no power when I first arrived. How one of the fundamental underpinnings of Western economies, real estate, did not exist in China and what that meant. How it rapidly developed after Deng Xiaoping pushed for reforms in 1992. The subsequent rise of the Chinese economy and the development of stock markets in a socialist economy.

But don't get me started. I was privileged to be in China when its history and economy took a U-turn from the dark days of the Cultural Revolution to the new China of today. It is now clear that China is well on its way to regaining the economic dominance it held for centuries. For me, the whole exercise of writing about the past thirty years has been a special experience, an analysis of forgotten memories, and a real joy. In the end, it feels a bit like driving away from a great movie and reminiscing about the scenario, the photography, the acting, the plots and the sub-plots. And then looking forward to the sequel.

Engaging in a cross talk session with old friend Ian Stones at a celebratory dinner, 1988

Dr. Robert A. Kapp
President, Robert A. Kapp & Associates, Inc

First came to China: 1977

Robert Kapp has four decades of involvement with China, in academia, trade relations and consulting, and is recognised for his contribution to furthering dialogue between China and the US. Among his many roles, he served as President of the US-China Business Council in Washington DC from 1994 to 2004 and was founding executive director of the Washington State China Relations Council. He currently runs his own consulting firm, Robert A. Kapp & Associates, which advises companies seeking to expand business with China.

A China life

Dr. Robert A. Kapp dedicated a quarter of a century to bridge-building work between the United States and China at the highest level. As President of the US-China Business Council, he was closely involved in the 'Politics of China policy', including the process that led to the establishment of Permanent Normal Trade Relations for China. Along the way, he also found time to acquire an international family

Let me begin with an admission: I have never lived in China. I have travelled to China countless times – I have no idea how many any more – but have never lived there: never gotten up in the morning, brushed my teeth, eaten some breakfast, headed for work, taken public transportation to and from the office, and so on. I have always been a visitor, and that is what I shall remain.

While I have not lived in China, I have lived what might be called a 'China life'. From my first day as a graduate student, in September 1964, I have spent nearly all my working hours studying about China, and two-thirds of my entire life working to improve my ability in the Chinese language, writing about China and, most of all, facilitating deeper and better relations between China and the United States.

This 'China life' of mine has taken many forms. Six years as a graduate student brought me a doctoral degree (PhD) from Yale University in modern Chinese history; for my dissertation, I wrote about Sichuan Province under warlord control between 1912 and the outbreak of war with Japan in 1937. With my PhD finished, I took a teaching position in Chinese history at Rice University, a high-calibre private university in Houston, Texas where, as the only China historian on the faculty, I taught 'Yao to Mao,' i.e. the full range of Chinese history from the time of the mythical founders of Chinese civilisation to the present day. Three years after reaching Houston, my wife and I left for Seattle, where I was offered a teaching position in modern Chinese history at the University of Washington.

To that point, I had had only one experience in Asia: in 1967 and 1968 my wife and I lived in Taipei while I conducted research for my dissertation. China remained largely an abstraction to me; then, and for another dozen years afterward, the People's Republic was closed to Americans. The closest I could get was a special trip for American holders of US government-funded scholarships, of which I was one. We flew to the island of Jinmen (Quemoy, as Americans then called it) in a creaking old C-119 propeller-driven cargo plane, just skimming the waves so as to avoid 'enemy radar'. Once on the island, we did the regular tour, which included a chance to peer at the People's Republic through huge binoculars inside an ROC artillery battery pointed toward Fujian, only a couple of miles away. But China, then in the throes of the Great Proletarian Cultural Revolution, was not, it seemed, going to make itself accessible to foreigners – period. Our tour to the edge of China ended in less than a day.

Once we reached the University of Washington in Seattle, in 1973, I joined a large academic faculty doing scholarly research and offering courses in many disciplines

Dr. Robert A. Kapp

University of Washington, Seattle, where I taught Chinese history from 1973

through the 'China Program' – courses in history, political science, economics, geography and many other fields. Graduate students abounded – I found myself with more than a dozen new 'dependents', whom I was supposed to coach and guide through their careers. Ironically, this move to the professional 'major leagues' did not work out as I had envisioned. My university and I did not take to one another. I discovered that I liked teaching more than research and writing, and that I greatly enjoyed helping the broader public to understand China. In 1980, I resigned from the university and left the academic profession. With that goodbye to academic life, I embarked on a series of assignments related to a unique kind of non-governmental, non-profit group in the United States – the 'business association'. My three executive assignments with such business associations would carry me from 1980 right through to the end of 2004.

However, before I left academia, I had my first opportunity to go to the People's Republic, with a faculty group from the University of Washington, in January 1977. The trip was momentous, and left lasting images deep in my mind. Even today, when I visit China, my memory invariably returns to the China of that first visit.

January 1977: a silent first visit

The trip was exciting – how could any of our University of Washington faculty delegation not be excited to be in China for the first time? It was also cold. And grey. And silent. Changan Jie in Beijing was still, except for the occasional bus horn.

Shanghai airport, where we waited for hours in the icy cold, was nearly deserted. Nanjing, where we landed unexpectedly, lay muffled in deep snow. In Wuhan, the doors to our hotel were chained shut at night; no one could leave. The streets of Wuhan were littered with abandoned city buses, their windows smashed out. On the Bund in Shanghai, and on Shamian Island in Guangzhou, the ornate structures built by foreign companies and residents in the decades before 1949 lay inert and dilapidated, with peeling paint, decaying roofs and broken ornaments.

Each of us in the faculty group came from a different professional background. There were a physicist, a civil engineer, a couple of medical doctors, a Russian studies expert, and so on. As we toured, I experienced very vividly a simple reality: what we see, and the

A China life

meaning we derive from what we see, depends on what we are trained to recognise.

Thus, walking down a street, our civil engineer would offer observations about the construction methods and materials used in buildings. Our MDs would notice the medical conditions of passers-by on the street. Our Russia specialist repeatedly 'recognised' what he was seeing in China because it so closely resembled what he knew from the Soviet Union. And so on.

As for me, I could read Chinese. In January 1977, there was a lot to read. Above all, I could read the highly colourful posters that adorned just about every wall space or display board. In a China that was cold, dimly lit and strangely silent, these dramatic posters critical of the recently 'smashed' Gang of Four provided a vivid break from the pervasive stillness around us.

I experienced very vividly a simple reality: what we see, and the meaning we derive from what we see, depends on what we are trained to recognise

In Beijing, our university group met with a number of Chinese scholars at Beijing University, led by the physicist Zhou Peiyuan. For those of us who had watched and read and listened as the Cultural Revolution had overrun China's best minds in the preceding decade, it was difficult to imagine what these sober and earnest academics must have experienced only a few years, or even a few months, before.

Also, during that first visit, I learned a lesson that served me well for many years:

First visit to Beijing, 1977: after the devastating Tangshan earthquake, many refugees were living in tents

Dr. Robert A. Kapp

'Never ask why'. During the extended 'brief introductions' that we encountered at every stop; during our air travel, when we landed in a city not on our itinerary, with no explanation; and even in conversations with our hosts, it seemed that we had entered a world where many things happened but very few things could be explained, at least to outsiders. Finding meaning in experience in China, at that early moment of renewed contact with the 'outside world', did not include much dialogue with Chinese friends about the question of 'why?'. I kept that reminder close to me for many years in China. Every now and then, even though China is so very much more accessible today to foreigners than it was in 1977, I still repeat it to myself.

1980: the year of big changes

In the spring of 1980, I finished up the academic phase of my life. From that September, I was scheduled to begin the work of starting up and developing a new private, non-profit private organisation, the Washington State China Relations Council (华州中国交流理事会). The Council was founded in late 1979 by a small group of private business people and state government officials in my home state of Washington, for the purpose of expanding our state's economic and cultural engagements with China.

The first PRC-flagged vessel to call at a US port, the *Liulinhai*, had called in Seattle before the US and China established diplomatic relations at the start of 1979. Early that year, Vice Premier Deng Xiaoping's historic visit to the US had taken him to Seattle. A sense of excitement and optimism prevailed in Washington State, on the Pacific Coast of the United

Vivid wall posters denouncing the recently 'smashed' Gang of Four provided rare splashes of colour

A China life

States. My job as founding head of the new China Relations Council was to seek out opportunities to develop mutually beneficial exchanges with China, help Washington State companies to learn more about China as they prepared to do business with the PRC, receive distinguished Chinese visitors and make sure that Washington State

On that first visit, I experienced a strangely pervasive stillness, even in Beijing

perspectives on US policy toward China could be heard. I remained at the Washington State China Relations Council from the fall of 1980 until the middle of 1987.

Before I stepped over to the new Council (which started with almost no operating funds), however, my wife and I became parents – in China. Nothing in my 'China life' has been more memorable, or more important to me. We learned later that we were the first American couple to adopt a child in the People's Republic. Our hearts are full of memories of the entire process, including the voyage to China to receive the little girl and bring her back to the US; telling all the stories would require a whole book. So I will just share one.

Upon receiving our daughter and completing the administrative formalities in the city of her birth, we had to go to Beijing so that our new daughter could receive a US visa in her passport. We made arrangements in advance for a place to stay in Beijing, and for someone to meet us at the airport there, and flew to the capital. When we arrived, no one met us. It was an awkward moment. We were loaded down with diapers and other baby gear, had been parents for exactly 24 hours, and did not have any idea what to do next.

Luckily, my very imperfect Chinese language helped us out. We made our way to the Friendship Guest House in northwestern Beijing and found a room there. Soon it was time for dinner. The three of us went to the dining hall; we were all tired. The dining hall was served by a group of very young girls, still wearing bangs and pigtails, as all young girls seemed to in those early days. They saw that we were exhausted, and went into action.

First, one of the waitresses, seeing that our child had only a little hair at that early age and that I was quite bald, beamed at us and said, 'Oho! This little girl looks just like her father!' Coming from a young and inexperienced girl, seeing surely for the first time a couple of Caucasian adults with a tiny Chinese child, these funny words were heartwarming. Next, the staff picked up the baby and took her off to the kitchen to show her to the chef and kitchen staff. We – parents for a day – never had a moment's uneasiness. The kitchen visit gave us a chance to eat quickly ourselves, and our daughter arrived back at our table as happy as could be. We were off to a good start as parents.

The following day, we had another delightful experience. We were walking down a street in Beijing, with the baby in our arms. The city was quiet, and older people were sitting quietly in front of their buildings in the summer heat, watching the passers-by. As we strolled past one elderly couple, they eyed us carefully. As we moved away from them, I heard the wife say to her husband, 'Did you see that baby with those foreigners? She looked just like a Chinese baby!' Another amusing moment in our first days of parenting.

> *I heard the wife say to her husband, 'Did you see that baby with those foreigners? She looked just like a Chinese baby!'*

The task in Beijing was to take care of the baby's US visa; our flight tickets back to Seattle were for a few days later, giving us just enough time to handle the formalities at the US embassy. At least, that was what we thought. After taking the baby to Tongren Hospital for the required physical check-up, we headed for the visa section of the US embassy. Only then did we learn that the necessary paperwork for the visa had not yet been received in Beijing from the US Consulate General in Guangzhou, which was responsible for such formalities.

This was a bad moment. The day was a Friday; the weekend was beginning. Monday in the US was the national Labor Day holiday. Our tickets to the United States were for a day or two later. We turned to the US Consul and asked, fearfully, how long it would take for the visa paperwork to arrive. He consulted an enormous volume of regulations, thumbing through what looked like thousands of pages, before looking up and saying, calmly, 'Could be a day, could be a month'. Our little baby, to that point so quiet and peaceful, began to howl.

We were in a jam. The three worst problems were these: we were running out of cash, we were running out of diapers and I needed to be back home in 48 hours to receive Bo Yibo, then Vice Premier of China, as he arrived in our city. What to do? We found a room for my wife and daughter in a China International Travel Service building in Qianmen, and I prepared to leave for the US without them, not knowing when I would see them again. My wife did not speak Chinese.

Before leaving, I called the wonderful Chinese friend whose efforts on our behalf had led to the adoption; she was a senior member of the All China Women's Federation, a friend and colleague of Mme. Song Qingling and a top figure in the Chinese People's National Committee for the Defense of Children. We had already taken our daughter to see this wonderful, generous and dignified lady after we came to Beijing. Now, I called to tell her that I had to return to the US, while my wife and child remained in Beijing to wait for the visa. I noted that I had arranged to transfer some money to my wife through an emergency assistance line maintained by the US State Department for such crises.

When she heard that, my friend told me that I should have come to her for money. I replied that I really couldn't imagine asking my dear Chinese friends for financial help, after all that she and others had already done for us. Mme. Zhang replied with a phrase that I will never forget: 'Dr. Kapp,' she said, 'Yours is already an international family!' And it was.

One of my best friends in Seattle was (and still is) an attorney who had served as a senior staff

A China life

member to United States Senator Warren Magnuson. Senator Magnusson had represented Washington State in the US Senate for four decades; with such great seniority, he was very powerful. From Beijing, I reached my friend on the phone, told him that the visa was held up in bureaucracy, and that I was returning without my wife and child in order to receive Bo Yibo the next day. That afternoon, I flew out of China.

When I reached Seattle sixteen hours later, I called Senator Magnusson's office, and his assistant informed me that the visa had already been approved and placed in our baby's passport. My wife and child would be in the States within two days. All ended well. Moreover, it seems that all ended well because my friend called his former boss, the Senator; the Senator contacted the US State Department at, shall I say, 'the highest level'; and the visa matter was instantly solved. The same afternoon that I welcomed Vice Premier Bo to Seattle, I welcomed my family home from China. It was the end of a short but unforgettable experience, and the beginning of a new life as an 'international family'.

The 1980s: building bridges

Quite by accident, the timing was right, in 1980, for me to move from an academic position into the new world of building bridges between the United States and China. Diplomatic relations began on 1 January 1979, and a bilateral Commercial Agreement was signed in 1980. China made the historic decision to pursue a policy of 'Reforming the Economy and Opening to the Outside World' at the end of 1978. In the US, and especially in the Pacific States including Washington State, a powerful wave of curiosity

Our international family: we learned we were the first Americans to adopt a child in the People's Republic

My Thirty Years in China | 101

Dr. Robert A. Kapp

Yang Xizong, Governor of Sichuan, entertaining our three-year-old daughter

and anticipation built up. Everyone wanted to see China, and many wanted to 'do business with China', even if no-one quite knew what that really meant. China itself, meanwhile, had begun to change from day to day.

I was very lucky. I had received extensive university training in Chinese language, history and other subjects – 'book learning', as Americans call it. I had a pretty good sense of China's post-1949 history and politics. But I was as ignorant as anyone else about the ways in which Americans could pursue commercial opportunities with China, and had virtually no day-to-day experience of living or working with people from China.

What made me lucky was the accident of timing. I have often laughed with friends, over the years, that in the early 1980s, if I spoke to a group of business people and told them that Beijing was in the north, Guangzhou was in the south and that the Yangtze River flowed from west to east, I could establish myself as a 'China expert'. Thus, despite my very limited China-related skills, I was able, with the support of key business figures in Washington State, to build the Washington State China Relations Council into an effective 'bridge-building' organisation. So began a quarter-century of bridge-building work between the United States and China. I remained in charge of the Council to 1987, and then resumed my guidance of it from 1992 to 1994.

The Council was tiny; for most of my years there, its staff numbered exactly two. Within a year of the Council's founding, I hired a young lady, just out of college, to be my administrative assistant. Hers was a Chinese-American family from a small town on the other side of the mountains that divide Eastern Washington State from Western Washington, where Seattle is located. Her sister had been one of my students at the University of Washington; when I needed someone to help me in the new organisation, I asked her whether she knew anyone just like her, and she introduced me to her sister Linda.

Never has anyone benefited more from

Everyone in the US wanted to see China, and many wanted to 'do business with China', even if no-one quite knew what that really meant...

102 | My Thirty Years in China

A China life

teaming with another person than I did with Linda. Her work was cheerful, socially gracious, meticulously accurate. She endured low pay and, in me, a difficult boss who constantly lost things ('I can't find my car keys!!!') or nearly forgot his tasks for the day. Linda was the real secret of the success of the Washington State China Relations Council. Later, when I moved to Washington DC to take up leadership of a much larger and more influential organisation, the US-China Business Council (美中贸易全国委员会), I invited Linda to 'go back East' to be my executive assistant. She agreed to serve for one year. Ten years later, when I decided it was time to leave the US-China Business Council and return to the beauty and quieter pace of Washington State, Linda was still with the Council. Our partnership, to me, was the gift of a lifetime; I cannot imagine what my work would have been like if I had not had the benefit of Linda's talent and dedication.

If I told people that Beijing was in the north, Guangzhou was in the south and that the Yangtze River flowed from west to east, I could establish myself as a 'China expert'

My work at the China Relations Council was stimulating, and offered much that was new. I initiated discussions in 1980 for the establishment of a special relationship between Washington State and a single Chinese province, Sichuan. This was a new project for China, and Sichuan was still a fairly closed place. But with perseverance and good will on both sides, the governors of Sichuan and Washington State signed a formal agreement in Chengdu in 1982. While that agreement did not produce any sudden or huge increases of commerce for either side, it did provide the basis for a number of educational and cultural exchanges that helped the people of Sichuan and Washington State to advance their knowledge and understanding.

At the same time, the Council, located thousands of miles from the national capital in Washington DC, worked hard to connect the interests of Washington State to national-level policy-makers. The late Senators Warren Magnuson and Henry M. Jackson, both representatives of Washington State, were particularly helpful to us in that regard. Both were recognised in China for their longstanding support of improved relations between our two countries. In the mid-1980s, I led a delegation of staff members from the Washington State delegation to the US Congress on their first visit to China; this, too, provided some memorable occasions.

I had, in those years, many opportunities to visit China, often accompanying or assisting delegations from my home state. Several successive Washington State governors travelled to China with delegations; my Council played its role in arranging itineraries, meetings and so on. Similarly, the Council received many delegations from the PRC and introduced them to our State, its leaders, its economic life and its educational institutions. Many of these figures were from our 'sister province', Sichuan; I have delightful photos of then Governor Yang Xizong playing with our three year-old daughter on his lap. Later, the then Vice Premier Yao Yilin came visiting, and we worked with our state government and other authorities on all aspects of the visit.

Dr. Robert A. Kapp

The back door of my car opened and out into the glorious, cool, clear morning air stepped veteran diplomat Hu Dingyi. 'Good morning, officer,' he boomed

But, looking back, it is the humorous moments that best flavour my encounter with China. Here are but two examples.

In the summer of 1980 I received the first visit of a Chinese Consul to our state. The Consulate General in San Francisco was newly established, under the leadership of Consul General Hu Dingyi. Washington State lies within the 'consular district' of San Francisco and so, on behalf of the Washington State China Relations Council, my wife and I drove 300 miles from Seattle to the city of Spokane at the eastern edge of our state, to receive Hu Dingyi and his wife and show them some of Washington's special places, including the great hydroelectric dam on the Columbia River, known as Grand Coulee. The dam is located approximately 100 miles west of Spokane, in a desert area of our state.

The guests arrived in Spokane, and after greeting them and dining with them, we retired for the night and prepared for an early start the next morning (a Sunday) for the drive to Grand Coulee. That next morning, very early, I rolled over in bed and accidentally demolished my eyeglasses. The lenses were not smashed, but the arms broke off, and I had no way to wear the glasses. Of course I had forgotten to bring a second pair. It was Sunday morning. The city was deserted. No stores were open. Soon we must meet our distinguished first-time visitors and guide them expertly to Grand Coulee and then to Seattle.

In our travel bags, we found some white medical adhesive tape, of the type used to hold bandages in place. We set to work on my eyeglasses – I should say, my wife did, since I am as blind as a bat without them – and managed to tape the arms back on, and then tape the glasses in place on my nose. I looked like the victim of a gruesome accident, but I could see well enough to drive.

Hu Dingyi and his wife were good-natured and understanding. Well over an hour late, we set off across the rolling wheat lands of eastern Washington, on the way to the great dam. I drove fast, since a receiving party was awaiting us at Grand Coulee. Too fast. Way out in the middle of the empty countryside, I saw flashing lights and heard a siren. A State Police car zoomed up to us and ordered me to stop by the side of the road. I had been speeding. The policeman peered in our window and started the familiar routine of charging a driver with speeding, making out an official ticket.

Then the new Consul General sprang into action. The back door of my car opened and out into the glorious, cool, clear morning air stepped veteran diplomat Hu Dingyi. 'Good morning, officer,' he boomed. And then began a delightful conversation: he was the brand-new Chinese Consul General, on his first visit to Wonderful, Beautiful Washington State. What a splendid morning it was, here in the fertile farmlands of 'the Evergreen State'. And so on. I stood quietly while Hu Dingyi taught me lessons.

The end of the story came quickly. The State Police officer told me not to drive so fast. He warmly invited all four of us to stop by his own hometown, a little village not far from Grand Coulee, to be special guests at a holiday parade scheduled for the next

A China life

day. Then he bade us good travelling, and we parted. As I said to Hu Dingyi more than once in subsequent years, I owed him a dinner – in fact, several dinners, given the likely fine that I would have had to pay if he had not saved my skin.

One more story from my days at the Washington State China Relations Council comes to mind. In the mid-1980s our then Governor, Booth Gardner, led a state delegation to China at the invitation of our Sichuan friends. The itinerary included Beijing, and when we got to the capital we learned that we would have a meeting with then Vice Premier Li Peng.

Just before the meeting, I briefed our governor. I made an important suggestion to him: if the conversation with Li Peng seemed to wane, and no-one seemed to know what to say, all the governor had to do was mention the name of Washington State's US Senator Henry M. Jackson, and the conversation would liven up. After all, Jackson was very well known in China (he was deeply hostile to the USSR, and that had endeared him to China's leaders from the 1970s). So, the governor could always overcome any momentary awkwardness by bringing Jackson's name into the conversation: the Vice Premier would instantly recognise it, and conversation could resume.

In due course we convened to meet Li Peng. All went smoothly for a time and then, as I had feared, the conversation seemed to lose speed, until finally it came to a halt. The governor looked my way, and I gave him a clear 'go ahead' signal. So the governor remarked, 'It may interest you to know, Mr. Vice Premier, that our state is

A visit to the Grand Coulee dam prompted a masterclass in diplomacy from Consul General Hu Dingyi

Dr. Robert A. Kapp

the home of the great United States Senator, Henry M. Jackson.'

The interpreter interpreted. Another silence ensued. Then the Vice Premier said to his staff assistant, 'Who is Jackson?' My advice was a miserable failure. Fortunately for me, the governor was a forgiving man, and we remained friends.

1987–1994: an interlude away from China

I was beginning to discover, at the Washington State China Relations Council, that I enjoyed starting things, and developing them, more than I did maintaining them. By 1987, moreover, I had been concentrating all my energies on China for 23 years: six in graduate school, ten in university teaching and now seven at the China Relations Council. To tell the truth, I was getting bored – with many things, but among them with China itself. I had learned the rituals, and had taught them to others. I knew when it was time to end a banquet. I knew how to make sure a high official's visit went well. I knew how to talk to the media. I knew how to help business people get a basic understanding of China as they prepared to build business there. I wasn't learning much myself that was new.

And I was finding that being 'Mr. China' had some disadvantages, too. I was besieged by young Americans seeking my personal advice on their careers in China or, even better, my personal intervention to secure jobs for them. I was only a little less besieged by people from China, seeking my assistance: to them, to their children, to their cousins, for educational opportunities, scholarships, visas and so on. I had become, as the Washington State China Relations Council thrived and US-China relations exploded, a kind of lightning rod for people who felt that I could do something good for them. I tried to meet their needs, but I grew increasingly fatigued, and dismayed that what I had earlier thought were highly individualised cases requiring my assistance actually were simply examples of a bigger, perhaps limitless, pool of needs and demands. I realised that I was 'burning out'.

> *Being 'Mr. China' also had some disadvantages. I was besieged by young Americans seeking my advice on their careers in China or, even better, my intervention to secure jobs for them*

It was time to step back from the whole China picture for a while. I became the head of another Washington State organisation, the Washington Council on International Trade (华盛顿州国际贸易委员) in 1987. Everyone called the organisation 'Witchit', because of its initials WCIT. A former official from the Office of the US Trade Representative assumed my place at the China Relations Council.

At the Washington Council on International Trade, I succeeded Dr. George Taylor, a revered figure in Washington State. Dr. Taylor had founded the Far Eastern Studies programme at the University of Washington in 1939 and had built it, by the 1970s, into one of the most prestigious Asian Studies programmes in the United States. In retirement from the University, he had served as the first president of WCIT. As president of WCIT, I stayed generally out of the China field, but immersed myself in international trade policy questions. I spent more time in Washington DC, building relationships for our state in the trade policy arena, both in Congress and in the Executive Branch of our government.

A China life

One of my projects at WCIT involved APEC, the Asia-Pacific Economic Cooperation organisation, founded in 1989. In 1991, a Washington State friend of mine, working in the nation's capital, tipped me off that the 1993 APEC meetings would be in the United States, and that the US Government would have to select a location. I went to work, with my supporters from WCIT, the City of Seattle and the Washington State government, and in due course learned the good news that APEC 1993 would take place in Seattle.

That led to two years of exciting work – raising money for hosting costs, working with the State Department and other US government agencies on plans for the meeting (which President Bill Clinton elevated to a new level by including 'Leaders' – mostly heads of government – for the first time), and cooperation with a whole new community of Washington DC-based groups focused either on the Asia-Pacific Region as a whole or on other countries (Japan, ASEAN, etc.) within the APEC region. I also found myself meeting for the first time the government affairs representatives of many very large American companies with Asia-Pacific interests, whether or not they had connections to Washington State.

Shortly after the APEC meeting was successfully concluded, I received word that Maurice R. Greenberg, then chairman of the US-China Business Council, was interested in whether I might consider coming to Washington DC to be president of that organisation.

Again, the timing was right. After the excitement and hard work – and success – of APEC in Seattle, I was asking myself, 'What's next?' Nearly seven years had elapsed since I left full-time work on China, and I was ready to plunge back into the field; I missed China, and I missed my friends in the China field. Moreover, my time at WCIT had given me much more understanding of national-level trade policy issues. Our daughter was just about to start high school; if there was a good time to move, this was it.

The China life in Washington DC

By April of 1994, I was in the US capital, ready to see what life would bring. I camped out alone for a few months, while our daughter finished middle school in Washington State. The usual anxieties of house-buying, house-selling and physically moving to a very new environment passed fairly well, although the summer heat and humidity in Washington DC were quite a shock after the cool, dry summers of the Pacific Coast. My wife and daughter arrived in Washington DC early that summer.

The US-China Business Council, when I arrived, was struggling. The tragic events of June 1989 had chilled both the political and the commercial climate for some time, and even though Deng Xiaoping's famous 1992 visit to Shenzhen had signalled the rebirth of China's economic reform and rapid growth, much ground had been lost. Economic conditions in the US had also affected companies' ability to support trade associations such as the one I was to lead.

The move to the US-China Business Council provided me with more than ten years of extremely invigorating, demanding and rewarding activity. I was able to help the Council to grow substantially and to serve more and more US companies engaged with China. To the Council's longstanding Beijing office, first opened in 1979, we added new offices, first in Hong Kong and then in Shanghai. The Council, founded in 1973 at the dawn of modern

Dr. Robert A. Kapp

US-China relations, was the principal organisation of American companies engaged in trade and investment with China. The size, and distinction, of its growing list of member companies lent weight to the Council's policy statements, whether directed to the American government or to the Chinese government. The Council worked hard to sustain the forward progress of US-China relations through some very tumultuous years.

Inevitably, and happily, my work at the Council drew me deeply into government affairs work. This included frequent testimony before Congressional hearings, particularly on the annual renewal of 'Most Favoured Nation' trade status for China between the time of my arrival in 1994 and the year 2000; the struggle for Congressional approval of 'Permanent Normal Trade Relations' （永久最惠国待遇） for China in 2000, after the US and China reached bilateral agreement on the terms of China's accession to the World Trade Organisation (WTO); and coordination of US business interests and policy positions as the US-China trade relationship grew, deepened and occasionally encountered serious problems.

Much of my work was centred on Washington DC. I had the benefit of very effective staff members working 'on the ground' in Beijing and Shanghai and coordinating well with our headquarters in the nation's capital. At the same time, serving as the leader of the US-China Business Council enabled me on many occasions to meet with leaders in the Chinese government, both in Beijing and in Washington. Indeed, my first guest at the USCBC, even before I had formally joined the organisation, was Bo Xilai, then Mayor of Dalian, and of course the son of Bo Yibo, whose arrival in 1980 in my hometown of Seattle occurred at such an exciting moment in my family life. I encountered Mr. Bo many times in later years, during his service as Minister of Commerce.

In Washington, I enjoyed steady and fruitful contact with successive Chinese ambassadors to the United States, as well as successive Ministers of Embassy (公使) and the leaders of the Commercial, Economic, Political and other sections of the Chinese embassy. I believe that we learned to speak honestly to one another in many situations that required sensitivity and mutual understanding. In China, as president of the USCBC, I accompanied leading American business figures to a number of visits with senior Chinese political leaders. In the US, my organisation regularly played a useful role in arranging for visiting senior Chinese leaders to meet and engage with American business leaders. Many of the activities I conducted in China with Chinese government agencies resulted from the gracious assistance of the China Council for the Promotion of International Trade (中国对外贸易促进委员会), our 'Counterpart Organisation' (接待单位) from the Council's beginning in 1973.

A roomful of CEOs sat in amazed silence as the President of China and a brilliant violinist who had left her homeland for the US recreated the music of a political era that had marked them both

Through my work at the US-China Business Council, I came to know a great many respected Chinese colleagues, and gained many rich memories. Some of the sharpest

A China life

As President of the USCBC, I was privileged to host President Jiang Zemin on his visit to the US in 1997

memories were of difficult moments in US-China relations. Others were of high points in the bilateral relationship. One of my warmest recollections dates from the visit of then President Jiang Zemin in 1997. The Business Council served as principal host, with the Chinese Chamber of Commerce in the USA, for a CEO-level dinner in honour of President Jiang at the famous New York Hotel, the Waldorf Astoria, on Park Avenue.

We made every effort to ensure that the dinner event would be gracious, lively and friendly. To help achieve that, I asked my brother, Richard Kapp, and several of his colleagues to provide classical chamber music as background for the dinner. My brother, who is no longer living, was a highly talented professional musician, both as pianist and conductor of a wonderful orchestra, the Philharmonia Virtuosi of New York. He agreed to provide, with four members of his orchestra, music for the enjoyment of our dinner guests at the Waldorf Astoria.

During the dinner, as I was seated at the head table, I mentioned to President Jiang that the musicians playing that evening were my brother and members of his orchestra. President Jiang decided to walk over and greet them. As the friendly greetings were progressing, Jiang came to the principal violinist, a woman with flaming red hair. In chatting with her, President Jiang learned that she was an immigrant to the United States from Ukraine. And so Jiang Zemin asked the violinist, Mela Tennenbaum, whether she knew any of the old Sino-Soviet 'friendship songs' of the 1950s. Indeed Tennenbaum did, and for the next five or ten minutes, a roomful of

Dr. Robert A. Kapp

Pemier Zhu Rongji came to Washington in April 1999, but on this occasion no deal was reached on China's WTO accession, to my great disappointment and frustration with US officials

American CEOs sat in amazed silence as the President of China and a brilliant violinist who had left her homeland for a new life in the US recreated the music of a political era that had marked them both but no longer dominated their lives. It was truly a delightful and memorable moment.

During my work at the US-China Business Council, I also had the pleasure of inaugurating, on the Council's twenty-fifth anniversary, a business-supported charitable programme called the US-China Legal Cooperation Fund. During the meetings between Jiang Zemin and President Clinton in 1998, the two sides agreed to deepen their cooperation in the field of law. I saw an opportunity for corporate members of the USCBC to contribute to something potentially of genuine value to China and to US-China relations.

Now in its tenth year, the US-China Legal Cooperation Fund continues to provide modest but helpful financial support to a wide variety of projects designed and created by US and Chinese partners. The projects supported by the Fund over ten years have ranged from topics closely related to commercial affairs to areas such as legal assistance for the poor, migrant workers' legal rights and many, many others. American companies have contributed generously to the Fund to enable it to continue its operations; to date, the Fund has conducted 19 semi-annual grant-making rounds, and has provided nearly US$1m in support to cooperative legal programmes linking our two countries.

The year 1999 was a memorable one for China and for US-China relations. Beginning in 1995, only a year after my arrival in Washington DC, tensions had arisen

A China life

between Washington and Beijing, mainly over Taiwan. Then, starting in 1997, American politics had witnessed a vast and heated debate over China, both among Washington politicians and in the US media. It is hard, now, to recreate the poisonous atmosphere that overhung US-China relations in that period. This was the era of allegations of Chinese involvement in American political campaign financing, of accusations of Chinese theft of US nuclear weapons secrets and secret rocketry information. Members of the US Congress, and some in the major media, hammered hard, over and over, at the dangers China presented to the United States. President Clinton, who, during his first campaign for the presidency, had blamed President George H.W. Bush for being too 'soft' with regard to China, found himself in 1997 and 1998 under heavy political attack on similar grounds.

Meanwhile, the long and difficult US-China negotiations over the terms of China's accession to the World Trade Organisation seemed to be making real progress. Amid the domestic American political controversy over relations with China, Premier Zhu Rongji visited Washington in April of 1999. On the eve of Zhu Rongji's arrival in Washington, expectations were very widespread that he and President Clinton would finally sign a bilateral agreement on the terms of China's accession to the WTO.

In the end, the agreement was not finalised. The American business community represented by the USCBC reacted with severe disappointment, and I felt it necessary to

A high point: shaking hands with President Bill Clinton at the White House in the fall of 2000, after he signed the legislation that established Permanent Normal Trade Relations for China

speak very bluntly to those American officials responsible for US trade policy toward China. In my ten years in Washington, that was perhaps the moment of greatest stress for me.

Soon after the collapse of the long-awaited US-China agreement on WTO terms, an American warplane struck the Chinese embassy in Belgrade, setting off a huge and angry reaction in China. Relations between our two countries essentially came to a standstill through the summer of 1999. Only at the APEC Leaders' meeting in New Zealand, in September of that year, did President Clinton and President Jiang meet face-to-face, and shake hands. With that, bilateral negotiations on the final US-China WTO deal resumed, and by November of that amazing year, US Trade Representative Charlene Barshefsky and Minister of Foreign Trade and Economic Cooperation Shi Guangsheng were able, at last, to announce a bilateral agreement.

> *I was extremely happy to be present at the White House for the signing ceremony that established Permanent Normal Trade Relations for China*

That set the stage for the bitter political struggle for Congressional approval of Permanent Normal Trade Relations in the year 2000. After much effort by many individuals and organisations, including my own, the critical vote in the US House of Representatives approved PNTR in late May. The US Senate followed suit early in the autumn. I was extremely happy to be present at the White House for the signing ceremony that established Permanent Normal Trade Relations for China.

The political battle for PNTR in the spring of 2000 taught me a great deal about the workings of the American political system. I remain grateful, to this day, for the many expressions of appreciation I received from Chinese colleagues and friends who, in later years, continued to remember my limited role in the effort to open a new era in US-China relations.

The new century: from Washington to the countryside

Once PNTR legislation was approved in 2000, the path lay open for China to negotiate in Geneva the final Accession Agreement that laid out in detail China's many commitments to change its economic and commercial system in order to meet the WTO's requirements for membership. Those negotiations were complex, and sometimes difficult, but by the end of 2001 China was a full member of the WTO.

With WTO membership achieved, China's integration into the global trade system accelerated. As it did so, its foreign trade relations grew very rapidly, and foreign direct investment began to pour into China in very large amounts. The US-China Business Council now focused its efforts on helping American companies both to enter China for the first time (as new business fields were opened to foreign participation in accordance with China's WTO commitments) and on supporting American companies seeking to expand their operations within China as the PRC economy roared forward..

China's laws and regulations governing international trade and investment underwent major changes in the post-WTO accession years; although the Chinese economy became more

A China life

and more open to foreign participation, great complexities and uncertainties remained for foreign business people seeking to navigate China's central, provincial and local bureaucracies. Meanwhile, in Washington, attention turned to China's record in fulfilling its formal commitments under the terms of its WTO Accession Agreement. This became a subject of close Congressional interest, particularly because the annual Most Favoured Nation hearings that Congress had held between 1990 and 2001 were eliminated with China's WTO membership and the implementation of Permanent Normal Trade Relations.

While controversies remained, however, the broad trend in US-China business and economic relations in the first half of the 2000s decade was favourable. Controversies did arise – over allegations of ill treatment of Chinese workers, over surges of imports from China that threatened to destroy US domestic industries, and so on. After 2003, there was the argument that China's 'peg' of its currency, the renminbi (RMB), against the US dollar was a predatory policy, designed by the Chinese government to keep Chinese export prices low, boost Chinese exports to the US to even higher levels and eliminate American competition in the US market itself. That theme has continued to resound in Washington for the past five years.

My job at the US-China Business Council, though, was becoming routine. Many

Greeting Hu Jintao, then Vice President of China, on his visit to Washington in 2002

Dr. Robert A. Kapp

of the political controversies over China were repetitions of old arguments. The tasks facing the Council in the field of US-China relations were familiar to me. Visits of China's new leadership team, including then Vice President Hu Jintao, Premier Wen Jiabao, Vice Premier Wu Yi and others, provided moments of excitement, but I recognised a familiar feeling that my work was becoming stale, and that the USCBC would benefit from new leadership – 'new blood', as we say.

Moreover, my wife and I increasingly longed to return to the Pacific Northwest, where we had lived for two decades before going to Washington DC. Our daughter had attended college in California, and then proceeded into PhD studies at Stanford University, near San Francisco. Most of our good friends were in Washington State. We were not growing any younger. It was time to move on. We decided to move to a small town of only a few thousand people, on the Washington State coast near Vancouver Island, Canada, a couple of hours' drive from Seattle.

My departure from Washington was very moving. My Chinese friends sent me a great many warm and supportive letters, which I cherish today. Ambassador Yang Jiechi, whom I had known from my first days in Washington when he was Minister of Embassy, and with whom I had shared some very exciting times, gave to me an exquisite example of his calligraphy, which now graces the wall of my office in my home. I was very touched, in 2005, by the concern that China's new Ambassador,

Premier Wen Jiabao was another visitor to New York as bilateral relationships continued to mature

A China life

Zhou Wenzhong, and Yang's predecessor Li Zhaoxing, by then China's Foreign Minister, extended to me when I experienced health problems.

The US-China Business Council staff, with whom I had had such close relations for such a long time, said farewell in the most gracious ways, but not always with grave solemnity. At a wonderful reception in my honour in Beijing, with many representatives of the Council's member companies in attendance, our China-based staff presented me with an extremely surprising memento – an original painting of 'Chairman Bob' commissioned for this special occasion.

And so, before daylight on the morning immediately following the US Presidential election of 2004, I got into my car, drove away from the nation's capital and arrived five days later at my new rural home on the other side of our country.

At home with our daughter, back in Washington State

I became a one-person consulting firm – many Americans do just that, when they finish their work in larger organisations. Since the end of 2004, I have provided consulting services to several large US corporations, to a leading American law firm and to an American non-government organisation with extensive interests throughout Asia. I have continued to visit China, though perhaps not as frequently as I did when I served the US-China Business Council. I remain actively interested in US-China relations, US politics as they relate to China and improvement of mutual understanding between the Chinese and American peoples. I am pleased to serve on several advisory boards of American educational organisations focused on China.

And I have the enormous pleasure of spending more time with my wife in a beautiful location. Our daughter has come a long way from the Children's Welfare Home in China where we first met her in 1980; she has earned a PhD and has put her skills to work in a fine American company. My wife and I look at our daughter and wonder at the good fortune that Fate has given us.

In short, a modest China life. I have sometimes wondered whether China was simply a passing phase in my life, a period of time with a beginning, a middle and an end, rather than a permanent, life-defining experience. In fact, though, it is the latter, a huge part of my life that will never fade completely into memory.

Tim Mathieson
Chief Operating Officer, Willis Insurance Brokers Co., Ltd.

First came to China: 1977

Tim Mathieson studied Chinese at university in England and first visited China as a postgraduate student in 1977. He has 28 years' experience in the insurance industry, covering marine hull broking, treaty reinsurance broking, energy underwriting and management aspects. During his career, he has worked in London, Switzerland and China. In 1981, he was responsible for setting up the first insurance broker liaison office in China and worked in Beijing from 1981–84 in this capacity. He has worked for Willis in China since May 2007, and is responsible for the overall operational aspects of the company's China business.

E-mail: mathiesonti@willis.com

The life of a *laowai* insurance broker

Tim Mathieson went to Beijing to set up a representative office in 1980 and has since seen China's insurance industry expand exponentially into one of the largest in the world. Now returned to the country once again, and based in Shanghai, he believes that life in the cities has improved dramatically for both Chinese and foreigners, although challenges remain

On an August afternoon in 1977 a very disparate group of a dozen recently graduated British Chinese studies students carried their bags over the border bridge between Hong Kong and Shenzhen and gained their first impressions of the People's Republic of China: young soldiers in their green Red Army uniforms, standing impassive guard; the background smell of poorly plumbed toilets in a hot climate; Chinese tea served in a room of imposing murals and large armchairs with lace antimacassars; the sound of shunting steam engines; and, distantly, the constant, inexplicable hooting of car horns.

Coming to China in those days felt a little bit like stepping through an Alice-in-Wonderland mirror into a land where life was vastly different from the 'real' world that we Westerners were used to. The difference in the standard of living was the first factor, but not a very important one, since overseas students were, relatively speaking, somewhat cosseted. The segregated dormitories for foreigners had students living two to a room – one Chinese, one foreign – rather than the six or more in a Chinese dorm, and the separate

A Peking University student attempting to blend into the background at the Great Wall in 1977

Tim Mathieson

An early expedition, in 1978, involved climbing the famous Tai Shan in Shandong province

canteen served better-quality food. Even so, life was fairly simple and the variety of food was limited, particularly in the winter when the only readily available vegetables and fruits were the ubiquitous *bai cai* (cabbage) and apples. The occasional arrival of a batch of poor-quality bananas from the south was a cause for some excitement in those days.

What were really strange for those early students were the social barriers between foreigners and Chinese. The room-mates at the universities in 1977 were of the old 'worker-peasant-soldier' variety selected during the Cultural Revolution for their political rather than purely intellectual capabilities. Nonetheless, they were a good bunch and sociable up to the point allowed by their political masters – which was not too far: they had to attend a weekly meeting to discuss what their room-mates were getting up to. Too much fraternisation, especially between the sexes, was definitely not allowed, and genuine conversations with people outside the universities were few and far between.

Foreign students countered this *de facto* segregation by trying gamely to blend into the background, buying Chinese-style Mao jackets and baggy trousers (choice of dark blue or army green) and caps with our allocated cotton coupons. However, it was a hopeless task and the lanky, long-nosed, pale-skinned, non-black-haired students stood out a mile and always attracted – at the least – inquisitive stares and, if stationary for too long, crowds of curious onlookers somewhat similar to those that would congregate around traffic accidents.

The course to be studied dictated which university the foreign student attended: linguistics in Shenyang, history in Nanjing, literature at Fudan University in Shanghai. Those who chose philosophy ended up at Peking University, with its campus set in part of the old Imperial hunting grounds, well-wooded and landscaped, with the willow tree-ringed 'Lake with No Name' at its

Lanky, long-nosed, pale-skinned students stood out a mile and, if stationary, attracted crowds of curious onlookers similar to those that would congregate around traffic accidents

heart. The course curriculum was, of course, exclusively geared towards Marxism, Leninism and Mao Zedong Thought and was – perhaps for obvious reasons – the only one on offer where foreigners were taught completely separately from Chinese students. The wisdom of this decision, from the Chinese authorities' point of view, became increasingly evident as the

The life of a *laowai* insurance broker

students slowly grew more sceptical and fractious as the year wore on. The large chunks of text deleted in red pen that we could see when our lecturers read out their notes either indicated that amendments were currently being made to the interpretation of socialist philosophy or that certain aspects were not for the foreigners' ears.

Eventually this particular student rebelled against the course content and in his final essay extended the dialectical approach espoused by Mao to Mao's own writings and was consequently told that he had made some 'errors of thought'. The opportunity to correct these errors was offered, but politely declined after it was confirmed that failure in the essay would not lead to expulsion from the end-of-year travel, which included Xi'an (a year after the discovery of the Terracotta Army) and a ride down the Yangtze River, long before the Three Gorges Dam was to change life forever on its upper reaches.

A rookie businessman in China

Three years later, that student was back in China, now as a rookie businessman opening a representative office for an insurance broker. Much had changed in the meantime, as the opening up of the economy started by Deng Xiaoping had really begun to have an impact. Initially many of those changes were primarily of a domestic nature: more economic freedom and therefore better incomes in the countryside, the establishment of some private companies, more cultural openness and so on. However, there were also an increasing number of foreign companies expressing an interest in the Chinese

Two insurance brokers in Beijing in 1981 outside the office/hotel, with the ubiquitous 'Shanghai' saloon car in the background. Twenty-five years later, David Brewer (left) became Lord Mayor of London

My Thirty Years in China | 119

Tim Mathieson

market, some of which had already started to put down roots in the long-term game of establishing a presence in – potentially – the world's greatest market. BP, Shell, Barclays and the Midland Banks, Rolls-Royce, British Aerospace and Sedgwick (the broker mentioned above) were amongst the 15 British businesses represented in Beijing. Although nowadays there are over 700 British companies in China, in 1981 you could fit the entire business community around one good-sized round table.

In those days, life for an insurance broking representative revolved around a three-bedroom hotel suite (although the word 'suite' rather overstates the quality of the accommodation) in a Soviet-era hotel on the outskirts of Beijing's city centre. The master bedroom was separated from the office-cum-spare-bedroom by a small sitting room, whilst a corridor alongside led to the bathroom. At least commuting was not an issue. The office was equipped with a phone, desk, electric typewriter, small filing cabinet and a 'Shanghai'-brand telex machine. When the telex machine was in full swing, the noise it generated could wake a sleeping representative two rooms away, so London soon learned to hold back telex messages until the small hours of the morning UK time, so that their man in Beijing could sleep more soundly.

> *Such was the difficulty of connecting phone calls that the telephone seemed to represent an infuriatingly large obstacle to open communication*

Electronic communications generally were a challenge. Such was the difficulty of connecting phone calls in those days that the telephone seemed in this sometimes topsy-turvy environment to represent an infuriatingly large obstacle to open communication. It would be rare to get through on the first – or even fourth – attempt and a full-time local assistant was an essential colleague solely for the purpose of making appointments. Much of the problem was undoubtedly due to the lack of infrastructure, but many representatives suspected that some of the problems were caused by surveillance of foreigners' calls. That little additional click on the phone line was a not uncommon occurrence.

Setting up and registering a representative office entailed, as now, numerous administrative and bureaucratic tasks, in which one's host unit – for example, the People's Insurance Company of China – played an important facilitating role. The whole process took several months, with many journeys to various government departments and with much documentation passing hands, including a power of attorney for the local representative so wide as to give a Head Office legal counsel sleepless nights.

Once these initial phases were past, the main focus of the insurance broker representative's life was the sole insurance company in China, the People's Insurance Company of China (PICC). In those days, its head office was a small building with a pre-fabricated appearance, located opposite the historic Bank of China head office building on the corner of Tiananmen Square.

In 1981 the PICC was, in effect, the rump of the pre-revolutionary Chinese insurance industry, stemming from the nationalisation in 1949 of the 64 pre-revolutionary companies into several state-owned entities that eventually became the PICC. Foreign insurance

The life of a *laowai* insurance broker

companies, which had around 22 per cent of the market in 1950, had all left China by the end of that decade and in 1959, as socialist dogma held sway, the PICC itself suspended most domestic operations. In the 1960s, in line with the more pragmatic economic policies following the economic disaster of the Great Leap Forward, insurance began to revive somewhat within China, but this was again brought to an abrupt halt in 1967 with the onset of the Cultural Revolution.

The PICC head office was in a small building with a prefabricated appearance

Only in 1979, with the post-Mao opening of the economy, were the conditions for an expansion in the insurance industry re-established. However, by the early 1980s there were still only around 200 people employed in the PICC, mostly dealing in insurances relating to overseas transactions, such as cargo shipments and ventures involving foreign investment. The need for insurance for the vast majority of China's industry remained an irrelevance, given that most enterprises were still owned by the State and that the 'normal' – from a capitalist point of view – rules of finance and accounting were not necessarily in operation.

The employees of the PICC in those early days were split, roughly, into three types of individual – reflecting Chinese urban society as a whole. The majority were comrades dutifully, but often unenthusiastically, fulfilling their assigned roles – mostly administrative in nature – in return for the fixed salary and other social benefits, including housing, that would be handed over by the State whatever the results of the business. This system was known as the 'iron rice bowl', where employment was guaranteed (though with little choice as to what job you were assigned), and all aspects of life from health care to education to accommodation were provided for by the State.

The need for insurance for the majority of China's industry remained an irrelevance, given that most enterprises were owned by the State and that the 'normal' rules of finance and accounting were not necessarily in operation

Amongst these folk there were a smattering of older, but extremely professional and astute insurance specialists, who had gained experience in the days before the Cultural Revolution – and in some cases before the People's Revolution of 1949. The third group

Tim Mathieson

was made up of the recent graduate intake – young, well-educated people who had been fortunate to enter university after the end of the Cultural Revolution and so had gained a good tertiary education. Many of this group, further trained by overseas visits and postings, today command the heights of the country's insurance industry.

Today the PICC has burgeoned into an organisation that, despite having lost its monopoly and now 'only' controlling around 50 per cent of the nation's insurance business, employs 80,000 people in 4,500 offices. It has a premium income of Rmb73bn (US$10.6bn) and writes most classes of business. It has restructured several times to reflect the normal state of insurance practice, including splitting its life and property businesses and spinning off reinsurance into a separate company.

> *China was being opened up by its own leaders, allowing the noisy, potentially disruptive invasion of Western, capitalistic ideas to stimulate its latent entrepreneurialism*

In 1981 it would have taken a brave, or reckless, analyst to have foretold this growth, so those insurance companies present in China were really there only to dip their toe in the socialist waters, with a view to long-term branding and possibly very long-term returns on investment. The result was that the investment was kept to a relative minimum – certainly in the insurance and general industry sectors, less so perhaps in the wealthier banking and oil sectors. This meant, *inter alia*, that this insurance broking representative was the proud possessor of the firm's only company bicycle. This was of limited use only, since the distances required to get to and from appointments with the PICC ruled out the bicycle in most cases, particularly during the cold winters or sticky summers. Eventually, a visiting company director, stranded on the wrong side of town by a lack of transport, put in a good word for a company car, but for a long while taxis (more of which later) loomed large in my life.

The task of 'establishing a presence' entailed frequent visits to the PICC's Head Office on technical or business matters, acting as a conduit for information between Beijing and London. Hosting visitors from Head Office and clients from around the world also consumed much time, effort and – since Maotai was the pungent, fiery spirit of choice at official banquets in those days – physical sacrifice. When these routine tasks were added to the day-to-day administrative jobs (arranging appointments, visits to the bank, tax office, etc.) one could, as one old China hand pointed out, spend all one's time just *being* in China.

There were nonetheless occasional breaks in the routine: a tree-planting exercise by the British business community, in support of the Government's efforts to improve the climate in the north of China, had us scrabbling round a scrubby hillside near the Great Wall on a cold spring day. Or – a highlight for this particular representative – participation in the trial run of the first-ever Hong Kong to Beijing rally, which took a small group of foreigners, including a Japanese film crew, through China's surprisingly mountainous and often staggeringly beautiful scenery. The fact that it took five days to travel roughly half the length of the country, traversing just six of the country's 30-odd provinces, brought home the enormous size of the People's Republic.

The life of a *laowai* insurance broker

A tree-planting exercise by the British business community near the Great Wall in 1983

Meanwhile, the swift progress of the two Subaru rally cars and support vehicles along roads and through towns and villages that had never in living memory seen a foreigner and often contained few mechanical vehicles of any kind seemed, to this businessmen at least, a fitting metaphor for the change that would soon be coming upon China from the outside world. This time China was being opened up not, thank Heavens, by the gunboats or bayonets of rapacious colonialist powers, but by its own leaders allowing the noisy, potentially disruptive invasion of Western, capitalistic ideas to stimulate the latent entrepreneurialism of the Chinese people.

Rapid growth of the insurance industry

The insurance industry in China in the mid-1980s continued to mirror – as it had done in the previous 20 years – the political and economic changes that were transforming the country. In 1988 the second post-Revolution insurance company – Ping An, also State-owned at the time – was established, with others following. In the 1990s, the insurance industry expanded 15-fold – that's an average of 15 per cent per annum compound growth – from a gross premium figure of Rmb9.8bn to Rmb160bn in 2000. This growth has continued and has accelerated into the new millennium, so that the Chinese industry now has 86 companies writing total premiums of over Rmb510bn.

As in more mature markets, life insurance now accounts for around two-thirds of the overall market, and there are 47 life insurers operating in China. It is perhaps also no surprise that the huge number of privately-

The phenomenal year-after-year growth, if maintained, will mean that within ten years China's insurance market will be the fourth largest in the world after those of the US, Japan and the UK

owned vehicles that have replaced the iconic, ecologically friendly Flying Pigeon and Phoenix bicycles that used to circulate quietly through China's cities means that motor insurance now accounts for two-thirds of the non-life market. Although China's insurance industry in 2006 was still roughly only a quarter the size of the UK's, the phenomenal year-after-year growth, if maintained, will mean that within ten years, China's market will be the fourth largest in the world after those of the US, Japan and the UK. Even then, the per capita spend on insurance will remain low by Western standards, implying that – as the Chinese economy develops further – the opportunities for the insurance industry will continue to expand.

> *Experience is a rare commodity, and competition in the industry is increasing. Someone with ten years of experience and a good track record can command near-Western levels of salary*

The explosion of opportunity resulting from the burgeoning of the insurance industry has provided jobs for over two million people in China. This has obviously been one of the success stories of recent years, similar to others in many different areas of the economy. However, remembering that in the 1980s there were only a few hundred insurance practitioners in the entire country, this rapid employment growth has created a large skills shortfall.

In the average London insurance business office, there will be numerous people with more than 15 years' experience and a reasonable number who have been in the industry for 20 or more years; in China such experience is a rare commodity indeed, with increasing competition between companies for those with five or more years of experience. Someone with ten years of experience and a good track record can now command near-Western levels of salary. Indeed, one of the largest insurance companies in China has recently been castigated for the numbers of its directors earning annual salaries of over US$1m – its chairman and CEO earns US$9.5m, a vast sum in a country where the average annual wage is around US$2,000.

The widening gap between rich and poor is another marked difference that has emerged in China over the past 30 years. In the more socialist-style economy of the 1980s, most State-owned enterprises typically ran an eight-grade salary structure that meant that a senior manager would earn perhaps five times as much as a new entrant to the industry. In addition, the bosses would also, of course, have had many other perks, such as better accommodation, access to a car, etc., all provided for by the State, but even so the differential between the most senior and the most junior employee would have been nothing like the factor of 4,750 illustrated above.

This gap is even larger when considering the standard of living in the countryside, where the average income is less than one-third of that in the cities. In 1978 the differential was 2.5:1, highlighting the fact that the old discrepancy in wealth between the cities – particularly near the coast – and the countryside is once again emerging. The solution of allowing people to drift to the cities has started – as testified to by the millions of migrant labourers working on construction projects in the cities – but cannot be allowed to get out of control for fear of

The life of a *laowai* insurance broker

Today cars have to a large extent replaced the ubiquitous bicycle, but at a serious environmental cost

creating large-scale unemployment and social instability in the cities. One area of particular concern has been the reduction in medical support to the countryside, following the partial privatisation of the medical system in the 1990s. It was noted that in some areas, peasants were unable to afford the Rmb1 fee for basic medicines and were therefore in some cases having to forego medical aid altogether. This has become an area of major focus for the government and is one in which the insurance industry will no doubt have a role to play.

Twelve years on

As always, the technocratic politicians in Beijing need to balance numerous, often contradictory, factors – and keep on getting the balance right to avoid tipping the country once more into chaos. The key is maintaining the economic growth, but the environment, education, land rights, corruption, unemployment, ethnic minority rights, religious beliefs are all, *inter alia*, aspects which also need to be taken into account. With all this breakneck – albeit unevenly spread – economic and social development, the changes that confronted this insurance broker when he returned to Shanghai in 2007, after an absence of over 12 years, should perhaps not have been unexpected, but were nonetheless astounding.

Forgetting the more obvious aspects of roads, traffic and high-rises, the most important difference is that the mindset in the major cities has undergone a sea-change. One needs to remind oneself that China is not a uniformly developed country and that cities like

Tim Mathieson

Signing the marriage certificate with an inky finger on my wedding day in Beijing

Shanghai do not represent most of the rest of the country. Nonetheless, in the big cities where most foreigners are employed, the level of service available to the inhabitants, including expatriates, is now infinitely better than it was 30 years ago.

Take the case of finding accommodation. In the 1980s there was little alternative – except for the most wealthy of companies – to the hotel-room-as-office scenario. Nowadays the plethora of choice, both for office and personal accommodation, would be daunting were it not for the services of relocation agencies. The one that I came across when searching the internet from London not only had the most informative website about Shanghai (www.entershanghai.info), but was able to provide advice and assistance on many aspects of moving to the city, including numerous accommodation options. The young lady who helped us with our relocation epitomised the best of the new China: smart, sophisticated, fluent in English and completely focused, in a very no-nonsense way, on providing the best possible relocation service. Months later, I know that I can still ring her or her colleagues to ask for assistance on any administrative aspect of living in China, and will be given help instantly.

China is no different from many other countries in so far as that old bellwether, the cab driver, is probably one of the clearest illustrations of the life of the city and the changes in the country as a whole. In the old days in Beijing, one of life's challenges was obtaining the services of a taxi. They could not be hailed in the street and the ranks were usually deserted, except at the major hotels, where the cab drivers were provided with a room or large hut where they could take a rest; the problem was that these beneficiaries of the iron rice bowl were often remarkably reluctant to emerge from this refuge, particularly if the weather was less than ideal. Nowadays, on the other hand, Shanghai cab drivers often work 16-hour days to make enough money to pay off the rent of the cab and earn a salary that is slightly above average. The taxi-driving community is not, of course, immune to occasional lapses in ethical standards, but the overall service provided – at all hours of day or night – is now exceptionally good.

Taxis have therefore become a convenient mode of transport – and it is the word 'convenience' that sums up so much of what is better, particularly for us *laowai* (foreigners), about living in China in the twenty-first century. Supermarkets sell products instantly recognisable to the average expatriate – and in many cases identical to those found at home, wherever that may be. Medical centres have opened, staffed with expatriate doctors, that are open seven days a week – and therefore provide a

The life of a *laowai* insurance broker

better service than most of us will have experienced in our own countries.

There are also now enough expatriates in the larger cities to encourage numerous foreign organisations to provide services to foreigners. The most obvious of these – and arguably the most important for many expatriates – are the international schools that have sprung up. There is now a very good choice of schools in cities such as Shanghai and Beijing, with new establishments opening up frequently and existing ones expanding to keep pace with the influx of foreigners. (Interestingly, though, foreign-run schools are one of the few exceptions to the principle that foreigners and Chinese are treated equally in today's China: Chinese nationals are not allowed to attend foreign schools, unless at least one parent is non-Chinese.)

> *In the big cities, where the majoity of foreigners are employed, the level of service that is available to the inhabitants, both Chinese and expatriates, is infinitely better today than it was thirty years ago*

Another example would be the procedures for hiring a local employee. Nowadays, all normal channels that one would find in the West are available: headhunters, job adverts in papers or magazines, job agencies, online recruitment, campus recruitment drives, etc. In the early 1980s there was just FESCO (the Foreign Enterprise Service Co. Ltd.), which had a complete monopoly on the hiring of Chinese staff to foreign organisations. The salaries were high by Chinese standards and the strong suspicion was that the primary quality looked for by FESCO in its employees was their political reliability, and that a significant part of the employee's role was to keep an eye on the foreigner. Nonetheless, many of the employees

A street market in Shanghai in the early 1980s. Since then, life for many Chinese has been transformed

were of excellent quality, made a great difference to the representative's life and, in some cases, went on to become senior members of their industry.

The ability to travel around China and to take in both the huge changes and also the unchanging facets of Chinese life has also improved immeasurably in the past 30 years. Nowadays there are very few restrictions on where foreign travellers can go, whereas in the 1980s for a foreigner to travel outside one's city of residence required administrative assistance from one's Chinese 'host organisation' and was limited to a number of 'open' cities. There were also restrictions on the hotels that one could stay in – of course only the better ones.

More bizarrely, from today's viewpoint, there was a different price for travel: a foreigner would pay two to three times the price of the Chinese seat (whether on a plane or a train) or for a hotel room, while if you fell into the Overseas Chinese category, the cost was somewhere in between. The advantage to the foreigner was that a seat or room could generally be found for him even at very short notice – not always the case today when, thankfully, all are treated equally.

> *A foreigner would pay two to three times the price of the Chinese seat or for a hotel room. The advantage was that a seat or room could generally be found even at very short notice*

Of course, the 'foreign guest' also paid for such services in Foreign Currency Certificates (FEC) – a parallel currency to the normal renminbi – which would be bought with foreign exchange and was the only currency that foreigners were supposed to use (and which the local Chinese were definitely not supposed to have access to). This system lasted for 15 years from 1980 to 1995. Yes, there was a time when the Chinese coffers were far from being embarrassingly awash with foreign exchange.

FEC was also the only currency acceptable in the 'Friendship Stores', purveyors of food and other necessities to the *laowai*, thus making these establishments effectively off-limits to the average Chinese. There were also other 'friendship' organisations catering to foreigners, and you may still come across remnants of these today: Friendship Hotels, Friendship Stores, the Friendship Service Organisation (FESCO – mentioned above – for providing appropriately vetted local staff to foreigners), and so on. Most of these have now fortunately transmuted into more normal organisations openly motivated by commercial rather than by political factors.

Is all this change really all for the better? There is an undoubted downside to the frenetic pace of modernisation in China. The pollution is the most frequently cited – and it is bad, but is also something that the authorities are actively and, in many cases, sincerely trying to address. Traffic congestion is another. More harrowing is the vast gap, already referred to, that has emerged between the haves and have-nots in China: desperate, elderly beggars outside the lavish elegance of five-star hotels remind you that, more so than in the 'old days', it is possible for people to fall into complete poverty with little hope of intervention from government authorities.

As in Eastern Europe, there are therefore not a few people who hanker back to the old days when, although people were less prosperous, there was at least a regulated equality

The life of a *laowai* insurance broker

Foreigners are no longer considered particularly special and can interact as equals with colleagues

to life. The old China hand may also from time to time, glass of imported French Cabernet Sauvignon in hand, become misty-eyed about the whimsical ways of the old China. The way, for example, that hotels or restaurants were run more for the benefit of the staff than for the guests; the complete indifference of shop assistants to completing (or often even initiating) a sale – although they were fantastic with the abacus; the usual horror stories of air travel; and the things that really were special, such as the network of *hutong* in Beijing, that are now mostly gone.

But if we're honest with ourselves, life here is now much more normal and much, much better for most of us, whether Chinese or foreign. Most important of all, we foreigners are ourselves no longer considered particularly special (whether especially good or bad) and can interact as equals in social or business circles with Chinese friends and colleagues. This is mainly, I believe, because the Chinese have – in one of their own phrases – 'stood up': they are no longer in awe of other countries or peoples, because they have been able to realise, in less than two decades, by their own efforts and on their own terms, the dream of making China once again one of the most important nations on Earth.

What better time to live here and witness – and participate in – this historic turning point? And if you want to catch glimpses of the previous, more socialist or traditional aspects of China, look closely at life going on around you, particularly if you go inland to the smaller cities: it's still there – the most recent piece of the great historical backdrop that will continue to make China such a fascinating place to live.

Pollution is the most frequently cited problem – and it is bad, but it is also something that the authorities are actively, and sincerely, trying to address

Chris Ruffle
Co-chairman, MC China Ltd.
Came to China: 1978

Chris Ruffle has built up the China business of investment management company Martin Currie since joining the firm in 1994. He has played a pioneering role in opening up the Chinese A-share market to foreign investors; his team is responsible for managing specialist China funds worth over US$5bn and is the largest foreign investor in the domestic stock market.

If you would like to learn more about the investment funds he manages, please see www.martincurrie.com or www.chinafundinc.com
Tel: +86 216 101 7800
E-mail: chris_r@heartland.com.cn

If you would like to see the Scottish castle, transplanted to the middle of Shandong province, please visit:
Treaty Port Vineyards Ltd.
Mulangou, Daxindian,
Penglai, Shandong 265612
E-mail: 0535 5719388
www.treatyport.com

On the road

A varied career has taken Chris Ruffle to far-flung corners of China and has involved memorable experiences ranging from factory visits in remote provinces to camel racing in Urumqi. Based in Shanghai, he is now also putting down roots with a personal project in rural Shandong

My involvement with China was not the result of any far-sighted plan, but merely of youthful rebellion. When asked what I wanted to study at university I picked the strangest subject I could think of: Chinese with Philosophy. And so I ended up studying Chinese at Oxford, one of only four students in my year in the whole university, in the late 1970s. Here the subject was taught with enthusiasm (to any of my teachers who happen to read this, my thanks). It was not a terribly practical course, but it is possible that knowledge of Neo-Confucianism and of the guerilla struggle in China between 1937 and 1945 has served me better in my subsequent career than more practical courses on Chinese business or society.

My link with China has survived from 1977, when I opened my first Chinese-language textbook, written in the Gang of Four era, to the present day, despite temporary excursions into soap-selling in Newcastle-upon-Tyne and the Japanese stock market bubble – slightly over 30 years in all. It has included time living in Beijing (1983), Shanghai (1984 and 2002 to the present), Taipei (1978–79, 1990–93 and 2000–02) and Hong Kong (1993–94), with many visits in between. It has taken me to all the provinces in China, with the sole exceptions of Hainan and Ningxia. It has involved metal trading, the sale of scientific equipment, stock research and investment. You will be pleased to learn that I do not intend to take you through the ins and outs of this chequered career, even if I could remember it all. I'll just share with you some of the changes I have witnessed during what must be the biggest transformation of a society in peacetime in history. And tell one or two stories.

Communications challenges

For a foreigner living in China, the biggest change has probably been in communications. Living in Beijing in 1983 was to feel isolated. Long-distance phone calls were still an event, both expensive and a strain on the vocal cords. Daily communication with the office was via telex; I would laboriously punch out a tape with details of the latest metal bids and offers on a 'Goldfish'-brand telex machine. A weekly letter was the main link with home. The internet has since shrunk the world for everyone, but that is particularly true for the expatriate in China. At this point I would like to thank Mr. Bezos, whose Amazon.com has replaced the stacks of books and tapes I used to drag back on each return journey to China.

Of course, even in the 1980s we were better placed than those intrepid businessmen and missionaries arriving on the China shore in the nineteenth century; in the event of a serious problem, the outside world was just a flight away. But flying in China in the era of Antonovs, Ilyushins and very old Tridents was an adventure in itself. On one flight my seat was a deckchair set up in the aisle (you held onto the

Chris Ruffle

Sightseeing during my first spell in Taiwan, at the Taroko Gorge in 1979

neighbouring seats for take-off and landing). As only one-way tickets were available at that time, the first task on arriving anywhere was to buy your ticket out. This was still the time of financial apartheid, when foreigners were obliged to buy their tickets with foreign exchange certificates (FECs) at double the price paid by locals. I remember also one memorable flight on British Airways to Hong Kong, sitting in the cockpit during the exciting dog-leg approach to landing at the old Kai Tak airport. As you now almost have to undress just to get through airport security, it is nice to think back to those more trusting days.

Travel by road has also seen enormous changes. In the 1980s it was to be avoided whenever possible, on account of the rudimentary roads between cities and terrifying driving practices (headlights being left off at night to avoid dazzling oncoming drivers, for example). The conveyances available, unless you were with a party official in his 'Red Flag' limousine, were also unappealing, usually an old Soviet-designed 'Shanghai' taxi, painted light-blue. Now the taxis are mostly VW Santanas, but they still have a tendency to melt in the rain. Planes or trains, whatever their inconveniences, were much to be preferred. Today an excellent network of highways covers the country, which makes road travel faster, if not necessarily safer.

Perhaps my most dangerous driving experience was on a visit to Inner Mongolia, driving south from Baotou to visit the cashmere company Erdos. The winding one-and-a-half-lane road through the desert might have been scenic, were it not for the massive coal lorries heading in the opposite direction to the railhead. I had visions of my VW Santana, weaving between the oncoming goliaths under the spirited direction of my Mongolian driver, being crushed like an insect on a windscreen. The previous day we had driven from Hohhot to Baotou. Only one side of the motorway had been completed,

> *I had visions of my VW Santana, weaving between the oncoming goliaths under the spirited direction of my Mongolian taxi-driver, being crushed like an insect on a windscreen*

On the road

so you could drive very quickly from Hohhot to Baotou, but only very slowly from Baotou to Hohhot. Driving at 90mph through the Gobi Desert on a one-sided highway listening to *Careless Whispers* (my Mongolian driver had a predilection for George Michael) was one of my more surreal China experiences. Fortunately my insurance company did not know the nature of my day-to-day work in China, or my premiums would surely have increased.

Only rail travel, with its hard class and soft class, and its lace doilies and thermos flasks for tea, has remained relatively unaltered, the result of under-investment. This, however, is also starting to change as the government starts to realise that China cannot follow the development blueprint of the US – there is just not the land to park the cars. So we are now seeing a lot of money going into developing metro systems in major cities and high-speed trains between them.

The necessities of life

In Beijing in winter in the 1980s, the normal answer from a waitress regarding what vegetables were available was *bai cai, you cai*, which basically translates as 'cabbage or cabbage'. Great pyramids of cabbages were piled on frozen pavements, to be consumed before the winter ended. Oranges, wizened and bruised, were distinctly exotic. To eat decent fruit and vegetables I happily volunteered for trips to Sichuan. On my quarterly furloughs to Hong Kong, I would immediately search out those necessities of life: chocolate, wine and a decent curry. There was admittedly one Beijing hotel, the Tianqiao Guesthouse, that served a curry dish, taught to its chefs, so the story went, by desperate crew members from Pakistan Airlines. Otherwise there was the Moscow Restaurant, near the zoo, which was probably the only place in the world where you could sit and eat borsch and Chinese caviar whilst watching elephants. If you really wanted to push the boat out, there was a steak at the newly opened and, for an office boy, wildly expensive Jianguo Hotel.

The Moscow Restaurant, near the zoo in Beijing, was probably the only place in the world where you could sit and eat borsch and Chinese caviar whilst watching elephants

Now of course all manner of exotic products and cuisines are available, at least in the largest cities, if you have the RMB to pay for them. The chocolate tasting of soap and the wine with a bouquet of diesel fuel can still be found, of course, but they are no longer the only alternatives. When I took a New York friend, and martini lover, to a bar in Shanghai recently, she started to explain to the bartender how to make her favourite beverage. She was stopped by a look of withering scorn that said: 'Please. This is Shanghai'.

I cannot remember there being much entertainment in China in the 1980s, beyond the self-generated variety. There was the odd excruciating Chinese opera, or local film in a cinema carpeted with sunflower seeds. I remember once a little boy standing up in the middle of a film and happily relieving himself in the aisle, forming a stream that looped down towards the more expensive seats. All in all, it was a good time for filling gaps in one's knowledge of the Russian classics.

Chris Ruffle

That venerable Shanghai institution, the Peace Hotel jazz band, must be mentioned. Apart from a few pre-Liberation billiard tables and the bowling alley in the Jinjiang Club (the old Cercle Sportif Français), this was about the only entertainment available in the city. The band was ancient and never any good. Their repertoire was so repetitive that you could tell where you were in the evening without referring to your watch (if it's *The Girl from Ipanema* it must be 9pm) The bar menu offered a series of cocktails made from Maotai, which has to be one of the nastiest drinks I have ever come across during my drinking career. Still, it was a place to let off steam and relieve the frustrations of living in China. Alongside language students from Leeds University at a corner table, there would be various expatriates back from working in the wilds. One moment that sticks in the memory is of a Japanese businessman performing a *paso doble*, plastic flower gripped between his teeth, suit jacket trailed cape-like in the dust.

Choice of entertainment

I have written so far about the Chinese mainland, but the Taiwan I visited in the 1970s, still under martial law, shared many of the prejudices of the Communists. Both had it in for dancing. I recall dance parties in private houses in Taiwan where the music was barely audible, kept low so that we would not be reported to the authorities by quisling neighbours. Similarly, in Beijing in the 1980s, trying to smuggle local friends into one of the few discos allowed in the international hotels was a sport in itself. Under both regimes, museums served a didactic purpose. Once, during an English lesson I was giving in Taipei, I mentioned a visit to Taiwan's military museum. I joked that the KMT army was one of the only forces I knew which always seemed to win a glorious victory and then retreat afterwards. My pupil, unsmiling, produced a KMT membership card from her pocket. On the card, under 'place of birth', it stated Jinan, though she had never been near the mainland.

The choice of entertainment has gradually improved. First classical music then, especially in Shanghai, jazz. The occasional daring Western pop star or group now ventures to China. But generally, the media still struggle under the suffocating weight of state censorship. I think I have seen more good Chinese films on visits to the Edinburgh Festival than I have in China. The number of foreign films imported each year for showing in cinemas is still restricted, and morally dubious scenes are removed.

However, this effort is completely undermined by the thriving pirate DVD business, which means that the Chinese can see almost any film, often before they are available in local markets, at a price

My membership card for the Mandarin Center in Taipei

On the road

Getting to grips with the language: attending a calligraphy class in Taipei in 1980

far more reasonable than the expensive cinemas. I find you must wait a few weeks after a film's release for the quality of pirate DVDs to stabilise, otherwise you can end up buying hand-held versions. An occasional problem is language – Batman in Russian with Chinese subtitles, for example – but often the only problem is the subtitle which now and then scrolls across the screen saying, 'For the exclusive use of the judging committee for the XXX prize'.

Attitudes to foreigners

It is seldom now that I hear the whisper 'foreigner' as I pass in the street. Usually it is from a young child, or when I am travelling in a more remote part of China. And the words used are the neutral *waiguoren*, *waibin* or *laowai*, rather than *yangguizi* ('foreign devil'). In some parts of Shanghai there now seem to be more foreigners in the street than Chinese (try the area around Dulwich School in Pudong), but to be a foreigner in China in the 1980s was to feel like an alien. I remember there were just 32 permanent British residents in Shanghai in 1983. During my time at the distinctly unfriendly Friendship Hotel in Beijing, or the Ruijin Guesthouse in Shanghai, the times of my comings and goings would be noted. All Chinese visitors had to register and the fact of their visit to a foreigner was reported to their work unit. It was just too dangerous for the average Chinese to strike up a friendship with a foreigner, unless it was by way of work,

> *To be a foreigner in China in 1983 was to feel like an alien. At the time there were just 32 permanent British residents in Shanghai*

or the Chinese was from a powerful background, or already in so much trouble that it didn't matter. I am grateful to those who did make the effort.

All this made relations with the opposite sex particularly complicated. Assignations were made to meet under the bridge in the park at a certain time. Motivations were open to question; somewhere in my piles of correspondence I will still have the letter with the immortal line 'I love you, and not just for your passport'! It also gave a new variety to brush-off lines; never before or since have I been dumped for being a 'counter-revolutionary element'. Together with the sexless blue denim clothes, and girls' severe haircuts and lack of make-up, it all made for an unpromising environment for a young man.

It was easier to meet people in Taiwan in that era, and I am pleased that I visited Taiwan when I was a student, and not the mainland – a far tougher assignment. By dint of much letter-writing, I secured a summer job with Jardine Matheson. This gave me a taste of what the colonial life must have been like. I lived in a 'mess' with a cook, cleaner and yard boy. The car in which we went to work flew a Scottish flag which caused the soldiers, who still guarded bridges and other strategic locations at that time, to slam to attention – very good for morale.

As part of Jardine's shipping and insurance business, I was included in various site visits, some more salubrious than others. I remember the visit to a tuna canning plant in high summer, with the ladies up to their waists in fish guts, trying to breathe as little as possible. Another time we visited a doubtful shipwreck (the insurance policy started at 12, the ship went down at one) and then retiring with the 'captain' to a portside bar, where I made good progress improving my Chinese with the bar-girls. My first visit to Taiwan was immediately in the wake of derecognition, when the US switched its diplomatic recognition to the People's Republic of China, so I had to be quick to assure taxi-drivers I was British, not American, to avoid invective. Tienmu, now a smart and expensive suburb, then had an abandoned feel, full of empty bars that had previously catered to US servicemen.

> *You had to avoid your companions toasting you individually, or you would be drinking on an 8:1 ratio, which could have only one outcome*

Doing business

It is difficult to believe that there was no such thing as a private company when I first worked in China. Trade with the outside world was done only through a limited number of government import/export bureaux. The end suppliers or customers were kept at a distance, and were often unknown. Sophisticated equipment just disappeared into the country's interior; occasionally our engineers were sent to install equipment but would not be told the location. To buy equipment from abroad at that time, companies needed an allocation of foreign exchange certificates. As obtaining these was a tedious, bureaucratic process, companies tended to apply for an amount sufficient to cover the most sophisticated type of equipment available. We tended, therefore, only to sell top-of-the-line equipment, even though there were models that would have been more cost-effective. After all, it was only state

On the road

On one unexpected occasion, in 1979, I found myself posing for a photograph with TS Lin, founder of Tatung, one of Taiwan's largest conglomerates

money. Several months later, visiting the installed equipment, we would find it unused, covered with a dusty silk cloth, like a holy relic.

Much of business at this time revolved around exhibitions, which were one of the only ways of meeting suppliers or customers and of promoting your goods. Attendance at such events was often huge; the trick was to distinguish legitimate clients from time-wasters and brochure collectors. It was tough work, as an interpreter, faced with a mob of attendees, leaning into the collective garlic breath, trying to sort the wheat from the chaff. The climax of each show was trying to sell off the equipment on the stand, so as not to have to ship it back – a pressure of which the Chinese buyers were well aware. Corruption seemed less widespread than now (though perhaps I was too naïve or too junior to spot it) and seemed to revolve around organising foreign 'jollies' or (let's be more decorous) fact-finding missions.

Then, as now, banquets played an important part in doing business in China. However, given the limitations on social contact outside such formal occasions, they played a more important role then. Certainly the drinking was more intense, centred on rounds of *ganbei* with Maotai liquor. I developed a range of survival strategies, the most important of which was never to allow your Chinese companions to toast you individually: you had to involve the whole table, otherwise you were drinking on an 8:1 ratio, which could have only one outcome.

The food was also more consistently strange, as official banquets offered the Chinese participants a rare chance to eat sea slugs, calf tendons, camel paw, giant salamander stew and the like. A polite show of enthusiasm for any such foodstuffs would only be rewarded with a second helping, so I perfected the art of pretending to eat, pushing the sea slug around my plate, without actually consuming any. The perils of over-enthusiasm were illustrated once by my boss during a spell in Hong Kong, out to dinner with an important potential client. He was a large and hungry man, who happily shovelled a large spoonful of what appeared to be blancmange into his mouth. Unfortunately it was *chou toufu* (stinky beancurd). He immediately knew he was in trouble. Spitting it out wasn't an option. His face turned a lime green before he manfully managed to swallow it down. And still we did not win the mandate.

There is a strong macho element in Chinese business drinking. I recall one lunch banquet in remote Qinghai, when I was trying to sell carbon electrodes, with an Italian representative of the supplier. The level of alcohol consumption reached that point where songs become necessary; the factory manager gave us a snatch from a Beijing opera, the Italian sang *O Sole Mio* and I contributed *On Ilkley Moor Ba' t'hat*. For his encore the factory manager stood, but planted his hand in a bowl of soup and had to be helped away from the table. After a short rest, still the worse for wear, we re-assembled, as negotiations were scheduled to restart at 2.30pm. A junior from the company came to tell us that the factory manager had, unfortunately, been called away on urgent business. We had scored an important moral victory, after which the factory had little choice but to buy our electrodes.

Sampling glazed apples, somewhere in the Beijing area, in the winter of 1983

One thing that has changed over time is the sense of time itself. Dealings in the 1980s were often characterised by a lack of urgency, which derived from a 'five-year plan' way of thinking, most famously characterised by the answer given by Zhou Enlai as to what he thought about the effects of the French Revolution ('It is too early to tell,' he reportedly told Henry Kissinger). Although there was officially little unemployment, there was huge under-employment, as large numbers of employees in state-owned enterprises seemed to do little more than smoke, drink tea and read the newspapers. Ambition was not thought of as a virtue and standing out from

On the road

the crowd was seen as positively dangerous. People might be poor, but there was an equality in their poverty, and fewer day-to-day pressures.

In more recent years all this changed. China developed a vigorous brand of Western-style capitalism, and the desire for short-term gains flourished. The social safety net fell away, and the 'iron rice bowl' was broken. The only health care available was what could be paid for upfront. There are signs that this has been recognised in the 'Harmonious Society' policies of Hu Jintao (a term which harks back to the teachings of Confucius, which are enjoying a revival). But the results of these remain to be seen.

Investing in the A-share market

From the 1990s I was a first-hand witness to this capitalist transformation as I built up a business investing in newly developing Chinese capital markets, particularly the A-share market, in which foreign investors still remain a rarity. My work involves visiting factories, shops and building sites all around China. Below I list some my stranger experiences whilst so doing. The origins of my interest in A-shares lie in the years 1993 to 1995, when the first wave of Chinese listings available to foreign investors (H-shares and B-shares) was found to consist almost exclusively of weakly managed state-owned enterprises. Looking for more entrepreneurial, management-owned companies, we found a number that were listed in the domestic market (it required political backing to get an overseas listing which, at that time, private-sector companies did not have). Thus started a programme of company visiting, which continues to this day. Visiting A-share companies, as you will see, is not for the faint-hearted; sometimes it has rather resembled an Indiana Jones adventure.

The first A-share visit: My first ever A-share company visit was in early 1996, to the TV manufacturer Changhong. The company is based in Mianyang in Sichuan province and used to make missiles (a large part of China's armaments industry was based in Sichuan, on the grounds that it was the most distant place from the then-enemy Soviet Union). The generals had by now beaten their swords into ploughshares, but were still deeply sceptical of this white man come to ask difficult questions. As I came through the office doors, they looked behind me to see where my Chinese colleague was, only to realise with horror that I was alone and that they would need to deal with me directly. Answers were as scarce as hen's teeth.

The worst visit: Shenzhen Development Bank holds this dubious honour. The visit was in the early days, before a US private equity firm took a stake in the enterprise. Even my questions on loan growth and deposit growth were refused, on the basis that this would be disclosing secret information. We never got as far as anything as potentially controversial as non-performing loans (or 'special mention' loans as they are now euphemistically known). On exiting the meeting, I found that all I had written down was the office address.

The silliest visit: I have two candidates. Both date from the early days of my A-share visits, when I used to visit all the listed companies in a given town. I no longer do that – it's a waste of time – but pre-screen more carefully. In the Sichuan city of Leshan there was a company called Emei Chemical, which operated salt mines. About five

Chris Ruffle

minutes into the discussion I had calculated that the company's total sales per employee per annum were just US$250. It had a nice factory canteen, however; I can still recall the fish stomachs with cauliflower dish they served for lunch. One time in Inner Mongolia, for the first meeting after lunch, I surprised the spokesman for Mengdian asleep, stretched out on top of his desk. I let him snooze on for a while before coughing discreetly.

My most exotic visit: This must be my visit to Lhasa Brewery. For a man from Yorkshire, the beer it produced was pretty weak stuff. Still, just being at 3,500 metres above sea level had the same effect as having drunk several pints of Black Sheep bitter. The management was also rather surly (there had previously been little call upon its PR skills). Still, the landscape was fantastic. My visit to the transformer maker Xinjiang Tebian ranks a close second. This factory is located in Changji, a two-hour drive from Urumqi, itself a five-hour flight from Shanghai. I timed my arrival to coincide with what I expected to be the start of office hours. Unfortunately Xinjiang, which is north of Pakistan, is on the same time zone as Bejing. Because of this, no-one turns up for work until after 10am and then works until 7pm. Dinner starts at 9pm. I consequently spent some time kicking my rather dusty heels in Changji.

The most beautiful visit: There are some spectacular sights in China. Some are justly world-famous: the Great Wall north of Beijing, the terracotta warriors of Xian, the sugar-loaf mountains of Guilin. But others I discovered by accident during the course of my visits. The listed companies of the old capital of Luoyang in Henan, a sad collection of unreconstructed state-owned enterprises, had not detained me long. So with time to spare I headed to a nearby valley of stone carvings, Longmen Shiku, which was

A view over Beihai Park, northwest of the Forbidden City in Beijing, and its surroundings, 1983

On the road

recommended by the taxi-driver. The park was empty and the sun was going down, highlighting the medieval Buddhist carvings. Spectacular. I can also recommend the old town of Pingyao, in Shanxi, one of the few towns to retain its Ming dynasty walls. As an excuse for a visit here, you can claim to be visiting nearby Taiyuan Stainless Steel….

A moment of celebration: opening a bottle of champagne at sunrise on the Great Wall, 1983

The most depressing visit: There is a depressing sameness to many Chinese towns: the same concrete structures, faced with toilet tiles; the same smell of boiled cabbage, grit and coal smoke. If I were suddenly to be deposited in one of a hundred Chinese cities, I would have difficulty saying where I was. The conditions in some of the factories I visit are hellish – one alloy casting company visited at the height of summer comes to mind. Even conditions in some of the offices might surprise readers; I have held a number of winter meetings in unheated offices in coat, scarf, gloves and hat. It makes one appreciate what a cushy number being a fund manager really is.

The tastiest visit: In the early days, my stomach clenched at an invitation to eat in a factory canteen. In recent years, with improvements in food refrigeration and transportation, the quality of food has improved immeasurably. A case in point was a visit to the sausage maker Shuanghui. When I mentioned that the smart new highway running past the factory door must be an aid to distribution the spokesman agreed, saying that he could now get his products to market in Beijing overnight. It made me think of sausages I had eaten in Beijing before the highway was constructed…. Strangely, the most depressing cities often have the best food (a form of consolation?). I am thinking here of lamb dishes in Lanzhou (an unlovely refinery town in Gansu province with a large Muslim community), the noodles in the coal town of Taiyuan and the spicy hotpots of muggy Chongqing. Perhaps my all-time favourite, however, is a visit to the listed Yuyuan's Nanxiang restaurant in Shanghai, which, in your author's humble opinion, makes the world's best dumplings.

Strangely, the most depressing cities often have the best food. I am thinking of lamb dishes in Lanzhou, the noodles in the coal town of Taiyuan and the spicy hotpots of muggy Chongqing

The most honest visit: This was definitely my meeting with Tsann Kuen, a Taiwan-owned appliance maker with a B-share listing. Having visited its busy Xiamen plant, I said

Chris Ruffle

A 1983 view of the Bund from the Pudong ferry, before the Shanghai skyline was transformed

that business appeared to being going well. The spokesman agreed and, when I followed up to ask why, therefore, profits seemed to have dipped by 20 per cent, he said that that was easy to explain. The parent company was planning to list in Taiwan, so the B-share listed subsidiary was busy transferring profits to the parent, paying more for R&D and various components! I have not included a section for the least honest visits, as it would be rather a long one. Many have been the visits when an upbeat assessment by the firm's management was not supported by my tour around the decrepit, over-manned plant, if indeed I was not prevented from seeing the plant at all by some thin excuse.

My prize for the most changed city goes to Urumqi, capital of Xinjiang. The dusty, remote town where I organised a camel race in 1983 is now a booming metropolis, fuelled by oil and gas

The most visited companies: These are in Shanghai, because foreign investors visiting China often don't venture inland. There are strangely not, as yet, a lot of good companies based in Shanghai, which was the base of the Gang of Four during the Cultural Revolution. Beijing also used to be similarly devoid of entrepreneurial companies, but that has changed in the past few years with an increase in local IT, telecoms and healthcare-related industries. Over the past ten years, our most popular sources of investment have been the provinces of Zhejiang (which has the highest proportion of private companies), Guangdong, Fujian and Shandong. We have sourced fewer investments from provinces where state-owned industries are dominant, such as Sichuan, Shaanxi and the northeast.

On the road

My worst buy: By dint of hard travelling and no small amount of luck, we have had a surprisingly small number of disasters in the A-share market. Of course, fund managers suffer from a kind of selective amnesia when asked about their failures, and I am no exception in this regard. The worst investment I recall is buying Shenzhen Airport a few weeks before the CFO was found to have put his hand in the till.

My best buy: This was Supor, a family-owned maker of kitchenware based near Wenzhou, which was eventually bought by French rival SFB. Supor was one of the companies that presented at our third A-share conference, held in co-operation with UBS in Shaoxing in June 2005. This conference absolutely caught the bottom of the market; the few hardy investors who attended would have made back more than five times their money in the next two years by investing in a portfolio of the companies presenting there.

The changing face of China

The effect of this economic transformation has changed the look of China. Above my desk I have taped a photograph that I took from a ferry on the Huangpu, when the 1930s towers were the skyline and the only reason for taking a ferry to Pudong was to enjoy the view of the Bund. The first new skyscraper in Shanghai, now dwarfed by its successors, was the unremarkable Union Building, which opened during my first stint in the city. This dull building stands in sad contrast to the more interesting work of pre-war architects. There is, of course, interesting architectural work in China (the Jinmao Tower is a favourite) but many of the prestige towers are just square blocks with silly tops to them.

The vineyard covers 21 hectares and is set to produce its first vintage in time for the Beijing Olympics

My Thirty Years in China | 143

Chris Ruffle

Beijing seems to have suffered more from development than Shanghai. The sense of the Qing dynasty city of long, low grey walls, sloping green roofs and hidden *hutong* is difficult to discern as ring roads spread like ripples across the dusty plain. The Friendship Hotel, once situated in a far corner of Beijing, within a short bike ride of countryside, is now almost downtown. The Beijing Exhibition Hall Hotel, where my first office was located, is long gone. On the city's roads, the bicycles of Western imagination first gave way to motorbikes and now to a gridlock of cars.

In Shanghai the nasty concrete building where I set up an office unfortunately remains, while the lovely Jinjiang Club, with its Olympic-sized swimming pool, has been subsumed into the Okura Hotel. In Taipei over the same period, the whole centre of the city has shifted east from the station and Changhua Road, with its stalls of delicious *midoubing*, to the Hsinyi area, where the rice paddies are now covered over by exclusive condominiums.

Even the countryside has not escaped. China Mobile's steel towers dot the countryside, multiplying, it seems, even faster than farmers with mobile phones. Where rubbish was once mostly organic, now supermarket plastic bags snag on trees and pile up in gullies. My prize for the most changed city goes to Urumqi, capital of Xinjiang. The dusty, remote town where I organised a camel race in 1983 for my board of directors (it was a slightly eccentric company) is now a booming metropolis, fuelled by oil and gas.

I can now own a part of China's built infrastructure myself (to be strictly accurate, I can own 70 years' use of the land for a residential building, and 50 years for industrial purposes). From the hotel apartment of 1983, I graduated to a rented apartment, my

Preparing the ground at the Treaty Port vineyard, 2007: the author (centre) with his wife Tiffany (far right), French wine-grower Gerard Colin and village heads Huang and Ruan

On the road

own apartment overlooking the river, and now my own house. After the challenge of outfitting this house (apartments in China are delivered as grey cement shells), I am now ready for my next challenge: a Scottish castle in Shandong.

Since 2004 my hobby, building a vineyard near Penglai, has brought home to me the continued power of the Party and the importance of connections in Chinese society. If you can win (and keep) the support of senior Party officials, things happen: roads get built, wells dug, trees planted. If you do not have support, you will struggle and be ripped off (or get ripped off even more; my wife calls our venture, Treaty Port Vineyards, my rural charity). The flexibility of regulations in the face of Party intervention allows thing to get done quickly.

I was excited the other day when I was approached by one of my farmers, who told me that the village elections were approaching and that he wished to be elected village head. I asked him why he wanted such a thing, given that the election was surely fixed by the Party. He disagreed, telling me that the villagers really had the right to choose whichever leader they want. When I expressed excitement and enthusiasm, dazzled by visions of thriving grassroots democracy, the farmer said, 'Well, if that's OK, could you please just lend me the money so I can buy the votes?'.

Finalising designs for the Scottish chateau

> ***Thanks to my wife Tiffany***, *without whom much of my work in China would have gone even less smoothly – even though, as a Taiwanese, how things work (especially in the Shandong countryside) is almost as foreign to her as it is to me.*
> ***Thanks to my parents***, *who have supported my often eccentric projects, learning a lot about two countries with which they have no connection, China and Scotland.*
> ***Thanks to my friends and colleagues***, *who have helped and have often covered for my lack of knowledge.*
> *And finally,* ***thanks to the Bradford Chamber of Commerce***. *This august body offers a scholarship to help local students improve their knowledge of foreign languages, so as to boost British trade. As a young man, faced with a panel of Bradfordian businessmen, I was told, 'At this point in the interview we normally bring in someone to test your oral standard. But as we were unable to find anyone who speaks Chinese, perhaps you'd just like to say something.' After I'd burbled on for a few sentences, the chairman said, 'Well, that seems all right to me', and gave me the scholarship. Gentlemen, I hope you consider your money well spent.*

Ian J. Stones
Business consultant

Lived in China since: 1978

Ian J. Stones came to China as an exchange student in 1978. From 1979 onwards he played a pioneering role in a number of different industries, including the oil and gas, aviation, automotive, financial and pharmaceutical sectors.

During his time in China, he has held senior corporate positions with Amtech, BP (Guangzhou), Citicorp American Technology Inc. (Beijing), Citibank, Pfizer (Dalian) and GM Asia Inc. (Hong Kong and Beijing). Since 1998 he has been a director and senior advisor for several firms, consulting on M&As, restructuring and crisis management, and currently sits on the boards of a number of Chinese and global companies.

His academic background includes training in biochemistry and Modern Chinese. His wide range of interests includes evolution and genetics, cognitive sciences, psychology, culture and institutional economics, marine biology, war games, history, antiques, archery and scuba diving.

Unexpected opportunities

Ian Stones was initially drawn to China via an interest in the martial arts, before travelling to Beijing in 1978 as a language exchange student. From there he embarked on a trailblazing business career, one that over three decades has given him a range of experiences and brought him into contact with people he could never have anticipated

It seems just like yesterday when, on a hot summer day in August 1978, I walked across the bridge into sleepy Shenzhen with a group of other British students. Each person in our group had different visions, different expectations and very different motives for being there. For me, the overriding thing I wanted, more than anything else, was to know the language of the mainland. The second thing driving me was a strong curiosity to see first-hand what the giant enigma behind the 'bamboo curtain' was really like.

China was the subject of so much debate back in England and subject to extreme interpretations and opposing points of view. No one knew that 1978 was to be the major turning point of reform that would lead to non-stop changes, setting China on its path to regaining its place as the largest economy in the world. I could never have dreamed that I'd still be here 30 years later and that I would have experienced first-hand every wave of economic and social change and reform since that pivotal year.

Above all, I could never have imagined the many people who would touch my life and who would become friends. As a young man who had grown up in Manchester, I couldn't possibly have dreamed that I would meet many historic figures and world-famous characters or that Chinese people from all walks of life would become some of my closest friends. Some of these people had lived through and witnessed turbulent times, or been actors in them, and they shared stories and living memories of events that spanned a century of historic events, stretching as far back as the end of the Qing dynasty.

> *No one knew that 1978 was to be the major turning point of reform, setting China on its path to regaining its place as the largest economy in the world*

I sometimes feel like I was a Forrest Gump figure, just by being here. I landed up in places and with people who you usually only see on TV or in history books, and at times I was in the middle of big events myself. Luck would put me in the right place at the right time, and sometimes in the wrong place at the wrong time. Through a few memories of my own experiences, I hope to give a flavour of how China has changed in the past three decades, and how many of its special people have touched me. If nothing else, I also hope to share a few laughs.

First contact with the language

It seems strange that a biochemist from Manchester, with no reason or opportunity to have any exposure to China, would become so passionate about the Chinese language. I'd become interested in Japan while on my university karate team, and the

Ian J. Stones

first three characters I could recognise were the kanji for 'karate', which literally means 'the Empty-Handed Way'. In friendly competitions or in cross-training with kung fu schools, our team would pick up a few Chinese words for techniques, often in dialects.

The fateful weekend that pushed me to dive into the Chinese language came when a close group of Malaysian and Singaporean friends asked me to fill an empty slot in a *mahjong* game, which – trustingly – I did. The so-and-sos used their language to cheat me, and even though I'd only lost 99 pence, I was so mad when I found out that I woke someone up to teach me all the *mahjong* vocabulary that night. I surprised myself by being able to memorise the names of all the pieces and tricks in one go, and most importantly the key responses to two phrases: 'What card do you need?' and 'What do you need to win?'. I had always considered myself hopeless at languages, but my new-found ability to learn a language so quickly convinces me that anyone can learn a language as long as they have the right stimulus and environment.

> *I asked them how to ask a Malaysian Chinese girl for a dance. The slap in the face she gave me had my 'friends' rolling about laughing. I can only guess what it was I really said to her*

These friends always made fun of us Brits and liked to joke behind our backs. They gave us Chinese names so we wouldn't know who they were talking about. I hated being left out of their jokes and so copied their phrases, and before long I could show off by holding simple conversations with them. One horribly embarrassing joke they played on me, which drove me to try never to lose face again, was at a dance, when I asked them how I should ask a Malaysian Chinese girl for a dance. The slap in the face she gave me had my 'friends' rolling about laughing. I can only guess what it was I really said to her.

Biochemist from Manchester, summer 1978

The last straw came when I and another friend trusted these guys and wore cool-looking T-shirts that they gave us with Chinese characters on them. We wore them proudly, but after being pointed at and laughed at all over Manchester's China Town, we found out that my friend's T-shirt said 'Red-Haired Devil Wanker' and mine said 'I Like Women with Big Tits'! After this I wanted to know exactly what each character meant.

While I was learning from these guys, often in the kitchen at our university hall or out having fun, I knew nothing about grammar, and used a spelling system to represent what I later found out were tones.

Unexpected opportunities

It was only after a couple of months that I found out I was learning the Hokkien (Fujianese) dialect. The famous Hong Kong waiter 'Mao Wong' (King of the Cats) in Charlie Chan's restaurant in Manchester – who spoke Cantonese – looked incredulous when I tried to order food in Hokkien and told me 'That's not Chinese!'. Until then I had thought that the Hokkien I was learning was standard Chinese and that everyone spoke it. Only then did I realise about dialects.

No one around me spoke Mandarin but several spoke Cantonese, so I tried to learn some Cantonese too. Even though several people suggested that it would be more useful to learn the 'standard language' (Putonghua), it didn't really seem useful to me. I joined my friends when they went out for their weekly kung fu movie fix at late-night showings of Hong Kong and Taiwanese movies, and began to hear the differences between Cantonese and Mandarin. I tried to memorise a few lines of the dialogue. Asian martial arts and exotic characters were at that time becoming cool and trendy, and I was one of many who were growing more interested. I was probably a shade more fanatical than most!

Preconceptions of 'Red China' in 1978

It is strange to hear CNN's Lou Dobbs still refer to 'Red China'. He's out of touch, but 30 years ago that's what people used to call it. In the UK in the 1970s, there seemed to be four very different Chinas, depending on who you talked to. The conventional wisdom was that it was an extreme leftist, Communist military state that was out of control and where people walked around in Mao suits waving the Little Red Book. Some people thought it was a workers' Utopia that was a better model for Western workers than the Soviet Union. Many older Chinese living in the UK seemed to be describing the mystical source of an ancient culture, values, manners and morals and thought that the revolution and the Communist period were a temporary anomaly. Many Asians seemed to believe that Taiwan represented the real China, and that one day the mainland would revert to being the true China again.

Like many peers who went through university in the 1970s I couldn't help but be influenced by the decade of strikes and labour activism. At Manchester, the student union focused on South African liberation and on supporting the British workers then involved in coal and power strikes. It was a period when we had power cuts and three-day weeks in the UK. Most students were polarised in intense debates and some joined groups studying the works of Popper, Marx, Trotsky, Mao, the feminists and other thinkers. To be able to debate issues better, it was popular to join study groups and attend lectures that debated politics and the works of economists and sociologists.

Sometimes we'd encounter extremist communist parties and anarchists, who would spend more time arguing with each other than focusing on the social issues we were originally there to discuss. The two main camps of Marxists hated each other. Some claimed to be the only true Marxists and dogmatically argued that the Soviet worker-led revolution was the only true way, while others claimed to be the only true Marxists and argued that the only true way was Mao's peasant-led revolution. Added to the mix were several exile groups from South East Asian countries and some extremist Islamic groups, which would guarantee fertile debates. Lectures by academics, experts of all sorts, politicians and exiles from Asia came from all over the political spectrum.

There have always been academic types who would analyse things but who would stand back and never take a position on anything. They were usually labelled as 'sitting on the fence', which is the safest refuge for second-hand experts who fear being proved wrong and who always say 'Let's wait and see!' rather than hazard a prediction. That approach is of no value to businessmen who need to make decisions today: there are too many opportunities to miss.

> *I used the time in the car to listen to Mandarin language tapes. I learned at least one new lesson every day, and would play those tapes over and over. I would try to practise in Chinese restaurants and enrolled in local karate or kung fu schools*

With all these different views, I couldn't know what China was really like, but I was growing more curious. Academics claimed to know all the answers, but I was amazed to learn that many of these experts and scholars had never been to China – or, if they were lucky, they might have been there on a ten-day trip. It showed how closed China was to the outside world.

After graduating, I worked in sales as a locum medical rep for MSD for two years, and while assigned to problem territories around the UK I'd often spend hours on the road and living in hotels. I used the time in the car to listen to Mandarin language tapes. I forced myself to learn at least one new lesson every day, and would play those tapes over and over. I would try to practise in Chinese restaurants and enrolled in local karate or kung fu schools, even if just for a couple of weeks. I moved to London and went to night school classes two nights a week. The teacher was a Chinese-educated exile from Malaysia who spent hours telling stories about words. I picked up a strong southern accent from him.

I wanted to attend the intensive nine-month course at Ealing College in west London, but could not afford it. However, without telling me, my father went to Manchester City Council and found out that they had lots of unused postgraduate grants available. He applied on my behalf and got the funding I needed.

One British teacher on the Ealing course had been to China in 1973. Her stories of her time in communes painted a very different picture from the lectures that the academics gave us. Twice a week we had classes in spoken Chinese given by Yan Hangtai, who had been an English-language broadcaster at Radio Beijing and was then working at the BBC World Service as a Chinese broadcaster. His stories were very different again. The language course at Ealing used a unique method based on 113 separate sentence patterns. This enabled students to master the grammar and took us from reading basic texts to newspapers and short stories within nine months. The course's shortcoming was that it focused on reading and translation, not on speaking.

Most analysis of China at that time was based on guesswork, sparse facts and maybe short visits. Supposedly the best sources of information were a priest in Hong

Unexpected opportunities

Kong and Taiwanese reports of Chinese radio broadcasts. The scarcity of information fed the mystery and the curiosity. China's perceived mystery, then and still now, has enabled many unqualified people to claim to be 'experts', but re-reading the works of some prominent scholars of the time only shows just how wrong they were and how little they really knew. In some ways, that phenomenon hasn't changed much.

Whenever we got a chance, we tried to mix with some of the small group of Chinese exchange students in London and would volunteer to interpret for visiting groups such as the Shenyang acrobatic troupe. My first impression of these visitors was how naive they appeared to be and, from my perspective, I thought they had simplistic views of the world. They were clean-living and frugal, and didn't go to pubs or to any of the student activities going on in London.

We had expected them to be as interested in current affairs and debates as we were, but they were actually discouraged from getting involved in anything remotely perceived as political or 'bourgeois'. They would happily talk about life in China, but never voiced opinions on politics. Their explanations of the Gang of Four were simplified, that they'd tried to take power and used the Red Flag to attack the Red Flag, but had been stopped. This was all a surprise, since my impressions of the Cultural Revolution had led me to expect Chinese to be very enthusiastic proponents of new ideas about Marxist and Maoist thought. I wrongly assumed that they would like debates. I knew next to nothing about their backgrounds and the lives they had led.

Hindsight is always 20/20. Today, we know the particular significance of 1978, as the beginning of Deng Xiaoping's visionary reforms. But at the time, most analysts expected China to follow a path similar to that of the previous 12 years – maybe a little less radical, but basically the same. After the deaths of Zhou Enlai and Mao Zedong in 1976, Hua Guofeng had become the new Party Chairman, and there were signs of a new personality cult developing around him. The propaganda machine was acting the only way it knew how. Many people assumed that Hua would become the new supreme leader and that we'd soon be hearing chants of 'Long live Chairman Hua!' and seeing Hua badges on lapels.

Most other leaders were Long March veterans, and many Western analysts still saw China as part of the big red Communist bloc, which included North Korea, Vietnam and, of course, the Soviet Union. China was associated with strong support for pariah states and regimes, including Albania and Pol Pot's Khmer Rouge in Cambodia. Although President Nixon had opened a dialogue early in 1972, the US had not yet established diplomatic relations. China was 80 per cent rural, had the world's largest standing army and was widely perceived as an Orwellian military state.

China's perceived mystery, then and still now, has enabled many unqualified people to claim to be 'experts', but re-reading the works of scholars of the time only shows just how wrong they were and how little they really knew

The Communist party of Malaya was believed to be backed by China, so the majority of Malaysians and Singaporeans were not allowed by their governments to go there, and risked arrest back home if they travelled to China. The works of Mao and Marx were banned in Malaysia and tightly restricted in Singapore. After the coup of Ferdinand Marcos in 1971, the Philippines clamped down on liberal dissent, and a group of Filipino students visiting China were unable to return home. Jaime Florcruz, now CNN's bureau chief in Beijing, was one of them; another, Eric, was to become one of my classmates.

The most 'optimistic' future predicted at the time was that a less extreme government might swing away from the Soviets and be more benign and less threatening to Hong Kong. China's minimal flow of foreign exchange was earned mainly through oil exports, with some from textiles and handicrafts. The country desperately needed foreign exchange to pay for oilfield equipment to help produce more oil. No one envisaged what was to happen in the next ten years, let alone what has happened in the subsequent twenty. I knew little, and believed that China would calm down and remain much the same as before. I thought it was a relaxed, rural-based economy that was building ten self-reliant heavy industries and which would remain closed off.

Exchange scholarship to Beijing

When I first applied to the British Council for an exchange scholarship, I didn't make the cut. Fifteen Chinese students were due to come to the UK and fifteen Brits would go to China; I felt I'd been rejected because of my Manchester accent and my background in science rather than the arts. All the students originally accepted had majored in Chinese at Oxford, Cambridge, Leeds or the School of Oriental and African Studies (SOAS) in London. At the interview, I'd felt intimidated as all the other candidates were carrying Chinese classics and reading novels that seemed far more advanced than anything I had ever read. Understandably, the interviews were in English. When the panel seemed to suspect my language ability, I nervously asked to be interviewed in Mandarin or Hokkien. They frowned. Of course they preferred English. In retrospect that says something – but I didn't feel good.

I'd only read one Chinese novel, *The Family* by Ba Jin. On paper, I'd only attended a nine-month course at Ealing, so I can't blame the selection committee: I hardly seemed to fit the profile of a China scholar. Later, however, the programme was expanded to 20 people, so I got to go. I was just 25 years old, and elated, and I was really determined to prove those fuddy-duddies wrong, since they'd made me feel bad and wouldn't dare interview me in Chinese. So far, my exposure to Western academics who knew China at second or third hand had been quite negative.

We got single-entry only visas, with no exit. This allowed us only to travel to Beijing: we would need to apply for an exit visa before we could leave again, which is inconceivable today. With no direct flights to Beijing, we needed to transit in Hong Kong and to walk across the border. For the two-day stopover in Hong Kong, I stayed with an old school friend to save the daily £25 hotel allowance. Instead, I spent the money on a short-wave radio and a couple of dictionaries. We were bussed to the Lowu border, which in those days was quiet but had strict security on both sides. Some tourists would travel to a few sites on the Hong Kong side, where they could peer

Unexpected opportunities

across the border and see PLA soldiers or peasants working in the fields, but that was as close as most people could get.

On the short walk across the narrow bridge out of Hong Kong were a number of Hakka ladies, offering to take our bags on bamboo poles. We walked into the Shenzhen immigration post, which was actually at the near end of the station. The crossing was quiet, and the station was almost empty. From the station waiting room, we could look out at the sleepy village of Shenzhen and see peasants working in the fields close by. After an hour, we took the train to Guangzhou, where we spent the best part of a day before being put on the train for Beijing.

The train was hotter than hell – around 42 degrees, dusty and sweaty. We shared four-person sleeper carriages. I was proud to find that I was one of only two people in the group who could speak practical, everyday Chinese. It seems that the others' courses had given them a great grounding in the classics, but they didn't know words like 'scrambled eggs', 'napkin', 'hot water flask' or 'towel'. Some would speak to the train staff using classical vocabulary rather than everyday language. Imagine Chinese visitors to England speaking Chaucerian prose to British Rail staff! From having been intimidated by all these Oxbridge types, I gained in confidence.

Beijing's dust and yellowish dirt was a big surprise: I'd expected a pristine and well-disciplined city. The single main street was wide, but others were a jumble. There were hardly any cars, but there were lots of bicycles and some horse carts. Junctions were chaotic, and thousands of bicycles would flow across them during the morning and evening rush hours.

Beijing had no high-rises except the new Beijing Hotel block, and was blanketed with sprawling *hutong* houses and alleyways. The city's many old buildings gave it a special character. There were many soldiers in uniform, while ordinary people seemed to wear only blue or green. Very few women wore skirts, and you could still see many old ladies around the Qian Men area who had bound feet. Most people worked six-day weeks and would finish work at 5.30 pm. At night the streets were quiet and dimly lit. In the summer, people would try to cool off by fanning themselves while sitting on small stools and chatting in groups till the evening air cooled down.

The Beijing Language Institute in 1978 was the first stop for all foreign students in Beijing, regardless of where they eventually wanted to study. Most were anxious to move on as soon as they could, and considered the institute a necessary evil before they transferred to a more glamorous place such as Beijing University or Fudan. Few stayed there to specialise in Chinese. In fact, however, this institute was the premium specialist university for teaching Chinese as a foreign language and for teaching foreign languages to Chinese. The course I landed in was actually designed for foreign teachers and interpreters of Chinese.

> *I was one of only two people who could speak practical, everyday Chinese. The others had a great grounding in classics, but did not know words like 'scrambled eggs', 'napkin', 'hot water flask' or 'towel'*

Ian J. Stones

The student mix was very different to that in the UK, with many Africans, Vietnamese, Laoatians, Palestinians, Albanians, Japanese and North Koreans. This was supplemented by a few exiles from the Philippines and a handful of Europeans, to make an interesting combination of cultures. At the time there were no American students, since relations with the US hadn't yet been normalised. We were assigned two people to a room and after a short time, if we wanted, we could share with a Chinese room-mate.

The school didn't care what qualifications we had earned back home. It would determine for itself what level we were, and put us through written, oral and interview tests to assign us to classes. In my entry essay I wrote how, as a biochemist, I'd been impressed that it was Chinese researchers who first discovered the structure of insulin in 1953 and that my thesis had been on the folding of penicillin. I was taken by surprise to be one of just two who were assigned straight into the fourth-year class, with classmates who had been studying there already for three years. All those tapes and the course in Ealing had really paid off but, honestly, I was way out of my depth and had a real struggle to keep up for the first couple of months.

Each building had its own story, often going back many generations. Our teacher showed us the carvings, gargoyles and even some of the carved calligraphy and people's names high up on the walls

At the institute, the conditions for learning the language were fantastic. There were just eight of us in our class. My Japanese, Tunisian and Filipino classmates spoke excellent Chinese and could express complex ideas quite comfortably. Every class was conducted in Chinese and included philosophy, literature, classics, famous authors, comic dialogue and the history of Chinese literature. The school arranged extra classes in subjects such as dialects and calligraphy. The teachers were all very dedicated and treated us very well. They'd take us to meet people or visit ministries to deepen our appreciation of whatever texts or topics we might be covering in class.

For example, one course was on Beijing dialect, which differs from Putonghua, and the language of the famous Beijing author Lao She, who wrote books and plays such as *The Rickshaw Boy* and *Tea House*. Our teachers took us to visit Lao She's home and meet his wife, and we were told of his tragic death a few years earlier during the Cultural Revolution. When we studied texts about culture, we were taken to the Ministry of Culture to discuss the concepts in more depth. For example, when we were learning to perform comic dialogues, Hou Baolin, the famous master of the Beijing dialect, was invited to the school to spend an afternoon with us. This kind of rich context made the subjects come alive, deepened our appreciation and made the whole experience much more memorable.

Our calligraphy teacher took us to Liulichang to meet old calligraphy suppliers and to talk with them about inks, brushes, paper and character styles. At the time, it was still the original street, with many buildings dating back centuries. Each building had its own story, often going back many generations. Our teacher showed us the carvings, gargoyles and even some of the carved calligraphy and people's names

Unexpected opportunities

high up on the walls. You wouldn't see them unless you knew where to look. Some of the old men would add more depth with the stories of the people and families who had lived in those buildings. Sadly, Liulichang has since been demolished and rebuilt as a tourist attraction. If you go there today, none of those old 'secrets' can be found any more.

We were taught calligraphy the old way, sometimes writing in sand, just as our teacher had learned when he was small. These activities deepened the learning experience and made it fun. Maybe this was in part our Chinese hosts trying to present a nice face to the world, but there was also a genuine hospitality towards foreigners, and our teachers were conscientious and devoted to their work.

Whatever we wanted to learn about, the school would arrange for us. Having studied competitive karate in the UK, I seized the opportunity to take lessons in several Chinese styles such as Bagua, Wingchun, Changquan, Taiji and even a little basic Shaolin. Every style has its own special characteristics, and it's a fallacy to think that any one is better than another. The teachers were great at communicating the different thinking behind each style. I was never any good at any of them, but the idea was to get a feel for them so that you'd know how to deal with them if you came up against them in competition.

Different worlds

Some of us really focused on the language. We would study all day for six days a week, except for Wednesday afternoons, and I filled every spare moment with optional courses and all the extra-curricular activities I could cram in. I thought I had only one year and intended to make the most of it. Few foreigners chose to eat in the canteen for Chinese students: we were allowed to eat there, but they were not allowed in our foreign student canteen. The Chinese canteen was crowded and the food wasn't as good, but the few of us who frequented it loved to mix with the Chinese students. They were happy to chat with us and practise their English, while we tried out our Chinese. One thing that felt strange, though, was that girls and boys would usually sit at separate tables. It wasn't a rule, but a custom. We didn't care, but we would attract some funny looks from some of the boys if we went to sit with the girls. It was new and, as always, intriguing.

Part of the fun was talking about things and ideas that showed how far apart our worlds were. Most Chinese seemed so fresh and naïve

Some Chinese students seemed to think that we British were a strange mix of downtrodden proletariat and colonial imperialists, while others were curious to ask about life in England

compared with us. They lived clean and simple lives, without all the distractions we had grown up with. A few had been in the army or had been in remote areas of China, so they'd had different experiences from the city dwellers. Some seemed to think that we British were a strange mix of downtrodden proletariat and colonial imperialists, while others were curious to ask about life in England.

Ian J. Stones

Our worlds had been very different. In the UK, student unions were hotbeds of activism and diversity. There were all kinds of people: long-haired hippy types, some who were on drugs, and it was no big deal if couples shared rooms with each other. The Chinese students all seemed clean-cut and clean-living and knew very little about the world we'd come from. They were not allowed to date or marry whilst at school, and risked losing their places if they did. We found out that a few were indeed secret couples, but they hid it very well.

There were some other cultural differences too. 'Excuse me, but where's the toilet?' was the question asked by one of our British schoolmates, just after he'd walked into, and out again, of the toilets on our dorm floor. Poor guy, he'd never seen squat toilets with waist-high half-doors before. You could see who was squatting in there. It was something that took him several weeks to get used to.

Our dorm rooms were quite bare, but they were fine. We lived a spacious two to a room compared with our Chinese schoolmates, who were bunked six or eight to a room. We were given a monthly allowance of Rmb120, which was four to five times what our Chinese schoolmates got. In those days whole families would be living on Rmb30–40 per month, so we were rich. One common question was 'How much does your family eat a month?'. The 'How much?' meant how much money, and many would answer 'Rmb30'. We bought Chinese jackets, trousers and shoes to try to dress and fit in like locals. We'd take part in collective callisthenics and *tai chi* exercises in the morning and we learned the habit of taking a siesta after lunch.

The dust in Beijing and the constant spitting of its inhabitants were very different from the pristinely clean image I'd gleaned from photos I'd seen in London. There was no grass anywhere, and many streets didn't have kerbstones. It was quite rough and, despite the few big landmarks, it wasn't a very modern city, as I'd expected. The only neon sign was at the International Club. *Dazibao* ('big character posters'), plastered haphazardly, decorated the whole city – on buildings, walls and trees, all criticising the 'Gang of Four'.

Beijing had two city walls at this time. The stone one was being torn down to make way for the subway. The invisible one was the perimeter beyond which foreigners were forbidden to

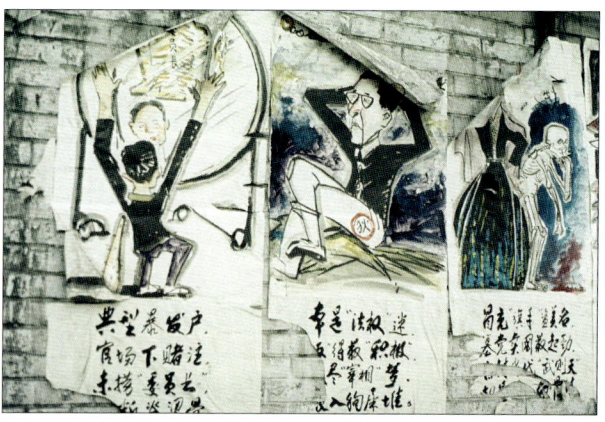

Posters criticising the Gang of Four were plastered everywhere in Beijing

156 | My Thirty Years in China

Unexpected opportunities

cross. Big signs made sure that we made no mistake as to where that invisible wall was. We couldn't go through it unless we had a travel pass.

Above the Tiananmen Gate hung the portraits of two chairmen: next to Chairman Mao was Chairman Hua Guofeng. For two years there had been a period of publicity promoting Hua, using similar cues and imagery as those of Chairman Mao. Everyone expected it would stay that way. People's homes and dorm rooms were often decorated with posters of Hua, Mao and other leaders. Four large portraits of Marx, Engels, Lenin and Mao on either side of Tiananmen Square gave the impression of a grand socialist state.

Between the old city wall (now the site of the Second Ring Road, which didn't yet exist) and what is now the Third Ring Road there were fields, farms and a few factories, where today there are high-rise buildings. Very few landmarks from those days still exist or are visible amidst the suburbs that have sprouted up and sprawled further and further out from the city centre. What is now the area around the university and the 'silicon valley' of Zhongguancun was then narrow lanes between tall avenues of trees and farms with horse-carts and small tractors mingling with students on bicycles.

What is now the area around the university and the 'silicon valley' of Zhongguancun was then narrow lanes between tall avenues of trees and farms with horse-carts and small tractors mingling with students on bicycles

We were free to go around within the city pretty much as we liked. But if you talked to a Chinese person on the street, even a fellow student, people would warn them to be careful and not to talk to foreigners. We noticed that often we were followed by people on the streets, in parks and in department stores. Not knowing who they were or why they followed you could make you feel quite uneasy. Some friends didn't care, but I was very sensitive to it and soon learned to play games with these shadowy pursuers. Sometimes we'd walk around a corner, turn round and wait to suddenly click the camera at them, deliberately trying to provoke them,

We were issued with ration tickets for cotton and rice. Cotton goods were very cheap but you couldn't buy them without ration coupons, and restaurants required 'rice tickets' whenever you ordered rice. You'd be asked how many ounces you wanted. Later, when I bought my first motorbike, I also needed to register for gasoline ration coupons.

The variety of experiences of our Chinese schoolmates reflected very different fortunes. Some older ones had done a few years in the countryside and had returned to the city. Others were workers or from peasant families, and a few were from privileged families. Some had competed in the newly reinstated entrance exams in 1977. There were people from all over the country, and they were all happy to be there rather than anywhere else. Their lives and experience were worlds apart from ours.

The calibre of the 1977 and 1978 student intakes was exceptionally high. These were the cream of a generation of people who suddenly had the opportunity to change their lives by going to university. Competition for entry those years was probably the toughest it had ever been. The students were interested in everything and full of curiosity. They'd ask us to give talks on all kinds of topics and seemed to remember every word we said. We got on well with just about everybody and had fun joking about our differences and our different experiences of life.

> *Striking differences in thinking – from feudal to Marxist, from internationalist to xenophobic, from curious to critical, and even blind worship of the West – could be found among my schoolmates. I hadn't expected this at all*

Sometimes something would suddenly hit home and make you re-examine your own cultural norms and question why you viewed the world so differently. It doesn't sound like much, but for me a small incident triggered a great deal of contemplation about values and norms. One day my Chinese room-mate suddenly blurted out '*Yingguo bu hao*' ('Britain is bad'). So I asked, 'Oh yes, why's that?' He said that in Britain, men and women lived together before getting married, and that was exploitation of women, so therefore Britain was bad.

The same guy had once told me that a certain girl at the institute was bad. His reasoning for this was that she'd sat at the lunch table with me and my Aussie friend. Since it was 'bad' for girls to sit with boys, she was therefore bad – that was his value logic. I was astounded that he thought her sitting with me showed she was 'bad'. What about him then? Was he bad too? I'd expected people educated in 'socialist values' in a place where 'women held up half the sky' to be much more progressive.

What I hadn't understood was that my room-mate was a 'worker, peasant, soldier' student, who had entered school before 1977 because of his working family background, which had nothing to do with any academic qualifications or competition. It was a bit like the comprehensive school argument in the UK. The theory during the Cultural Revolution was that it was better to be Red than to be expert, and it didn't matter what people's educational background was: as long as they were Red, they would come out just as well or better than people who had performed well in exams. The worker, peasant,

My graduation certificate from the Beijing Languages Institute, 1979

Unexpected opportunities

soldier system produced many good graduates, but it wasn't the same as selection via objective, competitive entry exams.

My room-mate was a great guy, but some of his thinking reflected what Chinese would categorise as 'feudal'. However, I didn't yet understand the very different viewpoints of the 'worker, peasant, soldier' students and those who'd had to compete for entry exams from 1977 onwards. Striking differences in thinking – from feudal to Marxist, from internationalist to xenophobic, from curious to critical, and even blind worship of the West – could be found among my schoolmates. I hadn't expected this at all. The Chinese were far from the monolithic stereotypes pictured in the UK.

Bourgeois thinking

Following this and other exchanges with my room-mate about 'Britain being bad', I tried to better appreciate the different schools of thought. According to the Marxist view we were taught in our philosophy class, society progressed from primitive communal, through a slave society, then feudal, capitalist and socialist towards Communism. In theory, China had skipped capitalism and jumped to the socialist phase. In our Western 'liberal' environment, women's liberation and equal rights were pretty well enshrined in institutions and common law, and were part of the accepted progression to a more open-access institutional environment.

I concluded that my room-mate was judging Western values from a traditional feudal perspective and that he and many others confused this with what he thought were progressive socialist views. This was completely different from the thinking of students of Marx and Engels in the UK, and I decided to discuss it with our 'media analysis' teacher. At the end of class, I raised the concept with him and said that I felt many Chinese seemed to view the West through feudal eyes rather than through socialist eyes. He excitedly jumped up and closed the door. He said in a whisper 'Many of us teachers think that way too, but we daren't say it!'.

The debate on the nature of Western thought arose again a few weeks later, when for some unknown reason the school suddenly stopped allowing friends from outside to visit us, except during a two-hour window on Wednesdays. No one had told us that the unpublished rules had changed. There were no notices and no announcements and, unlike back home, there was no consultation about the merits or demerits of such a regulation and no soliciting of opinions before the decision was made.

I had waited for hours for a friend to come, not knowing he'd been turned away. When I found out, and complained vociferously, I was told that this was a new regulation for our own good and that the British students were the only ones in the school who didn't know about it. Quickly, we established that no one had been informed beforehand, so we complained even more loudly that it wasn't democratic. The school cadre responsible said that we knew nothing about democracy because we had grown up in a capitalist society and had been influenced by Western bourgeois thinking. This was like a red flag to a bull.

We did some homework and presented that cadre with four quotes written by Western writers on democracy. He dismissed them as bourgeois capitalist thinking, until we pointed out that the authors were Engels and Lenin. He went white! It was a reflection of the times. Because of the extremism of the Cultural Revolution, we suddenly realised that he was in fear of being branded a counter-revolutionary for pooh-poohing Engels. Nonetheless, the regulation didn't get changed and we learned to live with it.

Actually, from 1981 these institutional and cognitive issues became hot topics among Chinese scholars, especially those who had read the works of thinkers such as Doug North, whose Nobel Prize-winning theories were first translated into Chinese that year. We didn't know it at the time, but leading Chinese scholars and economists were already devouring all kinds of theoretical works in their passionate search for new theory and ways to lift up the economy. What a challenge they faced!

Visits to the *hutong*

Our spoken language teacher at Ealing, Yan Hangtai – who had been at Radio Beijing before going to London – had given me the addresses of two people to look up in Beijing. One was his mother. The other was his English teacher, who turned out to be a very special lady.

One Sunday after settling in, I cycled into town to seek out Hangtai's mother. The address wasn't easy to find. She had no phone, so there was no way to call her. She was living in a single room in a courtyard house with several other families in Beiheyan, close to the Forbidden City. The signs through the maze of *hutong* houses and alleyways were confusing. Everyone I asked for directions insisted on following me, so I gathered quite a group behind me. Eventually I found someone who knew her. She was very excited to see me and was sweet and hospitable. She insisted on inviting

Dancing was not allowed in public until 1979, but we still managed to have parties in private houses

Unexpected opportunities

me to a restaurant with one of her friends, where I was shocked by the amount of food they ordered and felt somewhat guilty. But when we finished, the two ladies pulled out aluminium boxes and packed every scrap of the leftovers, including the little oil left on the plates. Nothing was wasted.

A week later I cycled to visit the second lady, Hangtai's former English teacher. It hadn't clicked with me that the fact she had a home telephone meant something. I was expecting to find a family crammed into another small room in a crowded courtyard. On the way, I bought Rmb3 worth of sweets as a gift. Again, it took a while to figure out where she lived. In the Western Old Curtain *hutong*, there was a huge door to what seemed like a big walled courtyard. There were high grey walls and big fancy roofing over the door. I was sure that this couldn't be the place, so I rode up and down and even round the next *hutong*, asking for Number 29. It turned out to be the big door after all, but it still didn't seem right. After I had rung the bell, an old man came to the door. I gave him the candy.

I had no idea that this was the home of Mei Lanfang's family and that the man who answered the door was

She lived in the main room at the back of the courtyard, in a room full of Chinese and Western antiques. She had a resounding aristocratic Beijing accent, with a twang of Manchu court speech about it

one of the servants. I thought that all Chinese lived very frugal lives and lived in small houses. Mei had been China's most famous Beijing Opera singer; we'd studied a short text about him at Ealing. Hangtai's teacher was Mei Lanfang's daughter-in-law and she had two pretty daughters, Honghong and Meimei, and one son. They lived together with their extended family in this beautiful courtyard house.

At Christmas 1978, I went back there for a party and took my Aussie schoolmate Michael De Clercq. Dancing was still not allowed in 1978, but we ended up having an all-night party, dancing till dawn. There were many more girls than guys; they loved ballroom dancing and even tried to teach us the jitterbug. We taught them disco and some John Travolta moves. Nobody outside could see what we were up to behind the high walls, so we weren't bothered at all. We all left on our bicycles around 8am. It was cold, with the morning sun just beginning to pierce the winter haze. Mike met his future wife that night, Wang Hong. As we rode out through Tiananmen Square, Mike and Wang Hong pedalled ahead of the rest of the group. It was love at first sight.

We became friends and would visit the Mei family quite often. Mei Lanfang's wife, Hu Zhifang, had been much younger than Mei Lanfang and was still alive. She lived in the main room at the back of the courtyard, in a room full of Chinese and Western antiques. She had a resounding aristocratic Beijing accent, with a twang of Manchu court speech about it. She told us that the best antiques had been put in a museum and that, after Red Guards had criticised her for keeping cats during the Cultural Revolution, she bred more until she had twelve of them.

Occasionally, for amusement, if she knew I was visiting, she'd invite me to her study to eat with her. She was full of stories about her husband and the famous people he had known (such as Charlie Chaplin), and she'd always finish her meals with a bowl of *douzhi*, a greenish, sour fermented beancurd liquid, particular to old Beijing. Sometimes, she'd be entertaining a group of former *xizi* (opera performers) and immaculately groomed old gentlemen, the cultural elite of a time gone by. One of them, Mr. Xu, was famous for his calligraphy. He gave me my own name written in many different character styles, one of which I tried to copy for my own calligraphic signature, although I could never match it.

This was my first encounter with historic characters. As I write, there's a film being produced in which the actress Zhang Ziyi will be playing the part of that wonderful, hospitable old lady. Her funeral was the first funeral I attended in China. I said my goodbyes to her, standing among many interesting people, some of whom were famous and some national leaders. I never dreamed that coming to China would bring me into contact with people like this – it was a world I'd never dreamed of.

My second brush with history came via a Japanese girl named Keiko, who had just started at the Institute. She spoke fluent English and was always bubbly, outgoing and friendly. She'd often joke around on the basketball courts and practise her English with us. The speed at which she learned Chinese was phenomenal. Late one afternoon, I was walking back to the dorms and noticed an old black limousine outside her dorm building, which was unusual. Some elderly and distinguished-looking Chinese were bowing and saying goodbye to Keiko. I was curious to know who they were, and she told me they were family relatives. One was Pu Jie, the brother of the last Chinese emperor, Pu Yi. Pu Jie had married Hiro Saga, a cousin to the Japanese Emperor Hirohito. I now understood why our Japanese schoolmates were very deferential around Keiko – she was related to both Japan's and China's imperial families. Before that, we had no way of knowing. Again, it was another world: I'd never have had the chance to meet people like this back home.

Beijing's John Travolta

A few months later, dancing was suddenly allowed and around the Spring Festival in 1979 there were dances all over the city. Honghong and Meimei took me along to the Beijing Authors' Society dance in the Capital Theatre on Wangfujing. The girls talked their way into the exclusive room on the third floor, which we learned later was only for senior cadres. This wasn't as crowded as the first floors, and everyone was dancing foxtrots and two-steps as though they'd practised for years.

Honghong asked to put on my new Western music tape, *Saturday Night Fever*. She grabbed me and we started a John Travolta routine; within seconds, the whole dance floor came to a stop and everyone surrounded us. Among the people watching were Madame Deng Yingchao, Zhou Enlai's wife, and Wang Guangmei, wife of Liu Shaoqi. When I knew this I was star-struck, but they were so warm and friendly. Before long, the dance floor was full of people copying us. They'd never heard or seen anything like it before, but it didn't take long before many of the girls had developed their own moves, much better than mine. This was nothing like the China I'd expected.

Unexpected opportunities

I found myself meeting people in the strangest ways. One night I went to a Beijing opera performed by Mei Lanfang's son and daughter, and got a lift back to the school with a distinguished-looking gentleman, though I didn't catch his name. Everyone recognised him except me. I later found out he was the Vice President of China, Wang Zhen!

My first good Chinese friend from school was Ding Haihua (Henry Ding), now a successful lawyer. He was one of the few who was not afraid to go around with foreigners, and was always enthusiastic about giving us new cultural experiences. On one occasion he suggested we go to a bathhouse, and once again my preconceptions would prove to be totally off the mark.

> *I'd like to believe I was the first foreigner to go there. The surprise of the regulars to suddenly see a foreigner for the first time – naked – and their curiosity about my anatomy suggested that I probably was*

Early one Sunday morning, we went by bicycle to what turned out to be the famous old Qing Dynasty bathhouse, Qinghuachi. Although it was famous to Beijingers, it didn't appear in any English introductions to Beijing that I'd ever seen.

Haihua insisted we should get there the moment it opened, so that the water would be clean and there wouldn't be many people there. It was an old marble and stone building with both large and small hot baths, and neat carvings in the nooks and crannies. The atmosphere was enhanced by natural light flickering through the steam and reflecting off the wet floors. The service staff were old Beijingers who had worked there all their lives. They spoke the true thick Beijing dialect and seemed to know everything that had happened in the city over the past 100 years. They even had stories of the foreign legations and the Boxer Rebellion, which had been passed down from an earlier generation.

It was unusual to see foreigners anywhere in Beijing, and I'd like to believe I was the first foreigner to go there. The surprise of the regulars to suddenly see a foreigner for the first time – naked – and their curiosity about my anatomy suggested that I probably was! It's one thing to be the centre of attention of a curious crowd when you are fully clothed, but it's very different when you are naked and have nowhere to hide. However, after seeing that I wasn't much different from anyone else, the curiosity faded and everyone settled back to enjoy the steaming hot pools and the place's special ambience. The service included a vigorous rubbing down and an acupressure massage, and lots of stories of old Beijing. By the time we finished, our clothes had been laundered and neatly pressed. It's a shame those old bathhouses don't exist any more.

During the spring festival of 1979, the school organised trips to five or six different cities and allowed us to break off into small groups, arranging travel passes and letting us travel without escorts. This had been rare before then. I wanted to see the prison featured in the film *Red Crag*, near Chongqing, so a few of us went to Chengdu, Chongqing, Wuhan and Shanghai together. We took the boat through the Yangtze gorges and in Wuhan found a hostel where we stayed for Rmb2 a night. On the trains and on the boat, curious people would surround us, eagerly asking the same questions:

'How much do you make each month? How much did your watch cost? What does your family do? Had we been to university?' – and so on.

At the Jing'an Temple in Shanghai I saw an 'imitation foreign devil' (*jiayangguizi*) for the first time. He was poised in stark contrast to the crowds clad in blue and green jackets. He proudly flaunted a wide-lapelled purple suit, with huge bell-bottoms. His hair was slicked back in something like a cross between Elvis and an Afro and he wore huge-rimmed sunglasses. To me he looked ridiculous and totally out of place but, actually, when you think about it, people like him have led fashion revolutions. He was daring not to conform and was not dependent upon a group for refuge. A couple of other 'imitation foreign devils' I ran across wore cool hats, white gloves and spats dating back to the 1930s.

> *We began to realise that, often, some of the people following us around were doing so for our own protection as much as anything else, which felt better than the paranoid perception of being watched all the time*

We were still followed sometimes, but we learned a reason why. In a busy Shanghai street, a British girl suddenly had her bag snatched. As she screamed, and just as I spun round, I saw a man grab the bag-snatcher and push him down a side alley. We chased them as the scuffle led into a small police station, and we began to try to sort it all out. We thanked the man who had accosted the bag-snatcher and asked how come he was so close by at the critical moment: 'It was my job, I was following you to protect you,' was all he replied. We began to realise that, often, some of the people following us were doing so for our protection as much as anything else, which felt better than the paranoid perception of being watched all the time. We were also naïve to have thought that petty crime did not exist in China. Most people were honest and we were generally very safe, but actually foreigners could make lucrative targets for pickpockets.

In March 1979, the Democracy Wall movement suddenly sprang up in Beijing. People would voice all kinds of opinions freely and post all kinds of *dazibao* posters. Democracy Wall was located next to the Xidan crossroads, a site that is now green space. For a few weeks, the atmosphere at the institute became quite lax. A few foreign students brought Chinese girls in from outside, and some even stayed in the dorms. They were very different from the girls we would usually see. It didn't last long, though, and things soon reverted to normal.

It could be rather serious for Chinese girls to be seen out alone with foreigners – the social pressure on them not to fraternise was huge. Police would routinely go to their homes after we'd visited and they would usually report back to the school. Most Chinese were afraid to invite you home, though some would tell the teachers beforehand to avoid trouble. For a while the rules seemed to have been thrown out, but not for long.

We were careful when going around with Chinese friends and were especially careful when we went to Wang Hong's home before she and Mike tied the knot.

Unexpected opportunities

Spending time with her family was like a breath of fresh air. We felt warm and relaxed there – but we still thought it was better to come and go in disguise. We did this too if we visited other school friends at their homes. In winter, it was easy. We wore big dog-fur hats pulled down so that the fur hid our 'round eyes' and mufflers so that people couldn't see our big noses. In the summer it was easy too. We switched to baggy trousers, loose shirts and big-brimmed straw hats pulled right down over our ears and noses. We tore eye slits in the brim, so we could see out while trying to prevent anyone from seeing our faces.

The trouble was in the spring and autumn, when people didn't wear thick coats or straw hats. We kept wearing our winter disguises into the early spring and probably started to look quite conspicuous. Generally, though, they seemed to work. Occasionally people would ask us directions, not realising they were talking with foreigners. Once Mike and I did the opposite. Instead of hiding our noses, we put on long fake plastic ones and went out on our bikes to show them off, much to the delight of lots of young kids.

Kung fu star

Sometimes being foreign was a big advantage that could lead you to do interesting things. For example, a film company was preparing to make a movie about a famous kung fu fighter beating up lots of foreigners. They needed a foreigner to play the chief villain, and wanted someone who spoke Chinese and who knew martial arts. At the time I was one of a very few who fitted their profile, so I went along to the studios for auditions.

Back then, I was quite baby-faced and the film-makers thought I looked too cute. They wanted me to be more rough and dislikeable, so they stuck hairs on my chest, thickened my eyebrows, drew a frown, and shaded my arms to make it look like I had bigger muscles. I was going to be a stereotyped vicious Russian villain, and looked pretty ugly by the time they'd finished with me. I met the handsome star of the film. He was great-looking, especially with his make-up on, and he performed a beautiful, stylised form of kung fu. They asked me to demonstrate my own style.

My *shotokan* katas must have looked jerky and rough to their eyes, which were accustomed to what were called the 'flowery styles'. Six older martial arts advisors in their tracksuits shook their heads as I performed a couple of advanced katas. One, Hangetsu involved deep breathing and slow, tense movements, combined with sudden snaps of speed. I think because they thought my *shotokan* looked stiff and jerky, I'd be a pushover. I was still made up like a vicious villain, and they asked us to spar. I didn't really want to and was a shade nervous, but years of training in the UK gave me some confidence and, when they insisted again, I agreed.

> *We thought it was better to come and go in disguise. In winter, it was easy. We wore big dog-fur hats pulled down so that the fur hid our round eyes and mufflers so that people couldn't see our big noses*

Ian J. Stones

After the first bout started, it took me only a few seconds to realise that I was able to kick the poor star all over the place. I thrashed him easily. One by one, the kung fu teachers wanted to take me on and put me in my place, but I could beat them all too. I realised it was not because they weren't any good; it was because, for years during the Cultural Revolution, China had stopped the tradition of free fighting. The old schools had been shut down and the styles were not taught publicly for more than ten years. These guys weren't accustomed to the bluffs, feints, combinations and reactive techniques of competitive martial arts.

Actually, it wasn't really fair. I had been a national-level karate competitor in the UK and had learned free fighting from the first team in the world ever to beat Japan on its own home turf

Actually, it wasn't really fair. I had been a national-level karate competitor in the UK and had learned free fighting from the first team in the world ever to beat Japan on its own home turf. I'd also won the British Universities individual and team free fighting tournaments in 1975. I probably should have told them, or been more modest in the first place. Anyhow, I got really cocky, though I think the film crew were pretty cheesed off. Only one other person was happy: the driver who'd taken me to the set, who thought it was hilarious. I think it might be a different story today, though.

In the end I didn't do the movie, because it would have taken too much time away from my new job, and so they found someone from Xinjiang to fill the part. Poor guy – he had to look awful and get beaten up! I don't think my ego would have let me do that. The driver, however, had the time of his life telling everyone he could what had happened. After a week he'd embellished the story so much, it was as though I'd taken on a room full of kung fu masters all at once, just like in a Bruce Lee movie. Even though this wasn't quite true, I kind of enjoyed my new reputation and the respect it brought me.

First job, and the first of many battles

Before the year at the language institute was up, Mike De Clercq got a job with a New York company involved in textiles trading. There were no representative offices then and, apart from one exception (Nat Wheeler from Kellogg), there were no other long-term foreign business residents. Traders would come in on single-entry/exit visas and would rarely stay for any length of time. Through Mike's boss, I landed a job with a Texan oilfield trading company, Amtech. A completely new chapter was about to begin.

The firm represented a large number of Western companies who were selling oilfield equipment to the Chinese Ministry of Petroleum. We soon started representing other large MNCs and brought many of their executives to China for their first encounters. I was earning US$900 a month – it seemed a huge amount. Mike and I both got suites in the old Peace Hotel, which cost us just Rmb16 per day, and every morning we'd race our bikes through the *hutong* to our offices in the Beijing Hotel a few blocks away.

A necessary characteristic for any 'China trader' in the late 1970s and early 1980s was

Unexpected opportunities

tenacity in the face of difficulties. We all had to battle to get things done that people take for granted today; it was no place for timid types. My first battle was switching from a student visa to a 'resident' one. In 1979, Mike was the first foreign student to switch to working in Beijing. I was the second and, after the difficulties I ran into, I believe I was probably the last. There was no precedent for it, and no procedures.

Our host organisation, Machimpex, was very supportive of our firm having someone in Beijing, especially someone who spoke Chinese, whom they could call and communicate with easily to follow up on contracts, deliveries and letters of credit. Their representatives went with me to the police office several times and provided letters of support. They argued more than I did. The police asked for the school to issue a certificate stating that I had left and that it supported my new job. The school insisted that my graduation certificate was all that the police should need, and that it had no precedent – and no intention – to issue such a letter for any foreigner.

After many visits, battles and arguments, I obtained a letter from the cadre at the school, but it took the intervention of very senior people at Machimpex to help get it through. There were no formal procedures like there are today, and over the next few years battling for just about everything became a constant challenge. Through this first of many battles, I got to know two people at Machimpex. One, Gu Yongjiang, would years later to become China's GATT negotiator as Vice Minister of Foreign Trade, while the other would later become the president of Machimpex Shanghai. Between them, they would sign billions of dollars of import contracts and oversee large-scale transfers of technology.

Despite what most people might think, you got a great sense of satisfaction from achieving what had been deemed impossible or doing something your competitors could not do. The new job was like a drug – it was extremely exciting. The 30-plus US oilfield companies we represented held continuous commercial negotiations and technical seminars with Machimpex and Techimport.

China's foreign trade system was organised along the Soviet model, and these large import/export companies imported all of the equipment used by China's oilfields. All imports and exports had to be conducted through a handful of state trading companies, under the Ministry of Foreign Trade. This was the main predecessor of the various incarnations of what is now the Ministry of Commerce. The 'end users'

The school insisted that my graduation certificate was all that the police should need, and that it had no precedent – and no intention – to issue such a letter for any foreigner

were units under the 110 ministries that existed at the time. The end users in most of our negotiations were usually oilfields, which were part of the Ministry of Petroleum. Sometimes we dealt with the Ministry of Geology or the Ministry of Coal as well.

Two buildings in Beijing housed the offices and negotiating rooms for the state trading companies. One was known as the 'Import Building', or Erligou, and the other was known as the 'Export Building' or 'Light Industry Building'. The nine-storey Erligou was more commonly known as the 'Tanpan Dalou' or 'Negotiation Building'; many foreign visitors called it 'Early Go'. This was to be the building where I would spend hundreds of days – sometimes engaging, sometimes educating, sometimes frustrating – very often under the high stress of protracted negotiations with tough negotiators and in competition with strong rivals.

Nothing was easy: China was genuinely a hardship posting. Unlike today, we couldn't own cars, and we had no telex or copy machines. There was no IDD – you needed to book international calls via an operator. We'd need to bring in coffee, office supplies, filing cabinets, film, writing pads and many other items we take for granted now. There were no phone directories. We couldn't hire Chinese employees. There was no such thing as income tax. We couldn't get multi-entry visas, and could not travel out of Beijing, even to Miyun Reservoir, without a travel pass.

If you didn't use China Travel or your host unit, you couldn't book flight tickets without going to the General Administration of Civil Aviation of China (CAAC) building in Dongsi, and you couldn't buy train tickets without going to the station. You couldn't book hotels in other cities, and couldn't book cars to meet you at the airport or station. It could take several hours or even days to get through to someone on the phone, so it could be easier to go across town to visit a ministry rather than try to call them. You needed a letter of introduction bearing an official chop for just about everything.

Outside restaurants, the only place we could buy decent foodstuffs was the Friendship Store. Coca-Cola was not on sale anywhere, and even in the Friendship Store there were only occasional batches of imported products. Most Chinese were not allowed in there. Anyone coming to the hotel to see us had to register with security, and if they were not from a ministry, and didn't have a chopped letter of introduction, the police might call on them a few days later.

We never could understand why the drivers on the streets would continuously hit their car horns. It didn't matter whether there was anyone anywhere near the car. Once, on the short trip from the Beijing Hotel to the Erligou, we counted as the driver hit the horn 203 times (this was one reason why later, in the 1990s when I was at GM, we specced our Chinese horns to be much more robust than the standard American type). Whenever we opened the balcony door, we would hear the racket from the streets – people used to call it the 'Beijing Symphony'. Then suddenly one day the government banned horns within the city limits. It felt weird, as though something was missing.

Nothing was easy: China was genuinely a hardship posting. Unlike today, we couldn't own cars, and we had no telex or copy machines. There was no IDD, there were no phone directories. We couldn't hire Chinese employees

A huge competitive advantage was your personal phone book. We would never give away the phone numbers of key contacts to anyone, unless it was a trade, and we'd lock our

Unexpected opportunities

telephone books and card cases away when people came to our suite for happy hour. Extension numbers were even more valuable, and the home numbers of senior officials were like gold. We even had lists of restaurant numbers that we'd trade as a currency. The handwritten names given to restaurants by the expats were things like 'The Yellow Sticky Pudding', 'The Squashed Duck', 'The Old Duck', 'Live Fish', 'By the Old Lake', 'Vegetarian', 'Mongolian Hotpot', 'Toffee Apple', or 'Crispy Rice'. None of these had anything to do with the Chinese names. When the first Fodor's Guide to China and the first China phonebook came out, the currency value of restaurant numbers dropped, but the numbers of business contacts retained their value for years.

> *A huge competitive advantage was your personal phone book. We would never give away the phone numbers of key contacts, and we'd lock our telephone books and card cases away when people came to our suite*

While getting to know Chinese negotiators and engineers, I was also meeting lots of Texans and needed to learn two more languages, Texan and 'Oilfield'. We were selling all sorts of equipment into the country – rock bits, downhole pumps, drill rigs, blow-out preventors, packers and desert trucks, and were buying barites and bentonite, used in drilling mud, for export to the US. Soon we were bringing global companies like Shell, Unocal and Agrico, and even directors of Boeing, to China for their first visits. I was still quite green and had been thrust into this commercial world with almost zero experience. Before long, however, I ended up interpreting at technical seminars and negotiating contracts worth millions of dollars on my own. It was another new world I'd never imagined and, once again, it seemed somewhat surreal.

There was only one place where we could send telexes, the infamous Dianbao Dalou (the Telegraph Building). We loved and hated that building at the same time. We needed to go there because from the hotel we could only send cables. Every night, our telexes were full of inquiries, requests for technical specs or prices and negotiations around contract terms and delivery dates. Usually we'd receive responses by telegram the next day, delivered to our room in envelopes, although often out of sequence. We might get the beginning and end of a message, but the middle part wouldn't come until much later.

Each night in the Telegraph Building, while typing out the telex tapes or waiting for our turn to transmit, we'd run into competitors and other traders. If you were unlucky, you might have to wait one to two hours to prepare a tape and send a telex. Sometimes a single telex might take an hour to type and then half an hour to send. We came up with lots of ruses to get to know the staff and to find ways to get put to the front of the queue. The information in telexes could be quite valuable to competitors, so one trick was to read other people's telexes from their used tapes in the waste bins. We soon learned that other people were reading ours too, so we'd deliberately prepare fake telex tapes to get competitors thinking we were up to something that we weren't, to send them on wild goose chases.

We'd also use codes, such as the names of roads in Texas, to disguise numbers, and funny names for people or companies. The Katy Road (the I-10 Freeway) meant 10 per cent, for example. 'Dallas' meant 45, from the I-45 Freeway. It was really competitive – but at the same time there was a kind of party atmosphere too, and some nights we'd share beers and snacks with Danish traders while we were hanging around waiting.

The world's best negotiator

Most of the negotiators from the import/export companies and the engineers from the ministries and oilfields were initially somewhat wary of us; but over a few years and hundreds of meetings we got to know each other well, and with some we became good friends. At first, some of the more political types would lecture us on politics before we'd start meetings. Others were very quiet and modest. When I first started, I felt a strong empathy with them because they seemed like my schoolmates or other friends. Later, some actually were former schoolmates who had been assigned there.

In these many negotiations, I learned from two people who I believe are the best negotiators I've ever known. One was Chinese, the other Texan. The Chinese was Tian Xuejin, who was the main negotiator for oilfield equipment imports for Machimpex. He had a photographic memory and could remember the names of people, companies, equipment, parts and prices like no one I've ever met since. He also knew exactly how to play competitors off against one other and how to wring out every cent on price. He was an expert at playing with anticipation and fear and at wringing a concession at the last minute.

The Texan was my boss Stan Mills, who spoke with a slow Texan drawl. Stan had experience negotiating all over the world and was always focused on closing. Every negotiation between Stan and Mr. Tian was different. They both knew that the other was a master at his game. Both would change their tactics and styles and do things differently to throw the other off guard. Sometimes they'd joke, sometimes they'd go silent; at times it would appear simple and quiet, and at other times they'd get mad, and might even storm out. Sometimes they'd act mad, sometimes hurt. Sometimes they'd swap cigarettes and take ages to light them.

They had lots of tricks. Stan had a T-shirt made with 'Price Too Low' printed on the front and 'Price Too High' on the back. On one occasion, after being told about 15 times that our price was too high, there was a long period of stony silence. Stan slowly unbuttoned his shirt to reveal 'Price Too Low' underneath. It caused an uproar. Even Tian couldn't keep a straight face.

One negotiating ploy was to keep clients waiting for days, or even a couple of weeks. Another was to invite them to Beijing a week before Christmas, so they started getting uneasy as 24 December drew near. If the clients did not trust us to negotiate it didn't matter, and occasionally we might not tell the negotiators that the client had left until after the fact. The one thing, though, that did drive me nuts about some negotiations was the way that the room would fill with smoke. They joked that I was smoking for free and should pay them for the privilege, but I'd sometimes need to open the window and take part in the discussions with my head half outside the window.

One thing about Tian was that anything would go until he reached a closing point,

Unexpected opportunities

but once he'd made a deal he would live by his word. No matter what happened, and even if a competitor tried to undercut our price afterwards, he would always keep to the agreed price and terms. We trusted him and would advise clients to ship against his word. He made the 'How To Negotiate With The Chinese'-type books by Lucian Pye and other professors look like children's cartoon stories. Some of these people had been in a negotiation or two, had drawn simple conclusions and published books on the strength of them. I would have loved to see them come up against Tian. Though neither Stan nor Tian would ever admit it, I think they liked each other. Through 30 years and hundreds of negotiations, I've never met anyone I'd consider an equal to Tian Xuejin. In my book he's still number one.

Stan Mills had all kinds of other tricks up his sleeves. No American airlines flew into Beijing, so travellers from the US usually had to transit in Tokyo and then do their best to get seats on Japan Airlines flights in and out of Beijing or Shanghai. Stan always flew first class and, unlike just about everyone else, he never seemed to have trouble getting the reservations he needed. I eventually found out how he did it. In his office, he'd have a pile of plain paper envelopes stacked neatly in a corner. One day he asked me to take a couple to the JAL office manager, who later came by personally to deliver Stan's confirmed tickets. The station manager opened the envelopes in front of me, and I found out what was inside: *Playboy*, *Penthouse* and *Hustler* magazines were the currency that got Stan priority on JAL.

The work was intensely competitive as others gradually entered the market. We learned all sorts of tricks to find out which Western companies were in town and who was talking to whom. For example, we got to know all the girls who worked at the counters at the old Import Building very well. They'd let us look at the meeting room bookings so we could see who was meeting who, in which meeting rooms and, if one of our competitors was meeting a buyer, we'd show up at the door to try to disturb the negotiations. Sometimes we'd deliberately stick our noses in to irritate competitors, and we'd always try to get a chance to compete for business. We lived on our wits quite a lot but, like everything else, it was always so much fun.

When we competed against other trading companies who were agents for competitors of our clients, we'd often play off each other with half-truths, lies and misleading information, trying to glean intelligence and unnerve one other. We acted cocky when we were nervous, and pretended to be worried when we got a deal. Sometimes we'd lie about when our clients were leaving. Sometimes we'd agree to allow the clients to go home on the same day, but could never be sure if the competitor was telling the truth. It was always critical to try to find out how big an order would really be and how close the competitors were to closing.

> *One negotiating ploy was to keep clients waiting for days, or even a couple of weeks. Another was to invite them to Beijing a week before Christmas, so they started getting uneasy as December 24 drew near*

Ian J. Stones

Man about town: an ad for the Lido Hotel Business Centre, 1986

One time, in a large negotiation for submersible pumps, we'd figured out that the total was around 80 pumps and that we were close to closing for 40. There were two other competitors and it was approaching Christmas. The negotiator seemed to be deliberately dragging things out to wear our clients down. They wanted to go home, but were worried they would lose out if their competitors stayed. Stan spoke with the competitors, saying that our client was leaving the next day and suggesting they could do the same. After a few calls back and forth, everybody said they would leave. But like any game, we had to be sure we could trust them, so Stan asked me to find out which flights their reservations were for.

No problem: the trick was to go to the one and only central CAAC office. The difficulty involved in booking and buying tickets and the need for letters of introduction actually made it possible to look up the details and check the handwritten flight reservations. We weren't supposed to be able to see them, but there was always a way – asking to check your own client's spelling, for instance, and flipping through the piles of papers to find competitors' bookings. On that occasion, we found out that the competitors really were booked on the same flight out, and they did all actually fly out the next day.

Believing the clients were sweating it out, the negotiator had expected us to call and request meetings, but we didn't. Three days later, when he thought our clients would be really wound up, he found out they'd all gone. He blew up and said that if we had colluded, he'd never do business with any of us again! His tactic hadn't worked on us and we only really dared to act that way because we could confirm that our competitors weren't lying – that time at least.

In 1980, the Ministry of Petroleum invited me to teach technical English two evenings a week. The class was 30-strong, but soon expanded as another 30 people would come to sit and listen at the back of the class. I didn't know it at the time, but all

Unexpected opportunities

the class had been selected to come for training before they became the founders and managers of CNOOC and its several regional companies. They were being prepared to work in cooperation with international oil companies in offshore exploration and development, and were so friendly and thirsty to learn. Within a couple of years, some of them would be my colleagues in BP. Years later, many became very senior business leaders and even ministers. However, no matter how senior they became, whenever we'd meet they would still smile and call me 'Teacher'. When I met many of them at CNOOC's 25th anniversary, it was like a class reunion.

Beijing's first bars and dance spots

Even though there were no bars or clubs in Beijing, the social life was great. Most of the expat community knew one other and we'd often see the same faces around town. A main hang-out was the coffee bar on the ground floor of the new wing of the Beijing Hotel. Everyone called it the Zoo, because sometimes Chinese people would come in groups to see us weird-looking foreign animals with strange clothes and hairstyles. It was definitely the best place to catch up with the gossip. If there were any new foreigners in town, you'd usually get to know them pretty quickly – you felt like you knew everything that was going on. If you happened to be alone, you'd always find someone to talk to.

There were no imported food or drinks available, but we easily adapted to that. There were other luxuries, such as big jars of black caviar you could buy in the Friendship Store for Rmb20 and Chinese champagne at Rmb4.5 per bottle – it tasted OK. Some embassies organised collective shopping runs to Hong Kong, and would sometimes bring us back a case of Guinness. The two things I missed the most were cheese and English beer. I used to gorge myself on cheeses and a variety of beers when I went back to the UK and would bring back half a suitcase full whenever I returned to China.

The Peace Hotel, where Mike and I lived, was in Goldfish Alley in Wangfujing. Now it's where the Peninsular Hotel and the New Peace Hotel are, but in 1979 it was a narrow grey *hutong* with walls on both sides and occasional gateways. The Peace Hotel café, which was located on the alley itself, started to become very popular with trendy Beijingers, some sporting leather jackets and greased-back hair. Some wore sunglasses with the sticker left on, to show they were new. A few fairly sleazy women used to gather there too; they turned out to be the first prostitutes I ever heard of in Beijing. They seemed totally out of sync with the rest of the city; I've no idea how they got away with it. The risk back then was being branded a *liumang* (hoodlum) and being sent for reform through labour, which should have been a big deterrent. Sadly, the Peace Café was only open for a few months before it was closed for the renovation of the hotel.

> *The coffee bar in the new wing of the Beijing Hotel was called the Zoo, because Chinese people would come in groups to see us weird-looking foreign animals with strange clothes and hairstyles*

In 1980 there were only three regular places to dance: the Minzu Palace, the

Ian J. Stones

International Club and a dance hall in the Friendship Hotel. Entry was restricted to foreigners and a few Chinese they would take in with them. At the Friendship Hotel some girls were brought in as dance partners, but they were under very strict instructions not to have any relations with foreigners, and to leave alone.

Getting what you needed

Nothing was simple back then: you had to jump through all kinds of hoops to get anything you needed, even just for normal office life. We take office equipment and furniture for granted today. We probably wouldn't think twice about importing something from Hong Kong and having a customs agent or freight forwarder handle the procedures for us. But 30 years ago it wasn't like this – it was very difficult, and we had to do everything ourselves.

The story of how we acquired a filing cabinet illustrates the difficulties of dealing with Customs. At the time we were involved in a joint venture with Smith Industries to represent their subsidiaries. Their vice president bought us a four-drawer filing cabinet in Hong Kong and shipped it by train to Beijing. This basic piece of office furniture couldn't be found anywhere in the Chinese capital, and we didn't want the nearest equivalent – all clumsy metal cupboards with flimsy brown paper envelopes piled up inside. The cabinet took three weeks to arrive. A postcard notice to collect it from Beijing Railway Station came by mail and, late the next morning, after meetings, I took a taxi to pick it up. With me I had around Rmb300 (US$200 in those days) and our company chequebook, so was ready to pay the customs duty. I thought I'd be in and out of there in a few minutes. Boy, was I in for some memorable lessons….

Lesson No. 1: Never try to clear Customs just before lunch. After finding the unmarked freight office at Beijing Station, I was given the documents to take to Customs and found the Customs office. Nine or so people were sitting at desks. Even though I was the only 'customer', no one stood up to attend to me. Eventually one young officer came to the counter. I asked how much the duty would be. He told me to come back after 2pm. I took a taxi back to the hotel, and returned in the afternoon.

You would never be sure if there really was a document or not. Transparency is an issue raised by foreign business representatives today. In 1979, 'You can't see the internal documents' was the norm

Lesson No. 2: Customs duties were very high. The filing cabinet and freight charges came to the equivalent of US$412, which at the prevailing exchange rate of Rmb1.58 to the dollar was Rmb650. This was already twice what the cabinet would cost in Hong Kong. After looking up the category in which it should be classed, I was eventually told that the duty would be 100 per cent, which meant that this simple cabinet would cost us the grand total of US$824. For anything we would want to import, duties ranged from 80 per cent to 280 per cent, including other taxes – although the categories weren't clear and were subject to interpretation.

Unexpected opportunities

Lesson No. 3: Foreigners are not allowed to see 'internal documents'. I was shocked by this amount and wanted see how they'd calculated the duties. I asked to see the booklets they'd been referring to and was told, 'Custom tables are internal documents, foreigners are not allowed to see them.' That term *neibu wenjian*, or 'internal documents', would become one of the most irritating phrases I would hear. It would be used in all sorts of situations, and you'd never be sure if there really was a document or not. Transparency is an issue raised by foreign business representatives today. In 1979, 'You can't see the internal documents' was the norm.

Lesson No. 4: Carry lots of cash – Customs don't take cheques. The duty came to Rmb649.50. Since I didn't have that amount of cash on me, I opened the chequebook. At that time, foreigners with accounts with the Bank of China were issued chequebooks that, surprisingly, you could use in taxis and hotels and even at souvenir stalls at the Great Wall. They were different from the cheques used by Chinese entities, and were generally accepted. The customs officer watched me write out the cheque, sign it and put the mandatory contact details on it. When I handed it to him he looked at it and, with a stony face, said, 'We do not accept cheques.'

'Why not?'

'It's a regulation.'

'Show me the regulation.'

'You can't see it.'

'Why not?'

'Because it concerns foreigners.'

'Then I can see it.'

'No, it's an internal document.'

'If the taxi-drivers, the Friendship Stores, CAAC and the Great Wall souvenir shops accept cheques, why won't the Customs?'

'We are the Customs, we do it our way.'

After 15 minutes I gave up. It was too late to go the Bank of China that day, so I went the next morning. The Bank's head office was the three-storey building just south of the Great Hall of the People on Tiananmen Square. The lady at the counter said there was no reason why Customs shouldn't accept a cheque. As we talked about it, she half-jokingly suggested I pay the Customs duty in small notes so that they would have to take time to count it, and it would teach them a lesson. I was given neat piles of Rmb1, 2, 5 and 10 notes (there were no Rmb100 notes then). My frustration had built up and, after telling my colleagues all about it, we eventually filled a paper shopping bag from the Friendship Store full of small notes, screwing up each note individually, fluffing up the volume and randomly messing things up with coins. We even threw in some US cents and Japanese yen coins for fun. I wrote '649.50 yuan' with a felt pen on the bag in big characters and went back to the Customs office.

The officer again went through the process to calculate the duty and told me the amount. I asked; 'Will you accept a cheque?'

'No.'

My Thirty Years in China | 175

Ian J. Stones

'Will you accept cash?'
'Yes.'
'Here is the cash.'
He saw the big bag full of notes and coins, and said, 'You must count the cash.'
'I've already counted it.'
'You must count it in front of me.'
'Why?'
'It's a regulation.'
'Show me the regulation.'
'You can't see it.'
'Why not?'
'It's an internal document.'
'Then it's nothing to do with foreigners.'
'It is.'
'Show it to me then.'
'No, it's an internal regulation.'
'Then it doesn't apply to me.'
'It's a regulation.'
'Regulations are *wangba pigu* (a kind of rhyming slang that meant 'turtle's ass').'

He was stony-faced, but others laughed to hear the slang. I left the bag of cash on the counter, sat down and got out a book. After several minutes, another customs officer, a young man, quietly walked over and said he would handle it. The young guy took ten minutes to sort out the notes, putting them in neat piles, and then three others each counted the money in turn. After half an hour they had finished the procedures, but they still took their time. When they finally handed me the paperwork, the officer said, 'You foreigners are really bad.'

'Why?'

'Another foreigner did the same last week, but he did it with one fen coins.'

I burst out laughing and said, 'Accept cheques then'. I left, and started to think how to get the filing cabinet to the hotel and – more difficult – how to get it past the front desk.

Lesson No. 5: Be careful who you upset – word of your deeds travels. Months later, this episode would come back to haunt me. When later I wanted to bring in a copy machine, I was told that my name and the story of my 'bad attitude' had spread all over Beijing Customs. The lady who told me advised I shouldn't upset anyone if I needed to get help from Customs in future. It was good advice. But nevertheless we were on our way to equipping the office.

We got tired of the run to the telex office, so next my boss said we had to find a way to get a telex machine of our own – even though no companies then had their own machines and the Beijing Hotel refused to let any of us have office equipment in our rooms. So I went to see an influential lady I knew who I figured would have the right connections; she said it would cost us US$500 and a couple of Win brand cigarette lighters (the top brand at the time). I agreed, and the next thing we knew, a very senior retired general from Hunan turned up at our office. He was around 75 and spoke with a loud

Unexpected opportunities

voice; he spent most of the time telling us stories of the Long March and civil war.

Eventually, he said getting the telex would be no problem, he'd go to see the manager of the hotel. In the end it actually took four trips to the manager. After a few days, the general came back waving chopped approval documents and a handwritten guarantee that we had to sign. He said the manager had agreed, but if any other foreigner found out we had a telex machine, we'd lose it. We had to guarantee that no one would find out and complain that they wanted one too. We had a soundproof box with sponge lining specially built to hide the machine in the office, which was still a hotel suite. And for all the help he gave us, the general got just the two cigarette lighters: the lady got the US$500.

One evening, when it was our turn to host a 'happy hour', a number of friends were sitting in our suite. I noticed slight vibrations coming from the box, indicating that a telex was coming in, but luckily no one else noticed it. I could hardly contain myself when Dick Glover, the first US China Business Council rep in Beijing said, 'Not even Deng Xiaoping could get a telex in the Beijing Hotel'. We couldn't risk Dick or anyone else knowing we had it, in case we lost it.

Office life in the Beijing Hotel

The next thing we desperately wanted was a photocopy machine. These were still extremely hard to get then, as they were considered to be a means of spreading propaganda, and each machine was required to have a code etched on its glass to identify it. A badly-made Chinese copier would have cost us US$40,000–50,000, and we would have had to register it with the police. To get some copying done, we could go to the US embassy once a month, at the time when the commercial counsellor needed to send commerce reports – so we would be welcome to trade some commercial information for the right to use their copy machine.

To get a copy machine of our own involved the same procedure as for the telex machine – though this time my contact wanted a tape recorder instead of lighters along with the US$500. She made a call and a guy from Customs showed up at her home and said we could import a copier. I was due to leave for the US on business and come back via Japan, where I planned to pick up the copy machine, so the officer said I should come back with it checked in as baggage, declare it on arrival and say I was intending to take it out of the country eventually. When it came to carrying out the plan, the officer seemed more nervous than I was. He put a triangular stamp on the Customs form in my passport, which meant you had something to take out. Once I'd been through all the rigmarole, there was the copier waiting for me outside Customs with a new customs form. My contact got the US$500 again and I believe the officer got the tape recorder.

Apparently we were the first foreign company in China to have a copy machine. When I took delivery of it at Narita Airport, Ricoh's international VP came to deliver it personally and to find out how I was going to import it into China, because this could possibly mean a big new market for them. I couldn't tell him. Once in the country, we had to smuggle the machine into the Beijing Hotel in a giant soft suitcase. We wheeled it through the lobby during the lunch hour, trying to look as innocent as possible. In the suite, the copy machine was disguised under a custom-made cover and pushed into a corner in the bedroom. It was another secret we didn't want people to know about.

We could make the system work for us in other ways. No one could book hotel rooms directly: they were assigned by the 'service bureau' according to availability on the day of arrival. It was pot luck, and many people would arrive with no idea of where they'd be staying, until their hosts actually took them there. People could be put in hotels anywhere around Beijing and, although everyone wanted to stay in the Beijing Hotel, that was almost impossible – except for a few of us. We found out that if a person didn't check out of their hotel room, it would be kept under their name indefinitely. As long as the bill was paid each month, the hotel never did anything.

We started to run our own room booking system: we paid the hotel Rmb50 per day for each room and Rmb100 for suites, but we could trade the rooms with other companies and did deals to cover the days they might be vacant

We realised we could take over rooms from people who left and then reassign them ourselves. Eventually we commandeered five rooms for our firm and, together with a few other companies, had 42 rooms in all. We started to run our own room booking system: we paid the hotel Rmb50 per day for each room and Rmb100 for suites, but we could trade the rooms with other companies in the hotel and did deals to cover the days they might be vacant. We could do time swaps when other people's rooms were in demand, and a few people kept long-term rooms and let us manage them while they were way. Sadly, it didn't last. After a few months, the hotel management figured out what we were doing and shut us down. We resorted to new tricks, but none were as good as our own bank of rooms.

Other strange things would happen in the Beijing Hotel. Ricoh's vice president had given me a very thin cigarette lighter when we met at Narita – it was unique, you couldn't buy them. One day I found it had disappeared from my drawer. I was pretty upset, and was convinced that someone from the hotel had taken it. I asked the people at the service desk on my floor if they'd seen it, but they just said they would look for it the next day. Their body language wasn't right. When I went back the following day, and asked them to give me the lighter back, they got very cross, saying I was wrongly accusing them of stealing it… but soon the lighter reappeared back on my desk.

I decided to do a little experiment. I left a voice-activated tape recorder in my desk the next day. When I came back in the evening, I listened to the tape and could hear people going through my stuff, for several minutes. I got pretty upset, and started to leave rude notes in Chinese in each of the drawers saying, 'Whoever goes through my stuff in these drawers is a real bastard'. The next day one of the guys at the service desk said it wasn't nice of me to leave such a note in the drawers. But when I asked him how he had read the note, he denied going through my drawers. They just could not understand that I felt strongly that it was wrong for them to go through my stuff.

Unexpected opportunities

Sometimes we got ourselves into trouble. One of the partners in the company, an ebullient Houstonian called Mike Pearce, was quite a character. One day the hotel staff were slow to clear away the tea cups after a meeting and were rushing to prepare for new guests about to arrive. This set Mike off, railing at the staff to clear the cups. One of the staff, who actually we really liked, jokingly replied by miming the action of throwing the cups out of the hotel window. So Mike got hold of one of the cups, opened the balcony door and threw it straight out. We heard it smash down below and carefully looked out to see a group of people surrounding the broken cup, soon followed by a crowd of security guards and police. They came to each room one by one to try to find out where it had come from. They searched all the rooms on our side of the hotel – but luckily the room boy never let on, despite the full-scale investigation. It could have been quite serious.

Another time, Mike Pearce camped out in the hotel manager's office for three days because the manager refused to meet him to discuss a number of complaints we had. Mike just stayed there all day, taking his work and papers with him. We started to put all his calls through to the manager's office, and Mike would answer. Nowadays, you don't find poor service like that in a Beijing hotel any more, and thankfully people like Mike don't need to resort to such extreme measures to get things done.

Rural encounters outside Beijing

Work-related trips away from Beijing also provided some memorable moments. In 1981, I accompanied a mining engineer and beneficiation expert to examine some remote phosphate mines in mountainous Guizhou province. We were taken to places way off the beaten track, and were told that one remote valley we were to visit had never been visited by foreigners, ever. Mike Dibble, the engineer from the US, was blond-haired, blue-eyed and had a very pale complexion. The first sign that foreigners were a novelty in this valley came while we were resting after lunch in a small hostel. We could hear a lot of noise outside, and found that thousands of people from all over the valley had come to surround the place. They filled the street outside, waiting to catch a glimpse of the two foreigners when we came out.

Later that afternoon we went to a mine high on a mountainside. It went underground for about a kilometre and a passage exited further along the steep valley. Mike and I walked along underground, wearing our

One of the staff jokingly replied by miming the action of throwing the cups out of the hotel window. So Mike got hold of one of the cups, opened the balcony door and threw it straight out. We heard it smash down below

mining togs and hard hats with lights attached. We gradually left the Chinese group behind, as they were busy chatting. Eventually the shaft turned sharp right, and we walked toward the wall of light and emerged out onto the mountainside. There were several villagers gathering herbs there. One man looked up and saw us, then screamed and started rolling down the hillside. The others all panicked, dropped their things and

My Thirty Years in China | 179

followed suit. The yellow-haired, blue-eyed monster with a light on its head must have looked like a spaceman! We also heard that there was a deep cave nearby called the 'devil's gate' which, because it was cool, was occasionally used as a temporary morgue. Maybe they thought we'd come from there.

In Britain we'd been told that every commune in China could make steel and that the government was not afraid of people making their own guns. My only encounter with a gun made by a commune was one Sunday in 1982. One of the favourite Sunday picnic spots among the small community of expats was one of the older Ming Tombs. Sometimes we'd go in small groups, and this particular Sunday around 30 of us from foreign businesses and embassies went there for the day. As usual, a few locals came along to check us out.

> *One man looked up and saw us, then screamed and rolled down the hillside. The yellow-haired, blue-eyed monster with a light on its head must have looked like a spaceman*

Two of these villagers were carrying a long, home-made musket, around seven feet long. I was curious, and followed them to ask how they'd made the gun and to see if it was legal. It was completely home-made, but they said they had registered it with the local police. The barrel was a long, rusted piece of steel tubing, reinforced around the breech and held together with nails and wire. They used a home-made black powder to charge the gun and then muzzle-loaded it with nails and gravel. The external firing pin triggered a home-made firing cap fashioned from a folded piece of a soft drink can, which contained the black powder and a flint.

Looking back now, I was stupid – I asked if I could shoot it. They were more than happy to let me have a go, and chose a rock about 30 metres away. I aimed and fired; the surface of the rock powdered and I was knocked backwards several feet. I lost the hearing in my right ear for about half an hour and it only came back slowly, with a constant ringing. The contraption was dangerous, and I'm sure there must have been breech bursts and many serious accidents in the past. Since then guns have become tightly controlled and those home-made guns have been banned – wisely.

One example of the eccentric character of the traders attracted to China in the late 1970s and early 1980s was Henrik, an individual from Denmark. He worked hard and played hard, and would sometimes do crazy things. One Sunday, some diplomats arranged a picnic at the Great Wall. Since most people didn't have cars, and we didn't want to go by bus, they arranged for a special train carriage to be added to the daily slow train to the Wall, and our picnic started as soon as we boarded.

At the Wall, it was actually about a 15-minute walk to the picnic spot, and some local peasants were offering donkey rides. Henrik asked how much it would be to buy a donkey, and got a deal for Rmb200. The old man was delighted. Henrik rode his mount to the Wall, with the old man tending to it, and some of the kids took rides on Henrik's donkey. In the late afternoon, after riding back, he half-seriously tried to get the donkey

Unexpected opportunities

The Ming Tombs outside Beijing were a favourite picnic spot for the small expatriate community

onto the train, but eventually ended up selling it back to the old man for Rmb150.

Henrik had another amusing habit that I've never seen in anyone else. He'd carry a novel around with him and, as he made his way through it, he'd tear out the page he'd just read and throw it away, so the book would get thinner and thinner until nothing was left. He'd say he never lost his place that way and saw no point in carrying around pages he'd already read!

One incident that none of Henrik's friends would believe who did not witness it themselves occurred in winter 1982/83, when Henrik became a real hero. There was a Sunday party taking place in an old compound near Yuan Ming Yuan, the Old Summer Palace, where BP and a few other companies had old-style houses. Some kids were playing on the frozen lake and we adults were chatting and enjoying mulled wine. Suddenly, there was lots of screaming: three kids had fallen through the ice into the freezing water and the mother closest by couldn't get near to the crumbling edge of the ice.

Henrik seemed a little drunk, but he didn't hesitate for an instant: he dashed across the ice and jumped straight into the water. He quickly threw the kids out one by one, after which it was quite a struggle to pull him out. His usually red face was almost blue, but Henrik was celebrated as a hero. His clothes were hung to dry and we all went inside to warm him up and make sure he

His clothes were hung to dry and we all went inside to warm him up and make sure he was OK. He was, but later when someone went to bring in his clothes, they were literally frozen rock solid and covered in a layer of ice and frost

was OK. He was, but later when someone went to bring in his clothes, they were literally frozen rock solid and covered in a layer of ice and frost. It never bothered Henrik that none of his Danish colleagues would believe the story, as it seemed so out of character. But it just shows that when unexpected things happen, you never know who might turn out suddenly to be a hero.

A fruit fest in quarantine

In winters in those days, there were only cabbages, tangerines and persimmons available in Beijing, so for Christmas 1981 a number of us planned a feast with all kinds of foods from our home countries. My job was to bring a suitcase full of mangoes, papayas and other exotic fruits back from Hong Kong. I didn't know, however, that new quarantine rules had been introduced because of fruit fly problems in California. At Customs, I was confronted by quarantine officials who told me that I had either to eat the fruit or throw it in the large disinfectant bins provided. When I insisted on reading the new regulations, I found that the fine print allowed the traveller to request that the fruit be kept in quarantine at the airport for three days. Aha, I thought, a loophole.

Happily, I insisted that they quarantine my fruit; the officials complied and gave me a receipt. On Christmas Day, our group of expats gorged on smoked meats, pickled fish, salmon and other goodies from our home countries. Mid-afternoon, we got into taxis and drove out to the airport. The quarantine officers had never actually expected me to come back, and had piled my fruit haphazardly among other bags and boxes of foodstuffs. I couldn't be sure what was mine and what was not. It didn't matter. For an hour we sat in the windowless quarantine room and gorged ourselves on all kinds of fruits. Afterwards we thanked the quarantine officers and conscientiously put the piles of peel and stones into the big waste bins. Until fruit became available on the domestic market, or unless it was imported through official channels, we had to bring in dried fruits or try to bring fruit back from visits to southern China.

For an hour we sat in the windowless quarantine room and gorged ourselves on all kinds of fruits. Afterwards we thanked the quarantine officers and conscientiously put the piles of peel and stones into the big waste bins

Something that few expats living in Beijing today would realise was that it used to take two days to get to Hong Kong. There were no direct flights, and the only flight to Guangzhou would arrive at 5.30pm, just too late to catch the last train or hovercraft. It would take four hours by road and the Shenzhen border would be closed. It was easy to go the other way, however, by morning train to Guangzhou and evening flight to Beijing. Then one day the Hong Kong hover-ferry started a 6.30pm sailing. It was about 50 minutes' drive from the airport which meant, in theory, that if your plane was on time and you grabbed a taxi fast enough, you might be able to make it and achieve the impossible. It was worth trying for the bragging rights. I only did it three times,

Unexpected opportunities

In 1982 I moved into the oil business with BP, and went scouring the Guangdong coast for base sites

once scraping in with just a minute to spare. These bragging rights soon disappeared, however, when more flights were put on and, eventually, when the first direct flights to Hong Kong started.

Over three years with Amtech, I'd become fully conversant with oilfield technology and had been involved in technology sales to refineries on behalf of Unocal and helicopter sales on behalf of Bell Helicopter. We'd concluded China's first ever aircraft lease, for a Bell 212 aircraft from Air Logistics that was to be based on Hainan island, flying the oil company Arco's crews to their drill ship. We'd sold desert rigs and trucks and had travelled to oilfields in the north, south, east and west of this vast country, when it was still closed to foreigners.

New job, new cities: Shanghai and Guangzhou

In mid-1982 I switched jobs and went to work for BP, which was then preparing to bid for the first offshore production-sharing exploration blocks in the South Sea and South Yellow Sea. I was the third expat, hired for my language and also because I had familiarity with Chinese oilfields and technology. I was very lucky to be sent to the UK for three months to be educated in all aspects of an oil company's business, spending two weeks training in each specialist department, from exploration economics to operations, contracts, planning and risk management.

One of my jobs was to fly occasionally to Shanghai to pay the rent on two houses and a jetty and warehouse that BP occupied there. One of the houses, on the outskirts of the city, was an Elizabethan-style building that used to belong to the Sassoon family, and which was now used by the company for its Shanghai office and accommodation. It was like a piece of England, surrounded by lawns and trees; it came with an old Western chef who had learned how to make curries in the 1930s and a pastry chef who was a master of both English and French cakes and desserts. Some Sundays we'd invite the whole foreign community in Shanghai for lunch on the lawn. Unbelievably now, at that time that was only 15–20 people in total.

After one busy period when two exploration wells were being drilled, the drillers

Ian J. Stones

Everything we did in Guangdong felt like pioneering

and geologists went home and the house was quiet for months. It suddenly came to life again for a visit by the British Prime Minister Margaret Thatcher. After arriving in Shanghai from Beijing, she was to visit BP for a briefing from our boss Simon Downes. She would be there for less than an hour, and the briefing would last 45 minutes. Three weeks before the memorable event, there were people everywhere, painting and repairing the house, trimming the garden, cleaning and polishing the furniture. Simon's 10-year-old son was excited. He was at the age when boys like guns and I'd joke with him that there were men in the garden with guns to spark his imagination.

On the appointed day, the Prime Minister arrived, accompanied by her husband Denis and a handful of others. As she sat down, our eager chefs brought out plates and plates of cakes, pastries and biscuits they'd prepared. We'd asked for tea and biscuits, but we didn't expect them to prepare a banquet. Simon began the presentation. I was at one side of the long room when I suddenly saw a small commotion. Simon's son had told the security officer that there was a man with a gun in the garden. I suddenly regretted my jokes, but was relieved to see the security officer take it in his stride.

> *I was at one side of the long room when I saw a small commotion. Simon's son had told the security officer that there was a man with a gun in the garden. I regretted my jokes, but was relieved to see the security officer take it in his stride*

That night there was a reception at the Jinjiang Club. I was sitting with two British businessmen who were going to be introduced to the PM. Having met her twice already by now, I was acting cool and experienced, but one of the pair was a nervous wreck. He was worried she would ask him something he couldn't answer or that he'd say something out of place. The other, a Scotsman, joked, 'Ach, whene' er ye meet someone famous, ye just say two lines o' Robbie Burns …. "Tho yer satins 'n silks may be fine, yer a***hole smells just like mine." Just say these words in your head when you're shaking hands,' he said, 'and you'll be fine.' Ten minutes later, they shook hands with the prime minister and both were smiling, with no sign of nervousness at all.

This would be the first of many high-level visits I'd either witness or be involved in.

Unexpected opportunities

Many people who are caught up in the planning, logistics and protocol of such events tend to lose sleep or get very nervous. Some people jockey for position to get a photo opportunity for their office wall, others go along for the social networking, while others just take a back seat and watch. The most important item on the agenda for Margaret Thatcher on that visit was to start the dialogue on the future of Hong Kong. After her meetings in Beijing, she met Mayor Wang Daohan and the Shanghai leadership, before leaving for Hong Kong. Over the next two years there were considerable tension and many rounds of negotations before the Sino-British Joint Declaration on Hong Kong was finally resolved.

After BP won contracts for several offshore blocks, I became part of the team that went looking

In 1982, Guangdong was still rural. Dongguan was still a small fishing village, Shenzhen was still a farming town. What today are Shekou and Chiwan ports were pleasant lychee groves dotted with small fishing villages

for sites for offshore logistics bases. We boated along the Pearl River estuary and along the Guangdong coast, and everything we did felt like pioneering. In 1982, Guangdong was still rural. Dongguan was still a small fishing village, Shenzhen was still a farming town and the border was strictly patrolled on both sides. What today are the huge Shekou and Chiwan ports were then pleasant lychee groves dotted with small fishing villages. We'd come across PLA soldiers all along the border areas among the bushes and in the trees. They were mainly guard against smugglers and illegal emigrants and would ignore us.

As BP ramped up for drilling operations and more people arrived, we started running into all kinds of problems every day. My job migrated into troubleshooting, and I was asked to fix anything that came up. It might be a problem with the tax office, a problem with a contractor, or a fishing boat sunk in the night. At one point, we couldn't sign contracts or pay suppliers because we couldn't get BP's business licence, nor the licences for our four international partners. My boss told me to drop everything and to go to Beijing to do whatever it took to sort it out. When I went to the State Administration of Industry and Commerce to try to establish what the problems were, it turned out that we simply couldn't meet the registration requirements, which were not designed for exploration companies. BP International's registered capital of £1m was too low for the size of the expected risk investment, and the potential business projections had probabilities assigned to them.

After hours of exchanges, explaining how the consortium was comprised of five members and how we carried out exploration, I felt I was making headway, but was still afraid that it might take weeks to resolve, which would really delay operations in Shanghai and Guangzhou. The next day, a Saturday, I got a call to come back to the ministry. When I got there, I found myself on national television receiving the five licences, numbered 000001 through 000005. I returned a hero to the office in Guangzhou, extremely proud and excited.

This episode showed that the Chinese authorities were changing their way of thinking and could be very flexible, doing things more quickly and opening up. It was always a challenge trying to beat the bureaucracy – but it was also an ecstatic feeling if you managed to do something for the first time or beat the system. In any case the system was continuously changing, and changing fast.

Worst memory: the *Glomar Java Sea* disaster

During my training at BP, I never expected that the operational crisis management training I received in Aberdeen would come in useful a year later in China. The *Glomar Java Sea* was a dynamically positioned drill ship, which had been drilling for Arco off Hainan island. In late October 1983 it was sunk by a typhoon in the South China Sea, about 70km south of Sanya. Eighty-one people were on board, half of them Chinese and half foreign.

At the time, I was in the thick of daily negotiations for helicopter lease contracts, which had run into all kinds of roadblocks. The CAAC Helicopter Company, based in Guangzhou, had never dealt with this kind of contract before and considered many of our terms unfriendly or one-sided. They were to do a back-to-back 'wet' lease for a Sikorski S-61 from British Airways and then lease it to BP. This meant that the conditions of the lease included experienced pilots from BA who had to fly as co-pilots under Chinese pilots in charge, along with BA ground crews who would provide technical services. Offshore helicopter operations are very specialised and, although there were some good Chinese pilots, they didn't have the minimum of 2,000 offshore flight hours that are usually required by global oil companies. Part of the contract was for BA to provide experienced pilots and technicians to support CAAC's personnel.

In late October, Typhoon Lex headed for Hong Kong and wrecked all the equipment aboard one of our supply boats. We'd been to the Shekou base to dress down the captain for not securing the equipment, but had been relieved when the typhoon turned west and headed south of Hainan. However, on the morning of 26 October we received a call saying that just before midnight all communications with the ship had been lost and that there were no standby vessels nearby.

Part of the unwritten code for oil companies is that they all pitch in when there's a life-endangering crisis. So when the call came in, we immediately agreed to mobilise the chopper and a workboat with sonar to assist in the search

Part of the unwritten code for oil companies is that they all pitch in when there's a life-endangering crisis for any one of them. So when the call came in, we immediately agreed to mobilise the chopper and a workboat with side-scan sonar to assist in the search and what we hoped would also be a rescue. We hadn't even finalised the contract for the helicopter, but we insisted on permission to take it out. There was confusion and misinformation everywhere. The CAAC manager told us that Chinese naval aircraft had found the ship, while other reports from foreign aircraft and ships indicated that

Unexpected opportunities

distress signals had been picked up. No one knew the facts and the local CAAC officials really didn't want us to take the chopper without the proper contracts.

However, after battling for approval, we flew to Zhuhai to pick up equipment, along with another BA pilot and a technician. We were lucky to have Captain Ye Guanwei, who had just arrived back from Aberdeen where he had been taking an S-61 familiarisation course. He was still wearing his suit when he arrived, but jumped into the chopper to take control as pilot-in-charge. The senior British pilot had spent eight years in RAF search and rescue helicopter operations in the North Sea, so we had had an A-team flying the aircraft.

We didn't have flight clearance to fly to Sanya. Normally the military needed to approve flights the day before but, by chance, the head of China's aviation authority, Shen Tu, was inspecting the airport. He told us to go, even though we didn't have clearance, since lives were at stake. But his message clearly didn't get through to the military: when we were 18 nautical miles out from Macau, the Chinese navy came on the radio and warned us that we were in unauthorised airspace and that we would 'suffer the consequences' if we flew any further. Just 63 minutes away from Hainan, Captain Ye said we had no alternative but to turn back. We'd lost a day of search time and were desperate to get to the location as quickly as possible. It wasn't until the next night that we got to Sanya, after flying to Zhangjiang and picking up people from Arco. On the way, at times, we were circled by air force jets. I was amazed at how friendly the pilots and air force controllers were over the radio.

> *When we were 18 nautical miles out from Macau, the navy came on the radio and warned us that we were in unauthorised airspace and that we would 'suffer the consequences' if we flew any further*

We spent five days searching for the ship or survivors, leaving at dawn, returning to refuel and flying till dusk. Often we were flying close to the surface of the sea, in the worst conditions imaginable. We were afraid to blink in case we flew past a head bobbing in the choppy waters. Of course it was a terrible time, but it was also very exciting to be flying in those waters between China and Vietnam and seeing Russian and Vietnamese naval vessels on the other side of the no-go line.

At the time there were tensions between China and Vietnam. However, on the fifth day reports from US aircraft said that fresh sea-dye marker and some debris had been spotted, so we decided to follow an intermittent distress signal and risk flying way over the no-go line, into Vietnamese airspace. Visibility was very low and surface conditions were rough, and we got conflicting messages from the Vietnamese who were monitoring us. Some encouraged us to fly further, others were threatening to take us down.

It was rough and dangerous and, despite all our efforts, we didn't find any survivors. It was a terrible tragedy and a major national news story. All of us who had been on that helicopter had the same recurring nightmares. We met up a couple of months later, and found we'd all had the same dream of being in the water ourselves and seeing the chopper coming in the distance, then flying past and leaving without seeing us. That was what we had been so afraid of: blinking and missing someone amongst the waves.

This accident drew attention to lots of operational problems, and no one wanted anything like this ever to happen again. Unlike in the aftermath of the Bohai No 2 rig disaster a few years earlier, when a rig had overturned in bad weather in the north, this time there were no scapegoats and no heads rolled. The oil companies, the Ministry of Petroleum and the helicopter and boat operators initiated a series of meetings and improvements. It always takes time, but important progress was made step by step.

I heard there was a young American interpreter on one of the search boats. Like me, he'd never expected to be in such a situation and he had a much worse time than we did. Even though we were sleeping in a filthy old place, with scorpions and snakes to guard against, at least we were on dry land. The guys in the boats had to face rough seas for days on end.

Biking in Guangzhou, 1984

I left BP in late1984 and went back to my original company, Amtech. This time I was to set up an office and support operations in southern China, based in Guangzhou and also covering Shanghai. We were selling oilfield equipment and services and representing Bell Helicopter and Air Logistics. Bell was supporting a number of 214ST and 212 helicopters operating in the south.

Unlike Beijing or Shanghai, the local people in Guangzhou didn't pay any attention to you, and you never felt you were being stared at. If you went out somewhere with Chinese girls, no one would bat an eyelid. Culturally it was almost like a different country. At the time, I thought it might have been partly because many people had TV antennae to pick up programmes from Hong Kong (you'd see them rising up on bamboo poles every evening) and partly because many had been exposed to family or friends from Hong Kong or Macau.

Also, I thought it might be partly because Guangdong people were more accustomed to foreigners after several years of the Canton Fairs. Recently I've seen some comparison metrics, showing that people from Guangdong score higher on individualist measures than other Chinese, using cultural indices. That's not derogatory in any way – the local people here just live and let live, and get on with their own business more than people in the north tend to do.

I'd run into police on motorbikes and they would challenge me to a friendly race along a straight stretch of road behind Baiyun mountain. Guangzhou made you feel welcome, and not like an object of curiosity or suspicion

I was the first person in the city to own a big motorbike – a Honda V4 400cc water-cooled machine, which I was able to import duty-free. It cost HK$22,000 and was worth every cent. When I went to register it with the police, they were reluctant to test-ride it because it was much bigger and more powerful than anything they were used to. Riding the bike around

Unexpected opportunities

In 1982 at the Zhanjiang ferry crossing, which was a regular journey for me in those days

the surrounding countryside and small towns, exploring new roads, was a great new escape. I used to love going for a good ride after finishing work, before going for a beer with my co-workers (the 'oilies').

One time I accidentally came across a small military post on Baiyun mountain, on a path to the peak. It housed a small battery of anti-aircraft cannon. I went back this way several times: at first the soldiers yelled at me to keep away, but after a while they got used to me whizzing past and we just waved at each other – I never got stopped. A few times, I'd run into police on motorbikes and they would challenge me to a friendly race along a straight stretch of road behind Baiyun mountain. Guangzhou made you feel welcome, and not like an object of curiosity or suspicion.

No one I've ever met comes near Fiona Ching for her spirit and determination never to give up until she had finished what she was asked to do. Fiona was a Shanghainese who'd gone to Hong Kong with her parents when she was small, and she grew up speaking fluent Shanghainese, Cantonese, Putonghua and English. In Guangzhou she helped me to set up Amtech's new office, and was a great asset in dealing with a few arkward characters in the oil companies and services companies we were selling to and with the many clients we represented. She was very attractive and that usually helped, but even then some people still complained to me about her.

We chose to set up office in a large suite in the Dongfang Hotel, which had been the main centre for foreigners before the White Swan and the China Hotel opened. The hotel would not allow the permanent installation of telexes in the rooms, but did have lines to cater for Canton Fair traders, who were allowed to install machines for the duration of the annual trade event. Fiona found out about the large number of lines and set about getting us a permanent line and machine. A few days later a poor lady from the Telex Bureau came along with a telex machine and some engineers and begged me to stop Fiona harassing her. She told me that everywhere she went, the phone would ring and it would be Fiona, and that she was only agreeing to this so that Fiona would leave her alone.

When the China Hotel opened in 1983 they had so many applications from people wanting to work there that they were able to choose the most stunning girls to be hostesses and receptionists – they were knock-outs

The second person who begged me not to let Fiona contact them again was the head of Pennzoil. One of our client's sub-sea well-head bids hadn't arrived in time to meet the US company's deadline, so with half a day to go they sent it by telex. We cut and pasted two sets of telex messages together and rushed to make up a half-respectable bid package. To meet the deadline, Fiona had to get the bid package to Zhanjiang by 10pm.

It turned out that the Pennzoil manager didn't get back until well after midnight: he'd been unable to fly in and had travelled by road from Zhuhai. Fiona had gone by road too. The executive hadn't been home long and was just going to bed when Fiona

At Zhanjiang in 1984, attempting to find a solution to another tricky technological problem

Unexpected opportunities

knocked on his door and delivered the bid. I cringed when he told me the story, but he did accept the bid. When I told Fiona, she laughed and shrugged it off. She'd done her job, and whenever she called Pennzoil again she just used her Chinese name. She was a gem and thrived on challenges. It sounded like a joke, but it was true that you had to be careful what you asked her to do. Even if you were joking, she might just accept the challenge and do it anyway.

The growing foreign community in Guangzhou was mainly involved in the oil-related business, except during the Canton Trade Fair, when the city would be full of people from all over the world. Quite often, in the early evening many of the 'oilies' would go to the bar in the China Hotel; another group would hang out at the White Swan. Unlike in Beijing, there was no problem with bringing Chinese friends along. When the China Hotel opened in 1983 they had so many applications from people wanting to work there that they were able to choose the most stunning girls to be hostesses and receptionists – they were knock-outs! They weren't hung up about mixing with foreigners either and, if we went out for dinner or went dancing with them, they wouldn't let you pay but would always want to pay for themselves. This was another difference from Beijing.

A move to the auto business

As well as being active in the oil and aircraft businesses, in 1985 our firm started to work for Chrysler, principally to advise on a proposed vehicle programme with Beijing Auto (which, after research, we advised them against) and then to assist with some potential vehicle and engine programmes with First Auto Works in Changchun. Ironically, when Chrysler bought AMC in 1988, they got the Beijing Jeep joint venture, with the partner we'd advised against in favour of FAW. This was the beginning of my many years of involvement in the auto business.

In Guangzhou and Shanghai we began working on fleet sales. In Guangzhou we ran up against a Hong Kong firm that was also selling Chrysler fleets but at quite high mark-ups. They had sold Chrysler K-Cars and some vans, mainly to the police in Guangzhou and Shenyang. When the police found that we also had a relationship with Chrysler, they'd sometimes bring cars round to us and ask for help with parts or repairs, especially when they found out that the prices we quoted were much lower than those of the Hong Kong company. Back then none of the global auto-makers had any decent after-sales capability, and Chrysler was no exception.

Seeing a police car coming, the cop waved the car through and as I drove past he saw it was me – the same foreigner he'd stopped three times. After that he always waved me past

While riding around Guangzhou on my Honda 400, I'd sometimes get stopped by police at one particular 'no left turn' intersection. I'd been pulled over by the same traffic cop three times, and each time I'd pretended not to speak Chinese. I'd smile, act dumb and he'd eventually wave me on, usually letting turn me left anyway.

One day, some people from the provincial police came to complain about the lack of parts and poor service they had received for their K-Car. They also complained about the car's handling and its lack of 'oomph'. Actually the car hadn't been specced as a pursuit vehicle, but the impression they had that American cars were fast left them disappointed with the K-Car. They asked me to take it for a drive with them to see for myself. Without thinking, I chose a route that took me to the same intersection where I'd been stopped several times before. Seeing a police car coming, the cop waved the car through and as I drove past he saw it was me at the wheel – the same foreigner he'd stopped three times! After that he always waved me past, but I never got to know him.

Competitive tension with the Hong Kong firm we were threatening was inevitable, but the company's boss thought up some underhand methods to try to put us out of business. Without my knowledge, he told some of his lower-level police contacts that I was a CIA spy and that I'd given the CIA photos of naval and air force facilities. He didn't realise I was British and that actually, after the *Glomar Java Sea* disaster, I'd given some pictures of Vietnamese and Russian naval vessels to the Chinese Ministry of Defence. He used this false claim that I was a spy with some of his contacts to have people planted outside my office. They would take any Chinese leaving the office for questioning.

I knew nothing about this, but one day two friends came to ask for help with fixing their Chrysler cars. One was the son of a senior army official and the other the son of a senior provincial police official. A few days later they came back again, and told me that everything had now been fixed. Last time, they'd been arrested as soon as they left my office. A scuffle had ensued, they called their colleagues, and the goons outside my office had been arrested themselves. I'd had no idea that they'd been there all that time – but, after that, there were never any problems again.

Another dramatic incident occurred in May 1986. The first regular cross-straits flights between the mainland and Taiwan are only just beginning now, but I bet few people know that 1986 was when the first cross-straits 747 flight took place. It literally came out of the blue. On 2 May, I'd finished business at the Guangzhou helicopter company and, while riding round near the forecourt restaurant, bumped into Mr. Yu Yan'an, the recently arrived head of Guangdong CAAC. He was walking alone. I showed off my Honda to him and joked that he had an easy job. It was because he always looked relaxed and smiling. However, the next day he looked rather more stressed out.

> We found the engine in the hold and I jumped onto the quayside crane to try to winch it out. Actually, I hadn't a clue how to operate the crane, but the people who came running up to stop me did

On 3 May, I was sitting on my bike on the tarmac chatting with the helicopter ground support crews. We always liked to watch choppers take off and land and would wave to the pilots. No one paid any attention to an approaching 747, until suddenly someone shouted, 'It's from Taiwan!'. Memories change our perspective of

Unexpected opportunities

time. In my mind, everything suddenly went into slow motion. The unbelievable had happened: a China Airlines jet was there in Guangzhou. It looked huge and it seemed to move very slowly. It took a while for people to realise what had happened.

Captain 'Johnny' Wang Shi Chuen had chosen to defect to the mainland, and certainly did so in style. For the next couple of weeks, Mr. Yu was embroiled in negotiations over returning the aircraft. It sat at Baiyun airport while historic talks took place with representatives from Taiwan, who had had no choice but to come to Guangzhou. How times have changed.

Logistical challenges

We'd need to find ways to support our guys working in remote locations. Field engineers in oilfields or other places could be living miles away from any city, in simple hostels with no Western food, TV, newspapers or any other entertainment, and could get pretty miserable after long periods away from their homes. Two Air Logistics helicopter engineers were based at Sanya airport on Hainan to service the Bell 212 that ferried Arco's crew to and from the offshore rigs. Today Sanya is a trendy seaside resort with lots of five-star resort hotels. In 1984, there were only two foreigners on the whole of Hainan island – those two engineers. They lived in a hut at the airport and would rotate two months on and one month off, so sometimes they'd be there alone for a month at a time. We'd try to get 'care packages' out to them at least once a week.

Once an inexperienced pilot accidentally over-temped one of the helicopter engines, which meant that a mandatory engine swap was required. We needed to get an engine from the US as fast as we could. The company would lose revenue every day the chopper couldn't fly, and its operations couldn't possibly be compromised. We had a replacement engine flown into Hong Kong but the freight forwarders couldn't get it onto any inbound flights, so they put it on a slow daily freight vessel, which arrived late on a Saturday afternoon. We had hired a minibus and had taken the seats out, and went to the jetty to get the engine.

We had all the Customs papers, but no one was working. We might have wasted another day, so we found the engine in the hold and I jumped onto the quayside crane to try to winch it out. Actually, I hadn't a clue how to operate the crane, but the people who came running up to stop me did. They helped us get the engine out. Once it was loaded, we also piled up the minibus with hot dogs, canned food, Cokes, beers, videotapes and magazines. The drivers drove through the night via Zhanjiang, made the ferry crossing to Hainan and drove down to Sanya. Late on Sunday, the two engineers heard the bus approaching in the distance, and jumped for joy when they saw what was in it. They got the chopper operational overnight and ready to fly on the Monday.

A few years later, we were supporting some Chrysler engineers who were working to commission an engine production line in Changchun, in Jilin province in the north of China, with First Automobile Works (FAW). In those days, working in remote areas or in smaller cities could be pretty tough. Guys would have no social life after work and no entertainment, so we did what we could to make life better for them. For the Chrysler guys, we had sent a big box of video movies that we'd gathered from friends. On one trip to Changchun, one of the foreign affairs staff from FAW told me that they'd had to hide the discs because one was Caligula, a film set in ancient Rome that included hardcore porn scenes. She explained that they were supposed to hand over such films to their superiors, to give to the police. But when I asked if they had done so, she said no – they'd all been watching it themselves in secret!

> *I choked and couldn't hold back my tears, but when I saw that just about everyone else in the room had tears in their eyes too, I didn't feel so bad. Lu Fuyuan was very well liked*

In 1985 Amtech was bought by Citibank, which was expanding its global trading services business – so I became a Citibanker. I flew to join our colleagues in Beijing for the announcement by John Reed in the Great Hall of the People, in June 1985. Citi was very well managed, with efficient systems and great training. By then I was 32 years old and had begun to learn the rudiments of banking. Paul Speltz was one of my colleagues there; he later went on to become the US representative at the Asian Development Bank, and is now president of Kissinger & Associates. Our boss was Anthony Leung, who later became Hong Kong's Financial Secretary. So I was working with some interesting people, in a new corporate culture, and soon got involved with Citi's products and training. It was another new chapter.

Chrysler, and some special people

We'd recommended to Chrysler that they work with First Auto, and that led to our firm being involved in setting up the sale and technology transfer for a used production line to build 2.2- and 2.5-litre engines, a model known as the 488, in Changchun. I became more involved as we started to support the commissioning of the line, and then began to discuss a body-in-white programme and eventually a vehicle programme. This process saw the beginning of friendships with two remarkable people. The first was Lu Fuyuan, one of First Auto's vice presidents, who later became China's Vice Minister over the auto sector and eventually Minister of Commerce. The other was Li Guangrong, whose family had at one time been associated with the KMT.

Both of these friends were true gentlemen. They were constantly studying the latest technologies and had perfect English. Both became mentors of mine in different ways, including helping to expand my vocabulary and giving me crucial advice when I ran into a couple of tricky problems. They loved books with a passion and whenever they went to the US their first stop would usually be a bookshop, where they'd be content to browse for hours. I'd sometimes bump into Mr. Lu at libraries on Saturdays and Sundays, such was his passion for books and knowledge. Even when he became the Minister of Commerce, he channelled his passion for study into the theories, policies, laws and issues of foreign trade and economics.

For a few years, I went regularly to Changchun and would often spend evenings

Unexpected opportunities

chatting with Mr. Li and Mr. Lu about anything and everything. Both later died of cancer. A couple of years ago, I was invited to attend a memorial held for Lu Fuyuan at the Great Hall of the People in Beijing. I was there along with a small handful of foreigners who had befriended him, among several hundred people who had worked with him or who knew him through their work. Many were elders from the auto industry and the heads of all of the big Chinese auto firms were there, along with several mayors. I was asked to speak, but I wasn't prepared and didn't speak very well. Actually, I choked and couldn't hold back my tears. I felt terrible, but when I saw that just about everyone else in the room had tears in their eyes too, I didn't feel so bad. Lu Fuyuan was very well liked.

As well as rising to be Minister of Commerce, he had been a member of the Party Central Committee. He was one of the new generation of up-and-coming leaders; an engineer, experienced in managing a big business, fluent in English, well read with a broad general knowledge, and very comfortable in the company of both Chinese and foreign government and business leaders. One thing that everybody said about him was that, no matter how senior he became, he would still welcome people he'd known in the past, no matter what their status was. He was a very special person.

Another person I got to know through working with Chrysler was Lee Iacocca, the corporation's legendary Chairman, who came to Beijing for a week in October 1988. At that time, many people were urging him to run for US President, so in Beijing he was accorded the highest level of security. Chrysler at the time owned Gulfstream, and at our request he

A special person: over the years I felt very close to Lu Fuyuan, who became a mentor to me

flew in on one of their demo jets, a G4. We arranged a demonstration day for the aircraft, flying around a 20 sq km airspace that included the Great Wall and the Ming Tombs. We got the approvals to do this just the day before, and felt like we'd brought off a coup d'état, being allowed to fly around that like that (incidentally, Jim Mann's book *Beijing Jeep* wrongly claimed that 'the Chinese' had taken Iacocca's plane for their own joyride and didn't allow him to fly it to Changchun – that was way off the mark).

Lee was down to earth and liked to chat with anyone. When we took him to the Ming Tombs, we arranged a big picnic lunch in one of the nicer undeveloped tombs. As we were preparing to leave, he looked at a village nearby and asked what kind of people lived there. When I suggested we walk into the village and talk to some villagers he was delighted, but I should have realised that this would send his American security guards nuts. They were furious at me for not warning them, so that they could reconnoitre the route.

Iacocca was determined to go, and in fact he ended up meeting one of the local villagers. The old woman, of course, had no idea who he was. She warmly invited him into her house, and I went in to interpret. When she offered him a cigarette, Lee gave her one of his trademark cigars, and they ended up chatting for ten minutes. He was fascinated by her kitchen, and what she liked to cook and what her family did. He swapped an Italian recipe with her. It was just fantastic. That night Lee was invited to dinner by Premier Li Peng. We'd had a professional interpreter lined up, but minutes

I was drafted in at the last minute to act as interpreter for Lee Iaccocca at a meeting with Premier Li Peng

Unexpected opportunities

before the dinner I was asked to step in. Hence you see me in the official photo sitting in the interpreter's seat. Actually, it was not useful to be thought of as an interpreter.

Lee was one of many global chairmen or CEOs I would be involved with in one way or another. He was the world's number one turnaround artist and the idol of many business leaders. He was a man of his times, and many Chinese government leaders and businessmen wanted to meet him. Nowadays, almost no chairman or CEO can afford not to come to China once or twice a year. They put considerable stress on their local government affairs staff, who have to make everything work and prepare briefing papers and Q&A sessions.

> *The old woman warmly invited Lee Iacocca into her house, and I went in to interpret. When she offered him a cigarette, he gave her one of his trademark cigars, and they ended up chatting together for ten minutes*

In some ways life is easier than it used to be, but nowadays many more executives want to meet with senior leaders, and that actually makes it harder. Over time I expect we'll see executives from China rising to lead more global corporations. I believe they'll behave differently in China from their foreign peers, but they'll have much to learn in dealing with other cultures.

Eventually, Chrysler lost the vehicle programme to VW-Audi; their then chairman Karl Han was more determined to win. A very senior Chrysler executive, not Iacocca, uttered words that he would come to wish he'd never said: 'The Chinese will never be able to build a car'. How many times have people made predictions like that and have later been proven utterly wrong?

Back channel diplomacy

Another person who became involved with our company was Leonard Woodcock, who'd been asked by Jimmy Carter when he was US President to normalise relations with China during what he expected to be his first term. Leonard had finalised the terms of normalisation in person with Deng Xiaoping in late 1978, and became the first US Ambassador to China when relations were normalised in early 1979. Leonard was a historical figure in his own right. He'd been close to JFK, and had gained fame and adoration as the thoughtful president of the United Auto Workers union. He was a rare visionary and strategic thinker. He used to help us with occasional red tape issues.

Not long after the Tiananmen incident in June 1989, Leonard took me along to the US Embassy, where we were told that they had no channels for communication to the central government. A day later, Leonard and I met with Party elder Hu Qiaomu, who for many years had been Chairman Mao's secretary. The main task was to frame the issues and nominate non-governmental negotiators to work out solutions. It was an education watching these two old gentlemen at work.

Neither of them had any official status any longer: Hu was supposed to be writing the official history of the Communist Party and Leonard was retired. Correctly framing the issues in a mutually agreeable framework was the challenge. They seemed to dance around the issues and talk about anything else but the subject for the first two hours; but when they got down to business they were both supremely well informed and got straight to the point. It was like watching two *tai chi* masters completely in tune with each other's movements but trying to throw each other off balance, just a little, while keeping a harmonious sentiment overall.

A month later, a few sensitive issues were brought up through my then business partner, Paul Speltz, who'd been close to President George H.W. Bush. At this stage, Nancy Pelosi had a bill going through Congress that threatened severe sanctions on China. Bush wanted to veto the bill, but first needed three concessions from the Chinese government. Without going into details, agreements were reached. To be honest, this process left me quite stressed and a little shell-shocked. I couldn't confide in anyone while it was going on.

Through my brief exposure to back channel diplomacy, I worked with Han Xu, China's former ambassador to the US, and Rong Yiren, then China's Vice President. This was weird, and something I'd never been prepared for. I learned a great deal, but it's not a game I would want to be involved in again. Still, Leonard was another walking history book, and I wish he'd completed his memoirs.

A new city, and back to my 'drugs' roots

Paul Speltz and I had done a management buy-out from Citi together in late 1987. We'd started doing other business in Japan and the Philippines, besides the auto, oilfield and aircraft businesses, but we gradually reached a parting of the ways in 1990. After selling my shares in the company, in 1991, I moved to Dalian to start another new chapter, taking up a very exciting new position with Pfizer. My job was to set up the medical, marketing and sales functions for the company's new joint venture and to integrate the sales and marketing for imports, which had previously been done out of Hong Kong.

It was a dream come true, and something I'd aspired to when I was a young medical rep in England – to be like the bosses I'd admired so much. Although I admired them, however, I felt I could do a better job at motivating people than they did with me and my fellow medical reps. At first I was worried about being away from the 'mainstream' action and comfortable life that expats enjoyed in Beijing. By this time Beijing was by no means any longer a hardship posting, and moving to Dalian seemed to involve going back to pioneering in a city where life would be harder.

We seemed to be able to hire the crème de la crème all over the country, and many of my happiest memories are of the enthusiasm and energy of the bright young people who joined the company at that time

Very quickly, I got to enjoy this coastal city, as it was just opening up. Dalian and the northeast of China had been left behind in the reforms, and when the moratorium on luxury hotels hit in 1989, Dalian had only two decent establishments. Shenyang

Unexpected opportunities

Moving to Dalian to work with Pfizer in 1991 opened up an exciting new chapter in my China career

actually had none at all. Being by the sea, Dalian's seafood was spectacular and the coast roads had great ocean vistas. The culture was a combination of the northeast and that of Shandong, which was just across the water and a source of migration. The people were taller than the Beijing average; the Dalian women were known for their attractive looks and their soccer skills, probably inherited from the racial melting pot.

The city's rich history was very different from those of Beijing, Shanghai or Guangzhou. There were strong Russian influences dating back to the early twentieth century, when Tsarist Russia had built a strategic railway down to Port Arthur, which was what the naval port was called then. The Russians had clashed with a rising Japan in 1904/05 and had lost two naval battles and a land battle, with the result that the Japanese replaced them for the next 40 years. They in turn left their mark on the city. There were some small Japanese businesses and restaurants, invested in by Japanese who either had strong empathy with the region or felt guilt for what their predecessors had done there.

I started with a blank sheet of paper, and over the next three years made many more new friends all over the country as we built up operations. We chose a strategy of having medical reps in 30 different cities, rather than concentrating on the three big cities, as several of our competitors were doing. We seemed to be able to hire the *crème de la crème* all over the country, and many of my happiest memories are of the enthusiasm and energy of the bright young people who joined the company at that time.

The pharmaceutical sector has more issues to deal with than any other industry. In addition to the usual production, marketing and business issues faced by most sectors, it also faces combinations of medical, regulatory, ethical, insurance reimbursement

Ian J. Stones

Training medical reps at Pfizer was always a lot of fun

and other policy issues that mean companies need to have people working on all fronts at the same time. The medical team had a busy time, since our strategy to take advantage of Pfizer's leading new drug pipeline meant that they had a string of new drug applications and clinical trials to conduct in key trial centres around the country. Building a new organisation from the ground up, with lots of deadlines to meet, was busy work and required long-term, detailed planning. Although there was a lot of work, we still managed to have lots of fun.

In 1991, the pharmaceutical sector was in the early days of transition from supply planning and allocation of commodities via a state wholesale system to the multi-channel competitive system it is today. Every six months, the big five Level One state wholesalers, the 282 Level Two companies and the several thousand Level Threes would converge on a chosen city for the big *dinghuo hui*, the national ordering meetings. These were a remnant from central planning days, but provided a good chance to network with wholesalers and industry peers. In Shenyang, I tried to buy a case of exploding beer glasses.

We were having dinner with the Wuhan Level One wholesaler. I'd just downed a glass of cold beer for a *ganbei* and had put the glass down. About 30 seconds later, just as I was about to respond to another funny toast, the glass exploded with a huge bang and showered sand-sized particles of glass all over the table. The room went silent for a moment while we all tried to figure out what had happened, then suddenly everyone burst out laughing.

The restaurant staff were very apologetic and started to clear away the table, saying they'd replace all the dishes and drinks. An older man in a white jacket came to my shoulder. He was carrying a notepad and started to ask me questions. 'What nationality was I? How old was I? What was my company name?', and details of my position and age and so on. I asked him why he wanted to know all this. He explained, 'This has happened several times before. Our procurement department won't listen to us. This is the first time it's happened to a foreigner, so maybe they'll listen now after I submit this report!' I immediately offered to buy a case of the defective glasses,

Unexpected opportunities

hoping to impress friends at parties and even to use them as gifts. Maybe if I'd been less eager, I might have succeeded. Actually the restaurant staff took it very seriously, and they were right to do so.

We had a young, well-built American guy named Kirk as our finance manager; he started seeing a local Chinese girl, Haixu. One morning, police showed up at Kirk's room at 7am and found him with his long-term girlfriend. They were both taken in for questioning. If this had been a prostitution case, the normal procedure would have been for the man to write a confession, pay a fine and get his wrists slapped; the girl might face some more serious punishment. But Kirk, naturally, refused to cooperate, adamant that he'd done nothing wrong. He contacted the US consulate to get a certificate of 'no objection' to marriage and started the civil registration process to marry Haixu. Even though the police certainly didn't get the outcome they'd expected, they were quite amused. I think they would have come to the wedding if Kirk had invited them.

I'd downed a glass of cold beer for a ganbei. About 30 seconds later, just as I was about to respond to another funny toast, the glass exploded with a huge bang and showered sand-sized particles of glass all over the table

Kirk and Haixu's wedding, however, was an example of one of several awkward situations I've witnessed with bicultural weddings, by virtue of being able to speak

Entering into the spirit of things, dancing at a party for Pfizer sales and marketing staff in 1993

Ian J. Stones

Chinese and therefore being able to communicate with both families. Kirk's parents, from California, were totally overwhelmed. It was their first trip to China, it had been made at short notice and the fact that their son was marrying someone they had never met before only added to the difficulty of the situation. Haixu's parents were local university professors, and were clearly very upset that their daughter was suddenly marrying a foreigner like Kirk who couldn't speak Chinese and whom they hadn't yet approved. At the wedding banquet, I sat between the two sets of parents, doing everything I could to get them to smile and talk to each other. It was tough and embarrassing for everyone.

The Party Secretary from Pfizer's partner company turned up to the wedding. Though he usually came across as a staid official type, on that day he read some beautiful poetry and made some very warm toasts. It was a surreal occasion: the wonderful poetry, the Communist Party secretary, the long-faced Chinese parents and the befuddled Californians. It was almost impossible, but the important thing was that Kirk and Haixu were both happy. I think both sets of parents got used to the idea eventually. They made a good couple.

Over the years it has become much more acceptable for Westerners and Chinese to marry – it's not a big deal any more. Now I think that more Chinese parents are positively happy, or at a minimum they accept it easily, when their sons or daughters marry foreigners. Maybe they think they'll be happier or treated better, maybe they're more willing to let their children make their own decisions. The failure rate for

Introducing the new Buick to President Jiang Zemin. One of his entourage called me 'Teacher'; he had been a member of my English class 17 years previously

Unexpected opportunities

marriages between foreigners and Chinese used to seem very high but, subjectively, I feel the success rate today seems much higher.

Back in the 1980s, however, I used to be asked quite often to help smooth out communication difficulties between foreigner-Chinese couples, with mixed success. One foreign student whom I'd known at the Beijing Institute, though not too well, came and asked for my help through the process of marrying a Chinese woman. He was worried and nervous. When I asked how long he'd known her, he said just three weeks and they'd met at the bus stop! He'd only met her two or three times since then, in a coffee shop and a restaurant. Because his spoken Chinese wasn't great, I arranged to meet her – and I'm afraid I took a dislike to her, mainly because it turned out she had a long-time boyfriend she was ready to dump to marry my friend, who she'd just met.

It was a surreal occasion: the wonderful poetry, the Communist Party secretary, the long-faced Chinese parents and the befuddled Californians. It was almost impossible, but the important thing was that the couple were happy

I thought it would be good for them both to wait, but there was no chance of that. When I couldn't persuade them, I did my best to help them sort things out to prepare for the marriage, despite my misgivings. I didn't really do much in the end, as they didn't need the help they thought they did. Sadly, and maybe predictably, it didn't end well. Soon afterwards they went to live back in the UK, and it didn't take long for them to split up. They both remarried afterwards, and I believe they are much happier now.

One hilarious occasion was in Guangzhou, when a good American friend asked me to go along with him and his intended to his first dinner with his future mother-in-law. During the meal, the three of them seemed not to want to look at each other or say anything. The future mother-in-law and I spent the whole of dinner, two hours, talking to each other – the loving couple themselves said almost nothing. They were holding hands under the table and kept exchanging the looks and glances that only people who are truly in love do. That couple are still happily together.

Autos again, and onwards

In 1994 I joined GM for four years as the head of GM Asia, having been recommended to GM by Minister Lu Fuyuan. We competed hard with Ford to win what is now the Shanghai GM project. Success has many mothers. Today many people like to claim credit for GM's success, but in reality it was a comprehensive team effort initiated by a special guy, Rick Swando. Rick started the whole thing and managed to gather the resources it would take to win the deal. Others came in later. My role in that project was to oversee a great team who did the market research, market planning, forecasting, marketing and distribution set-up. I also did my bit on the government relations side.

I left GM in 1998 and moved on again. Since then I've done many new things as a consultant and through partnerships with various friends. Through a number of crises and work-outs, some cross-border M&As and strategic projects, I've now started to jump onto the new wave of outgoing Chinese investment. Through work with the Conference Board I've been involved in helping to set up some cooperative economic research projects and have developed an intense interest in development economics and institutional economics, and in culture and institutional evolution.

Over the years, I've been lucky to meet quite a number of Long Marchers and many other figures who were walking history books about the battles and campaigns they'd been involved in. Their stories belonged to the early days of the Jiangxi Soviet, and continued through the Long March, the Yan'an base in Shaanxi and the anti-Japanese war from 1935–45, followed by the civil war up until 1949. Some fought in the Korean War, and some actually fought against one American general who came over as an advisor to Bell Helicopter. They bore no animosity to fellow soldiers.

These old veterans had experienced decades of war and had lived and fought through all kinds of hardships. They couldn't have known what the future would hold, but they fought for their ideals. Many experienced political ups and downs, which they took in their stride and never complained about. Their homes were usually simple: they would choose to live frugally, with just a few possessions, diaries and photos. Their values were different from those of their children's generation, which grew up in wealthier times. A trait they all seemed to share was universal optimism. As in other countries, there are now fewer and fewer old soldiers, and living memories are gradually being replaced by recorded memories. They are never the same.

> *These old veterans had experienced decades of war and had lived and fought through all kinds of hardships. They couldn't have known what the future would hold, but they fought for their ideals*

One close friend I lost recently was Wang Dayong. He died in 2007 and I really felt it badly, as I'd been with him the evening before he had a stroke while swimming. He never woke again. Dayong was a central banker and a macroeconomist. During the Cultural Revolution he been sent to the northwest of China and had resigned himself to settling into a new life as a farmer. He was that kind of person: he'd make the best out of whatever he did. He was prepared to stay there until university entrance exams were reinstated in 1977. Self-taught, he sailed through entrance exams and got into university, excelled there and gained his PhD in economics.

He soon became the top macroeconomic forecaster at China's central bank, and was well known for his interest and enthusiasm in anything and everything. In 1998 he transferred to China Development Bank with Governor Chen Yuan, and became involved in several firsts in China's banking sector. These included the first bank acquisition, when CDB bought the China Investment Bank, which had been set up in the early 1980s to handle World Bank loans.

Through Dayong, I was to meet many of the economists and thinkers who had brought China through its economic problems as it tested its reforms. Talking to

Unexpected opportunities

Li Lanqing, a former Vice Premier of the State Council, was another distinguished visitor to GM Asia

them made you realise how clever they were, and how they were constantly treading new ground when they could not know the outcome of the many things they were experimenting with. I remember many happy dinners discussing reforms, development and the growing international imbalances. I miss not being able to call Dayong to try to understand the economic ripples spreading around the world. He was well known among central bankers and economists everywhere, and they all miss him. He was another person in China who touched me deeply.

Proliferating expats and returning Chinese

Expats attracted to Beijing or Shanghai these days have it easy. Almost everything we had to fight for, they take for granted. Some executives posted here for a few years like to cover their walls with pictures of themselves shaking hands with the few ministers and perhaps central leaders they might have met once. Hardly any of them have ever been to those people's homes or met their families. Maybe they will one day, if they're lucky.

A new generation of China experts faces much more complex issues. It's impossible now to know everything about this country. Even in a single sector, such as finance, the changes and reforms happen on a weekly basis. If you blink, you're out of date. There are many competitive advantages to be gained by understanding the limits of what can be done and what cannot, and that is changing faster than ever before.

The youngsters the same age as I was in 1978 who come here now wander around freely and have fun in all kinds of places that didn't exist before. Beijing and Shanghai are

Ian J. Stones

becoming cosmopolitan cities, and a few other cities are on the way too. But actually China is a huge continental country, and can be looked at as a melting-pot of many different cultures and environments. When you spend time in the interior, in small cities and towns far off the beaten track, you can still find China's old variety. There are few traces of the China I came to in the late 1970s and the 1980s, but there's still plenty of culture, history and variety to experience.

China has always had its fair share of foreigners who are 'instant China experts'. I used to be one myself. Over time we are forced to become more modest. We learn new things every day, and the more we learn, the more we seem we need to learn. On the whole, more people are getting to know the country more deeply, and more are partnering and intermarrying. I feel sorry, though, for the many foreigners who come here for a few years, live in expat enclaves and leave without being touched by the richness of the country. Personally I feel very lucky, because when I travel from one end of Beijing to the other, I can look at every building and remember stories from all of them. My map of the city is full of memories of people and their lives.

The biggest changes have not been in the buildings, bridges, roads or cars, but in the ways that people think and relate. With greater wealth, values change. Rural people are becoming urbanites, and want fun

Any person who goes to live in a foreign culture experiences four phases of perceptual affinity or repulsion. Usually the first phase is positive, but over time most people go through a phase of strong negativity towards the new culture. Then it levels out and begins to rise back up again. This is where people differ the most in their responses. Some become more positive, some are neutral and some negative. I'm clearly on the positive side but, believe it or not, I know a couple of people who've been here almost as long as I have and they hate the place. They still choose to live here, but complain all the time. Compared with them, I've really been much luckier.

Evolving times

Looking back over the past 30 years, there's nothing that hasn't changed. China is like a continuously expanding ecosphere, growing in all directions at the same time and becoming more and more complex, as each of thousands or millions of entities evolves or co-merges or differentiates into more 'adjacent possibilities'. The more products and services that exist and interact in an economy, the more possibilities there are for new combinations and new businesses to grow.

In 30 years, China has come from having over 80 per cent of its population living below the World Bank's poverty line, and having just a few million dollars of foreign exchange reserves in 1978, to having lifted 700 million people out of poverty. With the biggest forex reserves in the world and a huge sovereign wealth fund, it is now the biggest source of capital globally and is poised to see more of its companies become global players very quickly. It has seen the greatest privatisation in human history.

Unexpected opportunities

The biggest changes have not been in the buildings, bridges, roads or cars, but in the ways that people think and relate. With greater wealth, values change. Rural people are becoming urbanites, and want fun and want to travel more. More foreigners and their Chinese friends can interact comfortably as friends, partners and equals, without suffering many of the old prejudices. We no longer need to disguise ourselves when we visit friends' homes. We can live among the Chinese as neighbours, and the neighbourhood police are friendly and helpful. In the context of institutional economics, the hassles and battles we used to face reflected high transaction costs and an inefficient business environment. China's institutions and culture are changing and, although many things might still irritate us, it is getting more efficient all the time.

In terms of longevity, a few foreigners came even earlier than I did. Some put down roots during the years of turmoil and can tell many stories of times that I never experienced first-hand. However, my 30 years pale in comparison with one man, a Manchu who had a much longer and much more unique perspective than I ever could. In 2003, through Juan van Wassenhove, an investment banker who was living in a courtyard house, I had the fortune to meet and befriend the then 94-year-old Guobuluo Runqi.

He was the brother-in-law of the last emperor of China, Pu Yi. His sister was the Empress Guobulo Wan Rong and his own wife was Emperor Pu Yi's sister. This earned him the appellation 'Guo Jiu' or 'Imperial Uncle', more simply translated as 'Uncle of the

Sharing an evening with my wife Sami and the sadly missed Wang Dayong, a true friend

State', since the emperor was deemed to be the state. His stories spanned 90 years from the final years of the Qing dynasty, Yuan Shikai, the warlords, the Japanese occupation, Manchukuo, the puppet emperor in Changchun, the tragedy of his sister succumbing to heroin, the civil war, and his imprisonment by the KMT and later the Russians.

He pursued his studies of Chinese medicine in China and in Tokyo. He showed us pictures and told stories from memory of what was happening before and after various photographs of Pu Yi were taken, as well as many anecdotes from the Forbidden City, including the story of their first bicycle and the sounds it made as they rode it through the courtyards and between the buildings. He'd had a turbulent life, which offered a unique perspective of a changing China. Like the old generals, he harboured no bitterness or remorse and seemed content, even though his eyes had seen many more changes over almost a century than I or any other person I know had seen – three times more than my mere 30 years, in fact. In another 30 years, today's youngsters will write their own stories. It's difficult to imagine the history that they will write, but I bet it won't be as interesting. I certainly hope so!

The funniest memory of all

I saved this for last. In 1984, I was with two engineers from an electric logging company and another from a diamond drill-bit company. We'd travelled 15 hours by car to Zhanjiang, because the flight was cancelled and there was no way to know when the next one might be. We were tired and somewhat the worse for wear, especially having had a few beers too many on the road and having been woken up every time the driver swerved to miss an unlit water buffalo.

We finally got to the last major hurdle of the journey, the Zhanjiang ferry crossing. It was around noon and we were hoping to be able to start meetings at 2pm. Usually, there were three drive-on drive-off ferry boats rotating across the straits in both directions and we wouldn't need to wait more than 10–15 minutes. For some reason on this occasion, however, only one boat was working – maybe the other crews were having lunch. This meant that there was a build-up of trucks, tractors, bicycles and carts carrying everything from piglets in baskets to oilfield rope, soap and dope, all vying for position at the front of the queue. It was jam-packed, but still people were trying to squeeze forward.

When the boat arrived, no one on board could get off and no one on the bank could get on, which just made everyone push even more. With no one to conduct traffic, it was total gridlock

You sometimes see this happen on the subway or with busy elevators. When the boat arrived, no one on board could get off and no one on the bank could get on, which just made everyone push even more. With no one to conduct traffic, it was total gridlock. Our small group of white-faced foreigners started swearing and shouting. My anger built up and I started to get really mad at the stupidity of it all. We were so near but now we were going to be held up – and it looked like it could

Unexpected opportunities

be for quite a while. The boat pilot decided to reverse and to pull round to another ramp. But as soon as everyone saw which ramp he was aiming for, that filled up chock-a-block too.

By this time our swearing, ranting and gestures had drawn quite an amused crowd. Quietly, a farmer driving a 'mechanical donkey' (a small two-wheeled tractor) took the opportunity to try to edge past us. He was amused by our ape-like behaviour too. Suddenly… BLOOOP! He'd disappeared over the side of the jetty – tractor, cargo and all. It wasn't deep; he could stand up, but he was stunned and had cut his forehead a little, and his straw hat was floating next to him.

Suddenly our anger turned into hilarious laughter. Some of the crowd rushed to help him, while many more surrounded us for what must have seemed like a great show. The more we laughed, the more my sides hurt. I tried to squat down to stop myself laughing, but slipped and fell over backwards into the mud.

That wasn't the end of it. Within a few minutes a crane truck nearby had lifted the tractor and cart out and dropped it on the jetty. Someone shouted, 'Check the oil!'. The poor guy did, and water spewed out. I laughed so much and, even though I was wet and muddy, I couldn't stop. The crowd must have thought we were either very callous or totally nuts. We got to our meeting an hour late. I was a mess, but we were all in a great mood!

Still here after all these years... The movie poster is for a recent release fortuitously entitled *Crazy Stone*

Roberta Lipson
Co-founder, Chindex

First came to China: 1979

Roberta Lipson co-founded healthcare company Chindex in 1981 and was the creative force behind the Beijing United Family Hospital and the United Family Hospitals concept. She is an expert in many aspects of healthcare in China, and has been an active member of the Beijing business community for almost 30 years.

Healthcare ambassador

Roberta Lipson first came to China with vague notions of connecting with the Chinese people, but found her true calling when she visited a local hospital. Since then, she and her partners have built a pioneering and thriving business that has helped to raise the standard of medical services in China

I couldn't really have known it at the time, but it so happens that my journey to China began in a Chinese restaurant in Brooklyn, New York when I was five years old. The family, having just been to see the re-release of the classic movie The *Good Earth*, based on Pearl S. Buck's famous novel, sat at the table discussing what it might be like if it were possible to visit China. My elder sister Pauline challenged my participation in such an imaginary adventure because I had refused to even taste the bland white rice, which was the hallmark of such establishments. Perhaps the challenge was laid to me there and then. The dream and fantasies were a recurring companion during my childhood years and added colour to the rather culturally homogenous suburbs of New York City. When my horizons widened during my college years, I was constantly fascinated by and attracted to the contrasts and similarities between my second- and third-generation Chinese classmates and my own third-generation Jewish immigrant experience.

The dream evolved into wanting to learn more about, and then visit and then somehow make a contribution to, a civilisation whose past greatness I would come to learn about through my university studies, and whose future potential I came to believe in through my own observations. Somehow I had the romantic notion that I could contribute in some way to China's modern transformation. Today I write from the perspective of feeling that in some way the company that I built together with my co-founders, colleagues and partners has indeed had some impact on the direction of healthcare reform and the improved quality of healthcare that is now available in China.

My first glimpse of China was in 1975 when, during a stop in Hong Kong together with my China studies compatriots on our way to Taiwan, I peered with great curiosity over the forbidden border to Shenzhen. That was

Armed with an MBA, two years' work experience and great enthusiasm for what I thought I might accomplish as a self-appointed 'ambassador to the people of China', I arrived at Beijing airport

as close as an American student could get to mainland China then. My experience as a student in the booming atmosphere of Taiwan in the 1970s only served to further whet my appetite to explore deeper into the Middle Kingdom. So, armed with an MBA, two years of Stateside work experience with a multinational pharmaceutical corporation and great enthusiasm for what, as a 24-year-old self-importantly filled with the momentousness of the occasion, I thought I might accomplish as a self-appointed 'ambassador to the people of China', I arrived at Beijing airport in the late summer of 1979.

Beijing, normally arid for most of the year and in those days brown as a desert, can be relentlessly wet for most of August, and on the night I arrived a torrential storm was raging. The bare cement floor of the arrival hall at Capital Airport was already soaked as rain blew in through the hole that was also the entry point for our waterlogged luggage. The hall was packed with passengers and their greeters, with luggage being thrown through the opening in the wall from the tarmac and with customs officials and border guards all milling around in the same (what I remember to be approximately) 200 square metre international arrival hall, which served the whole airport. The whole place was shrouded in a thick haze from the sickly sweet-smelling local cigarettes that were smoked by almost everyone present.

My host met me in an ample Shanghai Roadster driven by a white-gloved driver, and as we cruised into town down the tree-lined, two-lane airport road, the rain let up. The mystery of the night and my surroundings was heightened by the juxtaposition of friendly-looking – but conspicuously armed – young PLA guards at every bridge and crossing. We hardly saw another car on the road the whole way into town.

Some time later, in January 1980, Capital Airport's new Terminal 1 was opened with much pomp and circumstance, and it was a huge improvement in modernity, size and style. And while much more efficient, it too soon became flooded with passengers outbound and inbound – those lucky enough to get passage through the doors of the newly opened country. These included curiosity-seekers on both sides: foreigners eager to see what was behind the bamboo curtain that had been shut for so long, and also the locals who were eager to play a role in the development of the country that was now clearly set on a new, but not completely known path, and who were lucky enough to get what were than very rare opportunities to study abroad or participate in shorter-term 'investigation' missions. They would be able to see what the world had become in the past thirty years and help to determine which of its new technologies and social models might be appropriate for adoption or importation.

Because there were very few flights between cities each week, missing a plane was a major problem, but the airport was sufficiently friendly that a call ahead could keep the gate open a few extra minutes

I have many fond memories of escorting delegations of Chinese officials the other way through Terminal 1 on their way to investigate healthcare models and new technologies and products in America. Often the conversation would start with their burning questions, such as 'Why are American inter-familial relations so cold?'; 'Why do Americans only eat cold food?'; 'Why are there so many poor people in America living on the streets?'; and on to 'Why don't American hospitals smell badly?', before moving on to more serious and technical questions.

Healthcare ambassador

In the early 1980s, I escorted numerous Chinese healthcare delegations on visits to the USA

On the trip back to China, the conversation would often revolve around the visitors' admiration for what they saw in the US, and in the case of the heath delivery system, why much of it could not possibly work in China. My own thoughts in those days, upon landing back at Terminal 1 after short absences from China, each time revolved around the adrenaline-pumping excitement of leaving the completely familiar and coming back into a place which, while becoming more familiar, was still full of mystery and opportunity – for increased personal understanding of China and of the role I would ultimately be able to play in the exciting and unfolding story of development.

Despite the increasing number of foreigners visiting, and although we were often segregated from the average population, most foreign business people were treated with a great deal of respect and dignity. My frequent domestic travels took me through Terminal 1 often enough that I made many friends and in fact became somewhat well known to the ground personnel. Because there were very few flights between cities each week, missing a plane was a major problem, but the airport was sufficiently friendly that a call ahead could even keep the gate open a few extra minutes for those of us who were held up by meetings or negotiations that went over time.

By the late 1980s the door had opened wider to increased numbers of travellers. My role as leader of a company which by now employed scores of people in Beijing, many of whom were foreign citizens or transplants from other cities in China, was to make sure that all of our employees were safe in the midst of the chaos of the spring

Roberta Lipson

It has been a privilege to meet leaders such as President Jiang Zemin

of 1989 (which at that moment meant being sent back to their hometowns or countries). Our office was in the midst of the tumult in Beijing and, by day, we drove colleagues to the airport, where there were thousands of people vying for limited seats on flights out of the city. An intimate knowledge of the airport, and our many friends among the airport personnel, served us well.

Sadly, after that, yielding to long-distance parental urging, we took leave ourselves of by then what we considered a city that had returned to a calm and seemingly safe status, for what we hoped was a brief sojourn in Hong Kong. Nevertheless, from the time the door of the airplane closed behind us, we began to wonder whether China would return to its path of growth and development and the trend toward opening up to investment and trade, or whether the eight years we had by then invested in building a business would come to a sudden and sad closure.

The happy end of that story for us was a return to Beijing in less than two weeks. Although many lives and many social issues were profoundly changed by the events summer of June 1989, we were soon back to business and felt that our continued opportunity in helping to build healthcare capacity was not diminished by the other changes in society. The return to normalcy was slow and tentative. By mid-summer, I felt comfortable enough to insist that my parents make their long-planned visit to Beijing.

I experience a certain pride as a Chinese resident, and a bit of anxiety as an American, at the contrast between the grandness and efficiency of Terminal 3 in Beijing and the run-down terminals in my own hometown

By the time that Terminal 2 opened in 1999, Beijing – superficially, at least – was a far less exotic destination for Western visitors. Daily non-stop flights to several US cities made each trip less of an ordeal, and the improving conditions in urban China made daily life far more comfortable and far less of a hardship. It also meant that there was a

Healthcare ambassador

lot less distance between me and my Chinese friends and associates, many of whom now enjoyed good jobs or even ran businesses of their own, and enjoyed a far higher standard of living than previously.

This year, 2008, saw the opening of the world class Terminal 3. Although the days of the 'customised service' of holding planes for a few minutes at the gate for loyal passengers are long gone, I experience a certain pride as a Chinese resident, and a bit of anxiety as an American, at the contrast between the grandness and efficiency of Terminal 3 in Beijing and the tired, run-down terminals in my own hometown.

Transportation

In the early days of my stay in China, one could travel for many city blocks at the height of 'rush hour' and not see another car. But oh, were there bicycles! Taxis, though, were hard to come by. One had to call in advance and state one's nationality, which seemed to determine priority rankings in accordance with the political policy of the moment. Sometimes we had to wait long hours for a car to be despatched.

When we founded our company on a shoestring in 1981, we were thrilled to learn that a container of motorcycles had been imported from Japan and that they were available for sale to the first-comers with hard currency. After that, there were no more endless waits for taxis, but rather the opportunity to be waylaid on many street corners by friendly and curious traffic cops.

Over the next few years, increasing traffic made it more dangerous for motorcycle riding, and the fortunes of our company and the increasing trade allowed us to purchase an imported Toyota Crown sedan. The car had to be paid for in cash, at the small hotel room representative office of Toyota in Beijing. The landing charges, customs duties and fees had to be paid in cash at the port. Arriving in Tianjin port with thousands of dollars in small FEC notes made the transaction feel like one of grand international intrigue.

Today we are faced with a

With a visiting delegation to Boston, 1980

My Thirty Years in China | 215

different challenge: an over-proliferation of cars and clogged roads, and the attendant pollution. Although the new Chinese dream of an individually-owned house and car is being realised by more and more middle-class Chinese, increasingly the government, together with society, is starting to take deep note of the downside of the new private car society.

Communications

Likewise the communications systems when I arrived in China were very manual and of limited capacity and efficiency. Long-distance business was generally accomplished through clumsy old mechanical telex machines or cables (telegrams), which had to be sent through the post office. Some foreign offices by 1980 were fortunate enough to get a telex machine in their own facility, but with our start-up budget and fledgling status, we had to use the public Post and Telecommunications office.

Each morning and night, one of us would ride the motorcycle to the P and T office to cut the punch tape which carried all of the information that linked us to our overseas office, suppliers and business partners in the United States and Europe. Most of the machines were mechanical ones, with keys that travelled a good two inches before punching their intended holes. After a good work-out for our fingers, we deftly coiled the paper tapes that had accumulated in piles on the floor. The 'new kids' stood out for not having yet mastered the graceful coiling technique for the tapes, which seemed miles long and could be quite unruly to handle.

Then we had to wait (sometimes up to two hours) until it was our turn to get one of the very few lines to the States and send and receive the messages that were punched onto the long, uncoiling paper tapes. If one used the waiting time wisely, it would be to make friends with the telex operators behind the counter. This would not only ensure a much more enjoyable time, and an opportunity to practise Chinese while getting to know some genuinely nice people, but also that one's wait would be shorter in the future, because of the relationships that had developed. This was a lesson that stood me in good stead for future business practice.

Each morning and night, one of us would ride the motorcycle to the P and T office to cut the punch tape which carried all of the information that linked us to our overseas office, suppliers and business partners

Contact with my family back home was through a weekly Sunday phone call. This too had to be booked in advance through the long-distance operator. I had a standing Sunday morning call and it would be the same operator on duty each week who patched together the line. After my ten-minute talk with my family, the operator began to come on the line for her own chat, which often included commentary on my family news.

There was certainly a feeling that our communications were not private, but at the same time it did not bother us too much. We did have silly and naïve code words for

Healthcare ambassador

certain situations. For example, Taiwan was never mentioned, as we did not want to insult or be misunderstood by our hosts. So we always called it Bermuda instead. But even with that, the lack of privacy was pretty much accepted by those of us who were happy to work in this environment – perhaps because we believed in our good intentions and had nothing to hide.

Celebrating my wedding in March 1991 to journalist Ted Plafker

By the mid-1980s communications were getting better and one could even make automatic self-dial long-distance calls – at least to certain cities domestically. By the late 1980s we had a shoebox-sized car phone. By the 1990s we were already leapfrogging American telecommunications technology, and our cell phone service was a great source of convenience and pride. In fact, return trips to visit the States often generated frustration because we didn't have the same convenience of cell phone reach or connectivity that had long since become routine even in the most far-off parts of China. Not only does my cell phone work everywhere, but for years I have been online with my GPS card-equipped laptop computer in every corner of rural and urban China – a convenience that has only recently started to become available in the USA.

A hotel room is not a home

My first residence in Beijing was in a grand suite of the Beijing Hotel. I felt privileged to live in relative luxury, in a spacious room, with automatic window curtain controls that I could operate from the comfort of my own bed. Our rooms were cleaned, and laundry was picked up and delivered by friendly floor service personnel. These amiable lads knew every intimate fact of our lives, I suspect both out of friendship as well as because of their official duties. The relative luxury was tempered by the lack of privacy and by the somewhat depressing lack of wattage in the lighting. The whole time we were in the Beijing Hotel we never got to enjoy light from more than a 40-watt bulb. This could get somewhat depressing through the long, grey, coal-smoky winter.

However, it was great to be able to review the day's adventures and compare notes with our fellow foreign sojourners every night in the Beijing Hotel's bar, which for some reason was known as 'the Zoo'. The whole hotel had the social feel of a college dorm.

Roberta Lipson

With Ted and our three sons outside our *hutong* house in 1997

Many of us longed for the variety of food available in our college cafeterias, in contrast with the very slim pickings available in the hotel dining room. In fact, all winter there would only be one fruit or vegetable available at any given time, and the response to most picks on the long and varied menu would be *meiyou* ('We don't have it') when one tried to order.

By the early 1980s the variety of foods available, as well as the number of hotels open to foreigners, increased to at least four or five, and we were able to move to more economical hotel accommodation on the west side of town. After a few years of living in a hotel, though, I longed for the comforts of home. So when one of us trucked in a microwave oven, we transformed one of the hotel room office bathrooms into a kitchen. We even had a small cabinet built over the commode and bathtub to complete the kitchen-like authenticity. Although that touch of homelike atmosphere was helpful, after a few years we still really longed for a place we could call home.

As our business began to look viable, and it was clear that we would be staying in China for the long haul, a more normal living situation became a higher priority. So I began a letter-writing campaign to the government. I must admit I was somewhat surprised when I got a response from the secretary of the then Vice Premier Wan Li. He was sent to 'investigate' our living situation. The visit resulted in suggestions that landed us in a beautiful *hutong siheyuan* (courtyard house), which had space both for our office, whose staff had by then grown to almost 100 people, and a separate courtyard which was the real first home in Beijing for me and my business partner, Elyse Silverberg. After three months of renovations, the courtyard was 'traditional China on the outside and modern Western on the inside.'

We lived and worked happily in our traditional courtyard digs, and in fact were the envy of all who visited. In order to make it legal our landlord, the owner of our office/house, was made to go through a process of registering the property as a 'Hotel for Foreigners'. This was all made possible by the support of the Vice

Healthcare ambassador

Premier's office, which obviously saw our company's work and investment, though relatively small at the time, as sufficiently worthwhile to support.

We saw 11 happy years in our courtyard home, during which time I married and gave birth to three children. Our courtyard office grew to be the workplace of several hundred colleagues. We were finally forced to move out to make way for the high-rise development of our neighbourhood. We saw the character *chai*, meaning 'demolish', appear on our neighbours' houses one after another, and our landlord succumbed to the negotiated settlement in which he was given another prime property in downtown Beijing to develop. Our beautiful 100-year-old courtyard became the office for the property development company as, one by one, the neighbouring courtyards made way for skyscrapers. Unbelievably, our courtyard still stands today, an island on the edge of a sea of development. As the new steel and glass buildings edge closer, however, we

My sons were growing out of toddlerhood and I was glad to be able to provide them with a larger yard where they could run around. They had benefited greatly from the hutong. Their Chinese was definitely of the most Beijing local variety

We spent 11 very happy years in our courtyard office and family home in the Xiao Paifang *hutong*

know that the place we once called home will soon meet the fate of all the other original traditional structures for miles around.

On the positive side, the demolition of our neighbourhood cleared the way for our company to move into a more modern office building and gave us the ability to expand, without the space limitations of our courtyard perimeter. Although we missed lunches under our huge and ancient shade tree, it was time for our company to look to the future. And there was no longer time for such lunches anyway, and the tree was no longer ours. My sons were growing out of toddlerhood and I was glad to be able to provide them with a larger yard where they could run around. They had benefited greatly from the *hutong*. Their Chinese was definitely the most Beijing local, and they could squat and kibbutz games of Chinese chess and goh with the oldsters on the street corners. And so my husband and I found ourselves as home-owners, something that had only recently become possible for foreigners, in a semi-suburban gated community that looked strangely like the place where I grew up in Long Island!

With business partner Elyse Silverberg in 1989

Making healthcare healthier

The first time I set foot in a Chinese hospital I found my calling. My first visit to a major Beijing teaching hospital was an overwhelming experience. For me, it was not the thousands of bicycles that crowded the streets at rush hour, nor the bustling crowds at the Beijing train station that drove home the enormity of the task of modernising this country with such a huge mass of people, but rather the scene in the lobby of the hospital. I had never seen so many people crowded into such a space before, and on the wards there were beds not only in the rooms but lining the halls, and some beds were crowded with multiple patients. This was the best the country had to offer at the time. Yet I met incredibly talented and dedicated doctors who were working with only their wits and their hands, their stethoscopes and, in the most fortunate cases, a few very old X-ray machines, microscopes, EKG units and refrigerators. It was clear to me, coming from a recent career in the medical industry in the USA, that I could be of help in this situation.

So we founded our company, Chindex, with the mission of introducing appropriate technology to the medical sector, as well as a few other industry areas. Eventually the

Healthcare ambassador

company settled on the medical sector exclusively, but in those days there were such great needs in every sector, and so few companies from abroad engaged in meeting those needs, that we were happy to help where we could. How lucky we were to find a role that helped meet some of society's greatest needs and at the same time was a sound basis on which to build a business.

Together with my business partner, Elyse Silverberg (who has her own thirty-year story to tell), we founded Chindex in 1981. Using our life savings (which at the tender ages of 23 and 24 were pretty skimpy), we bought two typewriters, rented a hotel room in Beijing and a room in New York City, and began what sometimes felt more like a detective agency than a business. As we worked together with the Chinese foreign trade agencies (we were not allowed to have direct contact with our customers at the beginning), we had to decipher the purchase requisitions of the end users they represented, who were doctors in hospitals all over the country.

These doctors picked their shopping lists from the 'methods and materials' sections of research papers in journals, which were sometimes very old. The requisitions were handwritten with laboriously, sometimes inaccurately, copied English letters. Sometimes what they wanted was already obsolete, and so we had to figure out what modern product would best fill their needs. In the very early days, almost all of our business was done at the bi-annual Canton Trade Fair, a four-week event where business was done only with foreign trade officials. Our role was to help them find the products on the official requisitions, and then arrange for their importation.

Unfortunately we didn't get immediate cooperation from the US manufacturers, as they were often wary of getting involved in business with 'Red' China, suspicious of their prospective customers' ability to pay with anything but tea, and had reasonable enough concerns about how they would be able to support the products they sold. It was our job to convince these US companies that we could pay them 100 per cent upfront via letters of credit, and that we were building a company in China that could do the after-sales support.

Soon we hired a few engineers who we sent for training with the US manufacturers. Several far-sighted American companies became our business partners as we began to market and sell their products all over China. This became possible in the early 1980s as the government became slightly more open to direct (though still formal, government-controlled) contact between foreign

Celebrating the 20th anniversary of the company, 2001

suppliers and their customers.

One of the most memorable days of my career was spent as the sponsor of a medical conference. We had hand-carried five portable ultrasound machines and brought in some American experts to lecture and demonstrate the technology for an audience of 500 senior Chinese obstetricians. There were literally tears in their eyes as they saw for the first time, on the screen, in real time, moving foetuses and pathologies that they could only previously guess at through manual examination. After the lecture, most of the doctors would not leave, and for the next few days they brought their more difficult cases to be examined on the ultrasound machines. Hospital administrators vied to be the first ones to be able to buy the machines.

> *Our little company was staffed by scores of idealistic Chinese and young foreign people, each with an interest in and understanding of each others' culture, making us feel like we could be a model for world peace*

That day started my love affair with the business of bringing modern tools to the medical community of China. After that we took our show on the road, and I have amazing memories of travelling the country by train with my portable ultrasound machine, not only opening the eyes of doctors throughout the country to new possibilities, while furthering our business, but also making lasting friendships despite the barriers that were still very much in place.

When we made our first big sale (a nuclear medicine device for viewing the heart, costing several hundred thousand US dollars), we had the privilege of installing the equipment at the Air Force Central Hospital. Our visit on the first day of the installation had the pomp and circumstance of a state occasion. We were met at the door of the hospital by foreign affairs officers in full uniform and escorted through many corridors to a very large and impressive reception room which, in my memory, rivalled some I later visited in the Great Hall of the People. The general who was the president of the hospital sat at the front of the room on an overstuffed, anti-macassared armchair, and we sipped tea and talked in grandiose terms about China and 'the friendship of our two nations' and other ceremonial topics.

Of course this scene, which repeated itself hundreds of times in similar and other circumstances, made us feel VERY IMPORTANT. And in a way we were. Or at least it seemed that every encounter – be it with officialdom, or any Chinese person – was an opportunity to further our cause. Not only our cause of building our business, and improving the technological level of Chinese healthcare, but also making our small contribution to the positive development of the relationship between the US and China, theoretically making the world a better place. This may well seem laughable and naïve now, but in those days there were so few of us, and it seemed that every word we uttered had the potential to either advance or set back the 'cause' – and we all took it very seriously.

Our little company was staffed by scores of idealistic Chinese and young foreign people, each with an interest in and understanding of each others' culture, making us

Healthcare ambassador

feel like we could be a model for world peace. We were all on a mission and pulling in the same direction. This enthusiasm for our mission, although it now covers a much broader age spectrum of employees, continues today. And how could it not? Everything we do is intended in some way to improve how healthcare is done in China.

In 1985 I had an opportunity to experience the Chinese healthcare system from the inside, when I contracted type-A hepatitis. I was plucked from my hotel room by a doctor friend, who had noticed that my skin had begun to turn yellow. As the daughter of a high-level military officer, she dared to risk more personal contact than most locals would with foreigners at the time. When she called to check on me I was barely conscious, and she had me whisked off to the Officers' Ward of the Army's infectious diseases hospital.

At that time the hospital was still sparsely equipped technologically, but during the month for which I was restricted to the isolation ward, I learned how unbelievably caring the doctors and the nurses were. Although I knew I was getting special treatment – because I was a foreigner, because I was a trusted supplier to the Army's healthcare system, because I was brought in by the general's daughter and because I was in a special officers' ward – the concern that I was shown could not have been invented for me. Although the doctors of that time and even today are sometimes greatly lacking in tools and the hospital environments are less than ideal, there are many dedicated and devoted individuals who have soldiered through very difficult periods but have never lost their commitment to healing or their sense of caring.

In 1989, I was once again inside a Chinese hospital, but this time as a patient advocate

Being discharged from hospital after my bout of hepatitis in 1985. I received outstanding care while there

Roberta Lipson

The opening ceremony of the Beijing United Family Hospital in 1998

rather than as a patient, supplier or consultant. A good friend (a young official at a Chinese Foreign Trade Corporation) was pregnant. Due to the severe overcrowding of Chinese hospitals at the time, everyone needed all the help they could get to secure a bed in a top-rated hospital and, given our relationships, this was something I was able to help with at the obstetrics hospital in Beijing. However, because she lived far from the hospital and we lived close, she came to stay at our house as her due date approached. When her labour started in earnest, my fiancé and I drove her to the hospital. What then ensued was what I can only describe as a humiliating experience both for my friend and her husband.

It was 6pm when we arrived at the hospital and the dusty, smoky haze of a typical Beijing winter sunset gave way to the dim and dreary hallway of the hospital, already abandoned by the daytime workers and the hoards of clinic patients one would have seen just a few hours earlier. As my friend entered the intake exam room the nurses, who a minute earlier we could hear cheerily chatting with each other, became suddenly and completely absorbed in some piece of paper on their desks, and it took several knocks on the open door, a number of throat clearings and finally the surprise of me, a foreigner, tapping on a shoulder to get their attention. Despite the attention aroused by the unusual presence of a foreigner, the women clearly were perturbed to have been pulled away from their chat and, after begrudgingly asking about the contractions, which were then steady at five-minute intervals, sent us off and told us to come back when the contractions were three minutes apart.

After walking around the block with our mom-to-be for about an hour, the 'angel' of mercy who turned us away at the beginning reluctantly agreed to admit my friend, who at that time was so overwhelmed by the pain of labour, she could not walk very far without stopping to lean on a wall or on her husband until the contraction passed. Despite this state of affairs, she was asked to climb the stairs to the third-floor delivery rooms (the elevator being reserved for other uses) while carrying her own belongings, including her towel and washbowl, which she knew to bring from home. Neither I nor her husband was allowed to accompany her. We were dispatched to wait in a lightless corridor with about five or six other expectant young fathers.

Healthcare ambassador

During our wait, those who were not pacing the corridor and smoking endless cigarettes were sitting on the floor for lack of seating and smoking endless cigarettes, as they waited long hours with no word. I can only suppose that the nurses were so busy that they could not be bothered to come and deliver news to these anxious young men. At 3am I took matters into my own hands and ventured up to the delivery floor, where I was roundly criticised by the head nurse and sent back to wait until a collective news bulletin came at 6am, which included the information that our friend had delivered a healthy baby boy.

Two years later, I was to deliver my own child at the Boca Raton Community Hospital in Florida. The contrast between these two experiences convinced me to move forward with an idea that I had been toying with for a while. There was more that needed to be changed in China's hospitals than just the updating of the hardware and technology. There were serious issues of insufficient and misdirected investment, which I could not solve on a large scale, but there were also big improvements that could be made by upgrading the management, service model and the philosophy that surrounded the delivery of patient care.

As my friend entered the intake exam room the nurses, who a minute earlier we could hear cheerily chatting with each other, became suddenly and completely absorbed in some piece of paper on their desks

I could think of no better way to encourage change in this area than to model it, and at the same time provide a service to the growing international community who, like my small but growing family, still travelled out of China for any kind of serious healthcare need. When we developed a business plan for a clinic and hospital facility to serve the international community and whatever segment of the Chinese population may ever be able to pay for private premium services, it turned out to be not only a great opportunity to demonstrate a different approach to healthcare, but also a very solid business proposition, with the possibility of replication if it succeeded.

'It can't be done'

We started approaching various officials in the Ministry of Health with this idea in the early 1990s, but the suggestion of private, for-profit healthcare in a socialist country was one that was mostly dismissed as a non-sequitur and a non-starter. The concept, we were told, 'could not be'. We were either politely dismissed or summarily dismissed, until we met the foresighted leadership of the Academy of Medical Sciences, who helped us to make the case 'from the inside' to the highest levels of the Ministry of Health.

We explained that having such a facility was an opportunity to examine approaches to healthcare gleaned from abroad and to see how it played out right here on Chinese soil. Besides, we were only proposing a very small facility and at the time the officials took comfort that we would primarily be treating foreigners and, in fact, the existence of such

Roberta Lipson

In discussion with Wu Yi at the American Chamber of Commerce, 2007

a facility would prove a comfort to foreign tourists, investors and others considering travelling to Beijing or taking up temporary residence there.

We had been taking scores of delegations of Chinese public health officials and public hospital executives to the US each year to see for themselves some of the American palaces of modern healthcare. They would marvel at, among other things, the comfortable environment, the fact that there was no smell of either disinfectant or bodily fluids, and the level of consideration shown to individual patients, only to conclude that it could not be replicated on Chinese soil. Our hospital would prove that many of these elements of patient-centred medical care could, in fact, be delivered in China.

Once we had secured the agreement of the Ministry of Health, we had to conquer the hearts of the Beijing Health Bureau. That proved even more difficult, partly due to the relationship between the two regulating bodies. But it was necessary to have not only their blessing but their official stamp of approval (in addition to the other 180 stamps from various government agencies through the development process), as the final step to being given the licence to open the facility. We used the two years of design and construction to try to develop the concept at the bureau level, and finally the Commissioner agreed to a visit. He was clearly overwhelmed by what he saw. It far exceeded his expectations, and at the end of the visit he was totally won over. He said that our hospital was an opportunity to 'raise the bar' for the public hospitals in his jurisdiction, and has since become an avid supporter of our efforts.

Our little experiment in healthcare has grown to be a successful business, with facilities in four cities serving not only the expatriate population but a growing number of Chinese citizens who have acquired the financial wherewithal to improve their quality of life in many areas, including housing and education, and who now chose to buy better services in healthcare.

Going public

By 1994 we had enough confidence that the Chinese government would approve of our entry into healthcare services that we decided to raise money through the public markets in the USA. It was the very end of the IPO boom time of the 1990s and,

Healthcare ambassador

ironically, it seemed the fastest and easiest way to raise money. Perhaps it was too early in our company's history and caused too much dilution of ownership for me and my partners, but it was a fast way to get the funding we needed to build our first hospital. I and my fellow founders had ten years of maturation as a management team, and we felt ready to meet the challenge.

Very shortly after Elyse and I started out, our founding team had been completed by Larry Pemble, now our CFO, who was from the beginning our voice of financial discipline.

The IPO would allow us to take our company to the next stage of professionalism and development.

The suggestion was one that was mostly dismissed as a non-sequitur and a non-starter. The concept, we were told, 'could not be'. We were either politely dismissed or summarily dismissed

The vision of the future was all the more important as we were already providing the first private sector employment to more than 100 people (now the company has grown to 1,300). We had a vision that, in addition to providing a quality healthcare solution to tens or even hundreds of thousands of foreign residents of Beijing, we would eventually serve a larger market including Chinese citizens, by applying a formula that would allow our company to grow beyond our wildest dreams.

Over the years we have reflected on the wisdom of the decision to be a public company. Being public as such a small and 'exotic' company on the NASDAQ exchange was extremely – and increasingly – expensive. It took time and effort to comply with the reporting, audit and disclosure and eventually SOX requirements, but it also forced us to a new level of professionalism that might have taken much longer to develop if left to our own timetable.

We went public at a time in the USA when there was very little awareness or understanding about China and the potential for economic growth that it held. When we started the company, our big challenge was to convince suppliers

The Chindex management team: Elyse Silverberg, Larry Pemble and myself

Roberta Lipson

Receiving an award for corporate excellence from Colin Powell in 2002

that it was OK to sell equipment to China; now the challenge became to convince investors that it was not only OK but an excellent idea to invest money in companies that were dependent on China's future development.

In the long run, our NASDAQ listing made it possible for us to continue to raise money conveniently on public markets to pursue our ambitious plans for development. Since then we have built a company with a national footprint and two nationally recognised brands. Our Chindex Medical Products Distribution division operates a medical product and technology distribution organisation, one of the few with a true national reach. Our United Family Healthcare Services division has built, and operates, medical facilities including hospitals and clinics in four cities across China. The company is growing at a very healthy pace and we are excited about the prospects for the future.

Over these years we have had the opportunity to participate in many forums where we could share experience and best practices from abroad with the Chinese healthcare community, and also participate in a collaborative process with various Chinese ministries as they develop laws and policies related to healthcare. We have also been fortunate to be in a position to sometimes serve as a bridge between Chinese and US government departments.

Looking back, and looking forward

It has been an amazing thirty-year journey. I have had the privilege not only of watching one of the greatest economic, social and cultural transformations in the world, I have had the fulfillment of participating, together with my partners Larry Pemble and Elyse Silverberg, in the founding and building of what is now a substantial and vibrant company that has given employment and professional opportunities to thousands of individuals, has given solace and healing to millions of patients and has responsibly brought to China previously unknown medical technologies, products and service models.

It is a great source of pride for me and my Chindex colleagues to have had the opportunity to forge a corporate culture that models good business ethics, enlightened labour policies and social responsibility projects even before it was in vogue to talk about CSR.

Healthcare ambassador

I have had the great honour to sit with high officials and leaders of this country and, either directly or through my writing, share my humble opinions and recommendations on the direction of healthcare reform. Together with my husband, we are raising three children who, by virtue of their life experience, will be able to contribute to tomorrow's globalised world. I have participated in building a Jewish community in China, including its worship and educational institutions. I was instrumental, together with my mentor and company board chair Ken Nilsson and other wonderful volunteers, in building a foundation which has provided free medical care to more than a thousand orphans and needy children in China.

On the personal front, I have been able to connect with thousands of individuals with whom I was able not only to establish a trusting personal rapport but, in some cases, deep and lasting friendships. Also through those relationships, I was able to reverse some of the negative impressions of Americans and the general xenophobia that were the legacy of the anti-American propaganda that predated and to a certain extent survived the Cultural Revolution.

It was hurtful that early on there were people who could not imagine what a 'well-to-do' American would be doing in China if she were not pursuing some ulterior motive of pure greed, or worse. On the other hand, there were many more people who welcomed and appreciated our efforts. Looking back, I am proud of the time I have spent here, proud of my motives and proud of what we have been able to accomplish. And I am most proud of having made some little contribution to the great changes and improvements that have happened in this great and important country. Thirty years on, I feel like the journey is still in progress, with much more left to accomplish.

The company is growing and moving forward; plans for the future include a brand-new facility in Shanghai

Clinton Dines
President, BHP Billiton China

First came to China: 1979

Clinton Dines gained a degree in Asian Studies, focusing on Chinese Economics, from Griffith University in Brisbane, Australia and first came to China in 1979 on a postgraduate teaching programme. He has lived in the country ever since, and is now based in Shanghai with his wife and three children, the youngest of whom was adopted in China.

In his early career he worked for Jardine Matheson, the Santa Fe Transport Group and Asia Securities Venture Capital. For the past 19 years he has been the senior country executive in China for BHP and, since 2001, President of BHP Billiton China.

He was closely involved in one of the earliest joint ventures in China, in 1980, and has subsequently been involved in a wide range of initiatives and sectors across the country. He was instrumental in establishing the Australian Chamber of Commerce in China and is a founding governor of the Capital Club in Beijing and a committee member of the Shanghai Rugby Football Club.

A question of self-belief

When Clinton Dines arrived in China, he felt that his whole value system and world view were being challenged. However, he stayed on to witness first-hand China's dramatic transformation, and is now eager to see how the country adapts to a new identity as it begins to reassert itself as a major world economic power

The 20-year-old Queenslander who staggered across the railway bridge from Lowu into Shenzhen in February 1979, carrying two large suitcases and a newly acquired guitar, was really not at all ready for what awaited him in the closed, hostile, xenophobic but ultimately very human world that lurked mysteriously on the other side of the border. The reason for the staggering, apart from having too much luggage, was the fact that the idea of providing any infrastructural user-friendliness for incoming foreigners was then still a good decade or more in the future. There were no baggage trolleys, and once you crossed the big white line in the middle of the bridge, you weren't allowed to go back – so you had to lift and carry it all over in one go.

Upon arrival on the Shenzhen side, you and your luggage were very promptly separated by stern-faced customs officials while others, presumably immigration types, whisked you off into a series of small rooms where you and your documentation were scrutinised with an intensity and suspicion that made you feel guilty, even if you weren't. It took a couple of hours before we were all reunited with our luggage and escorted to our train. No explanations or apologies. Common courtesies were hard to find, instructions were brusque and peremptory. All designed, as one gradually discerned upon extended exposure to such behaviour, to establish the right kind of conditioned obedience to authority – to cow you into submission.

For a group of young Australians of that era, from one of the world's freest countries, where the state seldom imposed itself and then only with due and diligent respect for civil rights, let alone human ones, and who had embarked on a university-organised exchange programme to China with great anticipation and optimism, the experience of just getting across the border was somewhat subduing, and even slightly offensive. Dammit, we had rights... didn't we?

Within hours of arriving in China, after a long, slow train ride through hours of cultivated paddyfield countryside on our way up to Guangzhou (which even English-speaking Chinese still referred to as Canton at that time), we all rapidly fell into the rather unproductive but reassuring rhythm of resident or visiting foreigners complaining to each other about China and the Chinese. This happens naturally among the expatriated everywhere in the world, but the dominating chauvinism of China's culture, its seemingly unflappable preference for symbols over substance and the rather pointless Potemkin-style concealment of harsh reality, made China a venue with much to distress discomfited Westerners feeling the need for a bit of a grumble. This propensity of course continues unabated among foreigners, resident and otherwise, to this day, and is one of the factors that characterises and, in my view, impedes the development of decent dialogue between China and the West.

The Chinese, of course, are far from blameless in this eternal dance of mutual misperception. Then, they had to contend with a diabolical blend of the effects of extended isolation, the deliberate misguidance generated by the propaganda apparatus, a simple lack of factual information and a cultural predisposition that simultaneously imposed an absolute sense of superiority upon lingering doubts and demonstrable evidence of inferiority.

Lu Xun, the great Chinese writer, social commentator and satirist, once said something to the effect that the Chinese could only see themselves as being far superior to Westerners or far inferior, but never as equals. That's a clever observation. As their nation re-emerges as one of the world's great powers in the twenty-first century, the Chinese are going to have to get over this, or we will all have a problem. Luckily, there are a great many thoughtful and knowledgeable people in influential roles in Chinese society today who also see the need for China's relationship with the world to move to one of mutual respect. But there are bad habits, entrenched traditions and legacy dogma to be overcome on all sides.

First impressions

In these first days, as we slid down what in retrospect appears to be an inevitable slippery slide of antagonism with our Chinese hosts, our group was scattered to the various parts of China to which our programme took us. I and a classmate were shepherded out and packed off to the Teachers College in Nanjing. We all went into situations for which we were not well prepared and which challenged our world views and beliefs enormously. Of the twelve students who came to China on that programme in 1979, only three have subsequently had any further significant involvement with the country. Me aside, one came back to Beijing to do some months of postgrad study and another came back for two years in the 1980s to work with IBM. All the others left in varying degrees of dismay and have not, to my knowledge, been back. Why I stayed on is something that I contemplate regularly, mostly by virtue of people asking me 'How can you have stayed in China for nearly 30 years?'.

There are a great many thoughtful and knowledgeable people in influential roles in Chinese society today who see the need for China's relationship with the world to move to one of mutual respect

We arrived at Nanjing Teachers College and were immediately plunged into the sort of contrived adversarial political drama that I have since become used to in China and which our Chinese counterparts, fresh, and in many cases unreconstructed, from the Cultural Revolution, seemed to regard as normal process. We only found out much later, but as we arrived, not everyone at Nanjing Teachers College wanted to welcome us.

In 1979, after many years of political ostracism, English had again become the language to learn. The Foreign Languages Department at the College had something

A question of self-belief

An 'approved' concert at Nanjing Teachers College, 1979

like 90 teachers. Of those, the huge majority were quite old and taught Russian. China and Russia had officially stopped talking to each in 1960 and had fought border wars over territory, and Russia was still the cause of much trepidation in China – to the extent that the College, not alone among units in Nanjing, was still actively digging air-raid shelters when we turned up in 1979, because 'the Russians were coming'.

There were only about a dozen active English teachers, and most were no good. In a typically rigid Chinese approach to the situation, the best speakers of English, some of the older professors, had arrived at the level of seniority where they no longer had to actually interact with students in the classroom. The Foreign Languages Department had applied to be allocated some 'Foreign Expert' teachers of English from amongst the tiny numbers of teachers brought into China each year on exchange programmes, and who were carefully hoarded and controlled by the Foreign Experts Bureau in Beijing. The College leadership, the Nanjing Teachers College Revolutionary Committee, formed in 1966 – vigorous political animals with limited educational credentials, clinging tenaciously to their positions in the fading twilight of the Cultural Revolution and xenophobically anti-foreign to their bootstraps – dismissed the application out of hand.

The leaders of the Foreign Language Department, however, were not to be put off so easily. Prior to 'Liberation' (the Communist takeover in 1949), the Nanjing Teachers College had been Jinling Ladies University, a major national educational institution founded by American missionaries and supported by the Kuomintang government. Some of the leading lights, and the best English speakers, of the Foreign Languages Department were elegant older ladies who had been students at Jinling Ladies University pre-1949. And it so happened that the head of the Jiangsu Provincial Education Bureau was a former teacher at Jinling Ladies University.

The Revolutionary Committee was quietly bypassed, the Foreign Experts Bureau was discreetly approached, and two young, ignorant, untrained Australians whose

Clinton Dines

only qualification was a native-spoken, though broadly-accented command of the English language, were dispatched to Nanjing. In all honesty, I think the college got severely short-changed. But beggars cannot be choosers, and the Foreign Languages Department was there at Nanjing Railway Station to welcome us with open arms.

The Revolutionary Committee was notably absent from the Railway Station Reception Committee (not that we noticed), and we didn't get to meet any of them for several months, but they made their presence felt almost immediately. Our passports were taken from us 'in order to advise the relevant authorities of your arrival' and we didn't get them back for nearly four months, after a great deal of aggravated bargaining with bland, stonewalling officialdom. Also, within about 48 hours of arriving, the terms upon which we understood we would be living, working and studying at Nanjing Teachers College disintegrated before our perplexed eyes, to be replaced by a new set of arrangements which suited Chinese objectives admirably and ours not at all.

Thirty years later I would have a bit more to say about it than I did then, but we were young, in a strange place, inexperienced, unsure of our ground and trying hard, according to our backgrounds and values, to be polite and accommodating to our hosts. We were supposed to have been provided with Chinese classes – No. We were supposed to be in young teachers' accommodation with a Chinese room-mate – No. We were supposed to be entitled to save a portion of our stipend (all of Rmb260 per month) and exchange it into foreign currency when we left – No. We were supposed to teach 8–10 hours of English classes per week (which, considering that we were not qualified teachers, seemed not unreasonable) – No. They handed over a teaching schedule of 28 contact hours per week across three years of student programmes, plus programmes for young teachers. 'What are we gonna teach?', we cried. 'English' they said, looking at us hopefully.

Two young, ignorant, untrained Australians whose only qualification was a native-spoken, though broadly-accented, command of the English language, were dispatched to Nanjing

Of course, having just arrived and being young, completely out of our depth, overwhelmed, alienated and well bluffed, we didn't object. We accepted the situation, we knuckled down and we tried, as our values taught us, to be well-behaved guests for our hosts. We were true to the self-reliance and innovation of our new-nation, Anglo-Saxon creed: we shook off our initial dismay and puzzlement, we asked around, we made contacts and we went off and found some real English teachers, i.e. professional teachers of English as a foreign language, and prevailed upon them, surprised though they were to see us, to give us access to some of their teaching materials.

We scoured the very limited, but politically approved, English-language materials that were slowly resurfacing from under the floorboards (literally) in the Foreign Language Department, as the ideological shackles of the Cultural Revolution were gradually forced aside. Heavily edited old editions of Charles Dickens and Mark Twain were the pick of

A question of self-belief

The obligatory studio portrait with friends from the Teachers College, 1979

the bunch. The Marx and Engels were rather heavy going. We put our heads down and started work on writing full-blown, tertiary-level English language programmes so that we would have something to teach our not insubstantial bodies of students, whose genuine enthusiasm and naked hope for better things had been paraded in front of us as yet another lever on our good intentions. There were some great lessons here for us, in that the Chinese were so very pragmatic. Subliminally, we learned a a huge amount about China in those first few months in Nanjing, although I didn't really reflect on it much at the time.

One aspect of being abruptly dropped into such a challenging situation as a 20-year-old fresh from the peaceful, civil, caring, well-fed, liberal democratic backyard-BBQ-by-the-swimming-pool society that was Australia was the extent to which our reaction was initially intensely selfish. I recall how sorry we felt for ourselves, and how we translated that into hostility to the people nearest to us with whom we had regular contact: we bitched and moaned and hectored and lectured our Chinese hosts about the shortcomings of their country and society. We weren't even perceptive enough to realise that the people with whom we had regular interactions were the ones who were generally the most benevolently disposed to having us there, and who had taken substantial personal risks to get us there and to keep us there. I daresay that some of them often had second thoughts.

Every foreigner transposed into an alien environment has a period of adjustment, a period of dislocation and then a crisis of some description, varying from mild depression to full-blown nervous breakdown,

We didn't object. We accepted the situation, we knuckled down and we tried, as our values taught us, to be well-behaved guests for our hosts

depending on the individual and the circumstances. I still observe this phenomenon today with newly arriving expats, even in the relative comfort of Shanghai. About three or four months into the assignment, people have a patch during which they get a little depressed or a little weird. Most come out of it and either serve out their time with

Clinton Dines

gritted teeth or rebound and have a ball. It is a revealing and formative experience for most. As Mark Twain pointed out, 'Travel is fatal to prejudice, bigotry and narrow-mindedness' and, with few exceptions, everyone's adjustment crisis lays the ground for how they then proceed with the experience of living in another country.

I had a crisis, and it was very formative. I trace my interest and momentum for spending all of my adult life in China back to that moment in April 1979 when I came home from work, depressed and enervated from the effort of dealing for several months with the apparent and inexplicable hostility of the environment around me. I went wordlessly into my bedroom, closed and locked the door, sat on the edge of my bed and cried copious amounts of confused young man's tears of self-pity. Things got better for me from that moment on.

As I slowly shook myself out of my little cocoon of snivelling about how tough things were for me in Nanjing, I began, paradoxically, to have a heightened sensibility about how really tough things were for all of the Chinese around me. Two things began to stand out vividly in my perceptions: how fearful people were, and how hungry they were.

We joke these days about how all Chinese guys of that era wore their belts with the loose end finding its way through several additional loops all the way around to the small of the back. This may have indicated excessive optimism on the part of the wearer – or, more likely, a complete disregard for customisation on the part of Chinese belt manufacturers in a centrally micro-planned economy – but every Chinese person I knew at that time was lean and greyhound-gutted. There simply were no fat people. Even those one could describe as well-nourished were few and far between. Everyone was hungry. And this was in Nanjing, a major provincial centre, a former national capital, a city of some three million people in one of the wealthier and agriculturally fertile coastal regions along the lower reaches of the Yangtze River, Jiangsu.

While I'd been grizzling about the food, it hadn't fully registered with me to analyse the fact that we hadn't had any beef for several months, that the vegetables were limited, limp and monotonous, that milk products of any description were scarce (and usually putrid), that sugar was at a premium, that cooking oil was carefully hoarded. Such was the premium on the energy delivered by fat that, in the open wet markets with the flies buzzing around the few scrawny, unprotected animal carcasses, the little old ladies would argue vigorously with the butchers for bigger cuts of fat on their pork.

> *I locked the door, sat on the edge of my bed and cried copious amounts of confused young man's tears of self-pity. Things got better for me from that moment on*

There were no aerated soft drinks. Until the new Friendship Store (for foreigners only) opened, we couldn't find anywhere to get beer in a bottle. Finally finding bottled beer was cheering, until we remembered that we had no refrigeration to keep it cool. We did a deal with the only hotel in town that had a cold room

A question of self-belief

to house our beer. Some restaurants also served beer – in a large, open, room-temperature vat into which, having paid for your beer, you dipped your empty rice bowl, and most of your hand, through a layer of grease and oil floating on the surface. For a born Queenslander, raised with XXXX at the breast, describing this beverage as beer was a very generous and charitable gesture. But beggars could not be choosers in post-Cultural Revolution China in the 1970s.

In this era in China, everything was allocated by ration coupons, the ubiquitous *piao*. Even resident foreigners like us were brought into this system, although we were treated quite generously compared with the locals. We had *piao* for meat, for rice, for flour, for soap, for sugar, for cooking oil, for eggs, for cotton cloth, for cigarettes. We learned quickly that cigarettes were a very tradable commodity, and leveraged our privileged access to good brands – Chung Hua and Xiong Mao – via the Friendship Store into a discreet but workable mechanism for improving our food supplies. We had to arrange with other foreign friends to pick up tins of coffee for us when they visited Shanghai – the coffee itself was ghastly, but it was all we could get. There were very seldom any sweets, and chocolate was unheard of.

> *For a born Queenslander, raised with XXXX at the breast, describing this beverage as beer was a very generous and charitable gesture. But beggars could not be choosers*

At that time, Chinese people always greeted each other not with '*Ni hao?*' = 'How are you?' or 'Are you well?', but with '*Ni chi le ma?*' or '*Ni chi fan le ma?*' = 'Have you eaten?' For many years since, it has been clear in my mind that the Chinese obsession with food, most pronounced in the mainland but noticeable too amongst the diaspora, is a deeply ingrained experiential insecurity. To this day, the propensity to put on a huge repast when guests come to visit has as much to do with what is a genuine traditional Chinese urge to show hospitality as it has to do with the opportunism of being able to fill one's belly at the work unit's expense. The Chinese are not yet fully convinced that prosperity is here to stay, and with a significant proportion of the population yet to enjoy the solace and sense of comfort that come with a belly that is regularly full, should we blame them?

The other memorable feature of the situation that I observed more readily as I awoke from my self-centred sulking in Nanjing was just how pervasive Big Brother was. Essentially, everyone was afraid and edgy and mistrustful to a greater or lesser extent. Everyone was wary. No one, it seemed to me, trusted anyone very much, even members of their own families. Call it the State, the Party, the Work Unit, whatever –authority was deeply ingrained and embedded in all aspects of Chinese life.

I once observed two young students in one of my classes become attracted to each other and start to spend more time together. Unfortunately, I wasn't the only one who observed this and pretty soon their burgeoning affection was reported by the Class Monitor (read Party Commissar) and they were separated into different

Clinton Dines

classrooms, having been given stern lectures along the way. The young girl in particular was very distressed at what by any reasonable standard was an uncalled-for intervention in her life, but most of their classmates, hardened by many worse experiences in their earlier lives, simply shrugged, and those who were brave enough to comment to a foreigner like me suggested that the two youngsters should have been more careful to conceal their feelings.

> *That these people somehow felt they could trust me, of all people, was a responsibility that I wasn't ready for and which gave me some sleepless nights and shaped my behaviour thereafter*

The Work Unit (effectively the Party) controlled who you spent time with, where you could go (travel permits requiring a letter from your Work Unit were obligatory for even the most ordinary of domestic trips), which job you got, which house you were allocated and who you could marry. People these days bemoan the emergence of the cash corruption culture in contemporary China but, due to the pervasiveness of the State's decision-making control over everyone then, there existed infinite opportunities for those in authority to exact favour and indulgence from those whose lives they could ruin at a whim. The system was already inherently corrupt, even then; there just wasn't much cash involved. Cigarettes went a very long way in 1979.

Another interesting phenomenon that struck me after I had been in China for several months was the extreme, pent-up need that many people had to tell someone their story from the Cultural Revolution. These days, now that we've all had nearly 20 years of being bombarded by the publication of a virtual library-full of 'what-happened-to-me-in-the-Cultural-Revolution' books, we tend to take these stories for granted. There is also an aspect of the Great Proletarian Cultural Revolution fading into history as more recent events cloud the picture, including more recent major events in China. But at the time, and as a young Australian who had been educated with respect to China in the orthodoxy of Western academia in the 1970s, what I began to hear from some very brave people about their own tragedies in the decade or so before I arrived was something of a shock.

I later realised that it took people several months of observing and assessing me carefully to arrive at their decision to share their stories with a very young and plainly inexperienced foreigner. With hindsight I can see that this was a hugely risky proposition for them. But the bottom line was, they had something to say and they had not been able to tell anyone else. Over a period of several months, after I had been there for four or five months, several people found ways to approach me so that they could have enough time to broach their subject and tell me their story. Remember this was before I spoke Chinese reliably enough to comprehend anything as complex as a tale of human tragedy, so they all had to speak to me in English.

Paradoxically, even the officials of the College and of our Department would occasionally tell stories of the public demonstrations and orchestrated mass meetings on the campus in years gone by, and relate the episodes of brutality towards political

A question of self-belief

victims with a slightly sheepish and giggling embarrassment that clearly anticipated how we foreigners would view such admissions. But the personal stories, quietly and desperately told by people who had no one else to trust, were the ones that made an impression on me. Their stories were stunning and graphically informed my developing view of China, but the fact that their need to tell somebody had overridden their innate caution was a powerful object lesson for me, upon which I reflected in some puzzlement for many years. That these people somehow felt they could trust me, of all people, was a responsibility that I wasn't ready for and which, when thrust upon me, gave me some sleepless nights and shaped my behaviour thereafter.

This was also an era in which public display of affection was severely frowned upon, although Chinese society was, I discovered over time, remarkably licentious in many ways. Public morality was Victorian in its prudery. One never saw couples embrace, walk arms-around or even hold hands. The most you would sometimes see would be a woman holding the back of her husband's jacket sleeve as they walked along the street.

Only a couple of years later, my then girlfriend and I would entertain ourselves for an afternoon by walking up and down the Bund in Shanghai overlooking the river and changing the way we held hands or walked arms-around or arms across shoulders, as a gaggle of Chinese couples walked behind us copying what we were doing. They knew that the changes in their society now allowed them to publicly embrace each other but, unlike their parents, they had no memory or popular culture reference points to guide them as to how to do it. A pair of strolling foreigners was a ready enough benchmark for how couples behaved in the outside world. A small signal that change was beginning to take place was being permitted and, in the wake of Lu Xun, would reflect the traditional Chinese curiosity for what was happening abroad.

A new era

How do these memories inform a view of China thirty years later? What have I seen in the interim and why stick around to see it? I was amazingly lucky to arrive in China when I did, quality of life and deliberate ostracism aside. We were at the very beginning of the transformation that has made China a world-changing economic and geopolitical behemoth, which is challenging the established post-World War Two world order and causing all sorts of anxieties around our planet, in societies and government policy circles.

Many welcome the rise of China as a developing nation counterweight to the influence and style of the OECD, US-Western European model of global governance. But many in the developed world see a genuine threat emerging. Nobody quite knows what China's ultimate role or impact will be, but we all now have a sense that there is a fairly fundamental tectonic shift taking place, which emanates from China's recovery as a true major power.

Remember that China was the pre-eminent global power for hundreds of years – technologically and economically – until the decline that began sometime in the mid-Qing dynasty, around the late eighteenth century. The Chinese don't see their recent developmental surge as that of a developing country achieving high rates of

Clinton Dines

growth; they view it as a resumption of their rightful place in the world order, the re-establishment of the natural order of things.

At the beginning, it was hard for those of us who were immersed in China to be all that optimistic. The stifling control of the Party apparatus; the appalling ignorance born of isolation and lack of information; the creaking, out-of-date infrastructure and industrial structure. Nothing augured well or disclosed much potential for rapid transformation. So how did China go from then to now in just a generation or so?

A very tough and resilient little man named Deng Xiaoping was the visionary and architect behind what has happened, and is now of course revered by every Chinese person in

> *The Chinese don't see their recent developmental surge as that of a developing country achieving high rates of growth; they view it as a resumption of their rightful place in the world order*

a manner that is genuine, admiring and affectionate. Deng's model was simple. In the late 1970s he pointed out to the political elite and to the Chinese people at large that what had been happening up until that point had not worked very well. He understood that the previous 20-plus years had been traumatic for China, and that the previous 150-plus years hadn't been much better. They were all beaten down, fatigued, traumatised, scarred, enervated and afraid to even twitch. He understood, he had been there himself.

I played in an R&B band in Beijing in the early 1990s; we played two gigs at the Summer Palace

The political elite were good at keeping themselves in power and exercising control, but could deliver little else of any productive value. Deng knew that there was already a strong social and political consensus around the need for change – and he articulated it. Having pointed out that what had gone before had not worked, and having come up with some creative rhetorical devices that allowed Mao's thinking on economic management to be respectfully discarded, Deng then suggested some simple and commonsense reforms.

Rural communes went away and farmers were able to sell some of their produce on their own account at market prices. The doors were cracked opened to foreign investment. Factories were encouraged to upgrade their equipment. It all took a little while to build up a head of steam, with

A question of self-belief

agriculture and early industrial upgrading through the 1980s, genuine acceleration of market reforms, trade, investment, infrastructure development and industrial restructuring in the 1990s, and then a real take-off as the urban population became more affluent, financial reform gained traction and the economy achieved some virtuous balance and self-reinforcing growth momentum after 2000.

The changes have been phenomenal. I was able to go and see one of the very first 'free markets' in Nanjing in 1979. To give you some idea of how significant this was, many Chinese of my acquaintance whispered furtively about the impending advent of a 'free market' for weeks before it happened. It occurred to me that many of them, especially the younger ones, had absolutely no idea what a free market was.

When it finally happened, it was all a bit underwhelming. One day we went over to the street, a few blocks from the Teachers College, where the new free market was permitted to take place. On the first day the street was flooded with gawking locals, all

BHP Billiton is an Olympic sponsor and medal supplier; I was on the panel that chose the designs

keen to observe this new phenomenon in action. They cannot have been impressed. There were perhaps a dozen farmers (known as 'peasants' in the approved dialectic of the time) who had been persuaded to bring some product to town in order to kick things off. Each had a couple of items laid out on the wet, muddy pavement in front of them. There were no stalls or other particular infrastructure to indicate that this was a venue or event of any real significance. One suspects that local officialdom was standing back, careful to be aligned with the latest edict but unsure of the political sustainability of the concept and cautious by experience.

I saw a few eggs, some limp vegetables, a couple of chickens, a few items of clothing. The main comments from bystanders that day reflected outrage at the prices being demanded. Some of the shrewder heads remarked on the fact that *piao* were unnecessary in such a context. I honestly didn't know what to make of it, but I certainly didn't realise that it was one of the acorns from which China's current incredible economic transformation would grow.

Which goes to the heart of why I chose to stay on…. China has undergone a transformation in the past thirty years that surprises even the Chinese themselves in its scope, scale and impact. From a hugely disadvantaged standing start, hundreds of millions

Clinton Dines

of people have been lifted out of abject poverty. Many tens of millions have achieved substantive affluence. The economy has a prodigious mass and a self-sustaining growth momentum. Social change has been staggering and profound. Most Chinese people now have food and plenty of it, and China is a net exporter of food. The discussion nowadays is about the price of food, rather than its actual availability.

The youth of China now carry mobile phones (nearly 500 million of them), they SMS each other, they surf the internet (which is slightly curtailed, but by no means smothered by government restrictions), they wear whatever they like, go wherever they like and spend time with whoever they like. China will soon rival the US in terms of annual sales of private cars. Private ownership of homes and apartments has exploded since mortgages became available in the late 1990s. Chinese people can now get passports and travel overseas on vacation – and they do, in droves. There are more television stations to choose from than any one viewer could wish to watch. Most major cities and housing developments have cable TV. Print media provide a raucous plethora of newspaper and magazine choices and, as long as they don't try to challenge the Communist Party head-on, they get to write about a lot of the things that need to be discussed: social justice, the environment, education, corruption, the economy among them.

The Chinese economy is now the third largest in the world and is the critical trading partner globally for just about everyone. China's impact on us all is notable, and it has only just begun

The Chinese economy is now the third largest in the world and is the critical trading partner globally for just about everyone, whether you are buying or selling. China's impact on us all – every country, company and most of us as individuals – is notable, and it has only just begun.

I've been privileged to have ridden along as change of this order of magnitude has swept over nearly a quarter of humanity. The longer I stayed, the more I became convinced that I was witnessing history. Until the late 1990s, the extent or potential of China's metamorphosis was perhaps not very visible to the rest of the world. I see the first 20 years of the reform period as being a preparatory process of restructuring and foundation building, with a few mis-steps and bumps along the way, as the government and the people relearned the ropes of how a market economy and fully functioning society works.

Since about 2002, China has zoomed into the world's view with some suddenness, the roots of her apparently instantaneous advent misunderstood in many quarters and causing some anxiety in Western-world hearts and minds. These tensions are going to be a fact of life in global geo-economic and geopolitical terms from now on. The Chinese have come a long way since I first observed their baby steps towards something better back in the late 1970s, and they are not where they are today by accident. In terms of destiny, the Chinese feel that there is a historical inevitability to their country's resumption of global stature. They also feel that they have worked

A question of self-belief

hard, have suffered great privation and endured, persisted and prevailed against the odds, and have achieved a great deal in the past thirty years. The Chinese, at all levels of society, not just in the government or the Party, feel strongly that they are deserving of China's current new strength and stature, are deserving of some rewards and recognition, and possibly even of a little respect too.

Seeing these notions expressed by Chinese friends, colleagues and acquaintances, I find myself struggling to bridge or even discuss the bifurcation of sentiment that has recently characterised China's dialogue with the West. There is a great deal that both sides do not understand about each other's point of view. Both are right, and both are wrong. There is conviction and a sense of righteous indignation in views expressed by the West about China. On the Chinese side, there is a pervasive feeling that the major global powers are seeking to constrain China and curtail her right to develop and resume some of her long-lost pride and stature.

The West needs to accept that China is a fact of life and accord some recognition of her recent achievements. The Chinese need to come to terms with the responsibilities of great power and stature, and confirm to themselves what they have achieved to date. A confident nation is a responsible and benevolent nation. China is still struggling with the conundrum of inferiority and superiority that Lu Xun observed so acutely. Feeling equal is a matter of confidence: and China's next big developmental shift will be a cultural evolution towards the self-belief that underpins the great nations. And I will still be here, a privileged observer of a great human story.

With my son Seamus (right) and nephew Bernat at Wolong Panda Reserve in Sichuan province, 2006. BHP Billiton sponsors panda research in China

Caroline Chen Gaillard
Director, International Montessori School of Beijing

Came to China in: 1980

Educated in London, Caroline Chen Gaillard is the founder and director of the International Montessori School of Beijing (MSB), which she established in 1990. She is recognised in teaching circles in China for her expertise in early childhood education and for her work in introducing and promoting the Montessori teaching method. She has lectured frequently to early education groups in China, and was a speaker at the first Sino-US Early Childhood Education Conference. She has also written many articles on early childhood education and Montessori teaching methods for Chinese educational journals.

E-mail: carolineejhchen@msn.com
MSB website: www.msb.edu.cn

Lifelong education

Caroline Chen Gaillard came to China more or less by accident, but has ended up staying for nearly three decades. Beijing in the 1980s was a very different place from today's metropolis but, despite all the changes, she feels she still has much to learn from the city

Considering the fact that I have spent nearly three decades in Beijing, it would be fair to assume that my coming here in 1980 was a conscious decision and part of a well thought-out life plan. Actually, this is far, far from the truth.

Despite being British by birth and by school upbringing, the household in which I grew up was a distinctly traditional Chinese one – albeit one with a deep appreciation for the traditional British virtues shared by old China herself, namely honour, scholarship, industry, humility, self-discipline and compassion. My father's family were Shanghai textile tycoons who since the 1940s had sent their sons and grandsons abroad to study and, they hoped, to prosper.

Having no sons but only daughters, my parents were very strict and had no intention of letting us go off the proverbial rails. I had no idea of what I wanted to do when I graduated in History from the London School of Economics (LSE) in 1980, and really I ended up coming out to Beijing rather by accident.

On entering my final year at the LSE, and with all my friends and classmates pretty much intent on furthering their studies in economics, politics or law, I was at a loss for a plan that would gain the approval of my father. I had met a delegation of his professional contacts from Beijing in the mid-1970s and had gone rowing with them on the lake at Versailles, amid much jovial banter and merriment, and I recalled their rather throwaway suggestion that I come and visit my motherland upon graduating. Though I had no particularly great interest in going to the motherland in question, it was an answer to the eternal question that everyone seemed to ask of me. What was I going to do with myself, with my life? Answer: go off to China. In 1979/80 this silenced the questions. I didn't think any further than that. That was all the planning I had when I came to China nearly 30 years ago.

> *What was I going to do with my life? Answer: go to China. This silenced the questions; I didn't think any further than that*

The truth is that I would much rather have taken off to somewhere like France, but without having any well thought-out rationale for such a venture or having done any legwork or research, I knew better than to even think about bringing up such an idea with my father. Ironically, 30 years later, I am now married to a wonderful Frenchman – here the Brit in me has to interject and say, yes, hard as that might be to believe, they do exist! – and have a base in the heart of Dordogne-shire. Who knows, if the plane had dropped me off in Bordeaux-Merignac then, instead of Beijing Shoudu Jichang, my French might be a good deal better than it is today.

At least I might have been spared the years of being on the receiving end of mirth, derision, disbelief, condescension and even contempt for my heavily British-accented

Caroline Chen Gaillard

Mandarin. The heavens in their wisdom decided not to endow me with many talents, and speaking Mandarin was one of them. My sisters and I grew up speaking only English at home and at school. My father had learned good English in his schooldays in Shanghai, so when my eldest sister's teacher had encouraged my parents to use only English in the home, it was not an issue and was immediately accepted. This was England in the 1950s, and multiculturalism and global citizenship were unheard of in those days.

I have often lamented that point over the years and thought about the unknown schoolteacher who unwittingly put such a major obstacle in my path, for if I had learned Shanghainese at home, the path that I have followed for these nearly 30 years would have been so different, so much easier. Gosh, but would I have a mouthful of things to say to her…. Even more so now, knowing that my hearing would fail me at a relatively young age, requiring hearing aids in both ears, and that catching the right tones would be secondary to hearing them in the first place – how wonderful it would have been if this had all just come naturally to me. I would love to be able to rewind the tape back to that episode in the 1950s. But such are the quirks of fate.

Coal heaps and cabbages

Rewinding my mind's memories to the young students we were in 1980 floods my senses with vivid smells and sensations that are carved into my soul, probably forever. The crackling tannoy systems, admonishing us from what seemed like the crack of dawn when they called us to the early morning *caochang* calisthenics, followed us everywhere during our waking hours. Even when venturing out to the dusty, ramshackle local shops at Wudaokou, propaganda and stirring Communist music blared out at us. We soon learned when travelling by train around China in hard sleeper, the relatively luxurious standard of the day, that the top bunk of three was not the one to choose. Why? Simply because it was next to the train's loudspeaker tannoy system and the early morning, ear-piercing wake-up call at the start of the day.

The heavy pillows of buckwheat, the squat loos with their half-exposed stable doors, the smell of the drains – mind you, that smell is a feature that has remained, unfortunately, over all of the past three decades and is something that I would never miss, given the chance. The thick, shapeless, unisex denim overcoats, the vast seas of bicycles and their owners in endless shades of army green and blue on the donkey-laden roads of Haidian. The ubiquitous face masks of winter. Our black padded corduroy shoes which, when we bought them, like all items of the day from the little stores, came wrapped in paper and string.

The crackling tannoy systems admonished us from what seemed like the crack of dawn and followed us everywhere during our waking hours

Coal heaps and neatly stacked mountains of cabbages evoke in me an instant return to those days and the signs of the seasons. We may have had coal pollution in the air in winter, but we had the biggest and clearest blue skies, which present-day

Lifelong education

expatriates can only dream of. The seasons were so distinct that we could plan our diaries by them. People could confidently arrange picnics well in advance in the months of May, late September and October, knowing that there would be blue skies and a lovely day to be enjoyed. Mosquitoes were around for only a very short period, unlike in Beijing today, where we can be found with our aerosol sprays of OFF even in November.

With mobile phones being such a major part of our lives today, one wonders how we managed to socialise in those early days, but we did. And we had some really glorious times. We were privileged. Who could imagine anything more exciting than setting off by bicycle to the Old Summer Palace late on a balmy night, to find a comfortable patch of grass, gaze at the stars and discuss the burning issues of the day with students from any number of different countries and backgrounds? The sense of history, the here and now of it all. It might sound overly romantic or possibly even embellished by the passing of the years, but emphatically it is not.

We knew we shouldn't be sneaking into the Friendship Hotel outdoor swimming pool at midnight, nor going onto the ice at the Summer Palace in the winter darkness

Even during those talks there was such a sense of the moment. Priceless and timeless, very few experiences over the years have come close to them. There was a gentle 'naughtiness' perhaps, to our behaviour. We knew that we shouldn't be sneaking into the Friendship Hotel outdoor swimming pool at midnight, nor going onto the ice at the Summer Palace in the middle of the winter darkness. However, it wasn't due to any arrogance of youth but was rather the result of an innocent puppy-ish curiosity and delight in the moment. Who could possibly stand on the frozen lake, taking in the dark skyline of the Summer Palace, and not marvel at the awesome sense of history around you and your own little existence?

There was for me a greater sense of egalitarianism between my Chinese friends and foreign friends in the 1980s than there is now, strange as that might sound. Perhaps this is more a reflection of my youth at the time, but we were all very open with our hearts and minds. There was little or no artifice or posturing. We were all ringside observers as we watched this mighty country slowly but surely lumber forward. We might have giggled at some of the rather heartily titled propagandist magazines of the day, such as *China Reconstructs*, but every single person we knew was acutely aware that China wanted to climb onto the international stage, and was looking for pride and a belief in its rightful place there.

Nevertheless, there were still many people who were firmly entrenched in the old days of Soviet influence and who were strongly suspicious of anything that came overtly from the West. This we experienced from some of the older teachers and professors, but also in exchanges while working part-time for foreign companies, when as minions we would interact with august government departments such as Machimpex, Instrimpex and so on.

I well remember joking with other British students that maybe one day we would see Cadbury's chocolate for sale in China, or even Coca-Cola. It was purely a joke, an absurdity, to think that such a symbolic juxtaposition could ever take place; it was unthinkable to us in our little worlds of the day. How wrong we were….

When I talk to my pals from those days – and they are indeed great pals – we smile at those times. None of us were thinking about career moves; 'internships' and 'networking' were words not yet in vogue. We would have baulked at the idea of meeting people purely to see if they could be useful to us. Rather, we met people with sincerity, a curiosity, an openness. Perhaps these have been the ingredients that have helped our lifelong friendships to endure to this day, with enormous humour, compassion and affection. We even talk about ending up in the same Old Folks' Home one day, and what a hoot that would be.

> *There was not one foreign advertising hoarding in sight, and it seemed that things would stay that way forever*

China and our times here would be the number one subject on the menu. I suspect that our days of hunting down antiques, embroideries, rugs and rare books (as well as the near misses) would be close to the top of the list. These things represented history and beauty in our hands, a sense of magnificent, momentary ownership. Despite the need for travel passes and permission slips, we embraced the train timetable book and travelled the length and breadth of the country – unique times, unique memories. There was not one foreign advertising hoarding in sight, and it seemed that things would stay that way forever.

The changing face of the city

However, Beijing in the 1980s was characterised for me by the arrival of construction, of road building and coal pollution. The 1990s saw yet more construction, and the environment was poisoned by car pollution too. In the new century the construction continues, and there is more car pollution – and now global warming on top of everything. Getting out of the city and finding old picnic haunts, or finding new ones where one can be undisturbed for a few hours, becomes more and more difficult, yet more and more precious. I wonder whether, in my lifetime, I will ever see a Beijing not under construction.

I vividly recall being frustrated one day in 1980 as I was riding my bike to find my usual path cut off by huge tracts of land being dug up. I hoped it would be a relatively short-term problem, but I discovered that a road was being built, which was to be called the Second Ring Road. Experiences like this would become common over the next few years. On countless trips to the airport, ferrying people back and forth for a student job I was doing, I watched with some amusement at one location as what seemed to be matchboxes were stacked up on top of one another. Told it was to be a hotel, I wondered who would ever want to stay there, so far from civilisation – that was the Lido Hotel. Ditto Legend Gardens.

Driving in a British Land Rover one day over bumpy fields and paths, I found that a building had popped up out of nowhere. This was the Kunlun Hotel, and again my

Lifelong education

reaction was the same: who would want to move out so far? What innocents we were. I can even recall attending the opening night at the Jianguo Hotel and how we were taken on an impromptu tour of the place, and how we all gushed and ahhhhed at the splendours of its extremely modern, professional stainless steel Western kitchen. We had no idea of what was to come.

Laying the foundations of MSB

In these days of gap student briefings and trip preparation awareness, I do rather wonder what was going through my head when I came out to Beijing all those years ago. My mother was not in favour of my coming. She had greater wisdom and understanding of life than I did. I had no inkling that I would spend the next three decades of my life in this country. I think it has to be said that I often didn't think very much at all, but just bounded into things like a Labrador puppy at high speed, full of pep and enthusiasm and with a belief system of goodwill to others like the Brownie and Girl Guide I had been back at home in Britain.

As I began to put down the foundations of what would become the International Montessori School of Beijing (MSB) in 1990, and began to pioneer and champion that cause, I doubt that I was best served by that naïve enthusiasm. However, without this bouncing, jolly attitude I would probably not have persevered and sallied forth when I needed to, but would have walked away a long time ago. The path has been at times very long and arduous. Maybe there is something in the blood group theory which

When we set up MSB in the early 1990s, nearly everything had to be brought in from outside China

Caroline Chen Gaillard

Sports play an important role at MSB, where we try to create a whole-school environment

states that type As are not natural-born leaders, as we are perfectionists and live too much off our nerves. Funnily enough, a couple of years ago we realised that, however unlikely it might seem, nearly all the key staff and teachers at MSB were group As.

In the early 1990s, as MSB was getting under way, no one was interested in education, apart from the real educators and those with a heart for it. Any idea that education could be something remotely 'hot' as an investment was just laughable. We were poles apart from the new century, which is purely market- and investor-driven and where the real education of the child/student is almost purely coincidental. Nothing at that time was easy and everything we did at MSB was a first. This was very wearing as China's officialdom could be so frustrating and intimidating, but we certainly learned through our dogged perseverance and believed that all would be well, and it was.

> *In the early 1990s, no one was interested in education. Any idea that education could be something remotely 'hot' as an investment was just laughable*

Practically everything we needed for the school had to be sourced abroad and brought in. I cannot begin to count the number of friends of friends who had cheap holidays to Beijing whilst camel-ing art supplies, chunky wax crayons, coloured pipe cleaners and pom-poms for the school. What we lacked in business or legal acumen we made up for, in spades, with vision. Vision in glorious technicolour. We, and I do mean we, for we have many of the same old team still working happily together, believed in our commitment to the child. As soppy as 'mission statements' often sound, all we have ever tried to do over the years is to live our vision.

People often ask what MSB's special ingredient for success is, but it's nothing

Lifelong education

magical – just trying to treat others the way we would like to be treated ourselves. All those good old morning assemblies from my own schooldays must have paid off, for I know that I have begun to sound like them – perhaps that is why they are called the eternal truths. It has been known on numerous occasions for people to break out into singing *Kumbayah* when I have walked into a dinner party. I think I have heard all the joshing and joking and permutations about Montessori and MSB that there can be, over nearly 20 years. However, I take it all as a compliment – albeit with the odd roll of the eyeballs to the heavens.

In the early 1990s there was still something faintly reassuring about the government officialdom that we encountered. The tall thermos flasks, the lidded jam jars of tea on desks, the little makeshift bed tucked into a corner or the unembarrassed washing line of happily hanging smalls. This was familiar to us, it was still the 1980s. Government officials were for the most part easy to deal with and straightforward, and we were met with an almost avuncular kindness. There was an etiquette and we stuck to it, just like at an official banquet: no surprises, just the pleasantries with predictable timings for greetings, toasts and farewells.

Government officials were for the most part easy to deal with and straightforward, and usually we were met with an almost avuncular kindness

As the expatriate community was still relatively small in those days, everybody really did seem to know one another. The South African Centre, as it was then, was a great supporter of the school and assisted us with much behind the scenes, as did our first board, who gave unquestioningly of their time and hearts. Without all their efforts I wonder where we would be now. I believe that they recognised our lack of business experience but saw that our intentions were pure and so entered the fray on our behalf.

Just as we benefited from the generosity of so many people, we in our turn helped others where we could. Two mothers at the school, one American and one British, wanted to open a larger school in Beijing. MSB was the unofficial 'mailbox' for their communications for a long time in those early days, and when they were stuck with getting government approvals, we introduced one of our MSB parents, who worked for the World Bank at the time, and who then arranged a meeting for them with the education minister Li Lan-qing. This meeting led to the inception of the Western Academy of Beijing (WAB).

Crossing the cultural divide

The profile of our student body has changed gradually, beginning in the 1990s, with an increasing number of mainland Chinese families (although they all hold foreign passports or green cards). This has brought challenges as, at times, there has been a greater cultural divide to cross to meet parents' expectations, perceptions and sensitivities. However, this is an aspect of my present work that I really enjoy tackling, as I feel well placed to look at the raft of issues that get thrown up from day to day.

Caroline Chen Gaillard

Indeed, at the moment I am working with some of our mainland parents to develop better ways of bridging that divide. One of the parents told me that, despite her American graduate degree, she still finds herself in self-imposed isolation within the parent community at the school, because of a lack of self-confidence that is still a strong remnant of China's past history with the West. We want to succeed in creating a strong new, balanced identity for our children with this mixed heritage, and we will get there. Instead of trying to 'mould' our children into either a British or an American template, we want them to have their own unique identity, which will serve them well no matter where they go, and which will help them to deal with whatever life might throw at them, good, bad or plain challenging.

> *China's prosperity, coupled with the general 'me-ism' of the past decade, has given rise to a lifestyle in which much child-rearing is farmed out to paid help or the child is occupied with a constant barrage of entertainment*

For the school as a whole, teachers and administrators alike, China's economic boom has also given us a flipside of concern. For a good number of our parents (from all nationalities), China's prosperity, coupled with the general 'me-ism' of the past decade, has given rise to a tempting lifestyle in which many of our pupils' families can indulge. They are able to live lives in which much valuable (but often unglamourous) child-rearing work is farmed out to paid household help and/or the child's life is occupied with a constant barrage of entertainment. This is leading to children being brought up in some very dysfunctional family units. As unwelcome as this may sound, it is definitely our experience, often on a daily level for some of our children. We try to counter these influences by creating a whole-school environment of rich values and virtues, together with the dissemination of parental education, but it is a never-ending struggle.

Beijing in the twenty-first century has borne in on me, through hard experience and knocks, the realisation that the landscape I have known has changed dramatically and

The school aims to create a strong cross-cultural identity for all its pupils

Lifelong education

unalterably. The nest of rosy-pink glow, which I always thought of in my mind's eye as the backdrop for Beijing, has changed to a world of sharp jagged edges, and that softer side has gone forever. The seamier side of greater economic prosperity has brought wolves into the area of education. If my children were in their young teens again, I would consider only two schools in Beijing as they exist today. There are some good educators out there on the international educational scene, but they are in the minority. Everything is packaged and branded, with no real substance; it is crass marketing and not education at heart, while behind the scenes there is dirty business going on that could equal the imaginings of any TV soap writer.

Some of the schools in the marketplace these days have become like veritable holiday camps, wanting to offer everything for the family, like a giant Club Med. I caustically remarked to a friend recently, while we were looking at the latest advertising spread for one particular international school, that it would soon be offering courses on how to beat the menopause for its mums, along with retirement schemes and then a Co-op-style funeral service all rolled into one. Oh Beijing, is this what we started? Where will it end? At times like these, when I become terribly saddened about what I see, I remember the Old Summer Palace and just faintly I can revive my memories and sense of old Beijing's magic.

A time for reflection

In the autumn of 2007, my daughter Lizzy (in her third year at Edinburgh University in Scotland) came out to spend a year at Peking University as part of her undergraduate course. This has led to a good deal of reflection on my part as I watch the circle of life going on. I came out here as a 21-year-old myself, and my daughter coming back to her childhood home and turning 21 at the same time has led us both to compare our experiences. I have placed myself – as far as I can – in her shoes, and she in mine. It seems that in many ways our experiences of Beijing are of two very different Beijings, if not of different worlds. This is not due, I suspect, solely to the passing of time, but rather to the tsunami of Western culture that the economic boom has heralded in.

Since her days in sixth form at school, I had known that Lizzy was becoming more and more interested in China from a historical perspective, and so her decision to study Chinese at Edinburgh was a natural one. However, for the majority of the students in her classes here, and I suspect probably for many of the foreign students at all the other institutions in Beijing, the names of the game today seem to be career, internships and networking. All have their place, I'm sure, but I wonder if today's students know what they are missing out on.

I often comment to friends that there really should be another fifteen years in everyone's life between the ages of 20 and 40. I think that, as adults, we need that time to get it all together. From my perspective now, it has taken me these past 30 years to do this. The question that I ask myself now is what I am going to do with myself when I grow up at the age of 50? I have Beijing and both its Summer Palaces to thank for that part of the earlier growing-up process, and I suspect that the city will still lead me on to some new experiences.

Joerg Wuttke
Chief Representative, BASF China

First came to China: 1982

Joerg Wuttke is General Manager and Chief Representative of BASF China, based in Beijing. Since joining BASF in 1997, he has been responsible for helping guide the company's investment strategies for China, negotiating large projects and government relations.

His first professional encounter with China was in 1988 as the finance and administration manager of ABB Beijing. In 1993 he became Chief Representative of ABB China in Shanghai and in 1994 moved to the President's Office of ABB China in Beijing.

In 1999 he was a founding member of the German Chamber of Commerce in China and from 2001–04 was the Chairman of the Board. Since April 2007 he has been President of the European Union Chamber of Commerce in China, which has over 1,200 member companies in eight cities. He is married with three grown-up children.

Unwrapping the puzzle

Joerg Wuttke has spent many years trying to understand the complex behaviour patterns that drive Chinese people in business and politics. After nearly two decades, he feels he might be coming somewhere close

At the beginning there were Mao's words, and my older brother Roland waving the Red Book at us at home in 1968. I wondered why my father was so upset about it, as I frequently saw him studying the works of Confucius. I could not distinguish between the two famous Chinese, but saw that they had an impact on our dinner conversations.

China was always to me what Russia was to Churchill: a puzzle inside a riddle wrapped in an enigma. And in 1980 I wanted to find out more about it by signing up to study the subject of Sinology. This brought tears to my mother's eyes, as she assumed I had gone mad. In 1980, China was Mao. And to the professors and students who studied Sinology, it was literature and fine arts. No book on the Chinese economy existed, probably because the Chinese economy at the time was not worth the attention of even a single book.

In the summer of 1982 my friends and I boarded a train in Heidelberg, Germany to travel across the Soviet Union to China. After nearly two weeks we crossed the Mongolia–China border at midnight, and I shall never again in my life experience such a delicious Chinese dinner. It was not just the two weeks of Soviet diet that made us appreciate the exotic spices; it was also my first encounter with the richest and most diverse cuisine in the world.

Deng Xiaoping had opened up the country just four years earlier, and foreigners were still a rare and strange species. We toured China by train and, everywhere we went, from Luoyang in Henan province to Emeishan in Sichuan, people gathered around to look at this group of Western students. The brave ones approached us to test their English; the rest were limited to pressing their noses against the window of our carriage and staring at us.

In Beijing and Shanghai the streets

Wherever we went in 1982, people gathered around out of curiosity, and we became ambassadors for our country

My Thirty Years in China | 255

Joerg Wuttke

Dormitory accommodation was simple, but proved to be a good way to meet local people

were wide and almost empty of traffic. My new Chinese friends could not accompany me inside the hotels, as these were off-limits for ordinary Chinese. So I had to go inside and buy foreign cigarettes for them. To travel abroad was unthinkable for most Chinese, and we became ambassadors for our country, as well as journalists relating what was happening in Europe. Everywhere our group went, we encountered very curious people, who struck us with their simplicity and honesty. The doors of our dormitory were always left open, and nothing was ever stolen. China was a continent in awakening, and greed was still dormant.

We returned by train to Germany three months later, and I decided to quit Sinology and study Chinese in Taiwan and also economics, in order to feed my little family, which consisted of me, my wife and our newborn son Nawid. But when I approached various educational foundations and government funds in Germany in search of a China scholarship, I was turned down every time, unlike my friends who studied Sinology and the arts. Even today the answer of one professor rings in my ears, when I told him that I wanted to become a manager in China: 'What do you want to sell to those guys?'. So I gave up on the mainland, due to lack of funds, and moved with my wife and eight-month-old baby to Taiwan, where we could earn some money as language teachers and models.

From 1984 to 1985 I lived in Taipei. People in Taiwan were very curious about the mainland and the opening up they were hearing about, but nobody dared to speak about this openly. At immigration in Taipei the officer looked at my passport, saw the mainland chop and said 'This is not nice'. At that time Taipei was the place for fake garments and copied books. Heaven for a poor student, and how could I know that 20 years later mainland China would be flooded with fake products, which would be a major concern to the company I worked with?

My first business encounter with China was in 1986, when I represented a German publishing trust at the country's first international book fair. The event was very small, but the discussions on book licences were very lively. I succeeded in selling a

Everywhere our group went, we encountered very curious people, who struck us with their simplicity and honesty. The doors of our dormitory were always left open, and nothing was ever stolen

Unwrapping the puzzle

book with a rather strong religious content. The book was translated and advertised in the nei bu fashion: a Chinese word for 'internal', as the Party assumed that the average Mr. Wang or Ms. Li should not be exposed to a major dose of religious thinking from the Middle East. The publisher was confident of breaking even, as the estimated 'internal' readership was sizeable. I assumed that the book would be purchased on a nei bu basis only, but would

Today, Frankfurt's skyline pales in comparison with any Chinese provincial town, and there are probably more skyscrapers in Shanghai than in the whole of Europe

be distributed freely among friends. However, the events of June 1989 put an end to that: the book was never launched. Looking back, the late 1980s were politically far more liberal than is the situation nowadays, but Chinese people are better off now and can travel freely, provided they can obtain a Western visa.

In 1987 I lived in Beijing and Shanghai as an intern for my new employer, ABB, and hardly anything had visibly changed in either city in comparison with 1982. When I flew back to Germany I was struck by the high-rises in Frankfurt, as no building in China had more than about six storeys. When I take the plane today, Frankfurt's skyline pales in comparison with any Chinese provincial town, and there are probably more skyscrapers in Shanghai than in the whole of Europe.

The Great Hall of the People on Tiananmen Square, 1982. The streets were wide and almost empty of traffic

Joerg Wuttke

In winter 1987 I lived in the Shanghai Mansions across the Bund, a beautiful old building dating from the early twentieth century, where I could hear the horns of ships passing by. The walk to the ABB office was along the historic Bund riverfront on the Huangpu River, which empties into the mighty Yangtze downstream. Every morning I cherished the 2km walk, under trees and past old colonial buildings. As a journalist once put it, before 8am China is not Communist but traditional. You see early risers moving in smooth *tai chi* rhythms, alongside elegant sword dancers and men playing chess. Very often I stopped for a quick massage. There was no need to take off my shirt; I just sat there and chatted with the Shanghainese about the weather, soccer and my children.

When I returned in 1993 to live in Shanghai, the Bund had been turned into a wide thoroughfare; gone were the trees and the people. I was struck by a feeling of nostalgia and the knowledge that China had to change – but all too often the traditional China vanished only to make room for international-style skyscrapers. Whole areas disappeared in the late 1990s. In Beijing, too, the traditional courtyard houses downtown were demolished. To me, the soul of Beijing was under threat, although I knew that most of these dwellings were a disaster in terms of hygiene: they looked scenic, but not to the people living there.

Europe has maintained a certain feeling for its history and has kept many of its city centres friendly to the eye, some might say 'cosy'. In China, the infrastructure boom of the

I went back to Shanghai in 1987 to work. Over the river from the Russian Consulate lay the Pudong district of the city, at that time almost completely undeveloped

Unwrapping the puzzle

past 20 years has wiped out many historical references. Only the Forbidden City, the Bund and the palace of Shenyang still remind you of Chinese history. It has sometimes felt as though China wanted only to look into the future, and to build high and modern in order to forget about 200 years of misery, foreign exploitation, civil wars and political upheaval.

Very often I found that cultural awareness and Chinese tradition

The ABB office was located in the CITIC building in the Jianguomenwai district, right in the heart of Beijing

were far more evident and more a part of everyday life in Taiwan than on the mainland, where perhaps Mao's Cultural Revolution had broken the back of the urban middle class and had subsequently erased many traditions from the daily routine of the *lao bai xing* ('average Chinese'). So it is with great joy that today I see an emerging middle class on the mainland again embracing Confucianism and the Ming novels.

An auspicious beginning

My first real expatriate experience of living in China began on 8 August 1988, when I arrived in Beijing with my family, which at that time included a four-year-old boy and a one-year-old daughter. My ABB colleagues congratulated me on the excellent quadruple eight in the date, and declared that I would enjoy a very successful career.

ABB was at that time engaged in numerous infrastructure projects, which gave me a deep insight into how the Chinese leadership was preparing the country's future. Trains and subways were discussed, power plants and transmission lines negotiated over, and the country was the darling of international business people and the media, capturing the headlines as the 'Market of the Future'. How often I witnessed the media's rollercoaster of emotion, which swung from euphoria to deep resentment towards the Middle Kingdom. Businesses were lauded for entering this promising market, and years later lambasted for being so stupid as to lose money. As Churchill put it: 'There are a terrible lot of lies going about the world, and the worst of it is that half of them are true'.

And it was true that many European companies lost a lot of money, because they misjudged the market or had the wrong business partner. But in my 20 years in China nobody ever counted the virtual losses of companies that did not engage with the country, and which now face serious competition from those foreign companies that did successfully enter the market, or from Chinese companies which learned quickly

Joerg Wuttke

Getting around in Shanghai: taxis spotted in 1982 (left) and 1987 (right)

and acted with self-confidence.

During my days with ABB we engaged in many tough negotiations with Chinese utility companies as we tried to sell them power plants. Our counterparts were all seasoned engineers who not only had excellent technological knowledge but were also obviously tough individuals, as they had survived and kept the power plants running during the Cultural Revolution. Negotiations lasted sometimes for many long hours, in one case right through the night.

The head negotiator in the toughest encounter was Madame Sun, a formidable 60-year-old lady. She took no prisoners, especially if our team asserted a point and then could not prove it. On one occasion she thought she had caught out our specialist Mr. Herzberger again, and lambasted him for a technical detail that apparently he had forgotten. She pushed the file across the table, her face stern like that of a disappointed teacher. Herzberger went through the file, found the part that Madame Sun thought was missing, turned the file around and pushed it back to her. She looked at the file, looked up at her chief engineer, said something in a harsh voice and than slapped him across the face. She turned to our team again, and told us to carry on with the next topic as if nothing had happened. In many instances I encountered Chinese negotiators so passionate that they would have made any intercultural writer weep over his textbooks.

> *Our counterparts were all seasoned engineers who not only had excellent technological knowledge but were tough individuals who had survived and kept the power plants running during the Cultural Revolution*

The most significant event I witnessed in my nearly two decades in China was the 1989 Beijing Spring. After the events in the city centre, Beijing came to a standstill, and we felt trapped in our apartment. As I was responsible for the ABB Beijing office, I had to organise the evacuation of the expatriates and communicate with the company's head offices in Hong Kong and Switzerland. The phone was sometimes dead, so I had to send telexes, a mode of communication that probably today most people are unfamiliar with.

We returned to Germany a couple of days afterwards and, before we left the country, I gave an interview to the German TV channel ZDF, in which I forecast sadly that China might return to the dark ages. How wrong I was and, looking back, it strikes

Unwrapping the puzzle

me how often I misjudged China's capability to change and adapt. When I returned a week later, however, Beijing was still in shock. Businesses were idle, and the Chinese government was eager to reach out to the remaining Western business people in the city. A small group of Swedish business people, me included under the ABB ticket, was invited to dine with Politburo member Li Ruihuan, and it turned out to be an engagingly lively dinner conversation. The leadership clearly understood that they had to reach out to keep the economic reforms alive.

It was a hot summer, and in August 1989 I witnessed the visit to Beijing of East German Politburo apparatchik Egon Krenz, and bumped into his group at the Friendship Store. I thought about him again a month later in September, when he disposed of Erich Honecker as East German leader and was faced with demonstrations in Leipzig and East Berlin. The Soviets under Gorbachev made it clear that they would not intervene in the East German crisis, and the Berlin Wall fell peacefully on 9 November 1989.

It was not only politics that were exciting; daily living in China proved to be a challenge too. Everything took a lot of time, shopping was restricted because there were few interesting things to buy, and we couldn't wait to fly to Hong Kong for the occasional shopping trip. The biggest challenge was the medical services. My son Nawid, with the energy typical of a five-year-old but with the same lack of awareness of boundaries, fell off his bicycle, and I had to come home from the office to take him to hospital. The doctor was very competent, but the serious cut over Nawid's eye was

In the early 1980s the Bund retained its colonial charm – Shanghai resembled an ageing diva

Joerg Wuttke

stitched together with five stitches and a total lack of anesthetics.

A few months later, Nawid fell off the big ball on which he hopped around the compound, when he happened to be holding a pair of scissors in his hand. He fell right onto the scissors and ripped a large part of his mouth open. Again I was called from the office, and crossed town to pick him up and get him to another hospital – hoping that this one would have anesthetics, and fortunately it had. They put him on a dentist's chair to fix his face. The wound looked awful, wide and gaping; my wife fainted in my driver's arms when I asked her if she really was sure that there were no bits of his mouth left at home. Nawid recovered quickly, but a prominent scar on his chin still reminds him of this accident. The ambulance that was called before I left my office to rush home arrived an hour after we returned from the hospital.

Outings to the Forbidden City were easy as there were hardly any tourists then, and our children ran around the ancient palace as if it was their own private playground

Luckily the German embassy added a doctor to its staff after 1990, and he proved his skills several times when we had to call him to our house as my two-year-old daughter, adopted from India, had developed seizures. It was one of the most shocking moments of my life to helplessly witness my daughter's massive fits and not be able to stop them, until the German doctor gave her a tranquiliser shot. And these were pre-mobile phone days, so to get the doctor in the first place meant he had to be either at home or at the embassy. Today Beijing has excellent facilities to cater for all kinds of emergency. Gone are the days when foreigners flew three hours to Hong Kong to visit a dentist. However, I have visited a couple of Chinese friends in hospital recently, and many of the facilities reminded me of the 1980s. And this was in Beijing – it can be heartbreaking to walk into a provincial hospital.

Historical sites often provided the backdrop for family picnics, and the children were always in demand as everybody's favourite photo models

We greatly enjoyed living in Beijing, especially appreciating features such as the many trees that lined the streets at the time, before the ring roads were built.

Unwrapping the puzzle

Outings to the Forbidden City were easy as there were hardly any tourists then, and our children ran around the ancient palace as if it was their own private playground. Nawid had blond hair and my daughter Rekha, adopted from India, was very dark, so we

At home in Beijing in 1988. My son Nawid's bicycle would soon be the cause of a painful encounter with the local medical services

were everybody's favourite photo models. In later years, our fair-haired daughter Mirea was equally in demand with Chinese who wanted their picture taken with her, and often we had to rescue the children from excessive demands. We regularly had picnics in historical settings; today, of course, the sites are (rightfully) out of bounds, for their own protection.

We left China for good (or so I thought) in September 1990 and settled back in Germany. The atmosphere in business circles in Beijing and Shanghai was gloomy, and China was being criticised globally for its 1989 crackdown. But in 1992 Deng Xiaoping sent out a message, during his trip through the southern provinces, that 'getting rich was glorious'. The Chinese people and eventually government leaders picked that up as an indication that implementation of the 'open door' policy should proceed more quickly and that it should not be derailed. Ever since 1992 the Chinese economy has been booming, mostly in a double-digit GDP growth pattern, with the occasional bust in between.

So it came as no surprise that after about three years in Germany I was keen to return to China. ABB Shanghai was my new base, and I witnessed the transformation of the city from a dull and ageing former diva to a sparkling new star. In mid-1993 I was invited to the Pudong exhibition, where the Shanghai government rolled out its architectural vision of the future Pudong district. I was one of the very few

Today Beijing has excellent facilities to cater for all kinds of emergency. Gone are the days when foreigners flew three hours to Hong Kong to visit a dentist

foreigners attending – in fact a picture of my wife and I looking at a model of Pudong soon turned up in the Air China flight magazine – and I remember thinking that Shanghai had gone mad. But not only did the development take place and all the highways, bridges and skyscrapers get built in quick time; Shanghai once again became the fashion and lifestyle icon it had been in the 1930s.

Not only did the development take place and all the highways, bridges and skyscrapers get built; Shanghai once again became the fashion and lifestyle icon it had been in the 1930s

In 1994 we moved back to Beijing, and with my driver I drove my wife's car all the way up to the capital from Shanghai. It turned out to be an eye-opening journey, as the supposedly rich coastline turned out to consist of poor roads and backward villages. It took 36 hours of non-stop driving, whereas today you could probably do the trip in less than half that time. China's first-tier cities were pulling the rest of the country along, and setting the pace of its economic transformation. But this left many people behind and, while the rich got richer, the poor remained very poor.

In 1997 I became a member of the Rotary Club, one of whose main aims is to assist the development of poor people. I was privileged to manage two successful projects in remote Chinese provinces: three tent schools for Tibetan nomads in Qinghai province in 1999 and 2001, and a number of schools projects in the Tibetan Autonomous Region. In Lhasa, the Rotary Club supported a school for blind children. We assisted the project by helping to build support facilities for a workshop where older, blind farmers learned how to make yak cheese, adapting modern Swiss techniques. This project has not only created jobs for handicapped people on the roof of the world, but also supports the local yak farmers, who now have an additional outlet where they can sell their yak milk. The cheese is then supplied to restaurants in Lhasa.

In Qinghai province in 1999 and 2001, the Rotary Club helped to set up three tent schools for the children of Tibetan nomads

In Rutok County, a remote region in the western part of Tibet, an elementary school and a middle school were equipped with 20 computers, lots of musical instruments and a fuel generator to enable some 360 students, aged between seven and 11 years old, to engage in long-distance learning. It takes seven days by jeep to get there from Lhasa but, now that the IT infrastructure is in place, the children can learn online from qualified teachers based in the city. It was great fun establishing a virtual learning environment at the foot of the Himalayas.

Unwrapping the puzzle

As a Rotary Club member, I have been involved in projects to help poor people in Qinghai and Tibet

A contrasting highlight that the whole expatriate community remembers fondly was the 1998 performance of the Puccini opera *Turandot*, which was staged in the Forbidden City in Beijing. The Chinese film director Zhang Yimou built his trademark colourful stage settings, using some of the actual palace buildings, which were brought to life again for the first time in two or three hundred years. A cast of literally hundreds thronged the stage, and Puccini's music was wonderfully interpreted by the Indian conductor Zubin Mehta. This was a multicultural event with gorgeous music, and we were privileged to attend it twice. It served as a reminder that a love for art and music transcends national and religious differences.

Long-term commitment

In 1996 I changed company, and became General Manager of BASF China in Beijing. This was a real long-term commitment to China, as I had turned down an offer from ABB to move to Malaysia. Little did I realise at the time that, unknowingly, I had opted for the growth machine that China was to become and escaped the meltdown of the 1997 Asian financial crisis.

BASF is the world's largest chemical company, and works in an industrial sector that involves huge capital investments. In the late 1990s the company was negotiating three mega-deals simultaneously – a US$3bn integrated chemical site in Nanjing, two chemical projects in Shanghai together worth US$1bn, and a US$1bn nylon plant on the island of Hainan in southern China. The challenge was not only to negotiate these four projects with various partners and steer them through the maze of Chinese

Joerg Wuttke

government approval, but also to reassure BASF's shareholders that the company was not wasting its money in a region hit by a massive financial crisis. This required great leadership and communication skills from the then CEO of BASF, Dr. Strube, and from the lead negotiator Dr. Hambrecht, who succeeded him as CEO in 2002. The three projects in Nanjing and Shanghai were eventually built and started production in 2005, but the Hainan project was dropped in 1999 due to its lack of feasibility.

> *My experience after two decades is that many top leaders in China are extremely well briefed, diligent and hard-working. Hardly ever have I come across pompous, empty talk*

During the approval processes of these multi-billion dollar projects I got to know more about Premier Zhu Rongji, who encouraged openness and tried to modernise the Chinese economy. I still marvel at the way that Zhu acted to root out corruption, and how open he was to factual criticism and ideas. He was the most exceptional Chinese leader I have ever met. Zhu is now fully retired and has virtually vanished from public view, but I know that he is still looking at the development of the Chinese economy in his candid manner, and he is writing his memoirs.

Sometimes I wonder why China cannot permit such strong and presentable assets as Jiang Zemin and Zhu Rongji to travel the former world leader circuit and try to explain to the world just how China ticks. Both politicians could meet decision-makers across the world and listen to their concerns about China's integration into the global system and could maybe explain the thinking of China's leaders, without being constrained by the straightjacket of daily policy-making.

On one of the very rare occasions on which Zhu came out of his retirement, at a dinner at the German Chamber of Commerce, he remarked that his world had shrunk to the size of his *hutong* courtyard house in Beijing. He said that he loved to walk, but that he got dizzy after a few minutes circling the narrow space of his courtyard. Zhu had kept his trademark sense of humour, which made him such an engaging person to meet. I am sure that he was a difficult colleague to many and tough on his subordinates, but he got things done.

After nearly two decades in China, my experience is that many top leaders are extremely well briefed, diligent and hard-working. Hardly ever have I come across pompous, empty talk, and on the rare occasions that I have, it has been mostly at the provincial or city level. Even in the provinces, however, there are personalities who are not only charismatic but also serious movers and shakers. The former Jiangsu Party Secretary Li Yuanchao is such a man, with a very quick mind wrapped in a humble demeanour.

China's 'Iron Lady' Ms. Wu Yi, who retired in March 2008, was also exceptional in her openness and her quick wit. Over a period of more than ten years I met her on several occasions at different functions, as she progressed from Minister of Commerce to Vice Premier, and she struck me as a person who always wanted to go straight to the core of a problem and solve it. China's economic miracle is not only related to the entrepreneurial

Unwrapping the puzzle

Zhu Rongji was the most exceptional Chinese leader I have met, open to factual criticism and ideas

spirit of the average Chinese, but is also due to the fact that the Party has managed to groom excellent leaders. We could now witness 30 years of incredible political stability, which would be in stark contrast with the first 30 years of Communist rule.

In late 1999 I was one of the co-founders of the German Chamber of Commerce, which I chaired from 2001 to 2004. The Chamber is quite large and primarily tries to assist small and medium-sized German enterprises to find business opportunities in China. One of its other aims, of course, is to establish a lively information platform where German business people can exchange their views on China and learn to avoid the pitfalls, of which there are plenty.

The highlight of my chairmanship was in 2002, with the celebration of 30 years of diplomatic relations between China and Germany. Initially the Chamber committee was reluctant to organise anything special, but then the Vice Chair, Christian Sommer, and I decided to put on a show of what Germany can really offer. We chose a fun theme: an interactive park, with more than 100 German companies displaying products that invited visitors to play.

Bayer erected a small soccer stadium, obviously proud to show off the soccer balls produced with its chemicals. BASF built a children's laboratory, where six- to 12-year-olds could carry out chemical experiments under supervision, to help make them aware of environmental

> *China's economic miracle is not only related to the entrepreneurial spirit of the average Chinese, but is also due to the fact that the Party has managed to groom excellent leaders*

Joerg Wuttke

When I first came to China, bicycles were the main mode of transport

challenges and of how chemistry can contribute to solving them. It was heartwarming to see how engaged the kids were, their eyes shining, as they had never had interactive scientific studies at school, and these hands-on experiments were far more valuable than the front-loaded style of education that still prevails in Chinese schools.

Audi set up a small racecourse – but the cars only ran on leg power, and you could see adults pedalling hard to stay ahead of the pack. Around 180,000 Beijingers showed up to the event, and it was a huge success. But it took a toll on me, as besides having to run BASF's affairs in Beijing, I was also the chief organiser. I virtually stopped sleeping for months. And it was only possible because my friend Christian was a walking power station, solving with wit and charm the many problems that we faced, including a nervous German ambassador. The embassy staff also worked tirelessly day and night; at the end we had all aged, but enjoyed the ten days enormously. Germany, normally not easily associated with fun, displayed a humorous side to go with its trademark serious products and the conferences that took place in early October 2002.

Another perk of heading the Chamber was getting to meet German VIPs, and especially former Chancellor Helmut Schmidt. Although in his mid-eighties, he travelled frequently to Beijing to witness the changes taking place at first hand. In 2003 he came to the embassy to meet me. He is from Hamburg, and people from northern Germany are not known for their small talk. The moment I sat down, he challenged me on my vision of China in 2050. After an hour of *tour d'horizon*, the Chinese dignitaries arrived to attend the dinner that was planned. They had hardly sat down, having greeted the former chancellor with great warmth, when Schmidt asked them how their country could be managed sustainably without a religion to provide moral and social fibre. 'This has never happened in the history of mankind...' he asserted.

Audi set up a small racecourse – but the cars only ran on leg power, and you could see adults pedalling hard to stay ahead of the pack. Around 180,000 Beijingers showed up to the event, and it was a huge success

Unwrapping the puzzle

After the Chinese had absorbed this opening move, the former Chinese ambassador to Germany, the very eloquent and able Mei Zhaorong, started to explain the recent achievements of Jiang Zemin's 'Three Represents' as a basis for a sustainable political system. Schmidt was having none of this and brushed it aside with an 'Oh, this is nonsense', then rattled on to explain his own view of world history. The Chinese VIPs barely ever recovered from that; they probably missed the quick-witted Deng Xiaoping, who was able to challenge Schmidt intellectually when the two met in the late 1970s.

A changing society

In all these years in China, I have seen many changes in the lives of my Chinese friends. In the 1980s I was often invited to their homes, which were small and looked very poor. Dinners consisted of homemade dumplings and meat dishes, but meat was expensive in those days and I often felt bad that my friends had spent so much money to produce such heavenly beef and pork dishes. It was always a sign that winter was approaching when I entered the apartment block of a friend and saw heaps of Chinese cabbages at the entrance. Every autumn, convoys of trucks entered Beijing loaded with this vegetable staple. It has a high vitamin content, and could be stored on small apartment balconies – which were not used for recreation as they tend to be in the West but as an outdoor refrigerator piled high with cabbages that would last well into the next spring. The discussions we had over steaming food, in cold kitchens, were vivid, filled with a strong interest in foreign culture and books. My Chinese friends' rampant curiosity was enriched with a great sense of humour.

Today many of my friends live in big houses and have a nice car standing outside the front

Train travel in the early 1980s was more basic than it is today, but it was certainly well ordered

Joerg Wuttke

The discussions we had over steaming food, in cold kitchens, were vivid, filled with a strong interest in foreign culture and books. My friends' rampant curiosity was enriched with a great sense of humour

door, whereas in the past they would carry their bicycles all the way up to their apartments to avoid losing them. Conversations now revolve around business and money, recent or future trips abroad and problems of how to educate the children. I am sometimes nostalgic for the days when our discussions were supplemented with basic food but were richer in content. Discussions now are also far less political than they were in the 1980s, and people are satisfied with their government's achievements. Beijing offers strong economic growth, decent security and events that enhance the patriotic spirit. China is better off, no doubt, but gone are the days when curiosity was king.

I have always felt very safe in China, and so has my family. When the children were teenagers, with the usual desire to stay out late at weekends at parties or discos, we were very thankful to live here, as there was no need to worry about them taking taxis home in the small hours of the morning. Only rarely did I come across violent nationalism that made my beloved Beijing look ugly. In 1987 China lost a soccer match against Hong Kong in Tianjin, and hooligans marched through Beijing attacking cars with black number plates – a sign of foreign ownership,

With Nawid in the Forbidden City. China was a great place to bring up children: we always felt safe

Unwrapping the puzzle

and in those days most likely Hong Kong-owned. Another regrettable incident occurred in 1999, when NATO forces accidentally bombed the Chinese embassy in Belgrade during the Balkan crisis; the Chinese made all Caucasians feel guilty, and in some isolated cases beat them up.

The only time things got nasty for me personally was after a car accident. One weekend when I was out driving with the family, a Chinese driver cut a corner and hit my car head on. Immediately we were surrounded by bystanders who hurled insults at us and started rocking the car, which scared us quite a bit. Luckily a policeman arrived and sent the crowd on their way. The driver who had rammed me talked to the policeman non-stop, offering him cigarettes and trying to bond with him as a fellow Chinese against the foreigners. The policeman did his job quietly and than sent us home, with a reminder to show up at police headquarters the next day.

I went there with my translator and was put in front of the officer. Again, the driver who the day before had tried to buy favours with cigarettes launched into his story about how the Chinese should stick together and how the foreigner was at fault. The officer looked at him without even asking me a single question, took out the sketch he had made of the street and of the accident scene and then blasted the Chinese driver in loud and clear terms, stating that the accident was 100 per cent his fault, and that he must pay for the damage he had caused to my car. The driver uttered a dejected whimper, but was cut short by a final roar from the officer, who was physically seated higher than we were. My faith in the Chinese system was restored.

Not all accidents ended in such a satisfactory way. On another occasion, again on a weekend, I was slowly reversing my car outside a hotel when I heard screaming and shouting. I jumped out of the car and saw a man lying on the ground behind it. His three friends picked him up and, before I could say anything – and to my wife's surprise – they had opened the back door and jumped in, cradling the screaming man on their knees. They yelled at me to drive to the nearest hospital. My wife and I were in shock, as we had seen nobody behind the car while reversing and, in any case, were moving extremely slowly.

I drove to the nearest hospital, where the wailing man – who, however, bore no obvious signs of physical injury – was admitted. After being shown an X-ray that 'proved' – from an extremely hazy picture – that he had a fracture of the spine, we drove to another hospital to establish exactly how serious his condition was. On the way there, the group of men asked to be taken to the railway station so they could go back home to Changchun in northern China, and asked us for compensation. After all the hassle, and feeling very exposed, we settled on a sizeable amount. When I told my driver about the incident the next day, he was outraged that we had fallen victim to this particular scam. But these were pre-mobile phone days, and we had had no chance to call him.

> *The driver uttered a dejected whimper, but was cut short by a final roar from the officer, who was seated higher than we were. My faith in the Chinese system was restored*

2003 saw some dramatic events, beginning when a desperate man walked into our office building in Beijing to threaten the staff of the Reuters news agency with a bomb. Fortunately, when he surrendered a few hours later, it turned out to be fake. The year also saw the emergence of SARS, or severe acute respiratory syndrome. This episode first began with rumours and stories in late 2002, but developed into a fully-fledged crisis in spring 2003. It showed the Chinese government both at its worst and at its best.

The government first attempted to hide the fact that Beijing had any SARS victims; the civil authorities had no access to the army hospitals where the patients were being treated. After significant international pressure, the army hospitals opened themselves up to an audit by the World Health Organization, but before it began they put the victims into ambulances and took them off for a tour of the city's ring roads, until the auditors had left. It took a brave army doctor to blow the whistle and expose the cover-up. Then the government swung into action and cordoned off the cities. Hardly any flights touched down at Beijing airport, and the capital came to a standstill. The mayor of Beijing was fired, as was the vice minister of the Health Department.

From this point on, SARS was everywhere, on TV, on the radio and through every other propaganda tool available to the city government. The authorities gave the simple advice: be careful and stay at home. Nearly everybody wore masks. The result of the government's public awareness campaign, at least for those of us trying to lead normal lives, was full-scale paranoia. Many friends of ours wanted to leave the city, but not only was it difficult for them to obtain tickets, they also found themselves unwelcome in Europe, as their relatives were afraid of this disease from China and did not want to see anybody from Beijing. We found ourselves isolated on an 'island' for weeks. At the end of it all, Beijing had recorded a total of 2,521 cases of SARS and 191 deaths, but the authoritarian methods of the city government had paid off and contained the virus quickly. However, the episode left us all with a heightened sense of vulnerability, especially given the possible outbreak of avian influenza (bird flu), which was also very much in the news at the time.

> *It is part of community life to assemble around the coffin of a deceased friend, and we realised the artificial life of short-term postings to China largely excluded this important ritual from our own lives*

Like life for native Beijingers, expatriate life in the Chinese capital has also changed over the years. Those of us living in the city have been used to constant changes, as most foreigners come and stay for only a couple of years. It has become ever more of a struggle to make new friends, knowing in advance that we were going to part after only a short time. Luckily, some foreigners have made Beijing and Shanghai their homes and stayed for many years, as we have. This has helped to build a sense of community, bringing the usual life events of marriages, births and – more recently – funerals.

It has been a new experience for the close-knit expatriate community to gather to bid farewell to our friends and to comfort their widows. In 2007/08 both Ian Kay and Jim Brock died suddenly, Ian while rehearsing a Scottish dance for the Caledonian ball,

Unwrapping the puzzle

and Jim while leaving the office after helping everybody to understand energy politics in China. Both men were in their 60s, both extremely active in the community, pushing their schedules, and both died of heart attacks. We feel their loss keenly. These sad events reminded us that it is part of community life to assemble around the coffin of a deceased friend, and made us realise that the artificial life of short-term postings to China largely excluded from our own lives this important ritual of bidding farewell.

Flying the European flag

In 2007 I was elected President of the European Union Chamber of Commerce in China, an organisation with branches in eight cities and more than 1,000 members. The Chamber is the independent voice of European business in China, and its aims include seeking greater market access and improved operating conditions for European companies. This appointment put me at the forefront of lobbying on behalf of European business, and I found myself walking a thin line between criticising the Chinese authorities for their slow market opening and at the same time keeping EU officials informed as to how European businesses would gain from this political process.

The EU politician who I have met and briefed most frequently is Trade Commissioner Peter Mandelson, a fascinating, multi-faceted man. I have rarely met anyone who takes such care over the language he uses. I marvelled at his rhetoric, but had trouble convincing him that public speeches are sometimes only helpful if they are supported by a robust trade policy – one that would not only outline the benefits for China, but also indicate the possible trade mechanisms that would penalise Chinese exporters if trade between China and the EU became too lopsided.

Mandelson believed for a long time that the good rapport he enjoyed with Chinese Minister of Commerce Bo Xilai would get him a deal. But Bo took advantage of the well-meaning Mandelson, and in 2006/07 we felt that China took the EU for a ride. In mid-2007 it was getting to the point where China seemed unwilling to make any deal on trade and seemed determined only to ram through its own agenda, while deflecting any European attempts to settle issues of interest to Brussels. Mandelson listened carefully to the EU Chamber delegation that visited him in September 2007 and thereafter changed his tune. He began to defend EU interests in a more robust manner, and was also lucky that the Chinese installed the able Chen Deming as the new Trade Minister. The trade discussions that took place in early 2008 turned out to be more realistic and constructive, and the EU business community is now hopeful that some of the trade barriers and investment hurdles it faces will be addressed.

My colleagues and I felt that foreign companies were facing growing official resistance to investment and trade in China, as regulators issued new rules on investment and other activities. At press conferences to launch the trademark product of the Chamber, its annual Position Paper, I started complaining about rules on foreign acquisitions in China that are very restrictive, and criticised the unequal treatment meted out to foreign companies compared with their Chinese competitors in industries such as finance, energy and telecommunications, despite Chinese promises to open markets.

As well as launching the Position Paper, I launched a survey that was conducted against a background of strong growth in two-way trade between the EU and China, which revealed a ballooning trade deficit in China's favour (€160bn in 2007) and increasing activity by EU investors in China, particularly in terms of established investors expanding their operations to second- and third-tier cities. At a press conference held in November 2007, shortly before the EU–China summit, I was able to present to the media some very interesting aspects of European companies' current perceptions of the Chinese market:

> *The overwhelming reason for European companies being in China is to reach China's domestic market with their goods and services. Low labour costs are a relatively minor factor for them*

- The overwhelming reason for European companies being in China is to reach China's domestic market with their goods and services; this was even more the case than the previous year's survey suggested. Low labour costs are a relatively minor factor.
- Most companies are undertaking research and development in China or are intending to do so. Apart from reducing R&D costs by using local skills, the main reason for this is to adapt their products to China's domestic market (suggesting that product development is often the main focus of R&D operations, rather than innovative research).
- Companies' profitability in China tends to be reasonable, but not outstanding compared with their operations in other countries: most are as profitable or more profitable in China as they are elsewhere, but a significant number (41 per cent) actually say they are less profitable in China. A growing proportion of companies (28 per cent) reported losses. The picture improves in the case of companies that are larger or which have been operating in China for longer.
- Companies expect that competition in their sectors will get tougher in the years ahead.
- Despite all of the above, most companies expect to expand their activities in China, and most think that they will perform better financially in the future. The clear reasons for this optimism are continuing strong economic growth and the increased domestic consumption it creates.
- As companies hire more and more Chinese workers, shortages of qualified staff, specially at skilled and more senior levels, are an increasing problem. Improvements in pay and other benefits resulting from these shortages are socially beneficial; however, they tend to move the problem around without solving it – there are still not enough skilled workers to meet the overall needs of foreign and domestic companies.
- Not surprisingly, the scarcity of skilled Chinese workers means that localisation at the upper levels is not going as quickly as companies seem to want it to go. European companies in China with an exclusively foreign management board (38 per cent) still

Unwrapping the puzzle

As President of the EU Chamber of Commerce, I got to know, and brief, EU Trade Commissioner Peter Mandelson, a fascinating and multi-faceted man

outnumber those with an all-Chinese top team (12 per cent).
- While most companies believe that China will take steps to implement its WTO commitments, a sizeable minority (38 per cent) still think that it is only following the letter of the WTO rules while seeking to circumvent their implementation in practice. Most strikingly, companies' views on the benefits that China's WTO accession has brought to their businesses tend to be negative: 34 per cent said that it had made things worse, and only 16 per cent reported a positive impact to date.
- Companies are critical of the insufficient action taken by the government to address environmental problems, but tend to look forward with some confidence to improvements in this area.
- With regard to the investment environment, companies are for the most part strongly critical of the lack of transparency in the regulatory process, and of insufficient protection of intellectual property rights.
- A number of other factors also drew critical responses: for example, cumbersome registration processes and customs procedures; lack of alignment of technical standards; and discrimination in favour of local companies.

The overall picture that emerged from this survey was that EU companies are increasingly embedded in China as long-term corporate citizens serving Chinese consumers, attempting to localise their management despite recruitment and retention problems, and achieving a reasonable financial performance. They are strongly supportive of the Chinese government's intentions to improve the regulatory environment and to tackle environmental and IPR problems, but they would like to see more effective action on these issues, and soon. They want to be treated equally, but see evidence that at present this does not always happen. For now, their commitment to China remains firm, and indeed most look forward to expanding their businesses, and are not deterred by the increasingly competitive environment. Their bullishness is mostly based on the continuing strength of China's economic growth and the resulting growth in domestic consumption.

> *The engagement of EU companies in China is strong and long-term. EU companies remain committed to their China businesses and want to expand them. That also sums up my own personal experience as a businessman in China*

The engagement of EU companies in China is strong and long-term. It can be expected to grow further if high economic growth is maintained and if action is taken to improve a number of negative aspects of the investment environment. Lower economic growth, a deterioration or lack of improvement in the investment environment, or a combination of these scenarios, could trigger a shift in sentiment, but currently EU companies remain committed to their China businesses and want to expand them. That also sums up my own personal experience as a businessman in China. I had seen the low days in 1989, and now was privileged to witness China as business boomed.

Pondering the riddle

I had grown humble while witnessing the rapid changes taking place in China, while at the same time trying to remain critical, as a sympathetic guest of this splendid country. And often I asked myself where this would lead. I found a friend in Volker Stanzel, with whom I could reflect on these changes in all their complexities, because he was not only well positioned, as the new German ambassador, to gain a first-hand glimpse behind the Chinese political screen, but he also shared my fascination with, and passion and love for, China.

In the only quiet moment of the average week, we met on Sundays at The Bookworm bookshop and cafe, our usual hideout in Beijing, to reward ourselves with espressos and cheesecake, exchange notes and talk about our favourite topic: China. Sitting amongst the books, we felt that most books on China tended to fade very fast. Moreover, there seem to be only three categories of book about China: the 'how to get rich in China' book, followed by the 'I travel in China and will tell you what it looks like' book, and then the very serious books that are the preserve of academics only.

What was missing was a small book about diplomatic and business patterns of behaviour. As old China hands, we had encountered many examples in our nearly 30 years of China-watching, and felt that our collective knowledge could provide enough material for a small guide. An exhaustive analysis of patterns of Chinese behaviour was ruled out, as we were both far too busy in our day jobs.

Unwrapping the puzzle

So we came up with the idea of looking at China through a prism of set behaviours in politics and business. Not only was it an intellectual challenge to try to establish the themes, it was also a challenge to keep the book as crisp and concise as possible. Given China's long history and its vast size, it was agonising to select just nine themes. The headings we came up with, and the patterns they describe, are as diverse as 'fake and real', the development of law in China, ideology and the spiritual void that has been evident in recent years.

We tried to show how the Chinese elites evolved and to explore the similarities in the behavioural patterns of imperial mandarins and Communist bureaucrats. In a special chapter, we tried to answer the question of how a country as large as China could be managed effectively. This challenge has occupied the country's rulers through every dynasty in Chinese history, up until the present day. One chapter is dedicated to the principle of trust and the concept of *guanxi*, while another focuses on China's dreamers and democrats.

China is very open to ideas and influences from the outside world, yet members of the new middle classes focus on their private lives without challenging how they are perceived in society. We dwelled on the concept of chaos, as Chinese have always had a strong longing for order, and social conformity is seen as the price the individual has to pay to achieve this order. Chinese leaders have always used this fear of chaos to suppress opposition and challenges to their rule: for example, 'China could be in chaos given the magnitude of its problems, and already faces many challenges but we, the Communist Party, are the only organisation capable of managing the problem. Without us, chaos!' The final chapter examines the patterns of Chinese foreign policy.

After selecting our nine patterns of behaviour, we were all too aware that we might make fools of ourselves by pretending that those nine themes would cover the whole of China. However, 'Project Cheesecake' was under way, the patterns of behaviour were outlined and the chapters divided up between us. During the next few months we fought hard to carve out time from our hectic daily schedules to write something that made sense and that might be of help to readers.

We were worried that the book might end up full of shallow platitudes, with China straightjacketed into nine simplified clichés; very often we refer to 'the Chinese' as if there is only one single character in this country of 1.3 billion people. However, on completing the project we were sure that the analysis we had come up with was varied and vivid enough to show that simplicity and clarity could actually enhance the overall picture. Volker left China in autumn 2007, and we hope the book will see bookshops in Germany and elsewhere in 2009.

So, in the end, it is through words wrapped in a book that I have tried to understand China. I probably never will understand it completely, but I think I have come close.

> *We dwelled on the concept of chaos, as the Chinese have always had a strong longing for order, and social conformity is seen as the price the individual has to pay to achieve this order*

Jim Gradoville
President, United Technologies
International Operations – China

First came to China: 1983

Jim Gradoville graduated from the University of Notre Dame in 1976 with a degree in government and international relations and served at the Office of the US Trade Representative in Washington DC from 1980–84.

He joined Motorola in 1988 as Director of International Trade in Washington DC and in 1998 moved to Beijing and was named as Motorola Vice President, Asia Pacific Government Relations in 1999, responsible for regulatory and trade policy matters. He is now responsible for promoting United Technologies' corporate identity and presence in China, including building long-term strategic partnerships and positive relationships with the Chinese government.

Jim has lived and worked full-time in China since 1998 and lives in Beijing with his two adopted daughters, Wendi and Whalen. He is a former Chairman of the American Chamber of Commerce in China, and is active in many other aspects of the overseas community.

Building bridges

Jim Gradoville sees his life as a bridge between China and his native United States. Much of his China business life has been focused on improving trade links; away from the office, his pride and joy are his adopted daughters whom he hopes will be able to combine the best of both cultures. He is also immensely proud to have been chosen to carry the Olympic Torch for the 2008 Games

What's changed since I first came here? God... everything. My first trip here was in 1983. I took a vacation with my girlfriend at the time. It was just for a few weeks; I remember it was January and it was cold: it seemed everything was cold and grey. It was good to have that experience, and to see the place as it was then, with the lack of anything to do other than sightsee – the Forbidden City, the Great Wall. At the time, I was living and working in Washington DC, so I was used to a bigger city with a lot of choices, a lot of variety. On that first trip, I remember walking down the street, and I saw the Jinguo Hotel and thought 'Wow! It's so Western!' It was the only place like it; I was so surprised. It seemed so forbidding, but it certainly had a lot of character. Even though I didn't live here then and was just a visitor, the hotel wasn't very inviting. That's how things were – cold and grey.

I remember the airport when we arrived in Beijing: I walked out of the door and there were no cars, no people. It was really eerie. Now they use that as the private terminal at Beijing's Capital Airport. At that time, if you went anywhere, everything had to be pre-arranged, and we always had to be accompanied. Most people used tour packages – but we didn't. Instead, we did it city by city, calling ahead, making arrangements. We'd arrive at an airport and a car would pick us up, and made sure we got checked in to our hotel. So when we arrived in Bejing, we waited in that eerie emptiness two or three minutes, and then a solitary car came and picked us up and took us to the hotel. But, once at the hotel we were on our own and while I'm sure we were monitored along the way we still had a great deal of freedom to roam around, more or less as we wanted.

Starting in 1995, I began coming back to China with Motorola on business trips, when I

With Vice Premier Zeng Peiyan at an AmCham dinner, December 2003

My Thirty Years in China | 279

Jim Gradoville

was doing business development. My interest in China was piqued during those short trips, which lasted just a few days at a time. And it struck me how quickly the place had changed. In the twelve short years since I first came, Beijing had added the new airport and the Third Ring Road, and there were many more cars (about which I'll say more later). At that point, Beijing still wasn't as opulent as it is now – for example, the incredible variety in choices of food we have today – but it had changed a lot. People no longer just wore blue-grey clothes; there were cosmetics and colours and you could see the enthusiasm and excitement of the people. It wasn't completely different, of course – there was still a fair amount of grey around.

> *There was pollution, as there is today. At that time, though, it was more coal dust than smog. Trucks dropped coal off at every hutong area, and householders would pick up their share, and then shovel it into their furnaces*

It wasn't until the late 1990s that I finally got the opportunity to move to Asia full-time. It was supposed to be China – that's what I had wanted – but Motorola first moved me to Singapore. It was in 1998 that I was finally able to become a Beijing resident. For me, the whole situation was so unique, and so totally different from today. There was pollution, as there is today. At that time, though, it was more coal dust than smog. Trucks dropped coal off in every *hutong* area, and then householders would come and pick up their share, and then shovel it into their furnaces. What it did to the air was unforgettable. Working in the office, any papers that had been left on top of desks had to be shaken to remove the coal dust that collected on them. We just learned to deal with it: either you put things away, or everything would get sooty from the coal dust.

Now versus then

Choice: that's really the most important change. Relatively speaking, the Chinese people have been fortunate to the extent that they could travel out of the country to study or emigrate, especially compared with Russia, where people couldn't emigrate at all until the Soviet Union broke up.

In terms of work there's been a decisive increase in choices. The work situation has consistently improved over time. Business ties to state-owned enterprises were starting to be broken down even before I got here in 1998, and this allowed people to have the choice to work where they really wanted to work. They also got to choose to live where they wanted to live; to eat where they wanted to eat. The economy has been growing, so that improves things, of course.

In addition, the government has also really made it easier for us foreigners to work and live here. Just look at everything a foreigner can do now in Beijing. Even when I first started living here, people were still living in what I call the 'VCR world'. People had entire collections of videos: since we had nothing to do, we just watched movies. Maybe we would go to restaurant, or to a bar – and of course there were all the cultural sights – but otherwise, there was nothing to do. Now there's just so

Building bridges

much variety. Look at any of the several city magazines and you'll see an incredible array of options.

As I mentioned, the traffic and all the new cars are one key example of the changes Beijing has seen. When I moved here ten-and-a-half years ago, Motorola had a rule about driver's licences. This stated that employees couldn't get a driver's licence until they had resided in a place for six months. I had a driver at the time, but I wanted my freedom on the weekends. I didn't want to have to arrange every little thing in advance, like going to the market or going out of the city. I wanted my licence and I just couldn't wait.

At AmCham in October 2004 with WTO negotiators Ambassador Charlene Barshevsky, US Trade Representative and Long Yongtu, Assistant Minister, Moftec

So I got my licence and, since there were really no rules on the road, it was so much fun to drive. You could go the wrong way up a one-way street, you could drive on the sidewalk. Of course, rules existed but there were so few cars, and nothing was really enforced. For example, to get my licence, I had to take a blood test – but no eye test. I guess the logic was that if I was in an accident they would know my blood type, but they didn't even check if I could see.

Since I like driving, it was incredibly enjoyable; I could do pretty much anything. I remember driving off the Third Ring Road, and looking at the sea of bicycles. Today, there are so many cars, and drivers are incredibly impatient. They'll honk at pedestrians and cyclists, and I'm just amazed at how the culture of the road is so different. Some of the pedestrians remember how things were; they rebel by slowing down when crossing the street, and sometimes they don't even check to see if a car is coming. I imagine the walkers are saying to the drivers, 'Screw you'.

I remember, once I had been living here a few years (I think this was in 2001), when I saw my first red car in Beijing – it just blew me away. That image of red coming through the greyness – it reminded me of that scene in the movie *Schindler's List* when the little girl wearing the red dress walks into shot. I'm not saying that Beijing changed overnight, and the changes are still happening, but at the time it was incredible.

Changes in the business environment

Changes in the business arena are really visible. There's one story from 2000 or 2001 that illustrates how the need for *guanxi* in the past was much greater than it is today. At that point, I had started a new job at Motorola, running government relations throughout

Jim Gradoville

Asia-Pacific, when the Chinese government proposed some new regulations in the area of encryption. In pretty much any area of the electronics industry – mobile phones, to state one example – and also in programming and platforms (take Microsoft Outlook), you require a basic amount of encryption to prevent people from hacking in. It was a crucial issue to many companies.

The proposed regulation required that just about everything was supposed to be shared with the government. That meant everything, including IT networks. So a group of people got together: representatives from four or five associations joined up, including people from the American Chamber of Commerce (AmCham) and from the US Information Technology Office (USITO) and especially the US-China Business Council which took the lead. After surveying a lot of companies about the impact that those proposed policies would have, we sat around the table and drafted a position paper. In it, we concluded that it was beyond the pale of what we believed was appropriate.

What was noteworthy about that situation, from a business point of view, was that it was the first time that a group of companies had joined together, we were told, to state their case and explain the issues to the government. We simply went over to the Ministry of Foreign Trade and Cooperation (Moftec), sat down and had a meeting with government officials. We had taken a reasonable, well-informed position and explained how the proposed policy was going way further than it should. Nobody knew what to expect, but in the end it turned out to be a good meeting. Ultimately, they rescinded the proposal. However, since China has an interest in having the ability to have its own encryption, the issue keeps popping up again.

At the American Chamber of Commerce China Government Appreciation Dinner, December 2003

Building bridges

Now, eight years later, just look at the amount of interaction and the change. China's inclusion in the World Trade Organisation was a watershed event but it's important to remember that it's just the latest phase in almost thirty years of reform. Today, there's increased engagement, and it's official and much more standardised. Businesses have AmCham and the US-China Business Council and there exists a broad-based association of companies in general to represent business interests and speak for our needs. *Guanxi* is still important but it doesn't play quite the role it once did.

The challenge of doing business now has more to do with competition within this marketplace. In the past, the questions were 'How do I do that?' or 'How do I get around that?'. There are still many issues and problems that need to change. It's still not a transparent enough place, it still needs more clarity in terms of rules and regulations, and there are significant IPR and M&A issues. Also, even though the leadership has been composed of technocrats, engineers, mostly (which means they usually just say 'Give us the data'), sometimes there arises a conflict of interest between foreigners and their companies (or even Chinese and their companies) and what the government wants. Of course that happens. Regardless of that, however, it's more transparent than before, and it's easier to know the rules and regulations.

> *Increasingly, China is a more normal place to do business. The whole challenge of doing business now has more to do with competition within this marketplace*

Since I like to work on policy, China has offered me lots of opportunity to have an impact and learn along the way. In other countries, you can beat your head against the wall forever. Of course, the economic growth is great – and that is a huge part of why there's so much attention now.

However, there wasn't always this much attention and interest. When I held that business development job at Motorola, I was also working on Latin America. So when I finally made the permanent move east, I remember that people kept asking, 'Why China? Look at Latin America – the vibrancy, the culture. Why don't you go there instead?' I looked at people who came here ten, fifteen years before me – and just like them, the culture and the opportunity here intrigued me. I looked at this place and thought, 'This place will have a lot of growth, and change.' You could just feel it. The people were dynamic, they wanted to move quickly and to change things. It was always 'Let's go, let's go! Let's bring it together.' I compare that with my previous work on Japan, which is a very different system.

My first job after I graduated with a master's degree from the Lyndon B. Johnson School was in Washington DC, in a Presidential management training programme started under Jimmy Carter. I started working on US-Japan issues at that point, and when I went to the office of the US Trade Representative I continued that focus. We worked on 'Section 301' trade cases and ended up spending a lot of time negotiating with Japan's government on market access. There was a lot of friction;

Jim Gradoville

we basically had to force open trade with Japan. It was good training for my later business career. But China and Japan are very different. In Japan, you couldn't invest at all and the market was closed in many ways. When I was at Motorola, we had to use the US government's Section 301 measures to open every product line in Japan. People in the US government would say about Japan, 'They only understand power.' That was all muscle.

In comparison, China has opened itself to trade, in an amazing way. China had a closed market, but it was opening up. The way we approach the Chinese government is entirely different from the approach people used in Japan in the 1980s. It doesn't work in China to 'use a big hammer', to use the pressure of Washington. They don't respond in a positive way, and the US government is smart enough to know it doesn't work and instead has a more subtle, cooperative approach.

I admit I would never have been able to forecast growth as consistent as what's actually taken place in China. And people think it can't go on forever, this machine of growth. Frankly, I thought I'd have left China in three to five years at the most. It's turned out to be twelve years, so far.

Personal life

From my perspective looking out, you sit in China and watch the world go by. Watching what's happened internationally over the past seven years, one can't help but have a unique perspective on the US, on Europe, about development, government and change. I simply wouldn't have this perspective if I had lived in the US. I really value that. Sure, doing a job, you accomplish things – but that's true anywhere.

The things I've learned professionally are not just China lessons, but they are very important. The longer I'm here, the more I realise how little I know. I didn't study East Asia at school, so it's often on-the-job training: whatever came across my job, across my computer, through my involvement with AmCham and interaction with the China government. As a result, I've learned not to assume I know what was going on. I've learned that you can get a lot more done if you bring different people from different understandings or expertise to work on things together. I've also realised that everything doesn't have to get done in one day.

I've changed personally, too. Of course, becoming a parent: in terms of my kids I've changed, but that would be true no matter where I was. For my kids, hopefully this will broaden them, in a way I didn't have when I was growing up in Iowa. I love Iowa, but there just isn't as much stimulation and opportunity there as there is here.

China for me has been a good place to live, given my situation. There may be better places around, but as a single parent China is perfect. I have a great *ayi* (nanny): she's an excellent female role model for my two girls. I'm fortunate that my company has provided a driver, and he also helps by taking the kids to school and to their activities. As a single parent in the US, without that support and help, life for me would be extremely hectic. I'd always be afraid that I had too much going on. As a parent here, I can concentrate on my job, more than a single parent in the US could, and still have a caring environment for my children. That's a practical

Building bridges

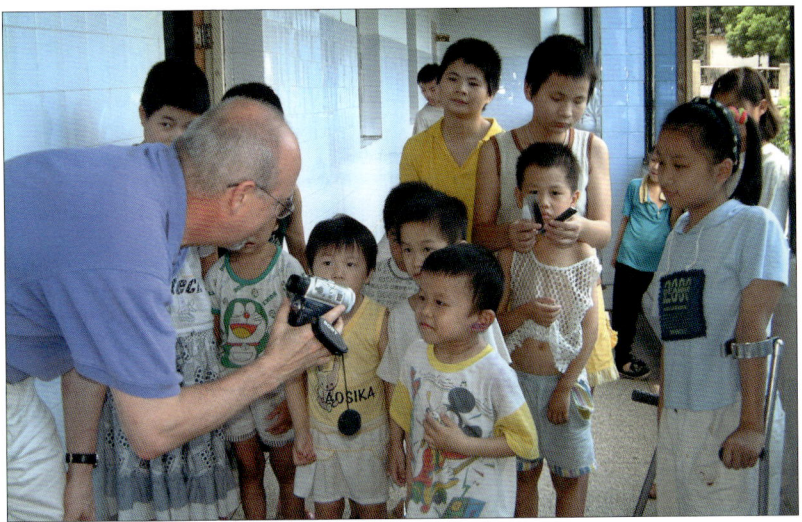

Visiting the orphanage in Jiujiang in June 2002, where I adopted my daughters Wendi and Whalen

thing, but very important.

When I started the process of adopting my daughters, I didn't anticipate everything that would come with it. I just wanted to start a family – it wasn't about saving the world or anything like that. But it's panned out to be really wonderful for me; I've learned so much. For example, people will comment, 'That's great, your kids are being raised bi-culturally.' But really, they're in a third culture. They are not Chinese, being raised in a Chinese family. And they're not American, because we're here. Their first language is Chinese, they go to a Chinese school, and they often go back with the *ayi* to her home in Hebei. We often travel around China, so they'll know the country, but it will be different than if they were living in a *hutong* in Beijing.

My kids will have to deal with that question, 'Am I Chinese? Am I American?' They'll have to go through that, and I'll have to deal

You can get a lot more done if you bring different people from different understandings or expertise to work on things together. I've also realised that everything doesn't have to get done in one day

with it when it comes up. Hopefully, though, these won't become life-consuming issues which might paralyse them from doing other things. I hope they'll be able to face them and grow from them.

By living overseas, they see that the world is not all the same everywhere. It's not one single way, and families are all different. Sometimes people ask my kids: 'Where's your

Jim Gradoville

mother?' 'We don't have one,' my littlest will say, or 'Well, my mother died. Then Daddy adopted me.' People don't know how to respond to that – so my girls will have to deal with this stuff. But I hope I'm giving them opportunities and love to build upon.

Olympic Torchbearer

Running with the Olympic Torch was such a great experience. It represents something greater than myself, and it is a singular honour that I'll never forget. I was very fortunate to have been chosen through the Lenovo competition. While attending the Special Olympics, I decided to apply. I said that I felt as if my personal and professional life in China had been like a bridge between China and America; professionally, in terms of my service with AmCham as Chairman promoting China's membership of the WTO, and with UTC and its legacy of energy efficiency and environmental conservation. Personally speaking, I view my family – my kids – as an example of that bridge between the US and China. The UTC employees voted online and the response was so positive that Lenovo selected me as one of the torchbearers.

We all look at the Olympics and the torch, and there are a lot of different perspectives out there. I look at the fact that the Chinese people, where I ran in Jingzhou, were just ecstatic. It was like a Notre Dame pep rally on steroids. Even though I was part of one of the last groups to run – we got dropped off along the 17km stretch depending on where we were each slated to run – the crowds were packed. It seemed liked there were hundreds of thousands of people and when they saw the bus filled with torch runners, the crowds just went wild.

One problem I faced was that my kids were not allowed to stay in my hotel with me; there was really heavy security. So I had to go out to meet my kids, and when I was out of my hotel, there were hordes of people who wanted my autograph. They wanted me to sign clothes, body parts, baby clothes. They were just thrilled to have any contact with the Olympics at all. In Jingzhou, few people will have direct contact with the Games themselves, so this was their one tangible, real experience, with all the pageantry, people and music.

With Wendi and Whalen and the Olympic Torch in Jingzhou, 2 June 2008

Chinese people are just so thrilled about the Olympics. For example, just

Building bridges

Running with the torch made me realise just how much the Olympics mean to ordinary Chinese people

after the run I was at a business meeting with aviation regulators and customers; we were discussing the new Pratt and Whitney Geared Turbo Fan airplane engine. They asked me to bring out the torch I had run with, and when I gave a little speech, the people in the meeting just came alive. These business professionals wanted pictures taken with the torch and wanted to touch it, to hold it, like an idol. So with every hint in foreign newspapers that people elsewhere are unhappy about the torch, or with anything that criticises the Olympics, Chinese people feel like they are being insulted personally, and treated unfairly. There's not one person with whom I've spoken who hasn't felt that way. Even Chinese living overseas agree with this point of view.

I've had many other positive experiences to live, learn and contribute to China, such as being a Board member for the Half the Sky Foundation, which supports orphanages throughout China

There were hordes of people who wanted my autograph. They wanted me to sign clothes, body parts, baby clothes. They were just thrilled to have any contact with the Olympics at all

and is now a model the government is emulating. Also, being the Chairman of the Board of The Beijing Center at UIBE University in Beijing. You see, I've gained so much from China. I really didn't expect it, but it's now defined my life.

Scott Kronick
President, Ogilvy Public Relations
Worldwide, China

First came to China: 1991

Scott Kronick has helped to build Ogilvy PR into China's leading public relations consultancy. With 21 years at the agency, 13 in Beijing, he has established offices in Beijing, Shanghai and Guangzhou and has built the firm into China's leader in terms of size, client base, talent and relationships.

As well as successfully helping to develop branding strategies for many leading Chinese firms and international firms seeking to enter the China market, Scott is a director of the Tsinghua-Ogilvy Programme for Public Branding.

This joint venture between the Ogilvy Group and Tsinghua University serves as a think tank on location branding for officials throughout China and on the way that China communicates with the outside world. In 2007 its work included addressing Western media perceptions of Chinese exports, while in 2008 it has focused on the XXIXth Olympic Games in Beijing.

E-mail: scott.kronick@ogilvy.com

Branding in China

As head of a leading public relations firm, Scott Kronick has seen huge changes in Chinese society and in the way that the country is perceived by the outside world. With the Olympic Games creating unprecedented levels of interest, he has been asked to help China refine its presentation skills for international audiences

It was a warm day back in the spring of 1992 that would change my destiny forever. I was in Bali on a company-sponsored trip when I met a woman I believed to be the most beautiful in the world. She did not speak much English and nor did I speak Chinese; she was from Taipei, Taiwan and I was from Flint, Michigan. There was an unspoken chemistry though, bridged by a computer dictionary that helped us get beyond simple sentences.

My China story, however, began in 1987 – two years after I graduated from Syracuse University in the United States. After spending a couple of years in a small public relations firm in New York City, I landed a job at Ogilvy & Mather Public Relations (O&MPR) in New York. I joined O&MPR for three reasons: first, they were known for being the leaders in creativity in the public relations industry; second, they had a global network that would allow me the opportunity to get transferred internationally; while the third, and perhaps most compelling, reason was that the Chairman of the Asia network of O&MPR was a gentleman by the name of Paul Verbinnen. Today, Paul is one of the principals of Sard Verbinnen, a well-respected financial public relations firm headquartered in New York. But in 1987 Paul was a star in the O&MPR global network. Interestingly, I had a similar educational background and career track as Paul; we both graduated from Syracuse University and worked for the same small PR firm after graduation. In fact, a few colleagues at that small firm had compared me with Paul, and I figured: 'Asia … how fascinating!'

From that point on I thought about Asia often. I read books about the coming 'Pacific Century'. Dr. Thomas Horton, then President of the American Management Association, as well as my client and mentor at the time, encouraged me to pursue an international career. His advice was: 'Get international experience. The CEOs of the future will have a global view.' At O&MPR, I worked hard to establish myself and after a year I put in my request for a transfer to one of our foreign offices if the opportunity presented itself. In 1988, there was discussion of a posting in Sydney, Australia, and I was ecstatic – this was around the same time as the first *Crocodile Dundee* movie was out. But that opportunity soon fizzled out.

In late 1990 a new position came up. I was called into our CEO's office and told that the O&MPR operation in Taipei was looking for someone to support the newly appointed General Manager. The CEO laid it out: 'We have an opportunity in Taipei for you – are you interested?'

'Yes, absolutely. I have always wanted to go to Taipei!' I responded. I then proceeded to run to my office to check out exactly where on the map Taipei was

Scott Kronick

located. I learned that the city was indeed the capital city of Taiwan, the place where nearly everything was made in the 1980s. Shortly afterwards, I was put in contact with the General Manager to plan my first trip to Asia.

Fast forward to July 2008. I am today married to Lisa Wei, the woman I met in Bali on my first Ogilvy company trip, and have two children – both of whom speak Mandarin as their first language. I have lived in Asia for 17 years, 13 of which have been in Beijing. And I have worked for the Ogilvy Group for 21 years, all of them with Ogilvy Public Relations Worldwide (Ogilvy PR), which is our company's name today. After consecutive four-year stints in New York and Taiwan, I was presented with the opportunity to open our offices in Beijing and Shanghai in 1995. I didn't hesitate.

Today, Ogilvy PR has more than 450 people working in ten offices in six geographies throughout China. I have been blessed with finding the right staff to help me build the Ogilvy PR business here over the past 13 years. We have a number of employees who have been with us for ten years or more, and many who joined more than five years ago. In the public relations industry, particularly in China, retaining employees is the most critical challenge; and having long-term staff has been our recipe for success. I am grateful to my colleagues who first and foremost have been my guides through the wonderful adventures I have experienced. These people also serve a portfolio of the largest and most amazing companies operating in China – companies that are driving a lot of the change that has taken place over the past 30 years. My family, the Ogilvy Group, my staff and clients largely define my past 13 years.

My combined 17 years in Taiwan and China are largely defined by a number of experiences that have made up what I would call my continuous Asian education. Friends who have lived in China as long as I have often remark, 'If you visit China for a week, you can write a book. If you live here for a year, you can write an article. And if you've been here for more than a decade, you know what you don't know and will never be able to write anything.'

The first time I set foot in Asia was

Our family group: me, my wife Lisa, daughter Jacquelin and son Samuel

Branding in China

in early 1991. I arrived in Taipei in the evening and was shuttled off to the Sherwood Hotel in an arranged car. My first impression, and one that will stay with me for the rest of my life, was of the number of motorbikes on the streets when I arrived – there were hundreds, if not thousands. The moped was the main source of transport for the masses in Taiwan, and I once read a statistic that there were more mopeds per square kilometre in Taiwan than in any other place on Earth. I made it a habit to carry around a camera to try and capture a record number of people on a single-seater moped. In fact, I once saw a family of six on a moped built for one.

If you visit China for a week, you can write a book. If you live here for a year, you can write an article. If you've been here for more than a decade, you'll never be able to write anything

The other distinct memory of my first full day in Asia was a stroll around the back streets of central Taipei and the smell of food stalls still open in the wee small hours of the morning. There were noodle carts and *dou jiang* (soybean milk) stalls and, much to my surprise, coffee shops. There was a drink at one of the shops composed of milk tea and rice balls that has since grown to be a personal favourite. The name for this drink is *jenju naicha*, which literally means 'pearl milk tea'. I have learned to appreciate many Asian delicacies in my years in Asia, but one taste I have yet to acquire is that of *chou doufu*, or 'stinky tofu'.

My first week in Asia was a success, complete with interviews, a review of the work going on in the Taipei office and spending time with the General Manager – a woman by the name of Ruby Fu, who has since become one my closest friends. This is not the Ruby Fu that the restaurant is named after, although if it were I imagine it would be a huge success because of the following Ruby has. She walked me through all aspects of what a posting in Taiwan would be like and then recommended to the Taiwan management team that they hire me.

I was immediately whisked off to Hong Kong to meet with the regional chairman for Ogilvy Public Relations in Asia. After an approximately one-hour flight from Taipei to Hong Kong, we made the notoriously frantic landing at the former Kai Tak Airport. Before long I was on the ground and on my way to the Conrad Hotel. Following a series of meetings in Hong Kong, including a breakfast at the Mandarin Oriental Hotel, I was congratulated on my future role in China: 'You are on your way,' remarked the late Steve Lyons, Ogilvy PR's Chairman for Asia at the time. 'You will be the Group Account Director at Ogilvy PR in Taiwan.'

The testing ground

The next four years in Taiwan proved to be the testing ground for my China experience. Beyond gaining a basic understanding of the language and culture, I found out what it took to run a public relations business in an Asian culture. I learned about the concept of *mianzi*, translated as 'face', which in the Western world is most simply understood as 'personal pride'. I experienced the kindness of Taiwanese people and grew attached to the concept of *fengshui*. But most importantly, I gained a bride who would root me even more deeply in Asia.

Lisa Wei grew up in a way that was vastly different from most people I knew in Michigan. She was the second child of a tight-knit family of five who lived in the Wen Hua district of Taipei, one of the oldest and toughest neighbourhoods in Taiwan. Lisa's family was lower-middle class, and at a very early age she assumed responsibility for raising her younger brothers and sisters while her mother and grandmother worked. In her youth, Lisa's only brush with Westerners was selling incense to foreigners at one of the oldest temples in Taiwan, for ten times the price she would give locals. She had also earned a black belt in judo and put herself through college. She was now hitched to a boy from the Midwest whose only connection with China when growing up was through fortune cookies and General Tsao's Chicken.

After one year of dating, from 1993–94, Lisa and I decided to marry. What followed was a procession of customs that would make even the most superstitious person wary. We had an engagement party, commonly known as a *dinghuen*. This was followed by an official marriage party one month later, held just after a crowded legal ceremony in late October 1994. The big day though was 2 December, our official anniversary, when we hosted a celebratory party. Prior to the party, I was shepherded to Lisa's home where I met the *meiren* (matchmaker) who would lead me through the affairs of the marriage. There was the giving of six gifts and of course the dowry – about which I learned only after I had proposed. I used to complain about how much I spent for my wife, but she would argue that high-priced pigs cost more than what I had agreed to pay.

Beyond the wedding fanfare was the traditional Chinese wedding photograph session, characterised by the bride and groom dressing in a million different outfits and posing as though we were auditioning for a part in the *Sound of Music*. And, of course, there were the cookies that go out to all of the friends and relatives we knew, or thought we knew. Needless to say, marriage in Taiwan was a distant cry from the suburbs of Michigan or the streets of New York.

Four months later I was off to Beijing to open Ogilvy PR's first office in the Chinese mainland. Shortly after settling into my room at the Hilton

Preparing for our wedding in Taipei. The matchmaker (*meiren*) is on the left

Branding in China

Hotel in Beijing, I was met by a man who would forever be a friend. Li Hong met me in the lobby and we were off to Beihai Park for a wonderful meal together. Although Li Hong had been appointed my Deputy General Manager by our joint venture partner, those who knew us realised we were equals. After spending nearly four years in the Chinese Consulate in New York as the Cultural Attaché, Li Hong had returned to China, and had left the Ministry to join the Foreign Enterprises Services Company (FESCO) – the appointed joint venture partner of Ogilvy PR.

My friend and coilleague Li Hong, the man who made so much of it happen

At dinner that first evening it was clear we were going to get along. I came to China knowing very little about the social environment, yet with a deep interest in the public relations profession and its evolution in Asia. Li Hong was a deeply rooted and networked individual in China and a fluent English speaker. In the infancy of the public relations business in China, client companies needed people who could get things done. I served as the guy who helped to take and interpret the brief, and Li Hong made it all happen.

Our first clients included BMW, BAT and Shell, of which BMW continues as a client today. As BMW established its representative office, we concurrently set up the Ogilvy PR office. In a city populated by bicycles and taxi-cabs that looked like they would break down at any time, BMW worked to set up an operation to service the growing number of imports in demand in China. In 1994, there were 480 BMW vehicles in mainland China, compared with more than 50,000 recorded by the end of 2007. The company's representative office had two people back then; today BMW China's operation is comprised of more than 10,000 people.

Back in 1995, it was common to have regular 'China days', characterised by having your best day and worst day on the same day. The early Ogilvy PR offices were housed in an old school that lent itself to the creative process, but fell far short of the creature comforts I was accustomed to. Upon learning that I would be using a squat toilet for the foreseeable future, I tried to get the landlord to build a Western-style one, but he would

Scott Kronick

not budge. I succumbed to buying a few stools with holes in them to alleviate the pressure I would have to put on my damaged knees if I had to squat. Making a phone call was equally difficult. The only mobile phones in the market at the time were bricks, and everyone used sub-standard fixed lines. As a sign foretelling the power that mobility would have in China, however, everyone carried a pager.

> *My baby daughter was beautiful. I smiled and got very emotional – only to be tapped on the shoulder by a Western guy who informed me that I was cooing over his child*

One of the fondest memories I have of Ogilvy PR's early days in China was of our group lunches. As we grew from a team of three people – Li Hong, me and one other founding staff member – to ten in the first year, we would frequently have lunch together. We would go across the street and buy lunch for the whole crew – most often for less then US$10. Coming from New York and also Taiwan, treating the whole staff to a complete lunch for so little was a delight. The US$1 taxi rides for distances less than 10 miles and the US$2 haircuts were also favourites in 1995, and the haircuts can still be found today. In the mid-1990s, however, entertainment was sparse. There were only a few bars or eateries – Poachers, Franks Place, the Hard Rock Café – and group entertainment most often involved karaoke at KTV clubs, where we would take turns butchering catchy tunes from the 1980s. There were also the beginnings of a strong

From modest beginnings: the Ogilvy PR team in 1995, our first full year of operation in Beijing

Branding in China

sports culture, and I joined both soccer and basketball leagues for those people or referees who would let me play.

My daughter soon arrived and life changed forever. On 2 December 1996, exactly two years after our wedding celebration, Jacquelin Kronick was born. Jacquelin came much earlier than expected, and since Lisa had returned to Taiwan to deliver, I happened to still be in Beijing when she went into labour. It was midnight in Beijing, and I begged her to wait. I arranged a flight first thing in the morning and, after flying from Beijing to Hong Kong and then on to Taiwan, I arrived around 3pm, only to miss my first child's birth by nine hours. I ran into the hospital first to see my wife and then into the nursery to set eyes upon my daughter. She was beautiful. The only mixed-skin child in the nursery

A formal occasion in 1998. Both our children have grown up speaking Mandarin as their first language

was lying there in front of me. I smiled and got very emotional – only to be tapped on the shoulder by a Western guy who informed me that I was actually cooing over his child. Hiding around the corner was my Jacquelin, and she was more beautiful than ever.

Today, Jacquelin is 11 years old, full of humour and a delight to be around. She is also very adept at walking and running, which I am ecstatic about considering that she didn't actually hit earth until the age of five. It is common for Chinese grandparents to not only help raise a child, but – and I kid you not – to also carry them around for the extent of their childhood. My mother-in-law also assisted Lisa quite a bit after her birth with her *zuo yuezi*, which literally means 'sit for a month'. This is a custom whereby a woman who has just given birth rests for one month, does not shower and does not eat anything other than Chinese medicine that smells horribly. I enjoyed Lisa's *zuo yuezi* period as much as she did, and in the end it was difficult to tell who gave birth, Lisa or me.

Business highs and lows

To understand how far China has come is to have experienced life here in the mid-1990s. Things had already begun to change before I arrived, as foreign direct investment grew from US$1.5bn in the early 1980s to US$40bn by the late 1990s. Jiang Zemin became General Secretary of the Communist Party in 1989 and then President four years later, and, together with soon-to-be Premier Zhu Rongji, his power-base was strengthening. With the focus in China on attracting foreign investment, there were discussions in corporate boardrooms about how a business could not be successful globally unless it had a strong China operation.

> *I tried to explain to a young staffer that 'the early bird gets the worm', and she told me she would rather be the 'late worm that misses the early bird'*

Our business also grew dramatically. We were largely helping multinational companies to introduce their brands in China, and focused our efforts on public affairs (government relations) and communications related to these brands. The most memorable times included almost sinking in a boat at an event held at the Summer Palace, where we were shipping promotional items across the lake and the boat could not hold the items together with my weight. There was the launch of the Land Rover at the Forbidden City, considered one of the first commercial events held at this historic venue. For Nokia, there was the first global launch of a mobile phone outside of Europe, held in China: evidence of how forward-thinking this company was and representative of why it is so successful in China.

In terms of managing a business, there were great highs and some lows. Running a business where people were optimistic and believed in the future was a dream. Keeping these people happy remains the key challenge, as the opportunities were, and continue to be, all around. Staff retention requires more than money and interesting work, as benefits, flexibility and future opportunities all play a role. I often joke with my parents that the 'great American dream is alive and well and exists in

Ogilvy has a strong sports culture and I play in both soccer and basketball leagues, when permitted

Branding in China

Befriending and growing together with the staff has been a particular highlight of my time in China

China'. Our first secretary left to start her own agency three years after joining us. Today, many early Ogilvy PR alumni have started and sold their own businesses, led other agencies or have assumed leading roles as corporate communications directors at client companies. There is an active Ogilvy PR alumni network and we gather annually to share our experiences.

Befriending and growing together with the staff has been a particular highlight of my time in China. The little things are so memorable to me. I remember the first US$5,000 we made – Li Hong celebrated after the money arrived, while I had forgotten about it after the bill was sent. Notes from staff who had learned English through tapes were signed 'Thank You and Goodbye'. As the staff began to earn, they also began to spend. Colleagues who lived with their parents in one-bedroom apartments and shared a communal bathroom were buying BMWs and second apartments – generally beginning to consume.

I cautioned them to 'save for a rainy day', and they responded that I should not worry, as they would simply invest in umbrellas. The logic often baffled me. I once tried to explain to a young staffer that 'the early bird gets the worm', and she told me she would rather be the 'late worm that misses the arrival of the early bird'. When I had just begun working in New York, I had the luxury of promoting a consumer confidence study that looked at the optimism of Americans in terms of their ability to 'live better than their parents did'. In China, you had nearly an entire nation, of hundreds of millions of people, with this exact opportunity.

My Thirty Years in China

Scott Kronick

Celebrating David Ogilvy Day in China, an annual event enjoyed by all at the firm

Socially, people were beginning to feel more at ease about mixing with Westerners and talking about the past. I cherished the conversations I had with my Chinese staff about the protests at Tiananmen Square and about the Cultural Revolution. In the mid-1990s people did not speak of past political events openly without some fear of repercussions – a dynamic that has changed dramatically today. I remember a conversation with one person who broke down in tears about their experiences at Tiananmen. I had a fantastic discussion with a staff member who described what he went through during the Cultural Revolution without any emotion, stating that the biggest crime was the near-doubling of the population during this time and adding, 'That is a wrong that cannot be undone'. These staff were all my own age – mid- to late 40s – and they described self-criticism sessions first seriously and then laughed at how ridiculous they were. They had all been young during this period and they felt at the time that the Cultural Revolution was just a big party. The older you get though, the more serious and depressing the stories become.

I have a good friendship with an older gentleman who was the child of a diplomat and used to swim with Chairman Mao – he was one of the first 'Red Guards' to go marching in 1966. His stories are equally fascinating. I think the biggest eye-opener for me in my early days in China came from a conversation I had with a woman who headed our research function at Ogilvy. She was explaining in the most objective, casual way why the one-child policy was a must for China. All of the very well-educated Chinese I respected had similar views on this topic: the one-child policy was a must for the sustainability of the Chinese people. I had grown up believing that the one-child policy was a gross injustice and a violation of human rights, but after these conversations I had a totally different view.

While the main part of the hospital was in fairly good shape, the nursery was dark and bare, and the respirator was old and squeaked like it was going to break down

My second child, Samuel, was born two years after my daughter, in 1998. It was his birth that introduced me to the true challenges of the Chinese social welfare

Branding in China

system. We decided to have Samuel in China at a famous local hospital. Lisa and I figured it would be fine; the doctor was reputable and this country had already delivered 1.3 billion people. Our kid should be OK. On 25 May, Samuel was born – a beautiful young boy, but he was gasping for air. He had pneumonia and was quickly carted off to a nursery.

While the main part of the hospital was in fairly good shape, the nursery looked like something from the early 1900s. It was dark and bare, and the respirator my son was on – one of the few in the hospital – was old and squeaked like it was going to break down at any moment. Reusable bottles were piled in a sink near to where Samuel was lying, complete with locally-produced rubber nipples, which looked similar to the bottles and nipples we used to feed sheep with at the zoo. During the course of the two weeks that my son stayed in the hospital we frequently brushed away cockroaches from some of the cribs where the kids recuperated. After several weeks, Samuel began to respond to the treatment and he was home with us in mid-June.

Samuel's stay in the local hospital was exacerbated by my weak language skills – I needed my wife to explain everything to me, and she was gravely worried – and also by the lack of any hope provided by the nursing staff. Perhaps this is the local training. But while we were desperate for some sign that everything was going to be OK, they stuck to the facts of what was possible, both positive and negative. Today Samuel is a very healthy 10-year-old boy, with an appetite bigger than mine. The only legacy of his birth difficulties is recurring asthma.

My son Samuel's birth was a traumatic time for us, but at last we were able to bring him home from hospital

Scott Kronick

For the entirety of the following year I was engaged in the planning for the first FORTUNE Global Forum (FGF) to be held in China, in September 1999. There were a number of milestones that came with the Forum, including the 50th anniversary of the founding of the People's Republic. This was the first event to be held in the Shanghai Exhibition Centre and was one of the largest gatherings of CEOs ever held (about 300); attendance at the FGF '99 exceeded the total of the previous four FGFs. The then Chinese President Jiang Zemin kicked it off, pledging to 'unswervingly open up and internationalise' the Chinese economy. Incidentally, Shanghai was the rumoured venue where Steve Case, founder and chairman of AOL, and Gerry Levine, CEO of Time Warner, met to put in motion the AOL/Time Warner merger.

Given the high-profile nature of FGF '99 and the support it was given both by China and internationally, the event was seen as truly transformational

The most memorable parts of this event, however, were the countless, marathon planning meetings that took place between the FORTUNE Global Forum team, the State Council Information Office, the Shanghai City Government and Ogilvy PR. Given the high-profile nature of the conference and the support it was given by the Chinese leadership and the global business community, this meeting was seen as truly transformational for China. It reinforced China's commitment to economic growth;

An early meeting with Li Tieying, former Minister at the State Commission for Restructuring the Economy

Branding in China

A gathering to mark a visit by Shelly Lazarus, CEO of Ogilvy (fourth left), for an Ogilvy China board meeting

in the prophetic words of Jiang Zemin that evening, 'The theme of this Forum, "Next Generation Asia", is of great significance, for the development of Asia bears on the development and prosperity of all countries and regions not only in this continent but also worldwide'. The conference set the tone for what would be an average of 10 per cent annual GDP growth over the next nine years in China.

Olympic triumph, and challenging times

China was humming along at a lively pace, but 13 July 2001 was a date that would change the country forever. After campaigning for years to become the host city of the 2008 Olympic Games, Beijing found itself a finalist, competing against Toronto, Paris, Istanbul and Osaka. While Beijing officials gathered in Moscow, I was at the top of the Beijing Hotel in the famous La Vie English tea house, overlooking the Forbidden City, with my clients and local and foreign journalists. We had a television set placed outside, while food and drinks flowed. With a slight interruption for rain, we were shuffled to the third-floor lobby where another television was set up. The announcer, outgoing IOC President Juan Antonio Samaranch, appeared on the screen and said, 'The Games of the 29th Olympiad in 2008 are awarded to the city of … Beijing.'

The room erupted and people celebrated all around. Outside on Changan Street and Tiananmen Square millions of people gathered in celebration. What was most memorable

Scott Kronick

A visit to the town of Qufu, in Shandong province, the birthplace of Confucius

was that there was mass hysteria, but an absence of overt drunkenness and no violence, as might have occurred elsewhere. Millions of people danced and I saw not one fight. Almost eight years after Beijing had bid for, and lost, the opportunity to host the 2000 Olympics to the city of Sydney, Australia, the Games would finally come to the most populous nation in the world, and plans to prepare Beijing for this historic event went into motion. At the same time, however, China came under fire for its human rights record, its environmental problems, its politics and more, and over the next seven years the country would face a number of challenges that it would have to grapple with as it became more integrated into the world.

Among the most challenging times I have experienced, both at work and personally in China, was in May 1999, when the US mistakenly bombed the Chinese embassy in Belgrade. It was a time when saying less meant more. The responses from my colleagues were very telling. The more sympathetic tried to explain the way the Chinese felt: that there was no way that the bombing was a mistake and that the US knew exactly what it was doing. There were others who advised me that, if Chairman Mao was still alive, we would be at war. From a public relations standpoint, many American companies were seeking advice on what to do and say. 'Should events be cancelled? Should we apologise?' From a social standpoint, this was an extremely interesting time.

The bombing took place on a Saturday morning China time. I was hosting a doorknock training session for the Board of the American Chamber of Commerce, as the Chamber was preparing for its annual trip to Washington DC to build understanding about China to help boost US-China relations. I ran the session with a colleague from our Washington DC office by the name of Frank Pizzuro and a few friends from Burson Marstellar, a respected competitor. Frank and I held the session in the morning and then we returned to my house for a bike ride. I put my then three-year-old daughter in the child's seat and we were off. We lived downtown at the time – right down the street from the US and British embassies. As we left our building and rounded a corner, we saw hundreds of students filling the streets in front of the British Embassy and behind the US Embassy. I was confused. I told Frank that this was the first parade I had seen in China and I was trying to figure out what it was for. I didn't think it was a protest, as gathering in protest is against the law in China. I soon found out differently.

Branding in China

Hundreds of students had been bussed in from their universities to present letters of protest to the embassies. They marched in front of the buildings screaming 'Down with America!'. In the early afternoon, the demonstration was nevertheless very peaceful. We watched from our bikes, with my daughter on the back seat, for nearly an hour. Soon, however, the peaceful protests took a violent turn. As the students marched in front of the embassies they began to collect rocks to throw. As the BBC described the scene: 'In Beijing about 100,000 people invaded the embassy district, massing on streets littered with rocks and broken bottles.'

> *What was most memorable was that there was mass hysteria, but no overt drunkenness or violence, as might have occurred elsewhere. Millions of people danced, and I saw not one fight*

Deciding that things were getting out of hand, I took my daughter back home and tuned into CNN to watch events unfold. I could hear the protesters from my window and heard cars honking outside our building, as one of the only open passageways to the embassy district was a small lane next to my house. I went back out on my bike in the evening to see what was happening and it looked like all hell had broken loose. There were flags being burnt in the middle of the street and hooligans lined up

Ogilvy CEO Shelly Lazarus took time off to see some of China and to climb the Great Wall

Scott Kronick

To mark my 21 years with Ogilvy, the staff threw a party and presented a special cake

in the streets. While it had appeared that the government wanted this to be a controlled protest, it was suddenly out of control. I soon returned home. My wife came back shortly afterward from a business trip, put her hair in ponytails like a college student and went out to report first-hand on what she saw.

Clearly the Americans were not the favourites at this time, and it took a while to bring US-China relations back to normal.

A different sort of event several years later evoked similar panic. It all began with a Chinese farmer who died after suffering from an unusual respiratory disease in November 2002. Shortly after, a Chinese doctor who had treated the farmer died from similar symptoms in Hong Kong, but not before infecting 12 other people staying at his hotel. The disease – severe acute respiratory syndrome (SARS) – began to spread exponentially and eventually thousands of people across Asia and China, particularly in major cities, were infected.

Despite public denials by the Minister of Health and different government authorities, what was happening throughout the city of Beijing was chaos. SMS messages were flying around reporting on the numbers of people infected. E-mails were being shared and everyone was wondering what was going on. Not until after a *Time* magazine piece was published on 8 April 2003 did things begin to change for the better. The article was based on a signed statement sent by a physician at Beijing's Chinese People's Liberation Army General Hospital (No. 301), who said that the SARS situation was much more serious than had been reported by the Ministry of Health.

Suddenly, information was flowing and there was a distinct difference in the way the government was communicating. Personally, as a manager, and as a parent, I was faced with questions as to what was the right thing to do. Many of our staff were frightened to come to work or to travel to clients' offices. As a management team, we decided to give staff the option to do what they felt was best. They could stay home and work from home. Their teams could rotate staff in and out of the office. Until

Branding in China

things subsided, we wanted our staff, first and foremost, to feel comfortable. For our clients, we invited medical professionals to a gathering at the Capital Club for a discussion of what to do and methods of prevention. And for those still working, we tried to focus on what were the best ways to help our clients and the government at this time of need. Some of the bigger donors included Nokia and Pfizer, who donated cell phones and gauze masks, respectively.

It felt like we were living in Wolfgang Peterson's 1995 film *Outbreak*, and for those who stayed there was a feeling of loneliness. And while SARS spread and the numbers of people infected climbed, the panic outside of China grew. There was a rumour that people living in China would not be welcome to travel abroad. Members of my team were 'un-invited' from attending global business meetings held during that time. I had friends whose family members suggested that maybe now was not the right time for a family reunion.

> *Members of my team were 'un-invited' from attending global business meetings during the SARS epidemic. Family members suggested that maybe now was not the right time for a reunion*

For my wife and I, who worked in different businesses but in the same office building, the problem was unusually acute. People were saying that if one person became infected in a certain location, then all of the people in that location must go into isolation for a certain period of time. In our case, both of us would be in isolation – what would happen

At the Boao Forum, 2007, with boss Chris Graves and economist and Nobel Prize winner Muhammad Yunus

to our kids? We worked out various scenarios in the event that we were separated.

I particularly remember a shopping experience during this period, when we went into a grocery store and the shelves were bare. I had seen this on television many times, but had never personally experienced it. There seemed to be a complete panic to stockpile food. My wife bought bags of rice and canned goods, and a disinfectant that was rumoured to keep the house germ-free. I had my Dad at home in the US go out and buy some 3M N95 masks, the highest-quality germ-free mask in existence, and send them out to China. During this period these masks were out of stock globally, and even hospitals on the other side of the world couldn't keep enough in stock.

Plunging into the property market

One highlight of my 13 years in China was becoming one of the first foreigners I knew to purchase a house. Friends who had lived in China for years did not trust the legal system and told me I was crazy, and to 'kiss goodbye' to the money I put forward. My wife, however, insisted, and we paid US$100,000 as a down payment on a two-bedroom apartment, with the condition that we paid the other half off within one year. One solution to this problem was to see what mortgage options were available to me. I went back to Flint, Michigan to Citizen's Bank and asked if taking out a mortgage

Branding in China

was possible. When I mentioned that the apartment was in China, they politely told me that they only loaned money to people living within something like a 100-mile radius. I responded, 'I guess that means Beijing is out of the question.'

After our very supportive parents came to the rescue, we owned our first house together in the Diyang Mansions, located in the Central Business District of Beijing. Although the apartment was far from being a mansion, it was wonderfully located in downtown Beijing, right next to the local school, Fang Cao Di, which my kids would eventually attend. The Diyang was well regarded among Westerners and well-to-do locals, in part because of its proximity to the school, and it attracted many people from the arts community. Our neighbours included Chinese actor and director Jiang Wen, gymnast and entrepreneur Li Ning, writer on the Ming dynasty Wang Shixiang, singer Ai Jing and a number of members of the Western news media. Articles were published in the local press about the great fengshui that existed at the Diyang, and our lives thrived. Years later, I loved watching my kids from the window of our apartment as they chanted school songs and did group exercises. The investment certainly paid dividends.

Living downtown had its advantages, but we also loved to travel outside of the city at weekends. My wife, tired of having a driver accompany us everywhere, insisted that I get my driver's licence. Although I worried a bit about the traffic, and all of the

Ogilvy China Business Summit, March 2008

neophyte drivers on the road, I agreed. It was a simple exercise anyway – all I needed to do was to drive 100 metres in a straight line and I would receive my licence. Or so I thought. It just so happened that in late 2003 – just the time I wanted to get a local licence – the rules changed. Policy changes were common in China, so this was no big surprise. The new rules, however, stipulated that I needed to take a 100-question test. There was no study book in English, as this was a new test, and I needed to get at least 90 per cent of the answers correct.

Test day came and I showed up on time. I was told I would have 45 minutes to finish the test and they would let me know immediately if I had passed. Tests were handed out and I began. After answering all of the multiple-choice questions I knew the answers to in the first 20 minutes, I still had approximately 20 questions that could go either way. I went back and took a few calculated guesses, turned in the questionnaire with minutes to spare and awaited the good news.

The questions that puzzled me had more to do with awkward translations than anything else. I remember one particular question that asked in rather broken English whether a person who had been in an accident and had a bone sticking out of their body should be moved or left in the street. There were other questions that would have kept even the best linguistic detectives on their feet.

As I waited outside the classroom, at a speed uncharacteristic of China, my answer came. As I stood with approximately ten other applicants, the proctor exited the room and announced my name: '*Ke Ying de xiansheng*'. I looked up eagerly. '*Ni guo bu liao*'. Or in English: 'You did not pass!'

I first felt embarrassed, as all of the other participants laughed, and then ashamed, as I had to explain to my wife and kids that I had failed. I would not be defeated though. I asked around to see if there was a book that I could use to prepare for another attempt. 'No problem,' answered a colleague, and he kindly purchased this for me.

The Beijing 'Traffic Regulation Manual' is a comprehensive traffic management book, with all of the questions and answers listed inside. The only caveat is that you need fairly good Chinese language skills to read this book – it did not come in English. No problem though, I thought, and I promptly had the questions and answers section translated. Among the questions:

The driving test was a simple exercise – all I needed to do was to drive 100 metres in a straight line and I would receive my licence. Or so I thought

'Categorised according to the specification terms, carriers for agricultural use refer to _____.'
 A. Three-wheeled, four-wheeled vehicles;
 B. Three-wheeled, four-wheeled ordinary goods carriers, four-wheeled vans, four-wheel tank carriers, and four-wheeled automatic unloading trucks;
 C. Three-wheeled, four-wheeled and six-wheeled vehicles.'
Or here is another good one:
 'True or false: When big trucks are loaded with goods, the height of the goods from the ground should be not more than 5m, the width of the goods should not be more

Branding in China

than that of the carriage, the front part should not stand out of the vehicle body by more than 1m, and the rear part should not stand out of the carriage by 2m or touch the ground.'

By now, word had spread to my colleagues and friends, and the pressure mounted. A test date was set and, with a translated portion of the book in hand, I crammed like I was back in college. This time, I showed up early and mentally prepared myself for the test. I went through the questions one by one and thought through each answer in detail. I then turned in the test at the completion of the 45 minutes and waited to hear whether I would be taking to the road, or having to face my family and colleagues another time with word of defeat. Fortunately, today the coveted licence rests in my car and, with a combination of pride and fear, I have become one of the best defensive drivers in Beijing.

This caricature emerged from a group training session

The first ten years of living and working in China were eventful, but the past three years have been particularly meaningful. After an introduction made by a friend to Tsinghua Professor of Journalism Li Xiguang, my connection to China grew even stronger. At the time, the Ogilvy Group was setting up an advisory board and I was tasked with putting the team together. I met Professor Li and immediately had the impression that he would be a perfect candidate for the Board. I followed up by inviting Professor Li to an Advisory Board meeting, and during the meeting he pulled our Asia Pacific Chairman, Miles Young, aside and said, 'Miles, you should do for the Chinese government what you do for companies. China needs branding.'

What transpired from this meeting was the creation of a joint venture between the Ogilvy Group and Tsinghua University, called the Tsinghua-Ogilvy Programme for Public Branding, with me serving as one of the directors. The Tsinghua-Ogilvy Programme is intended to serve as a think tank for the study and practice of location branding to share with officials throughout China. And, since the programme was founded, Professor Li has invited Ogilvy and me into many interesting conversations about the way that China communicates with the outside world. I have conducted more than ten spokesperson training programmes for Chinese officials, have shared a perspective with the Beijing Organising Committee for the Games of the XXIX Olympiad (BOCOG) and I have coached officials from the General Administration of Quality Supervision, Inspection and Quarantine in the midst of the China export crisis.

The invitations to share a perspective with government officials have been something I have welcomed. During the food crisis of 2007, I had the opportunity to coach one of the State Food and Drug Administration (SFDA) spokespeople. Sitting in a dimly-lit conference room at Tsinghua University, I was asked a number of very genuine questions: 'How do we build some understanding for the steps we are taking? How often should we communicate?' Professor Li turned to me for my views. After watching videos of the spokesperson and others who were communicating, I jumped at the chance.

'First, don't blame the foreign media. Whether they are right or wrong, nobody cares. Second, don't make guarantees. Nobody will believe you, and government spokespeople in the US would never make guarantees anyway. Third, all news does not have to be good. People do not expect everything to be rosy at all times. Fourth, communicate often, open and honestly. And fifth, be accessible.' We explained, 'You can't always control what will happen to you, but you can control what you do about it, and that's what matters.' This was a fascinating time. The bad news kept coming in but the spokespeople became much more accessible, open and focused on solutions, not on cover-ups. Slowly the tide changed and 2007 came to a close.

2008 has been all Olympics, all of the time. Working with more than ten sponsors, the Ogilvy

Looking out over central Beijing, at one of the most exciting times in China's history to build a business

Branding in China

Group has clients in every category across many different industries. With the intention of being the first agency to probe consumer opinions in 2008, we launched a survey in early January that collected 2,687 responses from Chinese citizens across 20 provinces. The findings showed that 74 per cent of Chinese were 'excited or very excited' about the Beijing Games. The survey also showed a high degree of 'national pride', with 72 per cent saying that they were proud of China. There is no question – China has Olympic fever.

You can't always control what will happen to you, but you can control what you do about it, and that's what matters

As the self-appointed Olympics coordinator for the Ogilvy Group since Beijing won its bid to be the host, I attended the 2004 Games in Athens and the 2006 Winter Games in Torino. I went largely to serve as Ogilvy's Olympics branding scout, and returned with a team to help service the clients we would represent. Since 2005 we have been coordinating Olympic marketing meetings for our clients, with a focus on totally integrated campaigns. Among the clients we work with regularly are UPS, adidas, VW, Great Wall Wine and Sohu, the Olympics online partner.

Anticipation and excitement

The past seven years have been full of anticipation and excitement, with anxiety also coming into the picture in 2007 and 2008. The spotlight has been placed on China, and it has been two years of a rollercoaster ride. Depending on who you talk to, the Olympic Torch Relay has either been a huge success or a huge failure. As our clients' public relations advisor, we have been in the midst of working through messaging on a weekly basis, similar to the way in which a US Presidential campaign is run. Despite what many cynics argue about the Olympics being a political event, I tend to believe in the mission of the Games, which is, as outlined in the Olympic charter, 'upholding ethics in sports, encouraging participation in sports, ensuring the Olympic Games take place on a regular schedule, protecting the Olympic Movement, and encouraging and supporting the development of sport'. At the time of writing, we are just days away from the Games, and the Beijing skyline is very different from that fateful day in July 2001. While there are expected to be more bumps in the road, the Games will go on and they will be fantastic.

I came to Asia 17 years ago with a two-year contract. I have witnessed unprecedented growth and have had the opportunity to build a business at one of the most exciting times in China's complex history. What makes China so interesting are the extreme contrasts. I remember seeing a person driving a BMW right next to a man riding a bicycle with a monkey in the front basket; or there was the peasant carrying bricks on a horse-driven cart while chatting on his mobile phone; or people dressed in formal suits with the brand label still exposed on the outside sleeve. I remember celebrating the opening of our office in Beijing with a bottle of wine that – because we forgot to buy a corkscrew – we had to pound against the cement wall to get the cork out. Today, the people who shared that wine with me dine at upmarket restaurants, buy fine art, drive their own cars and have multiple apartments. All this in 13 years. There is a famous Confucian proverb: 'A journey of a thousand miles begins with a single step'. My journey has been a marathon sprint, an experience and dream that I hope never ends.

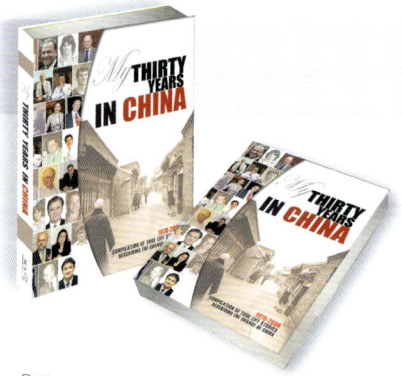

Have you been inspired by the stories in My Thirty Years in China, and would like to share them with others?

Order extra copies for your friends, customers and colleagues and enjoy a 10% discount.

Order Form

I would like to order____copy/ies of the My Thirty Years in China at GBP (~~19.95~~) 17.95 + GBP 5.00 delivery = GBP 22.95

Name:..Company:..
Address: ....
City:..Postcode:...Country:..
Tel: ....Fax:..
E-mail:..
Please charge my credit card: ☐Mastercard ☐Visa ☐Amex   3-digit security number:................
Card number: ....Expiry date: ....
Name of card holder: ....Total amount:..............................
Delivery address: ....
....Signature:..............................
☐Please invoice me. I enclose a cheque for.................payable to **ACA Publishing Ltd.**

Feedback

If you have any comments on the content of My Thirty Years in China, or your own thirty-year story to tell, please contact us. We are always looking for new and interesting stories and honest feedback.

Page number: ....Comment: ....
....
....
I am happy to discuss this further with you, please contact me on e-mail: ....
Tel: ....Fax: ....
Name: ....Date:..

ACA Publishing Ltd
Phone: + 44 20 7834 7676 / +86 10 8472 1250
Fax: + 44 20 7973 0076 / +86 10 5885 0639
Email: cbh@alaincharles.com